COLORADO'S FINEST
SMALL-TOWN RESTAURANTS
& THEIR RECIPES

DAVID GRUBER

FULCRUM PUBLISING

Golden, Colorado

Library of Congress Cataloging-in-Publication Data

Gruber, David.
  Colorado's finest small-town restaurants and their recipes / David Gruber.
    p. cm.
Includes index.
  ISBN 1-55591-456-X (pbk.)
  1. Restaurants—Colorado—Guidebooks. 2. Cookery—Colorado. 3. Colorado—Guidebooks. I. Title.
  TX907.3.C6 G78 2002
  647.95788—dc21

                              2001006711

Printed in Canada
0 9 8 7 6 5 4 3 2 1

Editorial: Daniel Forrest-Bank, Michelle Asakawa
Design: Trina Stahl
Cover illustration: Copyright © 2002 Mathew McFarren

Fulcrum Publishing
16100 Table Mountain Parkway, Suite 300
Golden, Colorado 80403
(800) 992-2908 • (303) 277-1623
www.fulcrum-books.com

Dedicated to my brother, William Jerome Gruber,
my only immediate relative.

He understands me better than anyone
and has been a major influence in my decisions,
furnishing me with half a century of good advice on life.

✌ CONTENTS ✍

Acknowledgments . *xi*
Introduction . *xiii*

ASHCROFT
   Pine Creek Cookhouse *(Mountain fare)* . 1

ASPEN
   Campo de Fiori *(Italian)* . 6
   Jack's at Sardy House *(American/Continental)* . 11
   Little Ollie's *(Chinese)* . 15

AVON
   Ristorante Ti Amo *(Northern Italian)* . 18

BASALT
   Café Bernard *(French inspired with a Rocky Mountain twist)* . 22

BEAVER CREEK
   Patina in the Hyatt Regency *(French fusion)* . 26
   SaddleRidge *(Contemporary American)* . 31
   Splendido at the Chateau *(Contemporary Rocky Mountain)* . 36

BRECKENRIDGE
   Breckenridge Barbecue *(Texas-style barbecue)* . 41
   South Ridge Seafood Grill *(Seafood and modern American)* . 45
   The Swiss Haven Restaurant *(Swiss)* . 48

BUENA VISTA
   Buffalo Bar & Grill *(Steaks and Seafood)* . 52
   Casa del Sol *(Mexican and New Mexican)* . 55

CARBONDALE

Taipei Tokyo *(Chinese and Japanese)* . 59
The Village Smithy Restaurant *(American)* . 63

CASTLE ROCK

Castle Café *(American comfort food)* . 67

CRAWFORD

The Dinner Bell at Smith Fork Ranch *(Elegant American)* . 71
Mad Dog Ranch Fountain Café *(American)* . 75

CRESTED BUTTE

Buffalo Grille & Saloon *(Steak, buffalo, seafood and pasta)* . 80

CUCHARA

The Silver Spoon Restaurant *(Steak, seafood, chicken and pasta)* . 84

DURANGO

636 Main—Ken & Sue's East *(American)* . 89
937 Main—Ken & Sue's Place *(New American bistro)* . 92
Christina's *(American and Continental eclectic)* . 96

EDWARDS

Sato *(Japanese and sushi with other Asian influences)* . 99
Wild Horse Bistro *(Mountain fare)* . 102

EMPIRE

The Peck House *(Continental and Colorado)* . 106

ESTES PARK

Cascades at the Stanley Hotel *(Western fare)* . 112
Grumpy Gringo *(Mexican)* . 115
Orlando's Steak House *(Steak and seafood)* . 119
The Other Side *(Traditional Western American)* . 122
Silverado at the Lake Shore Lodge *(Western bistro)* . 126
Sweet Basilico Café *(Italian)* . 130
Twin Owls Steakhouse at the Black Canyon Inn
    (Continental and Colorado) . 132
The Woodlands Restaurant *(Intercontinental)* . 136

EVERGREEN

Thuy Hoa *(Vietnamese)* . 140

FLORENCE

Rollin Rich's Steakhouse *(Steak and seafood)* . 144

FORT MORGAN
    Cables Italian Grille *(Italian American)* . 147

FRASER
    The Meadow View Restaurant at High Mountain
        Lodge *(Eclectic)* . 152

FRISCO
    Backcountry Brewery *(American comfort)* . 156

GEORGETOWN
    Panda City *(Chinese)* . 160
    Tasso's Bistro *(Continental with a Mediterranean flair)* . 163

GLEN HAVEN
    The Inn of Glen Haven *(English gourmet)* . 167

GLENWOOD SPRINGS
    Juicy Lucy's Steakhouse *(Aged steak and fresh seafood)* . 172
    Rendez-vous Restaurant *(French)* . 176

GOLDEN
    Hill Top Café *(Contemporary bistro)* . 179
    Old Capitol Grill *(Traditional American)* . 185

GRANBY
    Paul's Creekside Grill *(California-style bistro)* . 189

GRAND LAKE
    Caroline's Cuisine *(Contemporary bistro)* . 193

GUFFEY
    Peaceful Henry's *(Fine dining in casual rustic atmosphere)* . 197

GUNNISON
    Katie's Cookery *(Down-home cooking)* . 201

HAXTUN
    Haxtun Inn Restaurant *(Steak, seafood and burgers)* . 206

HESPERUS
    Kennebec Café & Bakery *(Mediterranean with Spanish flair)* . 209

IRWIN
    Irwin Lodge Restaurant *(Fine American)* . 214

KEYSTONE

Alpenglow Stube *(Contemporary Colorado)* . 219
The Bighorn Steakhouse *(Steak, chicken and seafood)* . 223
Edgewater Café *(American bistro)* . 227
Ida Belle's Cantina *(Mountain Mexican)* . 231
Keystone Ranch *(Upscale Rocky Mountain)* . 234
Ski Tip Lodge *(Coloradoan with multicultural influences)* . 239

LA JUNTA

Mexico City *(Mexican)* . 245

LAKE CITY

Facing West *(Savory San Juan fare)* . 248

LEADVILLE

Tennessee Pass Cookhouse *(High-country gourmet)* . 252

LOUISVILLE

Karen's Country Kitchen *(Healthful country)* . 257

LYONS

Oskar Blues *(Cajun)* . 261

MANITOU SPRINGS

The Cliff House Dining Room *(New American)* . 265

MORRISON

Dream Café *(New American)* . 270

NEW CASTLE

Elk Creek Mining Company *(Steak and ribs)* . 275

PAGOSA SPRINGS

J. J.'s Upstream Restaurant *(Seafood, steak and wild game)* . 279

PALMER LAKE

B & E Filling Station *(Continental)* . 284

PARKER

Italian Family *(Italian)* . 288

PINEWOOD SPRINGS

La Chaumière *(French and Continental)* . 291

PONCHA SPRINGS

Grimo's *(Italian)* . 295

RIDGWAY
    The Adobe Inn *(Northern Mexican and New Mexican)* . 299

SALIDA
    Antero Grill *(Modern American cowboy)* . 303
    Laughing Ladies *(Modern American)* . 306
    The Windmill *(Family Tex-Mex)* . 310

SILVER CLIFF
    Yoder's High Country Restaurant *(Home cooking)* . 313

SILVERTON
    Handlebars *(High-country burgers and barbecue)* . 317

SNOWMASS VILLAGE
    Il Poggio *(Italian)* . 321
    The Stonebridge Restaurant *(American West)* . 325

STEAMBOAT SPRINGS
    Mediterranean Grill & Tapas Lounge *(Mediterranean)* . 328
    Riggio's *(Italian)* . 333

TRINIDAD
    Wazubi's Blue Cup Coffee House *(Healthful foods)* . 338

VAIL
    La Bottega *(Northern Italian)* . 342
    La Tour *(Continental French)* . 345
    Larkspur *(American classic with French soul)* . 350
    Russell's *(Steak and seafood)* . 355

WINTER PARK
    Mama Falzitto's *(Country Italian)* . 359

WOODLAND PARK
    Austin's *(American)* . 363

Glossary of Restaurant Personnel Types . *368*
Recipe Index . *370*
Notes . *375*
About the Author . *383*

ACKNOWLEDGMENTS

I WOULD FIRST like to thank my wife, Linda, for her dedicated support while I wrote this guide, for her valuable assistance entering the restaurants' recipes into the computer and for putting up with me when I ignored her at restaurants to obtain information and at home during countless hours in front of the computer and on the telephone.

Second, I thank Angela Pedilla at the U.S. Census Bureau for providing me with the 2000 population statistics for Colorado towns. I was able to use the information for all but a few of the towns in this guide. My thanks also go to the following individuals for their information on restaurants in their local areas and their assistance in helping me decide which restaurants to visit: Dena Arner, manager of the Trapper Motor Inn in Estes Park; Chris Ryan, manager of Wild Horse Bistro in Edwards; and Sue Fusco, owner of 937 Main and 636 Main in Durango. A special thank-you goes to Julie Ward in the communications department at Keystone Resort for providing me with contact names and phone numbers, being a go-between and researching and coordinating much of the information that went into the Keystone chapter. I also thank the many people I met at arts and crafts shows over the past couple of years who gave me restaurant recommendations. Some of those recommendations are in this guide because of them.

Finally, I thank the restaurateurs themselves for taking time from their busy schedules to provide me with necessary information about their restaurants as well as their recipes. Without the assistance and support of those I mentioned, directly or indirectly, this book would not have been possible.

❧ INTRODUCTION ❧

WHEN I CAME OUT with my first book, *The Colorado Small-Town Restaurant Guide,* in 1991, I had just turned forty. As I finish writing this fifth book, I am now fifty. I have eaten my way through Colorado five times, dined at over 900 restaurants, put on twenty-five pounds, lost thirty and put twenty back on. My first four books were self-published under the pen name Benjamin James Bennis. With this fifth book, I thought it would be a good time to drop the pen name. I have had a terrific time traveling through Colorado discovering fine—and many times out-of-the-ordinary—places to eat and meeting some friendly people in the restaurant business.

Colorado's Finest Small-Town Restaurants and Their Recipes is for people who are interested in dining in some of the state's finer, not necessarily more expensive, restaurants. While this guide will lead you to some high-quality dining locations, it is not a "Best of Colorado" or "Top 100 Restaurants" list. Although fine food, superior service and appealing ambience were significant factors in deciding which restaurants to visit and which to include in this book, there were other influences at work in making those decisions. A remote location is, to my mind, a positive feature for a restaurant—its remoteness means it is unknown to many and is therefore a new experience. I gave special consideration to restaurants in buildings with historical value and to restaurants with unique qualities, having antiques, or with unusual items of décor. I considered a restaurant with character or a particular theme special. The Village Smithy in Carbondale, fashioned after a blacksmith shop, and Ida Belle's in Keystone, a model of an old mine, are two examples of restaurants with special character and a particular theme.

Finally, the setting of the restaurant and the scenic views it offers—the vistas of mountains, lakes, trees and valleys visible from the dining room—were all considered important qualities. This guide will lead you to ninety of the finest restaurants in Colorado.

This collection contains five of my personal favorites from my third guide, *Colorado Restaurants and Recipes from Small Towns,* which was nominated for the Colorado Book Award by the Colorado Center for the Book. Those five restaurants are Casa del Sol in Buena Vista, The Village Smith in Carbondale, The Peck House in Empire, Carolina's Cuisine in Grand Lake and Karen's Country Kitchen in Louisville. The other eighty-five restaurants are new discoveries that I have not written about in my previous four books. To allow for better coverage of the state, I included just one to three restaurants per town, with three exceptions: Estes Park has eight restaurants listed in this book, Keystone has six and Vail has four. In the past, I've viewed Estes Park as more of a destination than a stop along a route to someplace else, and for that reason I tended to visit it infrequently. I only included one restaurant from Estes Park in my third book, and none at all in the fourth. To make up for the town's earlier absence, I embarked on my first extended visit and was fortunate to dine at eight select restaurants. Keystone is pretty much the same story—no restaurants listed in my third book, and only two in the fourth. The fact that all six of the restaurants I've included in the present book belong to Keystone Resorts made it somewhat easier to coordinate writing about them. Vail also has had little representation in the past.

Colorado's Finest Small-Town Restaurants and Their Recipes is a cookbook as well as a restaurant guide. I intended this book for people who like to cook as well as for people who like to eat out at restaurants. If you like to do both, this book is definitely for you. This is a rare collection of recipes. Each one is a menu item written by the chef at each restaurant. You therefore have the opportunity to try a dish prepared by the chef at the restaurant and then recreate it for yourself in your kitchen. In most cases, a wine or other beverage recommendation follows the recipe.

This guide is arranged alphabetically by town. Each chapter begins with a brief history of the town, followed by the zip code, population and elevation. Unless otherwise stated, all population figures are from the 2000 U.S. Census. The restaurants that I reviewed in each town are arranged alphabetically. Following the name of the restaurant is its address, telephone and fax numbers, e-mail address and website. (Check the restaurants' websites for possible current specials.) Next are directions to the restaurant from a common starting point, such as a numbered exit from Interstate 70 or an intersection of major highways.

My review itself is divided into four sections. The first section, "Essentials," provides you with all the basic information you may want or need about each restaurant. Here you will find the restaurant's type of cuisine, the days and hours the restaurant serves meals, the price ranges for each meal, whether the restaurant has a nonsmoking section or is all nonsmoking, whether the restaurant offers take-out, what kind of alcohol the restaurant serves, which of the five major credit cards it accepts, its policy on accepting personal checks, its policy on taking reservations, whether it is wheelchair accessible, and other important information—such as whether the establishment has a children's menu or charges a service fee for large parties. The five major credit cards and the abbreviations used for each are as follows: MC for MasterCard, VI for Visa, AE for American Express, DS for Discover and DI for Diners Club. If a restaurant accepts all five major credit cards, you will see "All five" for credit cards.

The second section, "History and Biography," gives a brief history of the restaurant and the building it occupies. It also talks briefly about the backgrounds of the owners, managers and chefs at each restaurant. There is a story behind each restaurant, both in the people who operate the restaurant and its location. A fundamental understanding of who is preparing your meal, who manages the place and the place itself should enhance your dining pleasure.

The third section is where I review food, service and ambience. I tell you about my personal experiences with the food and service at each restaurant, and I describe the look, feel and ambience for you to envision. I also inform you about what to expect from the restaurant's menu. In many of the reviews I mention my wife, Linda. She has accompanied me on several visits and provided numerous beneficial comments and observations.

The last section, "Nutrition and Special Requests," is new to this edition. It is of interest to individuals with food allergies or dietary preferences or requirements (vegetarian, kosher, low-salt, low-fat and so on). The section discusses both the menu and the people who operate the restaurant and how each satisfies nutritional issues and responds to your special requests or needs.

My reviews are intended to provide you with complete information about a restaurant before you get there. This way, you can make your own intelligent decision about where to dine.

Reviewing restaurants is a subjective endeavor, and no matter how objective one may try to be, this business is still all opinions and personal perspectives. I have dined at all the restaurants in this guide at least once, at some more than once and at some with fellow diners. Without exception, I have approached each restaurant without prejudice or preconceived notions and attempted to be consistent and fair in all respects. I have no reason to judge any restaurant unfairly one way or the other. I am not a paid consultant or adviser for any restaurant. Many food critics differ on their opinions of the same restaurant, and your opinion may differ as well. Please keep in mind that I am reporting what I encountered at the time(s) that I dined at each restaurant. It should also be remembered that restaurants, like everything else, do change over time. The price ranges for meals quoted in this guide were accurate when I last dined at the restaurant. They may have changed since. Hence, these prices should be used as a guide only, not an absolute, and under no circumstances should they be presented to restaurant management as guaranteed prices.

ASHCROFT

ONCE A GREAT *mining camp rivaling nearby Aspen, Ashcroft degenerated into extinction by 1890 due to lack of rail service to the mines.*

Zip code: 81511 **Population:** 20* **Elevation:** 9,750 feet

PINE CREEK COOKHOUSE

12500 Castle Creek Road
Phone: (970) 925-1044
Fax: (970) 925-7939
E-mail: ast@rof.net
Website: www.pinecreekcookhouse.com

Directions: Take exit 116 from I-70 and go north to the traffic signal. Turn right onto Highways 6 and 24 and go to the next signal. Turn right onto Highway 82, go over I-70 and continue on this road for 11.7 miles to the intersection with Highway 133. Continue straight on Highway 82 for 28.6 miles to a roundabout. Enter the roundabout and take the second exit, Castle Creek Road. Drive 12½ miles. The restaurant will be on the right, about 2 miles past the old town of Ashcroft.

ESSENTIALS

Cuisine: Mountain fare
Hours: JUN to early OCT: Tue.–Sat. seatings at 12 noon and 1:30 P.M., Tue.–Sun. seatings at 6 P.M. and 8 P.M. Additional Sun. seatings at 10:30 A.M., 12 noon and 1 P.M. Closed Mon. Thanksgiving to mid-

---

*This figure is according to Pine Creek Cookhouse Manager Jeff Picasso; it includes twelve people Jeff can name plus an estimate of eight people operating the Elk Mountain Lodge. Ashcroft is technically a ghost town and, by five people, beats out Irwin as the smallest town in this book.

APR: Mon.–Sat. seatings at 12 noon, 1:30 P.M. and 6 P.M., Sun. seatings at 10:30 A.M., 12 noon, 1:30 P.M. and 6 P.M. Closed early OCT to Thanksgiving and mid-APR through MAY.

Meals and Prices: Lunch and Sun. brunch $12–$15. Dinner $23–$38 (soup and salad extra).

Nonsmoking: All

Take-out: No

Alcohol: Full bar

Credit Cards: MC, VI, AE

Personal Check: In-state with ID

Reservations: NECESSARY for brunch, lunch and dinner

Wheelchair Access: Yes

Other: Service charge of 18% for parties of six or more. Available for private parties. Directly accessible by vehicle in the summer. Only accessible by cross-country skiing, snowshoeing or horse-drawn sleigh a distance of 1½ miles in the winter. All staff members are trained ski guides.

HISTORY AND BIOGRAPHY

The Pine Creek Cookhouse has an interesting history. Half of the building, from the pine log pole in the middle of the room back to the kitchen, was built in Basalt, Colorado, in 1930 as a skeet-shooting lodge. It was moved to its present location in the early 1960s and used as a hunting lodge. During the 1960s, the building was also used as a camp for Cub Scouts and Boy Scouts. In 1971, Greg Mace purchased the building, expanded the building to its current size, added the deck and opened the first restaurant. In 1985, movie producer and current owner John Wilcox bought the restaurant.

Manager Jeff Picasso has been at the Cookhouse since 1999. His background is in breweries. He has worked at eleven breweries from 1989 to 1999 in Iowa; Munich, Germany; Phoenix, Arizona; Salt Lake City, Utah; Grand Junction, Colorado; and Aspen, Colorado. Executive Chef Michael Feil started at the restaurant in 2000. He is from Maui, Hawaii. A graduate of New York Culinary Institute in upstate New York, he worked in San Diego, California, before coming to the Aspen area. Chef de cuisine Richard Triptow has been at the Cookhouse since 1995. He grew up in a family-owned restaurant in Dallas, Texas, and cooked for three years at the Turtle Creek Restaurant in Dallas. He trained in Denver, graduated from the Culinary Institute of America and was sous-chef for five years at the Denver Buffalo Company. Chef Richard is also an artist, and his artworks can be seen in the restaurant. Chefs Michael and Richard are assisted in the kitchen by three Sherpa cooks from eastern Nepal.

FOOD, SERVICE AND AMBIENCE

The Pine Creek Cookhouse has a majestic view to the south of the Elk Mountains, Taylor Peak, Star Peak, Greg Mace Mountain and the Cooper Bowl. This is one of the three most spectacular vistas you will find at any restaurant in this book. (The other two are at the Irwin Lodge Restaurant in Irwin and Facing West in Lake City.) I spent a most pleasant summer afternoon here when I dined on grilled semi-boneless quail salad served in a sweet and warm maple balsamic vinaigrette. The tender charbroiled quail had great flavor and broke apart easily. Fresh raspberries, blueberries, kiwi, dried cranberries, sliced green apples, candied pecans, crumbled Gorgonzola, white mushrooms and an orange quarter completed this light and refreshing salad. Focaccia bread was served on the side.

Spotlighting the summer lunch menu are the hiker's banquet, an array of pasta salads, grains, greens, muffins, tofu and quinoa; great salads like the one that I had and hot smoked salmon Niçoise; and entrées including a grilled portobello mushroom melt, soft-shell crab on a sourdough roll and spinach crêpes. The winter skier's banquet is similar to the summer hiker's banquet. The entrées are headlined by Hungarian goulash and grilled vegetable pie. Sunday brunches are punctuated by halibut, leg of lamb, hot smoked salmon, frittatas and fruit crêpes.

For dinner, in the summertime you can look forward to wild mushroom strudel, pistachio-crusted venison tenderloin, herb-roasted chicken and walnut-basil–encrusted Rocky Mountain rainbow trout. In winter expect lobster pot pie, grilled Colorado lamb chops, Muscovy duck, herb-roasted free-range poussin, grilled vegetable pie, and polenta and goat cheese chile rellenos. Homemade Italian ice, chocolate raspberry bread pudding and rustic apple or bittersweet almond tortes are typical desserts.

Service was quick and accommodating. I was moved to a table outside when one opened up. However, there was no water refill, and the staff was slow picking up the check. The inside dining area is adorned with wood skis, snowshoes, photos of cross-country skiers, paintings of snowy peaks and valleys full of snow, a black stove in front of a rock wall and windows facing the deck that frames the magnificent view. The deck is covered by a white canvas awning. A covered concrete patio to the east side, with a green vinyl top and an adjacent barbecue grill, is used for private parties and overflow crowds. In the foreground, you can see a short waterfall emptying into a pond. If you are lucky, you might see some wildlife, such as black-tail weasel, ermine or deer. This is indeed a grand setting for some exquisite dining.

NUTRITION AND SPECIAL REQUESTS

The Cookhouse has a well-rounded menu offering vegetarian and vegan items; a low-cholesterol venison; and a salad bar featuring tofu, pasta salads and quinoa. The chefs handle special requests all the time. If you have a food allergy, let your server know so that your needs can be accommodated. Water, purified of course, is obtained from Pine Creek, which flows from Cathedral Lake.

Carne Asada over Seasoned Black Beans with Wild Mushroom–Ancho Chile Salsa

SERVES 4

1 beef flank steak,
    about 1½ pounds
Flank Steak Marinade
    (recipe follows)
Seasoned Black Beans
    (recipe follows)
4–6 cups mixed field greens

Wild Mushroom–Ancho Chile
    Demi-glace (recipe follows)
sour cream
    and fresh corn off the
    husk, for garnish
flour tortillas

1. Make the Marinade, Seasoned Black Beans and Demi-glace. Trim flank steak of fat and marinate it at room temperature for 3 to 4 hours.

2. Grill flank steak to medium-rare.
3. Ladle Seasoned Black Beans onto plate. Cover with single layer.
4. Add a mound of mixed field greens to the middle of the plate.
5. Slice beef thinly on a diagonal against the grain into 4 portions and mound over field greens. Ladle Demi-glace sauce over beef.
6. Garnish with a dollop each of sour cream and fresh corn. Serve with warmed flour tortillas (rolled or folded into quarters).

Flank Steak Marinade

3 fresh limes, juiced
1 tablespoon fresh chopped garlic
½ cup olive oil

1 tablespoon Worcestershire sauce
1 tablespoon soy sauce
salt and pepper to taste

Mix all ingredients well in a mixing bowl. Makes about 1½ cups.

Seasoned Black Beans

1 15-ounce can black beans
½ red onion, chopped ¼-inch
½ red pepper, chopped ¼-inch
½ bunch of fresh cilantro, chopped fine

2 teaspoons fresh chopped garlic
1 teaspoon ground cumin
1 teaspoon dark chili powder
1 teaspoon Mexican oregano
salt and pepper to taste

Mix all ingredients together in large saucepan and simmer for 10 minutes.

Wild Mushroom–Ancho Chile Demi-glace:

¼ cup fresh chanterelle mushrooms, sliced
¼ cup fresh morel mushrooms, sliced
¼ cup fresh shiitake mushrooms, sliced
½ cup dried ancho chiles, cleaned, seeded and chopped

½ yellow onion, chopped
½ bunch fresh cilantro, chopped
1 tablespoon chopped garlic
1½ cups hot water
1½ teaspoons beef base
1 cup prepared veal demi-glace

1. Mix all ingredients except the demi-glace in a large saucepan and boil for 25 minutes.

2. Add the veal demi-glace and stir until incorporated. Makes 3–4 cups.

Recipe by Richard Triptow

Wine Recommendation: California Sonoma Valley Fife Old Vine Zinfandel

❧ ASPEN ❧

THE POST–UTE *Indian history of Aspen falls into three eras. The first began in 1879 with the discovery of silver in the Roaring Fork Valley. It was during this era that mining promoter B. Clark Wheeler changed the town's name from Ute City to Aspen for the abundance of the appealing trees. With the demonetization of silver in 1893, Aspen's population diminished by 90 percent and the town reverted to ranching for its survival. Aspen had entered its second era as a sleepy cow town.*

In the 1930s the town began to stir with the prospects of skiing. However, it wasn't until World War II brought the 10th Mountain Division to the area that the movement for skiing in Aspen began to take off. This, combined with cultural and music festivals that originated in the late 1940s, launched Aspen into its current era. Aspen today is a world-renowned resort attracting celebrities from all parts for skiing in the winter and festivals in the summer.

Zip Code: 81611 **Population:** 5,914 **Elevation:** 7,907 feet

CAMPO DE FIORI

205 South Mill Street (in the Mill Street Plaza)
Phone: (970) 920-7717
Fax: (970) 920-3098
E-mail and website: www.campodifiori.net

Directions: From the northwest (Glenwood Springs), stay on Highway 82 as you enter Aspen. Make a right on 7th Street and a left on Main Street. Go 10 blocks to Mill Street (1 block past Monarch Street) and turn right. Go 1 block. The Mill Street Plaza is on the right; the restaurant is on the garden level.

ESSENTIALS

Cuisine: Italian

Hours: Seven nights 5:30 P.M.–11 P.M. Closed Sun. from mid-APR to mid-MAY and from mid-OCT to mid-NOV.

Meals and Prices: Dinner $11–$29 (soup and salad extra)

Nonsmoking: All including bar

Take-out: Yes

Alcohol: Full bar

Credit Cards: MC, VI, AE

Personal Check: Not accepted

Reservations: Highly recommended

Wheelchair Access: No, but staff will bring a wheelchair-bound person down the eleven stairs to the restaurant

Other: Service charge of 18% added to parties of six or more

HISTORY AND BIOGRAPHY

Campo de Fiori first opened its doors in 1994. Prior to that, these premises were occupied by The Village Restaurant, which opened in 1976, and Rebecca's Bakery, which closed in 1992. In 1994, Campo's current location was shared with Eddie Bauer storage space, a sewing studio and empty space. Campo has since expanded its tiny original location and now occupies two sides and a corner of the garden level, with the restaurant on one side and a bar and lounge on the other.

Luigi and Elizabeth Giordani are the owners. Luigi was a cook in Italy and graduated from the Istituto di Albighiero in Rome in 1985. He came to the United States in 1986 and worked in Philadelphia, Pennsylvania, and Newport Beach, California, before coming to Colorado in 1992. He was a chef at Farfalla in Aspen for two years before opening Campo de Fiori. Elizabeth has been in the restaurant business with Luigi since 1986. Sergio Acampora is general manager and partner and has been in the restaurant business since 1978. Executive chef Filberto Paglia studied cooking in Venice and has worked in restaurants since 1979. He came to the United States in 1989 and worked in Atlanta, Georgia, before coming to Aspen.

FOOD, SERVICE AND AMBIENCE

Campo de Fiori is a very pleasant open-air, open-kitchen restaurant especially nice for dining on warm summer evenings. The garden level is well shaded and by 6 P.M. the air begins to cool down in Aspen. The sliding glass doors to the restaurant open onto patio dining, so even if you are inside, you have some fresh air to breathe. If you are facing the back of the dining room you can watch the chefs at work in the kitchen.

When Linda and I dined here, I ordered an antipasto and the spinach-and-ricotta pasta dumplings; Linda went with spaghetti with fresh sardines, broccoli rapa (tiny broccoli buds), black olives and capers. We both preferred Linda's pasta selection. My light appetizer of a single layer of extra-thin-sliced roast veal served chilled with capers, mayonnaise, arugula and a slice of tomato, though minimal in size, tasted just fine. I liked the combination of cold meat, capers and mayo. The pasta dumplings were soft and overcooked, about 1½ inches long, cocoon-shaped, green in color and served in a small casserole dish. Their appearance and presentation did not agree with me. Linda's dish, in contrast, pleased her immensely—so much so that a week later she prepared her own version of the dish with the addition of anchovies. My recommendation is to avoid the pasta dumplings and go with the spaghetti or another pasta.

In addition to antipasti and pasta dishes, Campo's menu offers zuppe (soup), insalate (salad), risotti (risotto dishes) and secondi (second courses). Unless you leave your appetite at home, you should plan on adding an antipasto, soup or salad to your pasta or secondi selection.

There are several—in fact, fifteen in all—antipasti plates. A few of the ones that made my mouth water just reading about them were the portobello mushrooms, butternut squash, grilled artichoke hearts and shaved Parmesan cheese in balsamic vinaigrette and oil; grilled polenta filled with spinach and Gorgonzola and served with wild mushroom sauce; and lightly fried calamari. The minestrone soup is popular with regular diners. The restaurant also serves a chilled cantaloupe soup (in summer only) and a puree of white beans drizzled with white truffle oil. The salads offer great variety, featuring marinated seared duck breast, Gorgonzola, apples and caramelized walnuts; a wide selection of lettuces such as endive, radicchio and organic baby greens; and a mix of dressings including lemon-mustard vinaigrette, port vinaigrette and warm pine nut, raisin and balsamic vinaigrette.

The pasta dishes combine many favorites—linguini, fettuccini, rigatoni, penne and gnocchi—with ingredients such as sautéed shrimp, fresh salmon, asparagus, grilled sausage, prosciutto and vodka. The risotto choices also were tempting and featured porcini mushrooms, shrimp with white wine, Italian sausage and smoked mozzarella. Among the second courses were fresh fish and shellfish in a white wine and saffron broth, grilled filet mignon, marinated baby free-range chicken and roasted rack of Colorado lamb. Campo's fish is flown in five times a week from the East and West Coasts, Hawaii and South America.

Service during our visit was friendly, good-humored and plentiful. Several young (and handsome, according to my wife) men were on hand to remove plates, replace silverware and refill our water glasses. Songs of romance sung in Italian filled the cool evening air. One half of the back dining-room wall reveals the open kitchen while the other half displays a mural depicting a beautiful Italian villa with gardens and grapevines. The scene is supposed to resemble Tuscany. Above the opening to the kitchen hang brass pans and dried flower arrangements. Artistic stonework covers the lower wall in front of the kitchen. A grapevine is painted over the bar to the right of the dining room. Arched doorways connect the rooms and the inside to the outside. Dining is at mosaic tile tables created by Elizabeth Giordani. She also developed the grouted tiles in the arch outside the entrance and the tiles on the bar. The walls are a color wash of gold, burnt amber, light yellow and rust. The patio has hanging flowerpots and standing steel lamps. This is a true Italian restaurant from the food to the ambience to the Italian accents.

NUTRITION AND SPECIAL REQUESTS

Campo's menu uses free-range meats, organic foods, low-fat ingredients and virgin olive oil where possible and is health-conscious toward vegetarians and vegans. The chefs will accommodate special requests even when they do not have an item, so long as they are given advance notice.

Linguini ai Crostacei

SERVES 4–6

1½ pounds linguini pasta
4 tablespoons olive oil
3 cloves garlic, finely chopped
¼ teaspoon crushed red pepper
½ teaspoon salt
¼ teaspoon coarse ground
   black pepper
18–24 medium-size shrimp
   (deveined)

½ pound calamari, thinly sliced
16–20 scallops
18–24 clams
18–24 mussels
½ cup white wine
4–6 ounces crushed canned
   tomatoes

1. Fill a large pot with water and bring to a boil. (Campo's chefs add a couple of tablespoons of sea salt to the water to flavor the pasta as it boils.) Add the pasta and boil, stirring occasionally, for about 12 minutes.
2. While the pasta is cooking, prepare the sauce: In a large saucepan, heat olive oil for 30 seconds. Add garlic, crushed red pepper, salt and coarse black pepper, and sauté at medium to high heat.
3. Once the garlic becomes semi-translucent, add shrimp, calamari and scallops. Continue to stir for 4-6 minutes, until the shrimp start to turn pink.
4. Add clams, mussels, white wine and crushed tomatoes. Stir, then cover the saucepan and allow everything to steam for about 4 minutes.
5. Uncover the pan to see if your clams and mussels are open. If not, cover the pan again and wait a little longer.
6. Once the clams and mussels are open, your sauce is about ready. If it seems too liquid, leave uncovered over the heat until it is reduced to your liking.
7. Drain the al dente pasta in a colander and then immediately add it to the saucepan with the other ingredients. Stir until everything is mixed together. Serve immediately.

Recipe by Luigi Giordani

Wine Recommendations: Terre Ditufi Veraccia or Pinot Grigio Zamo and Zamo

JACK'S AT SARDY HOUSE

128 East Main Street
Phone: (800) 321-3457 or (970) 920-2525
Fax: (970) 920-4478
E-mail: hotlsard@rof.net
Website: www.jacksatsardyhouse.com

Directions: From the northwest (Glenwood Springs), stay on Highway 82 as you enter Aspen. Make a right on 7th Street and a left on Main Street. Go 8 blocks. The restaurant and hotel are on the left on the northwest corner of Main Street and Aspen Street, 1 block past Garmisch Street.

ESSENTIALS

Cuisine: American/Continental
Hours: Seven nights 5:30 P.M.–9:30 P.M., Mon.–Sat. 7:30 A.M.–10:30 A.M., Sun. 7:30 A.M.–12 noon. Closed late APR to early MAY.
Meals and Prices: Breakfast $7–$10. Dinner $14–$25 (soup and salad extra).
Nonsmoking: Smoking permitted only in the bar and on the lawn
Take-out: No
Alcohol: Full bar
Credit Cards: MC, VI, AE, DS
Personal Check: Yes, with credit card number
Reservations: Encouraged
Wheelchair Access: No
Other: Available for private dinners and wedding parties

HISTORY AND BIOGRAPHY

Jack's Restaurant at the Sardy House B&B is in a former Victorian house built by three-fingered Jack W. Atkinson, for whom the restaurant is named. In 1918, Medford Smith purchased the house for $800. He sold the home to Doctor and Mrs. Twining in 1935, who sold it in 1945 to Tom and Rachel Sardy. Tom Sardy was responsible for obtaining the land, coordinating county and federal agencies and raising funds for the airfield in Aspen, which appropriately bears his name (Sardy Field). In the late 1960s, he temporarily transformed Sardy House into a mortuary, though it remained a private residence until 1984. That's when long-time Aspen residents and current owners Daniel Delano and Frank Peters purchased the property and converted it into a business. Daniel and Frank combined the main house with the carriage house to create a bed and breakfast and restaurant. This is the one and only restaurant venture for these two gentlemen, whose background is in construction. Daniel had some prior food service experience working as a cook and waiter on sailboats in the Atlantic Ocean.

Peter Kelly has been the manager of Jack's since fall 2000. He came to Colorado in the summer of 2000 and worked at the Seven Lakes Lodge in Meeker before signing on with Jack's. He has been in the restaurant business since 1980, making his way down the Eastern Seaboard from Boston, Massachusetts, to Philadelphia, Pennsylvania, to Florida. Executive chef Alaxi Kokish has been with Jack's since June 2000, having spent seven years as the sous-chef at Carnavale Restaurant in Aspen.

FOOD, SERVICE AND AMBIENCE

Jack's provides an extremely pleasant setting for dining, especially out on the lawn. Linda and I had a late Sunday breakfast here outdoors. I went sweet while she went south. The homemade lemon syrup that accompanied Jack's French toast with strawberries and bananas clinched my decision to order that entrée. It also came with raisins, orange peel and powdered sugar and was simply scrumptious! Linda chose the chef's special, which on this particular day was a breakfast burrito with chorizo sausage, scrambled egg, finely chopped onion, green pepper and tomato. With cheddar cheese inside and melted on top, it was all in a soft flour tortilla with sides of sour cream, pico de gallo and strawberries. Fresh-baked blueberry bread accompanied our meals. I don't know which was best, the beautiful surroundings and majestic mountain view, the cool, refreshing Aspen morning air, or the food.

Some other breakfast highlights are fresh-squeezed orange juice, honey-cured ham, espresso, cappuccino, blueberry pancakes and eggs Benedict. For dinner, you can start with soup, a house salad with sun-dried strawberries, a smoked salmon salad with goat cheese, homemade garlic potato chips, naan bread, roasted red bell pepper, or homemade duck ravioli. Headlining the dinner entrées are pork tenderloin in a grilled fig bordelaise sauce, ahi tuna wrapped in crispy pickled eggplant, ginger garlic beef with a creamy peppercorn sauce and grilled leg of lamb over semolina gnocchi. Jack's has received the Wine Spectator Magazine's Award of Excellence for 1998 through 2001.

Service was helpful and courteous. We enjoyed a Frank Sinatra recording of "oldies but goodies" while we dined on the lawn. The elegant Victorian décor of Jack's Restaurant mimics the adjacent twenty-room Sardy B&B. A gazebo-shaped front porch frames the entrance. To the left is outside dining with four tables on a red slate deck and two iron tables and chairs with cushions under umbrellas. If the weather is right, definitely sit outside. If not, dining inside is also appealing. The two dining rooms and adjacent bar and lounge feature the maple-wood floors, fireplace and golden oak doorways of the original house.

In the front dining room is a sketch of original owner Jack Atkinson and a vintage photograph of four men and a boy holding up a string of fish. The man to the far right in the picture is Jack. The room is enhanced by brass and frosted-glass chandeliers, two marble tables, long white curtains in the bay window and a side table against the wall adorned with wine bottles, candles and dried flowers. The back dining room contains the fireplace, a china cabinet with glass doors containing some original house plates, brass and frosted-glass sconces and another big bay window with long white curtains. Beyond the second dining room is a small bar and lounge with a large cushioned sofa and two more marble tables. Throughout the restaurant you will find color sketches of flowers such as laelia amanda, cattleya and trianae massangeana. If I were entertaining out-of-state guests, this is the place I would bring them to in Aspen.

NUTRITION AND SPECIAL REQUESTS

Jack's accommodates special requests, though this is more easily done at breakfast than at dinner. When I dined here, several vegetarian items were available for breakfast and for dinner starters, but no vegetarian dinner entrées were on the menu.

Jack's French Toast with Strawberries and Bananas and Lemon Syrup

SERVES 5–6

5–6 tablespoons butter
Lemon Syrup (recipe follows)
1 cup heavy cream
¼ cup half-and-half
1 egg
½ teaspoon cinnamon

¼ teaspoon nutmeg
10–12 slices Texas toast
fresh strawberries and
    bananas, sliced
powdered sugar

1. Prepare Lemon Syrup.
2. Melt 1 tablespoon of butter in sauté pan.
3. Mix heavy cream, half-and-half, egg, cinnamon and nutmeg in bowl to make batter.
4. Dip 1 to 2 pieces of Texas toast in batter, then place in sauté pan. Brown both sides, about 2 minutes on each side. Remove from pan.
5. Add sliced strawberries and bananas to lemon syrup and warm on stovetop for 30 seconds.
6. Pour syrup with fruit over toasts. Sprinkle with powdered sugar. Repeat for the remaining bread slices.

Lemon Syrup

1 ounce lemon juice
1 cup simple syrup
1 ounce maple syrup

1 cinnamon stick
1 ounce golden raisins

Mix all the above together in a small saucepan and warm completely.

Recipe by executive chef Alaxi Kokish

Beverage Recommendation: Mimosa

LITTLE OLLIE'S

308 South Hunter Street
Phone: (970) 544-9888
Fax: (970) 544-0888
E-mail: None
Website: None

Directions: From the northwest (Glenwood Springs), stay on Highway 82 as you enter Aspen. Make a right on 7th Street and a left on Main Street. Go 12 blocks. Turn right on Hunter Street, 1 block past Galena. The restaurant is 2½ blocks up on the left, below street level.

ESSENTIALS

Cuisine: Chinese
Hours: Mon.–Fri. 11:30 A.M.–10 P.M., Sat.–Sun. 12 noon–10 P.M.
Meals and Prices: Lunch $6. Dinner $7–$16 (soup extra).
Nonsmoking: All
Take-out: Yes
Alcohol: Sake, wine and Chinese beer
Credit Cards: None
Personal Check: Roaring Fork Valley only
Reservations: Accepted for five or more for dinner only, not guaranteed
Wheelchair Access: Yes, by ramp
Other: Free delivery in Aspen, $10 minimum

HISTORY AND BIOGRAPHY

Little Ollie's opened in Aspen in November 1992, replacing a Thai restaurant. Owners John Ye and Charley Huang ("Wang") also own Little Ollie's in Cherry Creek in Denver and at the Park Meadows Mall in Lonetree, Colorado. John is the head chef for all three restaurants. He started in the restaurant business in China and came to the United States in 1989. He worked in New York City for a few years where he met his partner, Charley. Charley is the dining room manager for the Cherry Creek restaurant. John's brother, Michael, is the manager for the Aspen restaurant. He also began working in restaurants in China and worked in New York City at a Chinese restaurant and the Soho Kitchen and Bar, a French restaurant.

FOOD, SERVICE AND AMBIENCE

Chef John has created all the dishes on this authentic Chinese menu. I have dined at Little Ollie's in Cherry Creek and in Aspen and, although the two restaurants could not be more different in terms of ambience and size, both restaurants provide the same high-quality meals. Their portions are ample and a great value. You really get a big plateful, even for lunch. I ordered the Royal Shrimp off the lunch menu. It consisted of eight large, tender but chewy shrimp and about two cups of steamed vegetables—broccoli, cauliflower, carrots, zucchini, snow peas, baby corn, asparagus, celery and green onions—in an excellent white garlic sauce made with Chinese rice wine. It was accompanied by two sizable portions of fluffy, no-stick white rice and a vegetable spring roll, filled mostly with cabbage, all on the same plate. A small side dish of sweet apple and plum sauces completed the meal.

Ollie's menu consists of soups such as vegetable hot and sour, chicken egg drop and won ton; appetizers such as Chinese dumplings, crab rangoons and shrimp tempura; a variety of shrimp dishes from Yu Shan to Kung Pao; pork; poultry; vegetables; beef; and noodles or fried rice. You can order moo shu pork, cashew chicken, eggplant, tofu, Mongolian beef, lo mein or assorted seafood pan-fried noodles. The chef's specials include egg foo yung, sesame chicken, sizzling platters, fresh whole fish or Maine lobster in season, ginger shrimp and Peking duck.

Service was slow at the beginning of my visit—having someone notice me and seat me—and at the end, when my server needed to pick up my check. In between, it was smooth and fast. Staff members seem to operate in different gears, but slow or fast, everyone was very pleasant and friendly. The restaurant is one small garden-level room with a four-table patio. The white walls with vertical rectangular niches have some very realistic and appealing prints by a Yugoslavian artist showing Chinese fishing villages and docked fishing boats. Dark-green awnings shade the front of the restaurant, and umbrellas are provided for each patio table. Although this Ollie's is a fraction of the size of its two sister restaurants and lacks their elaborate décor, this is the original. It should not be missed by anyone who likes superior Chinese food.

NUTRITION AND SPECIAL REQUESTS

Little Ollie's chefs cook only with vegetable oil and do not use any canned goods. Everything is fresh. They will accommodate special requests and can prepare special dishes with a day's advance notice. There are numerous vegetarian items on the menu.

Baby Bok Choy and Black Mushrooms

SERVES 1

2 tablespoons vegetable oil
1 tablespoon sliced garlic cloves
¼ teaspoon salt
2 cups baby bok choy, chopped
10–12 Chinese black
    mushrooms

¼ cup Chia Fan cooking wine
    (prestigious Chinese rice
    wine available at Chinese
    markets), or substitute
    regular rice wine
⅛ teaspoon granulated sugar

1. Before cooking, place mushrooms in hot water with a tiny dab of baking powder and let set for ½ hour to soften mushrooms. Rinse mushrooms before using.
2. Heat vegetable oil in pan until you can smell the oil. Add garlic and sauté until you can smell the garlic.
3. Add salt.
4. Add bok choy and black mushrooms and sauté over medium heat for 5–7 minutes. DON'T OVERCOOK. The bok choy should be crispy.
5. Add rice wine and sugar. Cook for 1 more minute and serve.

Recipe by John Ye

❧ AVON ☙

AVON, NAMED BY *an Englishman for England's Avon River, was spelled Avin in 1889 when it was listed as a railroad station.*

Zip Code: 81620 **Population:** 5,561 **Elevation:** 7,440 feet

RISTORANTE TI AMO

40928 South Highway 6
Phone: (970) 845-8153
Fax: (970) 845-8113
E-mail: None
Website: None

Directions: Take exit 171 from I-70, west of Vail. Go west toward Avon for 1.8 miles. The restaurant is on the left in the Eagle-Vail Business Center.

ESSENTIALS

Cuisine: Northern Italian

Hours: JUL to end of APR: Mon–Fri 11:30 A.M.–10 P.M., Sat. 5 P.M.–9:30 P.M., Sun. 5 P.M.–9 P.M. Closed end of APR to mid-MAY. Mid-MAY through JUN: Mon.–Fri. 11:30 A.M.–10 P.M., Sat. 5 P.M.–9:30 P.M. Closed SUN.

Meals and Prices: Lunch $7–$9. Dinner $15–$19 (soup and salad extra).

Nonsmoking: All

Take-out: Yes

Alcohol: Full bar

Credit Cards: MC, VI, AE, DS

Personal Check: Yes

Reservations: Recommended for dinner and parties of ten or more

Wheelchair Access: Yes, by outside ramp

HISTORY AND BIOGRAPHY

The building that Ti Amo occupies was originally a warehouse constructed in 1986. The first restaurant located here was Walter's, serving German fare, followed by Cardinale, an Italian restaurant, and Chet's Restaurant; Vincenzo and Lisa Perucchini took over the location in July 1995 and opened Ti Amo. They came to Colorado for its mountains, which they say reminded them of northern Italy and so "felt like home."

Enzo first came to the United States in 1984 and ran a Dallas, Texas, restaurant. Lisa ran a restaurant in Austin, Texas. They worked together for the Macaroni Grill, a Denver restaurant chain, traveling around the country opening new franchises. In spring 2000, Enzo and Lisa sold Ti Amo to their son, Massimo "Max," and his best friend, Steve Negler. Max has been in the restaurant business since 1980. He previously worked in Dallas with his father and managed the Macaroni Grill from 1992 to 1997. Steve is from Boulder, Colorado, and has worked in restaurants since 1985, including stints at the Steak & Ale in Dallas, a Macaroni Grill in Denver and the Adams Mark Hotel in Grand Junction, Colorado. Paula Imhoff began managing Ti Amo in 2000 after spending fourteen years at Pepi's in nearby Vail. Executive chef Fernando Ocampo, from Mexico, has been in the restaurant business since 1991 and with Ti Amo since it opened.

Ti Amo has been voted Best Italian Restaurant in the Vail Valley every year from 1996 to 2000 by the *Vail Daily* newspaper. They base their success on four ingredients: good food, service, wine and atmosphere.

FOOD, SERVICE AND AMBIENCE

Dine at Ti Amo and experience for yourself what Vail Valley residents have been raving about. I stopped here for lunch and ordered the Spaghetti Ti Amo with the insalata mista. The small dinner salad consisted of a good selection of fresh field greens with diced tomato and onion in a balsamic vinaigrette. The spaghetti dish was a great mix of Italian and Greek influences, two of my personal favorites. It blended olive oil, Kalamata olives, pine nuts, oven-dried tomatoes and feta cheese with spaghetti. Slices of homemade bread were served warm in a covered basket. This was a delightfully delicious yet light lunch.

The recipes used at Ti Amo are from the Perucchini family in Italy and date back many years. Everything is made fresh and authentically. The Perucchinis say the food is made with love, and that is why the restaurant is named Ti Amo.

Minestrone, salads with Italian meats and cheeses and antipasti plates featuring portobello mushrooms, grilled eggplant and artichoke halves are a few of the starters for lunch and dinner. A panini sandwich is a good main course lunch selection. The secondi piatti, or second course entrées, offer chicken, veal, salmon, shrimp and pork either sautéed, grilled or stuffed, some with pasta, some with vegetables and a variety of sauces. The Italian-style desserts include cappuccino mousse, puff pastries, tiramisu, a berry torte, gelatos, sorbets and a crêpe.

My server was family-friendly and efficient. This is a very romantic place, with Italian opera music, wine bottles hanging from the ceiling and photos of young lovers and childhood sweethearts. At the entrance and front dining room are autographed photos of singer Al Martino, actor Zachary Ty Bryson of *Home Improvement* (who skis with Max's brother, Kevin), the whole *Home Improvement* gang, President Gerald Ford and Betty Ford, astronauts Scott Carpenter and John Glenn and skier Picabo Street. The walls in the second dining room, which contains all booths, are filled with old black-and-white photos of turn-of-the-twentieth-century Verona, Italy. Two comical caricatures are side by side. One shows a chef holding up a live turkey; the second shows a waiter serving the cooked bird. The back dining area is enhanced by color photos and posters of Verona and several bottles of wine hanging from black metal wine racks.

NUTRITION AND SPECIAL REQUESTS

Ti Amo offers vegetarian dishes, and the kitchen will take care of special requests. The chefs will prepare special meals for people with food allergies.

Petti di Pollo alla Fragole (Strawberry Chicken)

SERVES 2

2 chicken breasts halves, each
    4 ounces
1 cup flour
4 ounces (½ cup) butter
4 ounces (½ cup) julienned red
    onions
6 to 10 strawberries, sliced

4 ounces (½ cup) brandy
8 ounces (1 cup) heavy cream
pinch each of salt, pepper and
    red pepper flakes
10 ounces cooked angel-hair
    pasta

1. Pound chicken breasts to about ¼-inch thick and cut each into thirds. Lightly flour both sides of the chicken pieces.
2. Melt butter in a sauté pan over medium heat. Add chicken to butter; cook halfway through and turn. Add onions and sauté until soft. Add strawberries.
3. Deglaze pan with brandy. Cook off alcohol.
4. Add heavy cream, salt, pepper and red pepper flakes, and cook until sauce thickens and is pink. Serve over hot pasta.

Recipe by Vincenzo Perucchini

Wine Recommendation: Italian Zenatto Ripasso

BASALT

BASALT WAS NAMED *after Basalt Peak (10,800 feet), a basaltic lava formation in the area. The town was founded when the Colorado Midland Railroad was built through here. Basalt is located at the juncture of the Frying Pan and Roaring Fork Rivers, both known for world-class fly-fishing. The town's chamber of commerce office is located in an old train car in the town park.*

Zip Code: 81621 **Population:** 2,681 **Elevation:** 6,620 feet

CAFÉ BERNARD

200 Midland Avenue
Phone: (970) 927-4292
Fax: (970) 927-3585
E-mail: cafeb@sopris.net
Website: None

Directions: Take exit 116 from I-70 and go north to the traffic signal. Turn right onto Highways 6 and 24 and go to the next signal. Turn right onto Highway 82, go over I-70 and continue on this road for 11.7 miles to the intersection with Highway 133. Continue straight on Highway 82 for 11½ miles and turn left onto Basalt Avenue. At the roundabout go ¾ of the way around and then exit onto Emma Road (no street sign). Go to the stop sign and turn right onto Midland Avenue (no street sign, again). Go 0.2 mile, over the bridge, to the next stop sign. Go straight, continuing on Midland Avenue for 0.1 mile. The restaurant is on the left.

ESSENTIALS

Cuisine: French-inspired with a Rocky Mountain twist
Hours: Year-round: Tue.–Sat. 7:30 A.M.–2 P.M. (breakfast until 11:30), Sun. 8 A.M.–1 P.M. Closed Mon. MAY–OCT: 6 P.M.–(about) 10 P.M. Closed Mon. NOV–APR: 6 P.M.–(about) 9 P.M. Closed Mon.
Meals and Prices: Breakfast $4–$9. Lunch $6–$13. Dinner $14–$21 (soup and salad extra).
Nonsmoking: All
Take-out: Yes
Alcohol: Beer and Wine
Credit Cards: MC, VI, DS
Personal Check: Yes
Reservations: Recommended for dinner, not accepted for breakfast or lunch
Wheelchair Access: Yes
Other: No cell phones. Catering available. Children's pastas available. Shared entrées $3. Substitutions, special orders or split orders $1.50. Service charge of 18% included for parties of six or more.

HISTORY AND BIOGRAPHY

Café Bernard is set in a building dating back to the 1880s that was probably originally used as a mercantile. Bernard's opened in July 1990, replacing The Bakery, which occupied the premises beginning in 1986. Prior to that, this corner spot on Midland Avenue was used by Eileen's Restaurant and as a laundromat.

Café Bernard is owned by Bernard Moffroid and his wife, Cathy Click. Bernard started as a private chef in Aspen in 1982 for actress Barbi Benton and her husband, George Gradow. Bernard was born in Paris in 1939 and grew up there. He came to the United States in 1951. From 1986 until 1989 he cooked at the Pine Creek Cookhouse in Ashcroft, outside Aspen. In 1990 he went to work at the Main Street Bakery in Aspen, where he met his wife-to-be, Cathy. Soon afterward, they opened Café Bernard. Cathy prepares the breakfasts and pastries, including homemade multigrain bread, French bread and croissants. Bernard works the second shift and cooks during dinner.

FOOD, SERVICE AND AMBIENCE

Café Bernard is the kind of restaurant where a quick look at the breakfast or lunch menu may not seem impressive. Don't let that fool you. The meals are delicious and made with high-quality ingredients. Everything is made to order. They have their own bakery, make homemade jams and sauces and squeeze fresh orange juice. My chicken Dijon was a tender, flattened chicken breast with a warm, creamy, mild Dijon mustard sauce made from white wine, heavy cream and shallots. On the side were fresh julienne carrots, red peppers and yellow squash, sliced mushrooms, chopped broccoli tops and peppered potatoes sprinkled with parsley and slightly burnt, just the way I like them. Linda ordered the cold smoked pepper salmon (smoked locally), which was firm and very flavorsome—a perfect dish for a hot summer day. It came with gherkins and green and Kalamata olives on a bed of lettuce accompanied by tomatoes with mayonnaise and Parmesan cheese. Linda liked the combination of the tastes. Whether the recipe is simple or involved, Bernard and Cathy find the right mix of elements to create a very flavorful dish.

Some of the more notable items on their breakfast menu are big and fluffy waffles with homemade jam; French toast made with homemade baguettes; smoked trout hash; omelets with lox, onion and cream cheese; chicken with basil sausage; and Irish oatmeal made to order with steel-cut oats. Fresh pastries are made daily. Cold plates, hot food, salads and sandwiches make up the lunch menu. Choose from grilled Caesar salad with shrimp, calamari or chicken; hot spinach salad; mousse truffée pâté; or a vegetarian sandwich with goat cheese.

You can start your dinner with an appetizer of calamari in an anchovy sauce, smoked rainbow trout or escargot. Bernard's dinner menu literally covers the world. Starting in the Pacific and moving eastward, entrées include Vietnamese chicken, Australian baby lamb chops, Rocky Mountain pasta with sautéed smoked trout or salmon, grilled Atlantic salmon steak, Mediterranean shellfish with anchovies and capers in a garlic marinara sauce and curried shrimp, the house specialty.

Café Bernard's has a seasoned staff of servers who have been with the restaurant eight to ten years. The restaurant sits at the corner of an alley. Patio dining is on the alley side, as is the entrance to the restaurant. This is a small place with only three tables outside and eight inside, which is a good thing because all of their meals are made to order. The yellow interior walls are embellished with the works of a different local artist every four to six weeks. The day I was at the restaurant, the artist on display was Peggy Everett, who hails from Buffalo, New York, and now lives on a ranch in New Castle, Colorado. She presented giclée prints of original oils computer-generated on rag paper from England and hand-enhanced with pastels. Her prints included cows and horses in meadows and open plains, roosters, chickens and a fox. The entire back wall of the restaurant behind the counter is festooned with copper kettles, pots, baking pans in different shapes and sizes, ladles, spatulas and shakers. Off to the side is a Matisse poster of a goldfish in a glass. Café Bernard is quaint and classy, the people are charming and arresting and the food is prepared with great detail and attention.

NUTRITION AND SPECIAL REQUESTS

Bernard and Cathy will honor a special request as long as it does not interfere with the integrity of the food. For example, a Caesar salad, to be a true Caesar salad, needs to have the dressing mixed and tossed into the salad. Bernard will not serve Caesar salad dressing on the side.

Special orders are not guaranteed on Saturday and Sunday due to heavy volume.

Curried Shrimp

1 12-ounce package Greek orzo

1 tablespoon vegetable oil

2 quarts chicken or fish stock, warmed

16–20 very large shrimp, peeled

2 tablespoons clarified butter

1 red pepper, julienned

Sauce

2 cups heavy cream

1 teaspoon curry powder

2 tablespoons chutney

Korean Sriracha or favorite hot sauce, to taste (chef recommends 2 teaspoons)

Grated Parmesan cheese

Garnish

green onion, cut into ⅛-inch pieces

red pepper, chopped

1. Sauté orzo in vegetable oil until brown.
2. Add hot chicken or fish stock, 2 ladles at a time, stirring, until all stock is absorbed.
3. Cool orzo when done. Orzo can be prepared in advance and refrigerated. If refrigerated, warm orzo in a nonstick pan until ready to serve.
4. Sauté shrimp in clarified butter. Add red pepper when shrimp are mostly cooked. Cook shrimp until golden brown.
5. Make the Sauce: Reduce 2 cups of heavy cream in a saucepan over medium heat, constantly stirring; add curry, chutney and Sriracha to taste. Reduce until sauce is thick and dark. If sauce breaks down, add 1 teaspoon of cream to restore. Remove from heat.
6. To prepare individual servings: Ladle orzo into the middle of dish

and sprinkle Parmesan cheese over orzo. Add 5 sautéed shrimp in center of orzo. Ladle sauce to cover shrimp. Garnish with green onion and red pepper.

Recipe by Bernard Moffroid

Wine Recommendations: Seghesio Old Wine Zinfandel or a California or Oregon Pinot Noir

❧ BEAVER CREEK ❧

BEAVER CREEK RESORT *first opened for skiing on December 15, 1980. In addition to world-class skiing, Beaver Creek boasts a center for the arts, a small-world play school for children, a year-round ice rink, a multi-use 550-seat theater and a visual arts gallery. In 1989, Beaver Creek hosted the World Ski Championships. Twenty-plus years after the first skiers hit these slopes, skiers and snowboarders can enjoy 1,625 acres of village-to-village terrain from Beaver Creek to Bachelor Gulch to Arrowhead. McMoy Park gives snowshoers and cross-country skiers 32 kilometers of groomed and backcountry mountaintop trails. Mountain biking and hiking spotlight the summertime activities.*

Zip Code: 81620 **Population:** 5,561* **Elevation:** 8,200 feet

PATINA IN THE HYATT REGENCY ———

50 West Thomas Place
Phone: (970) 845-2842
Fax: (970) 748-0058
E-mail: None
Website: www.beavercreek.hyatt.com or ccarlson@beavepo.hyatt.com

Directions: Take exit 167 from I-70 and go south ½ mile through the roundabouts (four if you came from the west, five if you came from

---

*Population for the town of Avon, which includes Beaver Creek.

the east) to Highway 6. Continue south into the Beaver Creek Resort.
Go 2 miles past the Beaver Creek Welcome Station. Turn left onto Offerson
Road. Go ½ mile and turn right into the Hyatt Regency. The Hyatt
provides valet parking for $18, but if you eat at one of their restaurants
you can get your ticket stamped and parking is free. If you opt for public
parking, stop at the Welcome Station and get a map to direct you from
one of the public parking garages to the Hyatt.

ESSENTIALS

Cuisine: French fusion

Hours: Year-round: Seven days 7 A.M.–10:30 A.M. and 5:30 P.M.–
10 P.M. Also serving lunch from mid-APR to mid-NOV: Seven days
11:30 A.M.–2:30 P.M.

Meals and Prices: Breakfast buffet $13–$16. Lunch $10–$25. Dinner
$25–$38 (soup and salad extra).

Nonsmoking: Smoking permitted only at the fire pit

Take-out: Yes

Alcohol: Full bar

Credit Cards: All five

Personal Check: No

Reservations: Recommended

Wheelchair Access: Yes, by ramps

Other: Service charge of 18% added to all parties of six or more. Split
plate fee of $5.00. Half portions available for children. No cell
phones.

HISTORY AND BIOGRAPHY

The Hyatt Hotel and Patina Restaurant opened in 1989. In the beginning, Patina was an Italian restaurant. However, with changing clientele
and comments from guests it has evolved into the current multifaceted
restaurant. The restaurant is owned by Crescent Real Estate. Restaurant
manager Don Zigler came to Patina from Beano's Cabin in Beaver
Creek in August 2001. Executive chef Pascal Coudouy has been in the
restaurant business since the early 1970s. He studied in France and came
to the United States in 1986. He owned his own French restaurant in
New York City and also cooked at the United Nations. He has been at

Patina since 2000. Patina was recognized by Zagat as one of the Top 100 Restaurants in the United States in 1999.

FOOD, SERVICE AND AMBIENCE

I ordered the roasted-tomato soup and the pasta special of the day, linguini with rock shrimp. The soup had some ground black pepper, just the right proportion of spices, a definite roasted flavor and a dollop of grated Parmesan in the middle. The pasta dish came with several chopped pieces of shrimp, Roma tomatoes, pesto cream and pine nuts. The rim of this large bowl was sprinkled with fresh chopped basil and Parmesan. I really liked the pesto cream sauce flavor, which was not too heavy. The only thing missing was the bread, which my server forgot to bring. She also did not return to fill my water glass until I was finished eating. It reminded me of when Marie Antoinette said, "Let them eat cake." Here I had this delicious dish in front of me (the cake, or in my case, the linguini with rock shrimp), but no bread or water to go with it.

Patina serves a continental breakfast buffet that includes fresh seasonal fruit and berries, fruit-flavored yogurts, cereals, granola, baked goods and imported and domestic cheeses. For a few dollars more, you can get the continental offerings plus omelets made to order, pancakes, waffles, French toast, bacon and sausage links.

Lunch selections feature red lentil chili, grilled salmon or Asian grilled shrimp salad, a mountain burger, grilled vegetable and portobello sandwich, herb-crusted trout and seared halibut with Asian vegetables, and for dessert, banana spring roll, ice cream brownie sandwich and a banana berry smoothie.

To start off your dinner, Patina offers a raw oyster bar with crab legs, shrimp, lobster tail, clams and caviar. To maintain the freshest quality, Patina receives its fish and shellfish every other day from the East and West Coasts. There are several unique selections on the dinner menu. For appetizers, you can choose from jumbo asparagus with baby artichokes, towers made from shrimp and avocado or smoked salmon and potato, smoked duck and goat cheese spring rolls and rice-paper-wrapped crab cakes. More uncommon items appear among the soup and salad selections, including lobster bisque, tataki salad with seared ahi tuna and tofu Napoleon. Fresh fish, meat and poultry highlight the entrées, with items like lemongrass poached salmon, Szechwan pepper-crusted venison, soy-marinated duck breast and grilled filet of beef with foie gras.

Patina's dining room is long and rectangular. Windows along one of the long sides supplies some great views of the Beaver Creek ski slopes. I sat inside and listened to jazz while most others took advantage of the warm but windy spring weather on the outdoor dining terrace. If you enter the dining room from the hotel lobby, the first thing that you will see is a large mural of meadows, mountains, trees and sky covering two walls. From this entrance, there is a long buffet line to the right in front of a rock fireplace and a hunter-green tile wall. Cherrywood columns and ceiling trim complement the green slate floor and the red-and-green high-back cushion chairs. In the back of the restaurant are Neil Boyle paintings of an Indian in full headdress, another Indian on horseback and a cowboy resting. Patina provides class and a one-of-a-kind style of cuisine for skiers and travelers alike.

NUTRITION AND SPECIAL REQUESTS

Some menu items are marked "cuisine naturelle," a concept for foods that are fresh, fun, flavorful and as appealing to the eye and palate as they are nourishing to the body. Each dish is designed to limit excess sodium and fat and emphasize nutritional balance, flavor and wholesome fibers. Special requests are handled daily, and the staff "will do anything they can possibly do" to accommodate diners.

Oven-Roasted Lobster with Purple Potato Puree and Sautéed Baby Fennel in a Red Wine–Cinnamon Reduction

SERVES 6

Lobster

6 2-pound lobsters	4 gallons salted water

1. Bring the water to a boil and add lobsters. Cook for 5 minutes. Let cool and take off the heads and reserve for stock.
2. Cut the lobsters in half; partially remove the meat and line the shell with butter. Put the meat back into the shell and set aside. This prevents the meat from drying out when cooking.

Purple Potato Puree

½ pound purple potatoes	1 cup heavy cream
3 tablespoons butter	salt and pepper to taste

1. Cook the potatoes in a pot of salted water until soft.
2. Strain and whip the potatoes, adding butter, cream, salt and pepper. Set aside.

Red Wine–Cinnamon Reduction Sauce

1 tablespoon red wine	1 cup sugar
2 cups apple juice	2 cinnamon sticks
1 tablespoon lemon juice	

Combine everything in a saucepot and heat, reducing to 1 cup. The end result should have a syrup-like consistency. Remove cinnamon sticks before using.

Lobster Cake

3 medium-size shrimp	1 tablespoon fresh tarragon
1 cup heavy cream	1 tablespoon fresh chives
1 cup lobster claw meat	1 teaspoon lemon juice
1 tablespoon minced fennel	salt and pepper to taste
1 cup bread crumbs, divided	

1. Combine shrimp and cream in a food processor. Mix until mousse forms, and fold in the rest of the ingredients except for ½ cup of the bread crumbs. Form into 6 cakes.
2. Coat the cakes with the remaining ½ cup of bread crumbs.

Assembling the Dish

3 baby fennel   oil for sautéing

1. Preheat oven to 350 degrees. Place the lobster tails and Lobster
   Cakes in a pan and bake in preheated oven for 7 to 10 minutes, flip-
   ping the cakes after 3 minutes.
2. Cut the tops off the baby fennel and discard tops. Cut each fennel
   bulb in half. Julienne the bulbs, sauté in oil and season with salt and
   pepper.
3. To plate the lobster, place the sautéed fennel in the center of the
   plate, then place one cake and ¼ cup of the Potato Purée on each
   side of the fennel.
4. Pull the meat out of one half of the shell. Take the half with the
   meat still intact and lean it against the potato and the cake.
5. Place the removed meat on top and garnish with a fennel sprig. Spoon
   the Red-Wine Reduction Sauce around the plate, circling the lobster.

Recipe by Pascal Coudouy

Wine Recommendations: Sleepy Hollow or Chalk Hill Chardonnay

SADDLERIDGE ————————————

44 Meadows Lane
Phone: (970) 845-5456
Fax: (970) 845-5459
E-mail: None
Website: www.snow.com and www.opentable.com

Directions: Take exit 167 from I-70 and go south ½ mile through the
roundabouts (four if you came from the west, five if you came from the
east) to Highway 6. Continue south into the Beaver Creek Resort. Go
2 miles past the Beaver Creek Welcome Station. Turn left onto Offerson
Road. Go 0.4 mile and turn right into public parking at St. James Place.
Walk up to the front desk or concierge desk at St. James Place and
request a shuttle (no charge) to SaddleRidge. One should arrive about
every ten minutes. (You will have to request a shuttle back to St. James
after your meal.)

ESSENTIALS

Cuisine: Contemporary American
Hours: Thanksgiving to early APR: Seven nights 5:30 P.M.–10 P.M. Closed
to public rest of year. (Open then only for special private functions.)
Meals and Prices: Dinner $20–$32 (soup and salad extra)
Nonsmoking: Yes
Take-out: Yes
Alcohol: Full bar
Credit Cards: All five
Personal Check: Vail Valley residents only with ID
Reservations: Highly recommended
Wheelchair Access: Yes, by elevator
Other: Service charge of 18% added to tables of six or more

HISTORY AND BIOGRAPHY

SaddleRidge was built in 1987 as an executive retreat for Sherson–
Lehman Brothers. Ralph Laman was the designer. When American
Express purchased Sherson–Lehman Brothers in 1991, it sold Saddle-
Ridge, consisting of a clubhouse and twelve villas, to the Vail Ski
Association. Naomi Leff decorated the restaurant and the library down-
stairs, 80 percent of which is decorated with antiques.

Jeanne McCann is the SaddleRidge manager. She has been with the
restaurant since 1993 and worked previously at the Red Lion in Vail.
Assistant manager Joe Wilson has also been with the restaurant since
1993. He started in the restaurant business in the 1970s in Stowe,
Vermont, and came to Colorado in 1989. Executive chef George
"Geordy" Ogden is from Manhattan Beach, California, and has been at
the SaddleRidge since 1999. He came to Colorado in 1993 and worked
for one season at Two Elk and four years at Terra Bistro, both in Vail.
Sous-chef Eric Priebe started at the SaddleRidge in 2000. He previously
worked at the Ore House in Riverside, California, and also at Terra
Bistro in Vail.

FOOD, SERVICE AND AMBIENCE

SaddleRidge is in a colossal, majestic-looking building. The dining room is in a great hall with a 40-foot arched ceiling, enormous

chandeliers and a 30-foot-high wood-burning stone fireplace. But let's talk about the food first.

I ordered the Asian duck breast with horseradish mashed potatoes, roasted shiitake mushrooms, citrus slaw, soy ginger sauce, red onion and mandarin oranges. This dish was an excellent blend of contrasting tastes, with the citrus slaw and mandarin oranges facing off against the soy ginger sauce, shiitakes, onion and horseradish potatoes while the duck stayed neutral in the middle. The presentation concurred with this assessment: Duck slices were stood up against the potatoes, which were topped with citrus slaw; the sharp, mashed red onion, roasted shiitakes and mandarin oranges were on the side. Soy ginger sauce was drizzled around the edge of the plate. The medium-rare duck had just enough fat to enhance the flavor and my cholesterol level. I discovered that I preferred these horseradish mashed potatoes to the more prevalent garlic mashed potatoes. The bread served prior to the meal was a wheat and white mixture with a crispy crust, made locally. SaddleRidge makes its own soups, sauces and desserts.

The salads include some tempting items like smoked salmon, poached egg, capers, goat cheese, dried cherries and chili-spiked pecans. Spotlighting the starters are the seafood burrito, wasabi-seared tuna, a vegetable terrine and a duck quesadilla. Seafood, pasta, chicken, lamb, steaks and two vegetarian dishes highlight the main course selections. The dessert menu covers a wide range of tastes from sweet to sedate. You can order chocolate mousse Napoleon, caramelized banana split, pound cake with pear compote, assorted ice creams and sorbets or the assorted cheese board for two.

My server, Lauren, was not only very courteous, professional and efficient but also very informative about the restaurant's history. I could hear jazz music coming from the kitchen. Those chandeliers that I mentioned earlier are four to five feet in diameter, made by a blacksmith in Minturn, Colorado, and weigh 1,000 pounds each. They were originally the wheels used on railroad cars. The high dining-room walls are decked with the stuffed heads of elk, caribou, deer, buffalo and goats. Bouquets of wildflowers and red cowboy scarf napkins adorn the tables. Indian rugs and saddles hang from the high balcony, which is unfortunately not used for dining because it gets too hot up there. A bearskin rug hangs on the stairs leading up to the balcony. The back bar dates to the late 1800s and is from Ouray, Colorado. The front bar was constructed to match the back. Vintage photos of Arapaho and Sioux Indians taken by photographers Edward Curtis and Roland Reed further embellish the dining area.

Downstairs is the SaddleRidge library, which should not be missed. All the books in this library are from the 1800s. Here you will find $8 million in antiques and artifacts including General George Custer's hat and canteen, photos of Buffalo Bill and Teddy Roosevelt, Annie Oakley's shotgun, a print from a carving of George Washington used for the one-dollar bill (one of only five proofs used), photos of Crazy Horse and Geronimo and Buffalo Bill's desk. The SaddleRidge is historic, western and elegant. The restaurant is a worthy place to dine and explore.

NUTRITION AND SPECIAL REQUESTS

SaddleRidge offers two vegetable main course dishes. Geordy says he is always willing to do special requests.

Grilled Asian Duck Breast with Horseradish Mashed Potatoes and Asian Slaw

SERVES 4

Duck Breast and Marinade

1 orange	2 ounces Ketsap Manis
1 lime	(Indonesian sweet soy sauce)
2 ounces fresh ginger	2 ounces (¼ cup) water
1 ounce garlic	1 double-lobe Muscovy
½ ounce crushed Thai chilies	duck breast
4 ounces (½ cup) light soy sauce	

1. Juice citrus; chop ginger and garlic. Combine everything except the duck breast in a bowl.
2. Clean the breast of any silver skin on meat side. Score skin. Separate lobes.
3. Marinate breast for 4 hours to overnight.

Asian Slaw

juice of 1 orange	½ head Napa cabbage
¼ cup mayonnaise	2 carrots
1 teaspoon rice wine vinegar	1 red pepper
1/8 teaspoon sesame oil	zest of 1 orange
1 teaspoon soy sauce	1 zucchini

1. Whip together orange juice, mayonnaise, rice wine vinegar, sesame oil and soy sauce. Set aside.
2. Julienne cabbage, carrots, pepper, orange zest and the green part of the zucchini. Combine with the dressing. Set aside.

Horseradish Mashed Potatoes

1½ pounds red "B" potatoes, scrubbed	½ tablespoon shiro miso (white miso paste)
1 cup heavy cream	3 tablespoons butter
2 tablespoons prepared horseradish	salt and pepper to taste

1. Cover potatoes with water and boil until soft. Warm the cream.
2. Transfer drained potatoes, warmed cream and remaining ingredients to a mixing bowl. Whip using paddle attachment.

Garnish

roasted shiitake mushrooms (sliced or left whole and seasoned with salt and pepper; roast in 350-degree oven for 15 minutes)	green onions, cut into long pieces navel or blood orange segments

Assembly

1. Grill duck breast to medium rare. Let rest. Reserve marinade.
2. Bring marinade to a boil for 2 minutes. Strain.
3. Place potatoes on plate. Top with Asian slaw.
4. Slice breast thinly on a bias; arrange on potatoes.

5. Garnish with roasted shiitake mushrooms, green onion, orange segments and reserved marinade.

Recipe by George "Geordy" Ogden

Wine Recommendations: Oregon or California Pinot Noir

SPLENDIDO AT THE CHATEAU ────────

17 Chateau Lane
Phone: (970) 845-8808
Fax: (970) 845-8961
E-mail: splendid@vail.net
Website: www.splendidobeavercreek.com

Directions: Take exit 167 from I-70 and go south ½ mile through the roundabouts (four if you came from the west, five if you came from the east) to Highway 6. Continue south into the Beaver Creek Resort. Go 2.2 miles past the Beaver Creek Welcome Station. Turn right onto Scott Hill Road and go ¼ mile up the hill. Turn right into the drive for Splendido and go 300 feet up to the Chateau. There is valet parking except in the slow spring and fall seasons, when you park yourself in front of the Chateau.

ESSENTIALS

Cuisine: Contemporary Rocky Mountain
Hours: Mid-NOV to mid-APR: Seven nights 5:30 P.M.–10 P.M. Mid-JUN through SEP: Seven nights 6 P.M.–10 P.M. OCT to mid-NOV and mid-MAY to mid-JUN: Tue.–Sat. 6 P.M.–10 P.M.; closed Sun–Mon. Closed mid-APR to mid-MAY.
Meals and Prices: Dinner $27–$45 (soup and salad extra)
Nonsmoking: Smoking permitted only on the patio
Take-out: Yes
Alcohol: Full bar
Credit Cards: All five
Personal Check: Local only with ID
Reservations: Recommended, particularly during DEC–MAR and JUL–AUG
Wheelchair Access: Yes, by elevator

The Chateau was built by Vista Hospitality in 1990. The area now occupied by Splendido was originally intended to be a unit in the Chateau, but the owners, Magna Entertainment led by Frank Stronnack, decided the chateau should have a restaurant. In fall 1992, Chef Chad Scothorn from Beano's Cabin in Beaver Creek opened Chadwick's Restaurant. Chad and Chadwick's left in spring 1994, and in June 1994, Splendido opened.

Joanie McVey is the dining room director. She has been in the restaurant business since 1990, having previously worked at the Highlands Inn and the Rio Grill in Carmel, California. She came to Colorado in 1994 and worked as the food and beverage director at the Beaver Creek Lodge and the Lionshead Lodge in Vail before joining the Splendido staff in June 1997. Jim Williams is the maitre d' and assistant dining room director. He began his career in restaurants in 1975, also in California. His resume includes working as a cook at Jambo's in Merced, California, as headwaiter at the Ventura Inn in Big Sur, and as a waiter at L'Orangiere in Los Angeles and at the Highlands Inn in Carmel, where he met Joanie McVey. He came to Colorado in the winter of 1994 and managed Mirabelle in Beaver Creek before moving to Splendido in June 1994.

Executive chef and general manager David Walford was born in Great Britain and raised in Colorado. He started in the restaurant business in 1971, working in Vail restaurants while enjoying life as a ski bum. He trained at Auberge du Soleil in California's Napa Valley and at Miramonte in St. Helena, California, before working for a year in France. He then returned to San Francisco to work at Masa's. David was executive chef at Sweet Basil in Vail for nine years before becoming executive chef at Splendido in October 1994. In 1996 he was appointed to his current position. In October 2000, David received the Award of Merit from the Confrerie de la Chaine des Rostisseurs in recognition of his creative flair.

The chefs de cuisine are Michael Greenstein and Soa Yi. Michael has been in the restaurant business since 1990 and previously worked as sous-chef at Sweet Basil for six years and in Las Vegas, Nevada, for five years. He is self-taught and joined David at Splendido in June 2000. Soa started in restaurants in 1994, is a graduate of the French Culinary

Institute in New York City, and has been with Splendido since 1997. Pastry chef Trista "George" Wollesen has been in the restaurant business since 1990 and worked at Beano's Cabin before coming to Splendido in 1998.

FOOD, SERVICE AND AMBIENCE

Flavorsome combinations, high-quality ingredients and artful presentations are the three best descriptions I can think of for David Walford's cuisine. These qualities were present in both the appetizer and the entrée that I ordered. For a starter, I chose the crispy veal sweetbreads. These were extremely tender pieces of veal, lightly salted, with a crispy crust and a topping of celery-root puree. Grain mustard cream, a whole-grain mustard with a sour cream texture, was offered on the side. Three green beans and sherry vinegar reduction drippings completed the perimeter of the plate. My main course selection was the wild striped bass seared with porcini powder, which gave the exterior a crusty texture that I found very favorable. The bass was set atop leaf spinach. Porcini mushrooms were placed on top of a potato puree, and the plate's perimeter was laced with bordelaise sauce. The bass was firm yet broke apart easily with a fork.

Preceding my entrée, I was served a trio of appetizing homemade breads: lavosh, thin, crispy bread made with Parmesan and poppyseed; an onion-seasoned Tuscan bread and honey-wheat raisin. Duck strudel, compliments of the kitchen, was also brought to my table. It consisted of tiny crumbled duck pieces in a flaky strudel with a cream sauce. It also stimulated my appetite. Afterward, petit fours—chocolate tortes, a biscuit, a sugar wafer cookie and white and dark chocolates with walnuts—finished my dining experience.

For starters you can sample peach-wood smoked salmon, sautéed duck foie gras with caramelized mango, wood-oven roasted Maine sea scallops or Caspian Sea caviar. Spotlighting the soups and salads are clam-saffron bisque, roast beet and blood orange salad and warm Maine lobster with tomato. The main courses feature wild striped bass in bordelaise sauce, Atlantic salmon in lemon-caviar sauce, wood-oven roasted young chicken and red-wine braised beef short ribs. Pastry chef Wollesen's delectable desserts include banana-chocolate peanut butter tart, Valrhona chocolate fudge soufflé and homemade ice creams and sorbets.

Service was excellent. The table was cleared and silverware was replaced with each course change. The servers were dressed in black shirts and pants. Soothing flute, piano and harp music played before Taylor Kundolf took to the keyboard with his Broadway arrangements and classic cabaret piano-bar music. Taylor also painted a wall mural entitled "The Recipe," which is displayed in the back of the dining room, next to the open kitchen. It is an artwork in three dimensions with flaps that you can lift up, a pastel collage of recipes and painted fruits, vegetables and piano keys. This remarkable creation is complemented by brightly colored paintings of circus scenes, fish and flowers and fruity-looking orange- and raspberry-colored drapes. A sconce on one wall has two candles on either side of an immense bottle of wine. I sat at a table with white linen cloths and napkins, fresh Indian paintbrush flowers and a window view of the patio. Splendido at the Chateau has an extremely talented, artistic and creative staff of individuals who will treat you with the utmost consideration without a speck of pretentiousness.

NUTRITION AND SPECIAL REQUESTS

Chef Walford and his staff use all healthful ingredients, the best available. They will cook anything for anyone, provided they have the items in stock or you have called ahead. They are amenable to honoring requests for substitutions and making menu adjustments.

Wood-Oven Roasted Colorado Rack of Lamb

SERVES 4

2 8-bone lamb racks with
   long bones
Lamb Marinade (recipe follows)
kosher salt

freshly ground black pepper
Pomegranate Lamb Sauce
   (recipe follows)

1. Trim the fat cap from the lamb and clean the bones. Reserve the trimmings for the Pomegranate Lamb Sauce.
2. Marinate the lamb for 24 hours in the Lamb Marinade, then drain

(reserve 1 cup of marinade for Pomegranate Lamb Sauce) and wrap the exposed rib bones in aluminum foil.

3. Season the lamb with kosher salt and freshly ground black pepper.
4. Roast for 12–20 minutes in a wood oven fired with oak, or cook the racks on an outdoor grill. (The lamb can also be browned in a very hot skillet with a little oil and then roasted in a conventional oven at 450 degrees until medium-rare.)
5. Let rest for 10 minutes before carving. Serve with Pomegranate Lamb Sauce.

Lamb Marinade

4 cups pomegranate juice	2 tablespoons chopped fresh
1 cup olive oil	rosemary
juice and zest of 2 lemons	1 tablespoons chopped fresh thyme
½ cup finely chopped shallots	2 tablespoons crushed black
½ cup chopped garlic	peppercorns

1. To obtain pomegranate juice, split open 5–7 ripe pomegranates and scoop out seeds and flesh. Pulse in blender to release juice.
2. Strain mixture to remove hulls of seeds.
3. Combine juice with rest of ingredients and mix well.

Pomegranate Lamb Sauce

reserved meat and bone trimmings from the lamb	1 teaspoon black peppercorns, crushed
1 tablespoon vegetable oil	1 sprig fresh rosemary
2 shallots, chopped	6 cups lamb, veal, or chicken stock
4 garlic cloves, crushed	kosher salt
1 cup reserved Lamb Marinade	freshly ground black pepper

1. Cut the lamb trimmings into 1-inch pieces.
2. In large saucepan, heat the oil over medium-high heat. Brown the lamb for about 10 minutes. Transfer to a bowl and reserve. Pour off all but 1 tablespoon of the fat from the saucepan.
3. Reduce the heat to medium and add the chopped shallots, stirring often, until browned, about 3–5 minutes. Add the crushed garlic and cook for 1 more minute.

4. Return the browned meat trimmings to the pan and add the reserved Lamb Marinade, the peppercorns and rosemary. Bring to a boil and cook until the marinade is reduced to ¼ cup.
5. Add the stock and bring back to a boil. Simmer on medium-low heat until reduced to about 2 cups, skimming often to remove fat that rises to the surface.
6. Strain the sauce through a fine sieve, discarding the solids, and return the sauce to a clean saucepan. Season to taste with kosher salt and freshly ground black pepper.

Recipe by David Walford

Wine Recommendation: Rhône-style Syrah

❧ BRECKENRIDGE ❧

BRECKENRIDGE WAS ORIGINALLY *named Fort Meribeh after the only woman, a Mary B., in the original party of settlers led by General George E. Spencer in 1859. The town was later renamed after former U.S. Vice President John Cabell Breckinridge. Angered by Breckinridge's sympathy for the Confederacy during the Civil War, the town's citizens, ardent Unionists, changed the spelling. The first "i" was changed to "e" to disassociate the town of Breckenridge from the man. On July 23, 1887, the largest single gold nugget ever found in Colorado was discovered by miner Tom Groves at nearby Farncomb Hill. It weighed in at 13 pounds, 7 ounces! Today, Breckenridge has over 350 buildings on the National Register of Historic Places.*

Zip Code: 80424 **Population:** 2,408 **Elevation:** 9,602 feet

BRECKENRIDGE BARBECUE

301 South Main Street
Phone: (970) 453-7313
Fax: (970) 453-7413

E-mail: None
Website: None

Directions: Take exit 203 from I-70 and proceed south on Highway 9 for 10 miles into Breckenridge, where Highway 9 is also Main Street. At the traffic signal for Lincoln Avenue in the middle of town, continue straight for 2 blocks. The restaurant is on the right on the southwest corner of South Main Street and Adams Street.

ESSENTIALS

Cuisine: Texas-style barbecue
Hours: Seven days 11 A.M.–9 P.M. (10 P.M. DEC–MAR)
Meals and Prices: Lunch $6–$8. Dinner $11–$17 (soup and salad extra).
Nonsmoking: Smoking permitted only at the bar
Take-out: Yes, unless they are very busy
Alcohol: Full bar
Credit Cards: MC, VI, AE, DI
Personal Check: No
Reservations: No
Wheelchair Access: Yes, by a lift in the back
Other: Split platter charge $2

HISTORY AND BIOGRAPHY

Breckenridge Barbecue, opened in 1994, is owned by Breckenridge Brewery. A Wendy's fast-food restaurant and a bank were previous occupants of this space. The general manager is Michele Ranieri from Buffalo, New York. She has been in the restaurant business since 1990 and previously worked at The Village Pub in Breckenridge before joining Breckenridge Barbecue in 1996. The kitchen manager is John Thaler, a graduate of Johnson & Wales Culinary School in Providence, Rhode Island. He started out in the business in 1991, opening Houlihan's restaurants in Richmond, Virginia, and Charleston, South Carolina. He also helped to open Tripp's Steak and Seafood Restaurants in Durham and Raleigh, North Carolina. He came to Colorado in April 1999 and worked briefly at the Keystone Ranch before joining Breckenridge Barbecue in July 2000.

FOOD, SERVICE AND AMBIENCE

Breckenridge Barbecue has two things going for it: great barbecue and one of the best scenic vistas in Breckenridge, to be enjoyed from the two-tiered open deck.

First, the barbecue. I found their St. Louis–style, hickory-smoked pork ribs to have a pleasing smoked taste. The half rack was seven ribs with plenty of meat glazed with Breckenridge Barbecue's own barbecue sauce. The sauce is also served in bottles on the tables and comes in two versions: mild, with a good tomato and vinegar flavor; and my preference, hot, which had some zip without being objectionable. The beans with pork and onions were good, and the coleslaw had a favorable sweet taste. Rounding out the meal was a soft, crumbly, big chunk of home-made corn bread.

Breckenridge Barbecue also serves smoked chicken, brisket, pulled pork, turkey and spicy sausage links. For an appetizer you can order smoked wings, beer-batter onion rings, jalapeño poppers, a quesadilla or nachos. Spicy red chili, homemade soup and salads are also available. There are several sandwich selections, including chicken, pork, fish and smoked turkey, as well as sausage and burgers. For dinner, sirloin and rib-eye steaks, center-cut pork chops, a chicken platter and turkey are on the menu.

Eating barbecue can be a bit messy, which is why, after my meal was served, I was surprised to discover I had only one napkin at my table and had to request more. Service was a bit slow, but they eventually got the job done. Breckenridge Barbecue has dining on two levels; their esteemed deck is out back. From the entrance, there is dining to the left and straight ahead, with an open kitchen to the left and a bar in the back. The main level is decorated with photos of Breckenridge taken by local photographer Scott Duffy, including the 1996 Brecken-ridge Bumps & Jumps Contest, a close-up of a red rose, Blue Lake, columbines and other wildflowers. Added to this melange are posters of beer and breweries. About halfway through the main dining room and to the right is a staircase leading upstairs, where you will find wooden floors, booths, tables and chairs; a bar; pool table; big-screen television; and Foosball—it's an area for the sports-minded.

The Breckenridge Barbecue deck is much acclaimed and frequented by the locals and provides a majestic panorama of the Ten-Mile

Mountain Range to the west. Despite the fact I was here in April at the end of the ski season, each afternoon this spot was filled to capacity. Because there are no umbrellas on the tables, it can get pretty warm on sunny days. However, if you like barbecue and the weather cooperates, you can have the best of both worlds.

NUTRITION AND SPECIAL REQUESTS

Breckenridge Barbecue serves salads, a veggie burger and a portobello mushroom burger for noncarnivores. They are flexible on special requests.

Spicy Red Chili

SERVES 6–8

4 tablespoons olive oil	32 ounces tomato sauce
1 large yellow onion, chopped	2 tablespoons chili powder
4 green chilies, diced	1 tablespoon ground cumin
2 cloves garlic, minced	⅛ cup crushed red pepper
1 jalapeño, minced	salt and pepper to taste
2 pounds ground beef	

1. Sauté onion in hot oil in large pot until translucent. Add chilies, garlic and jalapeño. Sauté lightly.
2. Add the ground beef. Sauté beef until fully cooked. Drain off excess grease.
3. Add the tomato sauce, chili powder, cumin and red pepper. Allow to simmer for 20 minutes.
4. Add salt and pepper to taste. Serve, or cool and store in refrigerator for up to 3 days.

Recipe by John Thaler

Beverage Recommendation: Breckenridge Brewery Avalanche beer

SOUTH RIDGE SEAFOOD GRILL ────────

215 South Ridge Street
Phone: (970) 547-0063
Fax: (970) 547-0063
E-mail: None
Website: None

Directions: Take exit 203 from I-70 and proceed south on Highway 9 for 10 miles into Breckenridge. At the traffic signal for Lincoln Avenue in the middle of town, turn left and go 1 block. Turn right onto South Ridge Street. The restaurant is 1½ blocks up on the right.

ESSENTIALS

Cuisine: Seafood and modern American
Hours: Seven nights 5 P.M.–10 P.M. Closed MAY.
Meals and Prices: Dinner $7–$35 (soup and salad extra)
Nonsmoking: Smoking permitted only at bar or on patio
Take-out: Yes
Alcohol: Full bar
Credit Cards: MC, VI, DS, DI
Personal Check: In-state only with ID
Reservations: Recommended
Wheelchair Access: Yes
Other: Happy hour 4 P.M.–6 P.M. with raw oyster bar. Children's menu.

HISTORY AND BIOGRAPHY

The building that houses the South Ridge Seafood Grill was constructed in 1977. Tillie's, a burger and steak restaurant, held the space until 1997, when South Ridge took over. Paul Brenholt is the owner, manager and chef. He has been in the restaurant business since 1981, working in Dallas, Texas. This is his first restaurant in Colorado.

FOOD, SERVICE AND AMBIENCE

On the day that I visited, Apalachicola oysters from Florida were one of the grill's happy-hour specials. They were smaller than the Texas oysters that I had at Peaceful Henry's in Guffey and not as fresh tasting, perhaps because they were shipped from a greater distance. But hey, they were oysters and still delightful! For my entrée, I ordered one of Chef Paul's masterful creations: grilled yellowfin tuna on roasted red and green peppers, Kalamata olives, grilled zucchini and artichoke in basil pesto with citrus balsamic reduction. The tuna was seared on the outside and still a little pink on the inside, with a firm consistency. Green and red onions, tomatoes and a lot of capers complemented this light, unique creation.

Chef Paul's creative menu reflects an Asian influence, due primarily to his previous marriage to a Korean woman. His ingenuity shows in appetizers such as mussels steamed in Thai red curry–coconut broth, Chesapeake blue crab cakes with curry mayonnaise and spinach and artichoke ravioli in basil pesto cream. Among the soups and salads are chicken tortilla soup, poached Gulf shrimp in a Greek-style salad and a traditional Caesar salad with poached Gulf shrimp. His entrées have very lengthy, descriptive names. Two to try are Colorado-raised striped bass with a warm salad of potato, green beans and mushrooms in a whole-grain mustard vinaigrette and lemon-thyme aioli; and medallions of beef tenderloin with polenta-crusted potato cakes and bourbon–black peppercorn cream sauce. Completing the menu are surf and turf combinations, pastas and light entrées like black tuna tostados with marinated cabbage, grilled pineapple salsa and sour cream. Overall, I found the food at South Ridge Seafood Grill to be imaginative and inspired.

My server was prompt and frequent with the water refills and very helpful in answering or getting answers to my questions. Blues music played softly. From the entrance, the bar is to the right and the dining area is to the left, separated by a dividing wall topped with seashells. Overhead is a high copper ceiling with a colorful blue-and-gold mosaic in the middle. The dining-room wall to the left has some peculiar pictures of a man driving a red truck down a muddy road and a daydreamer with a rabbit. The rear wall has an entirely different appeal, with color photos of mountain goats looking perilously over a cliff, as well as a tiger and a cougar. A small patio to the right of the entrance is used in warmer weather.

Vegetarians note: South Ridge offers an entrée of grilled portobello mushroom over linguini, but other than that it is pretty much fish, seafood and meats. They say they will be very accommodating of special requests.

Sautéed Tilapia with Spinach, Crab and Pernod

SERVES 4

1 teaspoon oil	salt and pepper
1 shallot, minced	4 6-ounce tilapia filets, or other
½ clove garlic, minced	mild white fish
½ cup heavy cream	½ pound crabmeat
2 tablespoons Pernod or Sambuca	½ cup bread crumbs
1 pound fresh spinach, cooked	¼ cup grated Parmesan cheese
and squeezed dry	1 teaspoon dry basil

1. Heat a saucepan over medium heat; add oil, the minced shallot and garlic. Sauté for 15 seconds.
2. Off the heat, add the cream, Pernod and the spinach. Return to the heat, being careful of the liqueur flaming. Bring to a boil. Add salt and pepper to taste and remove from the heat.
3. Season the fish filets with salt and pepper. Sauté over medium-high heat for 30 seconds on each side and transfer to a baking dish large enough to hold the fillets side by side. Preheat oven to 400 degrees.
4. Divide the spinach mixture between the 4 filets and spread over the length of the filets. Do the same with the crab and then the bread crumbs, Parmesan cheese and dry basil.
5. Bake the fish in preheated oven for approximately 15 minutes. Serve immediately. Potatoes and a green vegetable are good accompaniments.

Recipe by Paul Brenhold

Wine Recommendation: Sonoma Cutrer Russian River Ranches Chardonnay

THE SWISS HAVEN RESTAURANT

325 South Main Street
Phone: (970) 453-6969
Fax: (970) 453-6969
E-mail: None
Website: None

Directions: Take exit 203 from I-70 and proceed south on Highway 9 for 10 miles into Breckenridge, where Highway 9 is also Main Street. At the traffic signal for Lincoln Avenue in the middle of town, continue straight for 2½ blocks. The restaurant is on the right.

ESSENTIALS

Cuisine: Swiss
Hours: Seven days 5 P.M.–10 P.M. Closed MAY to Memorial Day weekend and mid-OCT to Thanksgiving.
Meals and Prices: Dinner $13–$20 (soup and salad extra)
Nonsmoking: Smoking permitted only on patio
Take-out: Yes, except fondues
Alcohol: Beer, wine and limited mixed drinks
Credit Cards: MC, VI, AE, DS
Personal Check: In-state only
Reservations: Highly recommended
Wheelchair Access: Yes (no ramp; staff will carry). There are about a dozen steps.
Other: No separate checks. Service charge of 18% may be added to parties of six or more.

HISTORY AND BIOGRAPHY

The Swiss Haven Restaurant occupies a building constructed in the early 1970s and originally used to sell ice cream. In the mid-1980s the space was converted to house Giampetro's Italian Restaurant. The Swiss Haven replaced it in November 1996. The dining room to the left of the entrance was added in 1998.

Owner Matt Garrett started in the restaurant business as a cook in North Carolina in 1991. He is a 1996 graduate of the New England

Culinary Institute in Montpelier, Vermont. Matt worked at Café Alpine in Breckenridge from 1996 until 1999, when he took over The Swiss Haven. Manager Colleen Carney "loves her job" and loves being at The Swiss Haven. She also has been here since 1999. Kitchen Manager Jimmy Welch has been cooking since 1991, is from Virginia and came to The Swiss Haven in 2000. The restaurant has two sister restaurants by the same name and with very similar menus, but different ownership, in Denver and Steamboat Springs.

FOOD, SERVICE AND AMBIENCE

The Swiss Haven serves Swiss specialties with Italian and French influences. The restaurant's version of Switzerland's national dish, cheese fondue, contains the highest-quality imported aged Swiss cheeses along with dry white wine, Swiss Kirschwasser and fresh garlic. I tried another Swiss specialty, the raclette grill. An electric grill was brought to my table and plugged into a wall outlet. As the grill got warm, a wooden tray was presented, holding four slices of Swiss raclette cheese; two strips of Angus beef topped with black peppercorns, chopped garlic, minced onion and salt; four chunks of chicken with vegetarian seasoning; two chicken-and-apple sausage links; and a half-cup of cornichons, cocktail onions and baby corn. The meats were all raw and ready to be placed on the hot grill. A side basket with five warm, baby red potatoes was also served; these could be eaten as is, or cut and charred on the grill. To melt the raclette cheese, a small fireproof tray with a handle was provided that slid under the grill. After melting, the cheese could be scraped off the tray onto the potatoes and meats. This meal is for active people who do not mind mixing a little work with their meal. The cheeses and meats were all top-quality, and the seasonings in and on the meats created some very flavorsome tastes.

Two of my arts-and-crafts-show partners joined me for dinner. They elected to try two other house specialties: the Monk and the Mount McKinley. The Monk was a really moist and tender sliced chicken breast sautéed in white wine with a zesty lemon-pepper sauce. My partner noticed more lemon than pepper flavor. The McKinley was a sautéed, then baked, firm yet flaky, wild Alaskan salmon filet. It was marinated in a citrus mustard and plated with a creamy sauce de Provence. Both dishes came with rosti potatoes, which are twice as thick but not as crunchy as hash browns, mostly not browned and on the bland side. However, that could be corrected by adding some of the main dish's sauce. Both of my partners enjoyed their choices and said they were enough food without soup or salad.

For starters, you can try a homemade appetizer like sautéed Provençal mushrooms sautéed in sherry, white wine and Provençal herbs; or kachniche, which is French bread soaked with white wine and topped with prosciutto, pears and melted Gruyère and Vacherin cheeses. Your homemade soup options are tomato basil, cream of potato and bundner gurstensuppe, a hearty barley packed with vegetables and smoked bundnerfleisch (a Swiss salt-cured, air-dried beef). The salads come with homemade dressings and include Caesar, spiced walnut with Gorgonzola cheese and geimeister, a seedless cucumber wrapped around baby greens with assorted veggies.

All of the restaurant's cheese fondues are served with cubed French bread and include some combination of Gruyère, raclette, Appenzeller, Vacherin and Emmentaler cheeses. The meat and seafood fondues come with steamed vegetables, wild grain rice and four homemade dipping sauces: chive and garlic, European cocktail (a creamy, thick shrimp cocktail), apricot and lemon Provençal. Highlighting the house specialties are jungfrau (grilled Swiss-style veal bratwurst or chicken Parmesan bratwurst), gottard (penne pasta, bacon and raclette cheese in a creamy béchamel sauce), Mont Blanc (strips of beef tenderloin in a paprika stroganoff sauce) and zuriberg (thinly sliced free-range veal in a creamy mushroom sauce). The crème de la crème of The Swiss Haven's homemade desserts is the Swiss chocolate fondue with fruit platter. Other homemade desserts include the three-layer Swiss chocolate terrine, apple strudel with warm vanilla sauce and white chocolate cheesecake with strawberry sauce. You can complement your dessert with a specialty drink like the Peppermint Patty (hot chocolate laced with peppermint schnapps) or a brandy or cordial.

Our food was served quickly, and our server was very helpful in explaining how to use the grill and cook the food. Ravel's *Bolero* was appropriate background music. Photographs and examples of the Swiss cut-paper art of scherenschnitt, depicting Switzerland's landscapes and icons, adorn the restaurant. Included in the montages are the

Matterhorn, dairy cow herds, Zermatt, the Bernese region, Staubbach Falls in Lauterbrunnen Valley and profuse displays of columbines. A poster of St. Moritz, a vacation photo of a Swiss lake and a photo of the eleventh-century Le Chateau de Chillon on a rock outcropping on Lake Geneva further enhance the national décor. The bar area in the back is decked with turn-of-the-nineteenth-century photos of skiers. The small side dining room to the left, called the "cow room," displays photos of dairy cow herds in Swiss Alpine settings. The patio in the back offers a fantastic panorama of the Tenmile-Mosquito Range. Seating is at tables in this brightly lit restaurant.

NUTRITION AND SPECIAL REQUESTS

The Swiss Haven is primarily a fondue restaurant, so you'll do best here if you like and can tolerate cheese. Broth is used in place of butter and other fats on the other entrees. The staff will accommodate special requests but recommend diners stay close to the menu. Though vegetarians will enjoy the cheese fondue and salads, vegans (who eat no dairy) should consider dining elsewhere.

House Cheese Fondue

SERVES 2

7 ounces dry white wine	1 teaspoon fresh minced garlic
3½ ounces Gruyère cheese, grated or cubed	grated nutmeg and white pepper to taste
3½ ounces Vacherin cheese, grated or cubed	French bread, cut into cubes, for dipping

1. Combine all ingredients except bread in medium saucepan and cook over medium heat. Stir constantly until hot and smooth.
2. Transfer to fondue pot with burner. Serve at table with cubed French bread for dipping.

Recipe by Matt Garrett and Colleen Carney

BUENA VISTA

BUENA VISTA, SPANISH *for "beautiful view," is located near the geographic center of Colorado in the Upper Arkansas River Valley, and lives up to its name. Twelve "fourteeners" (14,000-foot peaks), including the Collegiate Peaks, are located in the Buena Vista region. Its residents made it the Chaffee County seat in 1880 by stealing the courthouse records from Granite and transferring them to Buena Vista. The records were subsequently stolen from Buena Vista in 1928 and moved to Salida, the present-day county seat.*

Zip Code: 81211 **Population:** 2,195 **Elevation:** 7,955 feet

BUFFALO BAR & GRILL

710 Highway 24 North
Phone: (719) 395-6472
Fax: (719) 395-4762
E-mail: kelly@chaffee.net
Website: None

Directions: From the intersection of Highways 285 and 24, 2 miles south of Buena Vista, go 2.4 miles north on Highway 24 to the traffic signal at Main Street. Continue north for ½ mile. The restaurant is on the left.

ESSENTIALS

Cuisine: Steaks and seafood
Hours: OCT–MAY: Sun. 4:30 P.M.–8 P.M., Mon.–Thu. 5 P.M.–8:30 P.M., Fri.–Sat. 5 P.M.–9 P.M. Closes one hour later each night from JUN through SEP.
Meals and Prices: Dinner $6–$17 (includes soup or salad)
Nonsmoking: Yes
Take-out: Yes

Alcohol: Full bar

Credit Cards: MC, VI, DS

Personal Check: Accepted

Reservations: Recommended in the summer

Wheelchair Access: Yes

Other: No separate checks. Service charge of 15% added to tables of eight or more. Available for business parties. No parties over twenty during the summer. Logo pint glasses and shirts available.

HISTORY AND BIOGRAPHY

The Buffalo Bar & Grill uses a building constructed in the late 1960s. The original occupant was Gianelli's Italian Restaurant. Several more restaurants followed, including Emoline's, the Three Thieves, the Aspen Leaf and the Pine Cone. In November 1994, Larry and Katie Kelly opened the Buffalo Bar & Grill after spending months totally remodeling the interior.

Larry has been in the restaurant business since 1970. He learned the business in San Francisco, California, then owned and operated a restaurant in Lake Tahoe, Nevada, for twenty-three years before coming to Buena Vista. His wife, Katie, has been in the business since 1975 working alongside Larry. Larry and Katie manage the restaurant, and Katie is the head chef. She is assisted in the kitchen by chef Mark Carey, who has been cooking since 1976 and with the Buffalo Grill since 1997. He was certified at Buckhill Falls in Pennsylvania in 1979 and worked in New Jersey and at the Wine Cellar in Fort Collins, Colorado, before coming to Buena Vista.

FOOD, SERVICE AND AMBIENCE

The Buffalo Bar & Grill specializes in charbroiled steaks, chops, chicken and fish. In fact, when I arrived, the smell of charbroiled steaks outside the restaurant was absolutely mouth-watering. My 8-ounce top sirloin was a lean two-inch-thick cut, cooked medium-rare, just the way I like it, with a superb charbroiled flavor. It came with bread, soup, a medium-sized baked potato and a side dish of green beans and red peppers. The soup was a nicely seasoned cream of potato with large chunks of potato in addition to mushrooms, scallions, and shredded cheddar. This meal was savory and flavorsome without being overly filling. If you have a big appetite, you may want to order the 12-ounce top sirloin.

The staff prepares the sauces and salad dressings in their kitchen. They also smoke their pork ribs and chicken using select hickory and fruit woods. Their selection of steaks includes rib-eye, bacon-wrapped filet mignon and teriyaki-marinated coulotte (a type of top sirloin) steak. Other meaty choices are charbroiled pork chops with or without homemade tangy barbecue sauce, ground chuck or buffalo burgers, green chile chicken and chicken Parmesan. From the sea, you can choose shrimp scampi, deep-fried shrimp, sourdough prawns or halibut. Lighter, smaller portions of many of the entrées are available. For dessert, delight yourself with a slice of homemade pie, such as oatmeal, cherry, mixed berry or piñon nut and chocolate chip; or try the homemade tiramisu or a non-homemade cheesecake such as chocolate swirl, pistachio or orange creamsicle.

My server was casually dressed in shorts and a T-shirt. After a fifteen-minute wait to order my meal (the waitress did apologize) service ran more quickly. Surfing music and other rock-and-roll tunes from the early 1960s played throughout the restaurant. The Buffalo has two dining rooms separated by a bar and lounge. The restaurant is appropriately decorated with western accoutrements, old sporting gear and stuffed animals. Embellishing the pine log walls, posts and ceiling beams are several pairs of old wooden skis, wood and metal ice skates, parts of a horse's harness, a wagon jack, stirrups, spurs and a logger's saw. A wooden figure of a frontiersman holding a rifle rests atop an iron wood-burning stove. Behind the rifleman is a sign that reads "We pay for dead stock—Quick, Reliable Auto Truck Service, Larry Kelly, Proprietor." Adding further enchantment are an antler chandelier, a stuffed buffalo head, a picture of buffalo and prairie dogs facing off against each other and black-and-white as well as color photos of buffalo on the plains. For great charbroil in a western mountain setting, visit the Buffalo Bar & Grill.

NUTRITION AND SPECIAL REQUESTS

The Buffalo Grill has but one vegetarian dish on its menu: homemade cannelloni. The menu is neither low-calorie, low-fat nor health-conscious—after all, this is a steak house. However, the owners will work with any request and honor substitutions where possible, for example, substituting oil for butter in a sauté.

Santa Fe Chowder

SERVES 6–8

½ pound chorizo (Mexican sausage)
½ onion, chopped
1 cup mushrooms, sliced
1 can chopped green chilies
  (8 ounces)
2 cloves chopped garlic

2 cups chicken broth
1 cup heavy cream
1 teaspoon ground cumin
½ teaspoon Tabasco
¼ cup shredded cheddar cheese
¼ cup sour cream

1. Sauté the chorizo, onion, mushrooms, green chilies and garlic until the chorizo is browned and the onion is softened.
2. Add the rest of the ingredients; stirring to blend, and simmer for ½ hour. Do not boil. Serve.

Recipe by Chef Mark Carey

Beverage Recommendation: Corona beer

CASA DEL SOL

303 Highway 24
Phone: (719) 395-8810 or (719) 395-6340
Fax: None
E-mail: None
Website: None

Directions: From the intersection of Highways 285 and 24, 2 miles south of Buena Vista, go north 2.4 miles to the traffic signal at Main Street. Continue north for ¼ mile. The restaurant is on the right at the southwest corner of Highway 24 and Arkansas Street.

ESSENTIALS

Cuisine: Mexican and New Mexican

Hours: Seven days 11:30 A.M.–3 P.M. and 4:30 P.M.–9:30 P.M. (8:30 P.M. from end of SEP to mid-APR). Closed Tue. from JAN to mid-APR. Closed for 2 weeks in mid-NOV and mid-APR.

Meals and Prices: Lunch $4–$8. Dinner $10–$15 (includes chips, salsa, soup and salad).

Nonsmoking: Yes

Take-out: No

Alcohol: Beer, wine and margaritas

Credit Cards: MC, VI

Personal Check: Yes, with two forms of ID

Reservations: Highly recommended JUN–SEP

Wheelchair Access: Yes

Other: Children's menu

HISTORY AND BIOGRAPY

The building occupied by Casa del Sol is a "tale of two centuries." The front dining room was originally constructed of logs in 1880 as a blacksmith shop, and the back dining room was added 100 years later, in 1980. Paul and Marjorie Knox purchased the structure in 1974. Their son, Jeffrey, started out in the early years waiting tables and then moved on to cooking. Today, he has taken over the restaurant while Paul and Marjorie operate The Adobe Inn next door.

FOOD, SERVICE AND AMBIENCE

I thoroughly relished my two dining experiences here, and part of the reason is Casa del Sol's recipes. For the past thirty years, the Knoxes have been traveling throughout Mexico sampling the cuisine and bringing back authentic recipes from Sonora, Jalisco, Guerrero and Chihuahua. On my first visit, I delighted in their most popular dish, the Pechuga Suiza—a lightly toasted flour tortilla stuffed with chicken, Monterey Jack cheese, mild green chilies, onion and sour cream: a delectable combination. On my second visit, I ordered the enchilada Casa del Sol, filled with ground beef and topped with cheese and red chile sauce on top (a real "nose-runner" but short of a "barn-burner"). All meals made to order with fresh ingredients is another reason why this is one of my favorite Mexican restaurants in Colorado. Chips with homemade salsa—thick with tomato, onion and green chilies and hot with jalapeño—are served with each meal. For dessert, I recommend the fresh rum butter pecan cake served warm with a scoop of whipped ice cream on top. It was soft (easily pierced with a fork) with a sugary top—delicious!

Other Mexican delicacies found on the lunch and dinner menus include chicken, cheese, beef and crab/seafood enchiladas with frijoles; shrimp quesadillas; a green chili bowl; and tacos and burritos. Highlighting the dinner menu are traditional Mexican dishes such as chicken mole—a broiled breast topped with a mild, exotic sauce of green chilies, tomatoes, onion, garlic, almonds, spices and chocolate; carne Asada—a broiled New York strip smothered in green chili; a cheese enchilada with a special homemade, mild sauce made from the flavorful pulp of Rio Grande Valley chilies; and a fluffy egg chile relleno. American dishes are also offered, including broiled New York strip and shrimp scampi cooked in garlic butter. Homemade soups include French onion for lunch and beef consommé with sherry and meatballs for dinner. For dessert, homemade hot fudge sundaes, ice cream and sherbet are available for your enjoyment.

My service was cheerful and efficient. Because everything is cooked to order, you may wait a few extra minutes for your meal if the restaurant is full, but it will be well worth it. Mexican guitar and classical violin music provided pleasing entertainment when I visited. Aged and weather-stained plywood in the rear dining room gives it an old look. Kachina and papier mâché dolls, Mayan masks, Mexican rugs, several gold-framed mirrors, and small tapestries enhance the Mexican décor. Orange is the predominant color, with matching wood tables and chairs, paper napkins and placemats and curtains all ablaze. A narrow circular stairway leads up to a pair of booths with two small windows overlooking the highway and a view of Mt. Princeton to the west. An enclosed brick courtyard was added in 1987 with a fountain, aspen and fir trees and a red-rock walkway. Diners are seated on wooden benches under canvas canopies and on cushioned iron-frame chairs under umbrellas. A separate enclosed dining room off the courtyard features cowhide chairs, an iron Cameron stove, a shelf with Mexican pottery and colored-pencil sketches of assorted wildflowers and plants. Take pleasure in "a little bit of Mexico in the Rockies" with Casa del Sol's bona fide Mexican cuisine.

NUTRITION AND SPECIAL REQUESTS

At Casa Del Sol most items are baked, a few are pan-fried, and none are deep-fried. Special requests for no cheese or no sour cream are handled routinely. However, like most Mexican restaurants, the offerings are not health-conscious. Those with special dietary needs or allergies may want to reconsider dining here.

Pechuga Suiza

SERVES 1

1 flour tortilla	1 tablespoon diced onion
1 cup grated Monterey Jack cheese	1 tablespoon diced mild green chilies
½ cup cooked white chicken meat, small chunks	butter for sautéing
	2 tablespoons sour cream

1. Preheat oven to 425 degrees. Cover half of flour tortilla with ½ cup of cheese and all of chicken meat. Sprinkle diced onion and green chilies on top. Fold tortilla in half.
2. Melt a small amount of butter in a sauté pan. Add the folded tortilla and brown on both sides.
3. Transfer tortilla to ovenproof plate. Spread sour cream on top. Sprinkle remaining cheese over tortilla.
4. Place plate in preheated oven. Bake for 5 to 10 minutes, or until cheese begins to bubble.
5. Remove from oven. Serve with lettuce and tomato, your favorite refried beans and Spanish rice.

Recipe by Jeff Knox, who obtained this recipe on a trip to Guadalajara, Mexico

Beverage Recommendation: Regular or strawberry margarita made with Cointreau

～ CARBONDALE ～

CARBONDALE WAS NAMED *by one of the town founders, John Mankin, for his hometown in Pennsylvania. There is good fishing nearby on the Roaring Fork and Crystal Rivers.*

Zip Code: 81623 **Population:** 5,196 **Elevation:** 5,170 feet

TAIPEI TOKYO

1194 Highway 133
Phone: (970) 963-1888
Fax: None
E-mail: None
Website: www.taipei-tokyo.com

Directions: Take exit 116 from I-70 and go north to the traffic signal. Turn right onto Highways 6 and 24 and go to the next signal. Turn right onto Highway 82, go over I-70 and continue on this road for 11.7 miles to the intersection with Highway 133. Turn right onto Highway 133. Go 1.1 miles to the first traffic light. Continue straight through the signal for 0.1 mile. The restaurant is on the left at the intersection with Euclid Avenue.

ESSENTIALS

Cuisine: Chinese and Japanese
Hours: Seven days 11 A.M.–10 P.M.
Meals and Prices: Lunch $6–$8. Dinner $8–$20 (includes steamed rice. Most Japanese dinners served with soup and salad).
Nonsmoking: All
Take-out: Yes
Alcohol: Full bar
Credit Cards: MC, VI, AE

Personal Check: Yes, with ID
Reservations: Accepted
Wheelchair Access: Yes
Other: No MSG. Local Discount Card.

HISTORY AND BIOGRAPHY

Taipei Tokyo opened in 1997 in a building formerly used as a cowboy store with antiques, and as an apartment. The owner is Jenny Wang (pronounced "Wong"). She has been in the restaurant business since the 1980s and previously worked at the May Palace in Vail. She also opened and owned the Chinatown Restaurant in Glenwood Springs. Her daughter, Suzan Wang, manages Taipei Tokyo. She started in the restaurant business in 1990 working in a hamburger shop in Glenwood Springs. She also helped her mother open the Chinatown Restaurant and worked there for seven years. The Wangs opened Taipei Tokyo II in Glenwood Springs in July 2001.

The head chef is Michael Chen (pronounced "Chan"). He began working in restaurants in 1992 and worked at Little Ollie's in Aspen for five years before coming to Taipei Tokyo in 1999.

FOOD, SERVICE AND AMBIENCE

Linda went Japanese with vegetable tempura, one of her favorites. I, naturally, had to go with Chinese (so we could sample both cuisines) and ordered the twice-cooked pork. Although my dish was marked with a red star on the menu to indicate it would be spicy, I did not find it to be so. You can, however, request your own meal to be more or less spicy. Soups came with both meals. I had the spicy hot and sour soup with tofu. Linda had the mild bean curd miso soup.

The twice-cooked pork was thin, tender sliced pork with crisp vegetables, diced onions, bell peppers, portobello mushroom and green cabbage. The vegetable tempura presented big pieces of fresh vegetable—onion, asparagus, mushrooms and broccoli—deep-fried in tasty and crunchy tempura batter. It came with a whole orange cut up bouquet style and a side bowl of salad—lettuce, cabbage and carrot in tempura sauce. The Takara plum wine we chose to drink with our dinners was sweet and flavorsome and, I thought, better than its competitor's brand.

The menu is about 70 percent Chinese and 30 percent Japanese. Highlighting the Japanese side are seaweed, squid and tofu salads; miso soup; udon noodle bowls; and sushi and sashimi. If you choose Chinese you can go with Peking shrimp or duck; Mandarin, Mongolian or Szechuan beef; Kung Pao or sweet and sour chicken or pork; cashew or curry chicken; egg foo yung; chop suey; or chow mein.

Service was fast and courteous. Japanese vocal music was playing during our visit. The décor consists of the four P's: pottery, potted banana and bamboo plants, peacock feathers and a panda bear, stuffed, sitting in the lounge to the left of the entrance. Red Japanese lanterns hang from the ceiling, contrasting nicely with the golden wallpaper and columns.

NUTRITION AND SPECIAL REQUESTS

Taipei Tokyo has several vegetable entrées with steamed rice, as well as vegetarian spring rolls, vegetarian noodles, moo shu, egg foo young and chop suey. Suzan says they will honor special requests for dishes without salt, certain vegetables, garlic or sugar.

Ginger Chicken with Black Bean Sauce

SERVES 1–2

The wok is the traditional cooking pot in Chinese cooking, but you can still cook good Chinese food without one. If you are using a nonstick frying pan, you can get wok-like results if you are patient and also very quick with certain steps of the process of cooking Chinese. The times mentioned in this recipe are set for regular cooking pans. If you are using a wok, you need to speed everything up.

8 ounces chicken breast, sliced
    into half-dollar pieces
¼ cup cornstarch
vegetable oil, enough to
    grease pan
½ tablespoon ginger root, peeled
    and sliced into strips

1 to 1½ cups assorted fresh
    vegetables (such as snow peas,
    mushrooms, asparagus, bell
    peppers, onions, celery)
Black Bean Sauce (ingredients
    follow)

Black Bean Sauce

vegetable oil, enough to grease pan

½ tablespoon ginger root, peeled and sliced into strips

2 cloves garlic, minced

2 teaspoons Chinese fermented black beans

2 teaspoons soy sauce

¼ cup chicken broth

½ teaspoon sugar

½ teaspoon ketchup

½ teaspoon oyster sauce

¼ teaspoon white vinegar

2 pinches of white pepper

½ teaspoon minced green onions

1. Prepare the chicken slices by lightly coating them with cornstarch, shaking any excess starch off each slice. It is important not to over-coat the chicken; it should not be breaded but rather given a coating that will not be noticeable to the diners, allowing the meat to pick up the sauce of the dish and tenderizing the chicken. Lay the slices in a dry bowl to be covered and placed in the refrigerator until they are ready to be used.

2. Lightly coat a pan with vegetable oil. Bring to high heat and add the sliced ginger while constantly stirring so it does not burn. It is important that the pan be very hot when the ginger is added.

3. When you see the ginger begin to scar, reduce the heat to medium and add the chicken slices. Just before they are done, add the vegetables and stir-fry for 30 seconds.

4. Cover the pan and set aside. The vegetables will continue to cook from residual heat while you prepare the sauce.

5. Make the sauce: Lightly oil another pan and turn the heat to high. This part is very fast. When the pan is very hot, add the ginger root and garlic, constantly stirring so they do not burn.

6. Stir in the black beans and soy sauce and sear for 5 seconds. Quickly add the chicken broth, sugar, ketchup and oyster sauce, constantly stirring until the sauce bubbles.

7. Add the chicken and vegetables, vinegar and white pepper. Stir for 30 seconds until all ingredients are combined.

8. Transfer to a platter and garnish with green onions. Serve immediately, accompanied with steamed rice.

NOTE: *You may add chili sauce or powder to this sauce if you want a spicy dish. Usually the ginger will be spicy enough for most diners. Also, note that no salt is added to this dish, mainly because the fermented beans and the soy sauce are usually salted already.*

Recipe by Susan Wang

Wine Recommendation: Sake

THE VILLAGE SMITHY RESTAURANT ———

26 South 3rd Street
Phone: (970) 963-9990
Fax: (970) 963-3575
E-mail: None
Website: None

Directions: Take exit 116 from I-70 and go north to the traffic signal. Turn right onto Highways 6 and 24 and go to the next signal. Turn right onto Highway 82, go over I-70 and continue on this road for 11.7 miles to the intersection with Highway 133. Turn right onto Highway 133. Go west on Highway 133 for 1 mile to the first signal. Turn left onto Main Street. Go 0.6 miles. The restaurant is on the right at the corner of 3rd Street.

ESSENTIALS

Cuisine: American
Hours: Seven days 7 A.M.–2 P.M. Breakfast all day. Lunch from 11 A.M.
Meals and Prices: Breakfast $6–$11. Lunch $6–$8.
Nonsmoking: All, including the patio
Take-out: Yes, except on weekends. Includes baked goods and desserts. Whole pies or cakes can be ordered to go with 24-hour notice.
Alcohol: Beer, wine and limited well drinks
Credit Cards: MC, VI
Personal Check: Local only
Reservations: No, but call ahead for groups of more than six. They will try to accommodate.
Wheelchair Access: Yes
Others: Additional 15% service charge added to parties of six or more if separate checks are requested. Half orders charged ¾ full price.

Senior citizen discount for those 65 years young or older. An anvil symbol is used on the menu to designate those items most popular with the locals.

HISTORY AND BIOGRAPHY

The Village Smithy began as an old blacksmith shop (hence the name Village Smithy) around the turn of the century. Some of the locals still talk about the days when horses were brought in here. In 1914, Roy D. Pattison came to Carbondale and took over the blacksmith shop from his uncle, H. C. Pattison. Two additional blacksmiths followed before a few unrelated businesses occupied the premises: a shop that made looms; a woodworking shop, then a kitchen, for the local school; and the Western Slope's largest tropical fish store. Chris and Terry Chacos, a couple of former registered physical therapists, opened the Village Smithy in May 1975. Chris retired in 1998 and sold the restaurant to his son, Charley. Chris still helps out in the kitchen and with the specials and designs the soups and menu. Head chef Conrad Delores started at the Village Smithy in 1988 as a dishwasher.

FOOD, SERVICE AND AMBIENCE

This is a great little mountain sojourn for breakfast or lunch. Friendly people; good, nutritious and innovative food; and, in the summer, a most appealing lawn and patio for dining and viewing Mt. Sopris. It's a must stop if you're between, or near, Glenwood Springs and Aspen. I had lunch here on two occasions and have enjoyed an appetizer, homemade soup, salad with homemade dressing and a sandwich. For a scrumptious treat that will tantalize the taste buds without interfering with your appetite, try the Smithy's lightly breaded, nongreasy jalapeños stuffed with black beans and sour cream. Their beef-vegetable soup is chock-full of vegetables and meat. You can order salad with a novel tamari dressing prepared with soy sauce, lemon, garlic, honey and yogurt (the blue cheese dressing is also homemade). The savory southwestern chicken sandwich was top-quality, moist chicken breast marinated in Mexican seasonings and orange juice, grilled and served with a whole green chile and Monterey Jack cheese. Very tasty!

Breakfast presents a number of unusual and delicious treats. You can order an omelet with items like specially seasoned spinach, tomatillo green chile, fresh avocado or fresh pesto with roasted red pepper. Pancakes come baked with homemade granola or bacon, green chiles and cheddar cheese. The French toast is dipped in nutmeg egg batter and deep-fried, or made with raisin bread and served with sliced bananas, walnuts and chicken-apple sausage links. Other specialties include chile rellenos and eggs, tofu scramble and garden burrito. On weekends, the selection is expanded to include eggs Benedict made with avocado, spinach, artichoke hearts, salmon, homemade salsa or pork green chile. Espresso drinks and fruit smoothies also are available.

For lunch, indulge in one of the Village Smithy's big bowl salads, featuring teriyaki-marinated grilled chicken breast, marinated yellowfin tuna with avocado-orange salsa, or cranberry-ginger marinated grilled turkey. Choices from South of the Border, homemade soups, sandwiches from the grill or pantry and burgers complete the lunch menu.

The folks who work here seem more like family than a staff of employees—the camaraderie is obvious. The host had an infectious smile and was very helpful, bringing me a to-go menu without my asking. The artwork in the dining room changes every six weeks and is created by local artists. In the past, the walls have exhibited pieces by local high school students, color photography, oils, watercolors and even rugs. The restaurant has a modern look and doesn't resemble a blacksmith shop. The front of the menu contains a fitting quote by Thoreau: "To affect the quality of the day is the highest of arts." A meal at The Village Smithy may well enrich the quality of your day.

NUTRITION AND SPECIAL REQUESTS

The Village Smithy has a natural and healthy menu, and the staff is most accommodating with special requests. The locals have really designed their own menu here. Rocky Mountain beef, locally raised on family ranches in the Roaring Fork Valley, is proudly served. Canola oil and olive oil are used in all the cooking and homemade salad dressings. Baked goods and desserts, salsas and hollandaise sauce are all made from scratch.

Blueberry Corn Cakes

1 tablespoon baking powder
1 tablespoon baking soda
¼ cup sugar
1 teaspoon kosher salt
¾ cup all-purpose flour
1½ cups yellow cornmeal

2 cups buttermilk
2 large eggs
¼ cup canola oil
1 cup frozen blueberries,
    thawed and drained

1. Preheat skillet or griddle to 350 degrees.
2. Combine all dry ingredients in a large mixing bowl.
3. Combine buttermilk, eggs and oil in another bowl. Lightly whisk together.
4. Pour the wet ingredients over the dry ingredients and gently whisk them together, mixing just until combined.
5. Ladle ¼ cup batter onto the griddle for each pancake, leaving room for spreading.
6. Immediately drop a few blueberries evenly onto cooking pancakes. Flip when the pancakes are very bubbly and the edges are dry.
7. Serve the cakes blueberry-side-up when the bottoms are golden brown. Serve with maple syrup.

ALTERNATIVE FILLING: *For Santa Fe Cakes, replace the blueberries with bacon, mild diced green chilies and cheddar cheese. These are wonderful with maple syrup and/or hot sauce but may not be for everyone.*

Recipe by chef Sandy Baker

Beverage Recommendation: Fresh-squeezed orange juice

❧ CASTLE ROCK ❧

CASTLE ROCK WAS *named by Dr. Edwin James, botanist on Major Stephen Long's expedition in 1820. He named the town after the large, castle-like rock formation nearby. Castle Rock is a community nestled among thousands of acres of rolling hills, scrub oak and ponderosa pine that used to be the hunting grounds for Ute, Arapahoe and Cheyenne Indians. In 1869, Jerimiah Gould took out a claim on a 160-acre tract of land that included the impressive rock formation and geological landmark. Two sets of railroad tracks ran through Castle Rock connecting Denver to Colorado Springs. In the last quarter of the nineteenth century, Silas W. Madge quarried lava stone in the area for use as building material.*

On June 16, 1965, a cloudburst dropped fourteen inches of rain onto Plum Creek, south of Castle Rock, causing a terrible flood reaching up to Denver. It killed six people and caused a half-billion dollars in damage. In March 1978, the county courthouse was destroyed by a fire lit by a distraught lover who tried to free her imprisoned boyfriend. The courthouse was replaced but has since been moved to the north end of town. Each year for the holiday season, a Yule star is lit on top of the large rock marking the town. In the summer, Castle Rock is home to a PGA golf tournament—the International at Castle Pines. Another major attraction are the factory outlet stores just north of town.

Zip Code: 80104 **Population:** 20,224 **Elevation:** 6,200 feet

CASTLE CAFÉ

403 Wilcox Street
Phone: (303) 814-2233
Fax: None
E-mail: None
Website: www.castlecafe.com

Directions: *From the north on I-25,* take exit 182 and head east. The street will bend to the right (south) and become Wilcox Street. The restaurant is on the right on the corner of 4th Street, 1 block past the traffic light at 5th Street. *From the south on I-25,* take exit 181 and head north on Wilcox Street. The restaurant is on the left on the corner of 4th Street just past the Old Courthouse.

ESSENTIALS

Cuisine: American comfort food
Hours: Mon.–Thu. 4:30 P.M.–9 P.M., Fri.–Sat. 4:30 P.M.–10 P.M., Sun. 11:30 A.M.–8 P.M.
Meals and Prices: Dinner $10–$20 (includes soup or salad)
Nonsmoking: Smoking permitted only at the bar
Take-out: Yes
Alcohol: Full bar
Credit Cards: All five
Personal Check: In-state only with ID
Reservations: Not accepted
Wheelchair Access: Yes
Other: Split plate charge of $5.99

HISTORY AND BIOGRAPHY

The Castle Café, originally the Keystone Hotel, was built in two sections, the first in 1901, and the second in the 1910s. This was a wild place back then, with brawls and inebriated cowboys riding their horses through the bar. About 1910, the Castle Hotel and Café became a stopover for travelers between Denver and Colorado Springs. A dance hall was built over the bar and served as a community center during the 1920s, 1930s and early 1940s.

Over the years, several restaurants and other businesses have occupied this space. In the 1950s it was a restaurant serving chicken, and then a grocery store. Prior to the Castle Café opening in November 1996, it was a saddle and leather shop, Justin's Bar and a bicycle shop. The upstairs has been—and is today—used for apartments.

The owners of the Castle Café are Tom Walls, Brad Brown and Brad Anderson. Tom is the only operating owner. He is also part owner of the

Trinity Grill, the Rocky Mountain Diner and Chopper's Sports Grill, all in Denver. Tom has been in the restaurant business since 1971 and used to be operating owner of Pasquinel's Restaurant in Aurora, Colorado, from 1977 to 1985.

General manager David Doty has been with Castle Café since it opened. He grew up working in his father's restaurant in Minnesota. Executive chef Jerry Good is a graduate of the Culinary Institute of Arts in Hyde Park, New York. He began working at the Trinity Grill in 1982 and now oversees the food operations of Tom's four restaurants. Head chef Jeffrey Enger, a Castle Rock native, has been cooking since 1995 and joined the Castle Café at the beginning of 2000.

FOOD, SERVICE AND AMBIENCE

Castle Café specializes in family-style pan-fried chicken, steaks and fish. Linda and I both ordered fish. She had the pan-blackened campfire trout, which arrived with a crispy exterior and a nice interior texture and was accompanied by mixed vegetables, homemade mashed potatoes and brown gravy and lemon mayonnaise on the side. My pan-fried, breaded catfish was moist and light with a slightly spicy jalapeño mayonnaise on the side. It came with fluffy rice pilaf. We also tried two of their soups. The chicken noodle was thick with lots of celery, noodles and chicken. The tomato basil soup was a little spicy and delicious with pieces of tomato. Hot homemade rolls were also served.

Table snack appetizers headline their menu and include Yuppie-I-O Dip with artichoke, Parmesan, spinach and corn chips; jalapeño onion rings; house-smoked rainbow trout; and Rocky Mountain oysters. For a lighter meal, you can order a Cobb salad, spinach salad with roasted goat cheese, a steak burger, or a chicken grill. The pan-fried chicken comes with cracklin' gravy and takes approximately thirty minutes to cook to order. Other entrées highlighting their menu are chipotle chicken with penne pasta, grilled pork chops, roast duck enchiladas, a variety of steaks and buffalo meatloaf. Save room for dessert—they are all homemade. We had a choice of bread pudding, four-layer chocolate fudge cake, blueberry cobbler or strawberry shortcake, all with or without vanilla ice cream.

The hostess helped our server, who was quite busy. Our dinners were brought out before the forgotten soup and rolls. We really did not mind eating everything together, though, once the soup and rolls did arrive. The Castle Café is a true historical and western treasure with old photographs of Castle Rock from the early twentieth century, paintings of cowboys and Indians in southwestern settings and regional décor. Enhancing the setting are a stuffed buffalo head and two stuffed heads of pronghorn antelope, plentiful on the western plains. Behind the bar at the entrance is a smaller room that can be used for private parties. You cannot go back in time, but you can visit places that will transmit some feelings for days gone by. The Castle Café is such a place.

NUTRITION AND SPECIAL REQUESTS

The Castle Café chefs use safflower oil in their cooking and will accommodate any requests they can, like substituting homemade mashed potatoes for rice.

Yuppie-I-O Dip

SERVES 8–10

8 ounces cream cheese, brought to room temperature
1½ cups grated Parmesan cheese
1½ cups mayonnaise

7 ounces canned artichoke hearts, drained and coarsely chopped
¼ pound fresh spinach, chopped
¼ of small yellow onion, julienned

1. Using the medium speed on an electric mixer, blend the cream cheese until it is smooth.
2. Add the Parmesan cheese and mayonnaise slowly to the cream cheese. Continue blending. Meanwhile, preheat broiler.
3. Add the artichoke hearts, spinach and onion last, then mix by hand with a spatula.
4. Place the mixture in a shallow ovenproof casserole dish. Spread out evenly about ½-inch deep and broil until golden brown. Serve hot with corn chips or vegetable sticks.

Recipe by Jerry Good

CRAWFORD

CRAWFORD WAS NAMED *after frontier capitalist, speculator and former governor of Kansas George A. Crawford, who started many towns on Colorado's Western Slope in the 1880s. Crawford is located at the northern rim of Black Canyon of the Gunnison National Park.*

Zip Code: 81415 **Population:** 366 **Elevation:** 6,520 feet

THE DINNER BELL AT SMITH FORK RANCH

4536 East 50 Drive
Phone: (970) 921-3454
Fax: (970) 921-3475
E-mail: smithfork@tds.net
Website: www.smithforkranch.com

Directions: From the intersection of Highways 550 and 92 in Delta, go east on Highway 92 for 21 miles to the fork in the road in Hotchkiss. Take the fork to the right, continuing on Highway 92 for 11 miles into Crawford. Just around the corner from Pam and Joe Cocker's Mad Dog Ranch Trading Post on the right will be the Mad Dog Ranch Fountain Café on the right and Dogwood Avenue on the left, between a church and a post office. Turn left onto Dogwood Avenue. Go 2.4 miles, then turn right onto East 50 Drive. Go 3.9 miles. The log cabin restaurant and big dinner bell will be set back on the right, the SFR logo sign is by the road, and there is a gravel parking lot on the left. If you get to the one-lane bridge, you have gone too far.

ESSENTIALS

Cuisine: Elegant American
Hours: MAY to mid-JAN: Wed.–Sat. 5:30 P.M.–10 P.M., Sun. 10 P.M.–2 A.M. Closed mid-JAN through APR.

Meals and Prices: Sunday brunch buffet $16. Dinner $13–$22 (soup and salad extra).

Nonsmoking: Smoking permitted only on deck

Take-out: No

Alcohol: Beer, wine and limited well drinks

Credit Cards: MC, VI, AE

Personal Check: In-state with ID

Reservations: Highly recommended

Wheelchair Access: Yes, including the bathrooms

HISTORY AND BIOGRAPHY

The Smith Fork Ranch is named after the Smith Fork of the Gunnison River, which flows along the ranch's border for nearly two miles. The lodge, cabins and dining hall for their guests were built in the 1940s by Grant and Mamie Ferrier and their four children. They ran the operation successfully for over thirty years before selling the ranch to absentee owners in 1979. After that, the ranch was neglected and fell into disrepair. In July 2000, Marley Hodgeson, Jr., his wife Linda, their daughter Lindsay, and their son Marley III purchased the ranch. After a year of remodeling, The Dinner Bell, which had been previously used only as a dining hall for ranch guests, was opened to the public as a restaurant. This is the Hodgeson family's first restaurant.

Operations manager Randy Czech and Marley III manage The Dinner Bell. The two ran the New England Brewery Company in Norwalk, Connecticut, before coming to Colorado. Randy has been in the restaurant business since 1991. He previously worked at Marlow's, the Barolo Grill and Cliff Young's, all in Denver. Marley, who is also the head chef at The Dinner Bell, was a grill chef at the Barolo Grill and at the Phantom Canyon Brew Pub in Colorado Springs.

FOOD, SERVICE AND AMBIENCE

The Dinner Bell's menu is short on quantity but high on quality. I began my dinner with one of their special salads of crisp, fresh field greens; sliced avocado, tomato and onion; feta cheese; finely chopped yellow pepper sprinkled on the rim of the plate; and crunchy, toasted chopped-walnut vinaigrette dressing on the side. Simultaneously sweet and tart, this was a fine mix of a salad. White sesame-seed bread, honey butter with chives and extra-virgin olive oil was brought to the table. For my main course I chose the roasted pork tenderloin: four lean, bold medallions stuffed with sweet apricot chutney offset by dry ginger–red wine sauce. This was a wonderful complement of flavors for a pork dish that must have come from a sturdy pig. The vegetables on the side were great-tasting, too. The mashed potatoes were lumpy with skins combined with finely chopped mushrooms and garlic. The julienned red, yellow and green bell peppers were sautéed but still had their crunch and flavor. The baked half-tomato with porcini mushroom cap, garlic clove and stuffed Parmesan cheese was also savory.

For an appetizer, you can choose from grilled chicken skewers with fruit salsa, lime and jalapeño marinated shrimp, white or smoky signature chili, or smoked portobello mushroom with warm Brie and cranberry salsa. The other salad on the menu was composed of wild rice, minced vegetables and toasted nuts with honey-Dijon dressing. For a lighter meal, you might try the buffalo quesadilla or grilled buffalo burger. The short list of entrées features blackened chicken fettuccine, a vegetarian portobello mushroom baked in puff pastry, roasted Cornish game hen, sesame-crusted 12-ounce New York strip steak and grilled boneless trout. Desserts include Paonia, Colorado, fresh fruit (in season) with a light butterscotch glaze, banana torte, light and white avalanche cheesecake, pecan shortbread and baked fudge terrine on a thin pecan and coconut base. Also, if you are in the mood, the restaurant offers a top-shelf selection of fine single-malt Scotches. Highlighting the brunch menu are fresh berry blintzes, a cooked-to-order omelet bar, raspberry-jalapeño-glazed ham, red pepper and lemon grilled Cornish game hen, Cajun chicken fettuccine, banana cream, salads and desserts.

Service was helpful, friendly and intelligent. I did experience a short delay when I had to return my plate because the wild mushroom garlic mashed potatoes were served cold. No music was played. The Dinner Bell is a small one-room restaurant in a pine log cabin made with jackboard walls, a style of old barn wood, with chinking between the logs. The wood was taken from a dilapidated old barn on the ranch. To the side of the dining room is a wood deck with a log wood railing, black iron tables, box elder trees and scenic views of Sleeping Indian Mountain and Saddle Mountain. The dining room is decorated with black iron figures of an elk, fish, bear, eagle and a cowboy on a horse, all in wilderness scenes. The bench seats and backs are covered in Ghurka leather, a superior leather tanned by a patented process. The sides of the booths are made from calfskin. Oxen yokes hang on the light fixtures on either side of the entrance inside and an authentic red-and-black wooden wagon-wheel chandelier hangs from a black iron chain. Additional lighting is provided by black iron and gold mica sconces on the inside walls and black iron and glass lanterns on the deck walls. In summer, flowers grace the front of the restaurant and the base of the vintage dinner bell, which hangs from a rusty steel bar between two carved pinewood posts. This is a peaceful, remote and relatively unknown location. It should be high on your list of adventures in fine dining in off-the-beaten-path locations.

NUTRITION AND SPECIAL REQUESTS

The Dinner Bell uses a lot of local ingredients. They have a vegetarian appetizer and entrée on their limited menu. The few special requests they receive are mostly from vegetarians.

Roasted Pork Tenderloin Stuffed with Apricot Chutney in Ginger–Red Wine Sauce

SERVES 4–5

2 pounds pork tenderloins

Apricot Chutney
(makes about 4½ cups)

1 teaspoon salt

1 large tart apple, chopped

¼ cup black currants

½ teaspoon pepper

1 cup diced apricots (½ cup
    fresh, ½ cup dried)

¾ cup vinegar

½ tablespoon powdered ginger

1 tablespoon curry powder

1 large onion, chopped

½ cup water

Marinade / Sauce
(makes 3½ cups, enough for 1 to 4 tenderloins)

1½ cups dry red wine

⅔ cup brown sugar

½ cup vinegar

½ cup water

¼ cup vegetable oil

3 tablespoons soy sauce

4 cloves garlic, minced

1 teaspoon powdered ginger

½ tablespoon ground pepper

5 teaspoons cornstarch

1. Make Chutney: Simmer all ingredients over medium heat until thickened.
2. Make a small slot lengthwise through the tenderloins, using either a filet knife or a sharpening steel.
3. Stuff the tenderloins with chutney. Place tenderloins in a bowl or nonreactive pan.
4. Combine ingredients for Marinade, except cornstarch. Pour over tenderloins. Cover with plastic and marinate, refrigerated, 6 hours or more.
5. Preheat oven to 325 degrees. Drain meat, reserving marinade, and pat dry. Transfer tenderloins to a roasting pan.
6. Roast tenderloins in 325-degree oven for 45 to 60 minutes, depending on size of tenderloins (165 degrees on a meat thermometer).
7. Heat 1½ cups marinade (or more) with 5 teaspoons cornstarch (or more, depending on amount of marinade) in saucepan over medium heat, stirring constantly, until thickened to make sauce.
8. Serve tenderloins sliced diagonally with generous portions of sauce.

Recipe by Marley Hodgeson III

Beverage Recommendation: Selbach-Oster Spätlese Riesling

MAD DOG RANCH FOUNTAIN CAFÉ ——————

131 Highway 92

Phone: (970) 921-7632

Fax: (970) 921-4857

E-mail: mdrfc@cocker.com

Website: www.cocker.com

Directions: From the intersection of Highways 550 and 92 in Delta, go east on Highway 92 for 21 miles to the fork in the road in Hotchkiss. Take the fork to the right, continuing on Highway 92 for 11 miles into Crawford. The restaurant will be on your right just around the corner from Pam and Joe Cocker's Mad Dog Ranch Trading Post.

ESSENTIALS

Cuisine: American

Hours: Seven days 7 A.M.–9 P.M.

Meals and Prices: Breakfast $4–$5. Lunch/Dinner $5–$18 (entrées include soup and salad or baked beans).

Nonsmoking: Smoking permitted only on the patio and in the park

Take-out: Yes

Alcohol: Beer and wine

Credit Cards: MC, VI

Personal Check: Yes

Reservations: Recommended for weekend dinners and for parties of eight or more

Wheelchair Access: Yes

Other: Private dining room available for banquets, business lunches and private parties

HISTORY AND BIOGRAPHY

The Mad Dog Ranch Fountain Café opened in the summer of 1996 in a building formerly occupied by a bank and a general store. The building was vacant when legendary rocker Joe Cocker bought the place as a birthday present for his wife, Pam. This is Pam and Joe's first restaurant. When they are in town, Pam hosts and works the front of the restaurant, and Joe stops in for lunch, dinner and sodas. Three of the head servers manage the restaurant. Chef Christopher Snow has been at the Mad Dog Ranch since August 1999 and in the restaurant business since 1989. His career has taken him from Boulder and Snowmass Village, Colorado, to Washington, D.C. He is a graduate of the Western Culinary Institute in Portland, Oregon, and the Italian Culinary Institute for Foreigners in the Piedmont Region of Italy.

FOOD, SERVICE AND AMBIENCE

The Mad Dog Ranch is a fairly spacious restaurant with a soda fountain bar on one side and a covered patio adjacent to a well-manicured park with hundreds of big, beautiful black-eyed Susans. The menu presents a mix of primarily American cuisine from omelets and deli sandwiches to pizzas and steaks. I stopped in for lunch and ordered the special: a southwestern chicken sandwich with peppered Monterey Jack cheese, jalapeño-peach chutney and avocado, without the sprouts. The ingredients were all fresh, the chicken was tender and the chutney added a pleasant sweet and spicy flavor. It was a little messy to eat, but a lot of good things are that way.

The breakfast offerings include eggs and meats, a breakfast burrito, omelets, corned beef hash, French toast and Belgian waffles. Nachos, spicy chicken wings, spiced calamari with sweet chili sauce, burgers, chicken breast sandwiches and pizzas with a lot of common items plus chèvre cheese, pesto, Kalamata olives and pine nuts are all available for lunch or dinner. There are a few salads to choose from, such as the Mad Dog Ranch, with ranch dressing and chipotle chilies; smoked turkey Cobb; Asian chicken; and Caesar with or without chicken or shrimp. The dinner entrées feature steaks grilled over an open flame, garlic-and-herb-roasted chicken, grilled Atlantic salmon with pesto crust and daily pastas. For dessert, try cheesecake, lava (chocolate) cake or pie, and do not forget the soda fountain treats: ice cream and sherbet in a dozen or more flavors, banana splits, malts, shakes, floats, old-fashioned sodas, smoothies and Java Joe's cappuccino brain freeze!

Service was attentive and friendly. My server was very apologetic when I had to return my cold French fries. The restaurant has a number of very appealing features. The ceiling fans are all connected by a rubber belt and pulley system run by a battery-operated motor hanging on the wall. I particularly liked the dark-blue glass found on the lampshades hanging over the counter, in the crown molding, in the front window and in the stained-glass windows next to the doors leading to the patio. Other attractive characteristics include brass sconces, wood-frame chairs with cowhide seats, a birdhouse collection on the shelves behind the counter and a glass-enclosed cabinet with ceramic vases filled with lemons, olives and anchovies pickled or packed in oil. The old-fashioned and authentic-looking soda fountain is behind a roped-off area to the right of the entrance. Just beyond is the entrance to the patio and park, which you must visit; weather permitting, you can dine here. In the back of the building is the private dining room, its walls covered with Joe Cocker's platinum and gold records and CDs. You may not get to see Joe or Pam Cocker (they were on tour in Canada when I visited), but you will get to enjoy some good American cuisine, see a piece of original Americana rejuvenated and experience the prettiest piece of real estate in town, all compliments of an Englishman and his wife.

NUTRITION AND SPECIAL REQUESTS

A number of vegetarian items are on the menu, including a veggie omelet, veggie hash, a garden burger, a garden Reuben sandwich and sun-dried tomato ravioli. My request to substitute salad for the fries was denied by my server, who informed me they do not do substitutions. I later found out from the chef that this was a mistake and I should have been able to substitute. He said they do get a fair number of such requests and will do whatever they can to accommodate. Mad Dog's burgers and steaks are made from locally raised organic beef. The soups and spicy baked beans are homemade.

Gnocchi with Cannellini Beans and Pesto

SERVES 4

½ ounce olive oil
1 ounce minced yellow onions
6 ounces tomato cancasse
   (peeled, seeded and diced
   tomatoes; if unavailable,
   substitute canned chopped
   tomatoes), divided

8 ounces vegetable broth
16 ounces cooked potato gnocchi
8 ounces cooked cannellini beans
2 ounces pesto
salt and pepper to taste
fresh grated parmigiano
   reggiano to taste

1. Add oil and onions to sauté pan. Cook until soft.
2. Add 4 ounces of the tomatoes, sauté and mash slightly with a fork. Add broth, gnocchi and beans. Bring to a simmer.

3. Add the pesto. Season to taste with salt and pepper.
4. Divide between four bowls and garnish with remaining tomatoes and parmigiano reggiano.

Recipe by Christopher Snow

Wine Recommendation: Italian Lagaria Merlot

ᕦ CRESTED BUTTE ᕤ

CRESTED BUTTE, *the wildflower capital of Colorado, was founded by Howard F. Smith, who bought the first mill here. The town was named for a nearby mountain whose top resembles the crest of a rooster's head. Ute Indians used the area around Crested Butte as summer hunting grounds. They were displaced by the gold and silver booms of the 1880s. Crested Butte was incorporated in 1880; the following year the town was connected to Gunnison, twenty-eight miles to the south, by the Denver and Rio Grande narrow-gauge railroad. Also in 1880, coal was discovered in the area and it helped sustain the town until 1952 when the last mine was closed.*

The economy struggled through the 1950s but was revitalized with the birth of the ski resort on Mount Crested Butte just three miles to the north. In 1974, the entire town of Crested Butte was designated a National Historic District. One point of interest that you should catch while you are here is the world-record elk rack displayed at the Chamber of Commerce building at the four-way stop in town, at Elk Avenue and Highway 135. (It may move to the Crested Butte Heritage Museum once the museum relocates from its present location in the old Spritzer Bar.)

Zip Code: 81224 **Population:** 1,529 **Elevation:** 8,885 feet

BUFFALO GRILLE & SALOON

435 6th Street
Phone: (970) 349-9699
Fax: None
E-mail: None
Website: None

Directions: From the intersection of Highways 50 and 135 in Gunnison, go north 28 miles on Highway 135 to Crested Butte. Go 2 blocks past the first stop sign. The restaurant is on the left on the corner of 6th Street (Highway 135) and Sopris Avenue, one block before the stop sign for Elk Avenue.

ESSENTIALS

Cuisine: Steak, buffalo, seafood and pasta
Hours: Mon.–Sat. 11:30 A.M.–2:30 P.M. Seven nights 5:30 P.M.–9:30 P.M.
Meals and Prices: Lunch $7–$9. Dinner $15–$36 (includes starch, vegetables and soup or salad).
Nonsmoking: Smoking permitted only on patio
Take-out: Yes
Alcohol: Full bar
Credit Cards: MC, VI, AE, DS
Personal Check: Yes
Reservations: Recommended
Wheelchair Access: Yes, including the bathrooms

HISTORY AND BIOGRAPHY

The Buffalo Grille & Saloon is in a building originally occupied by the Backcountry Gourmet Restaurant, which opened in August 1996. In June 1998, the Buffalo Grille, owned and managed by Jimmy Clark and Kathy Benson, replaced the Backcountry Gourmet. Since 1945, Jimmy's family has owned and operated a dude ranch in Montana that serves 60,000 meals within a five- to six-month period every year. Chef Mike Larson developed the menu and has been with the restaurant since it opened. He has been in the restaurant business since 1986, previously cooking at Giovanni's in the Grand Butte Hotel (now Club Med) and

Jeremiah's, both in Mount Crested Butte. He also worked at the Mangy Moose in Jackson, Wyoming, and owned the Gonzo Café in Moab, Utah.

FOOD, SERVICE AND AMBIENCE

The Buffalo Grille is a fine dining establishment where you will find some of the best and healthiest buffalo in Colorado plus numerous alternative options. I took a natural liking to the entrée titled "Buffalo New York Strip," 10 ounces of sweet, tender buffalo with a savory rosemary and portobello demi-glace. Although the buffalo was grilled, it was almost as good as charbroiled, blackened on the outside, pink on the inside. There were a couple of ounces of fat for added flavor. The buffalo chip potatoes were a combination of two slices each of white and sweet potatoes seasoned with salt, pepper, garlic and spices. The medley of vegetables—asparagus, cabbage, carrot, onion, red pepper and onion—were boiled, then grilled for enhanced taste. For presentation, the rim of the plate was sprinkled with chopped red cabbage and chives. The soup of the day, cream of mushroom with roasted red peppers and a few drops of chèvre cheese, was creamy, thick and exceptionally delicious.

Highlighting the appetizers for dinner are fried rock shrimp with polenta, beer-broiled buffalo bratwurst, stuffed artichoke baked with Asiago cheese, grilled duck breast with orange jicama salad and stuffed portobello mushrooms. The salad selections include Greek, Caesar and the house salad with grilled buffalo, shrimp or chicken. Buffalo Grille stew is also available. The dinner entrées offer a wide variety from the range, sea, henhouse and pasta corral. For a beefsteak, you can try the New York strip, the dry-aged T-bone, or tenderloin medallions in a rich brandy-peppercorn sauce. The other buffalo steaks are ribeye, tenderloin tips in a sun-dried cherry demi-glace and filet mignon on a bed of portobello demi-glace sauce with Gorgonzola crumbles. New Zealand red deer is the foreign exotic on the menu and comes as a rack with a lingonberry demi-glace, as saltimbocca medallions with prosciutto ham and mushrooms, or as a tenderloin seared with shrimp. From the sea you can choose tempura-coated shrimp with coconut batter, skewered and grilled; shrimp scampi; chili-rubbed grilled salmon; or fish and chips. Choose from chicken Florentine with prosciutto ham and portobello mushroom or roasted chicken stuffed with chèvre and chives.

Fettuccini tossed with Gorgonzola and asiago cheeses and topped with seared buffalo completes the dinner menu. For dessert, sample one of the Buffalo Grille's cheesecakes, chocolate tortes, or ice creams.

The lunch menu offers light fare of ground buffalo or chicken quesadillas, artichoke dip and bruschetta with tomato along with the soups, salads and stew available at dinner. Spotlighting the sandwich board are grilled tuna with basil aioli and tomato-caper relish, ginger sesame–seared ahi tuna with sweet soy, a lean organic tatanka (Lakota Sioux for buffalo) burger, buffalo or veggie cheese steak, Creole eggplant, a veggie (classic garden) burger and the classic beef Reuben.

My service was professional and courteous. No music played. The western artworks depicted cowboys on bucking horses, buffalo, two Indians crossing a snow-filled field and two cowboys on the high plains riding in a circa-1920 automobile and hauling a cart with a horse, captioned "Life in the Fast Lane." The bar to the right of the entrance displays a stuffed buffalo head. The dining room has a classic look with rustic overtones. Ten tables topped with glass over cream-colored tablecloths and cream-colored napkins set the tone. Windows extend around the two exterior sides of the restaurant and lead out to a heated patio with umbrellas over tables and a fountain spewing water from three cowboy hats. Weather permitting, you can dine under an umbrella while taking in the fountain and local mountain peaks.

NUTRITION AND SPECIAL REQUESTS

The buffalo served at the Buffalo Grille comes from the family's dude ranch in Montana. These buffalo are allowed to roam freely over grasslands that have always been free of pesticides and other chemicals. The result is stress-free buffalo with tender meat not subject to growth hormones or stimulants. This is 100-percent natural buffalo that is highly nutrient-dense because of the proportion of protein, fat, minerals and fatty acids to calories. It also has a greater concentration of iron than regular cow beef.

In addition to the buffalo, the Buffalo Grille uses top-quality produce, fish and other meats. Granulated salt, grill spice, garlic and pepper are used in the food preparation. However, the staff are flexible about withholding seasonings and will cook whatever a guest desires, within reason. They will also accommodate vegetarians by leaving meat out of a dish or using grilled portobello mushrooms or squash.

Stuffed Portobello Mushroom

SERVES 1

1 portobello mushroom cap
(discard stem or use in
another recipe)
olive oil
grill spice, granulated salt,
pepper and garlic to taste
clarified butter
2 ounces creamy chèvre
cheese

1 ounce Monterey Jack cheese,
shredded
1 ounce sun-dried tomato, pureed
1 small zucchini, ends cut off,
sliced ¼-inch
4 slices tomato
7 cloves garlic, roasted
1 ounce balsamic vinaigrette
pinch fresh basil

1. Preheat oven to 350 degrees. Rub the mushroom cap with olive oil and seasonings.
2. Sauté the cap in clarified butter for 2 minutes on each side. Remove from the grill and place on pie tin.
3. Fill the mushroom cap with the cheeses and sun-dried tomato puree.
4. Bake in preheated oven for 4 minutes. While mushroom cap bakes, rub zucchini with olive oil and seasonings. Grill for 2½ minutes on each side.
5. Remove cap and zucchini. Cut each into 6 pieces.
6. Placed tomato slices in middle of plate. Top with garlic. Alternately arrange the cut-up mushroom cap and zucchini around the tomato slices. Sprinkle the balsamic vinaigrette on top of the tomatoes. Sprinkle fresh basil over entire plate. Serve.

Recipe by Mike Larson

Wine Recommendation: Sonoma Valley, California, Benzinger Merlot

CUCHARA

CUCHARA, SPANISH FOR *"spoon," was named for the Cuchara River, which took its name from the spoonlike shape of the valley through which it flows.*

Zip Code: 81055 **Population:** 250* **Elevation:** 8,650 feet

THE SILVER SPOON RESTAURANT

16984 State Highway 12
Phone: (719) 742-3764 or (800) 680-3764
Fax: (719) 742-6020
E-mail: jdepweg@yahoo.com
Website: www.silverspoonrestaurant.com

Directions: Take exit 50 from I-25 in Walsenburg and go west on Highway 160 for 0.9 mile to the first traffic signal. Turn left on Main Street and go 0.2 mile (2 blocks). Turn right onto West 7th Street (also Highway 160). Go 12.2 miles to Highway 12 and turn left. Go 3 miles into the town of La Veta. Continue on Highway 12 through the town on Main Street, making a right at the end of Main Street onto Grand Avenue, then going 1 block and turning left onto Oak Street. From here it is 11 miles to Cuchara. When you get to the town and see "Dakota Dukes" on the left, continue on Highway 12 for ¾ of a mile. The restaurant is on the left.

ESSENTIALS

Cuisine: Steak, seafood, chicken and pasta
Hours: Mid-OCT to mid-MAY: Seven nights 4 P.M.–9:30 P.M. Thanksgiving to mid-MAY: Fri.–Sat. 5 P.M.–9 P.M., Sun. 5 P.M.–8 P.M. Closed Mon.–Thu.

---

*Population estimate from Silver Spoon owner Adam Depweg.

Meals and Prices: Dinner $11–$25 (includes soup and salad)
Nonsmoking: Smoking permitted only in gazebo and on patio
Take-out: Yes
Alcohol: Full bar
Credit Cards: MC, VI, AE, DS
Personal Check: Yes, with ID
Reservations: Appreciated
Wheelchair Access: Yes
Other: Available for private parties and receptions. Meal splitting discouraged. Split entrées, $4 fee; with two soups and two salads, $7.95 fee. No split charge for two children splitting an adult entrée with one soup and one salad. Service charge of 18% added to parties of six or more. No separate checks on parties of six or more.

HISTORY AND BIOGRAPHY

The Silver Spoon Restaurant began in 1983 as Vietti's Streamside Restaurant, owned by Don and Betty Vietti. Vietti's replaced a miniature golf course and clubhouse. From 1988 until 1993, the property lay vacant. Then, in December 1993, Adam and Jill Depweg opened The Silver Spoon. Adam had been in the restaurant business from 1976 to 1984, working at Bennigan's and Steak and Ale Restaurants in Dallas, Texas. He also previously leased and operated two restaurants at the Cuchara ski resort and owned the Sports Pub & Grub in La Veta at the same time he purchased The Silver Spoon. Adam is the chef and handles the kitchen. Jill is the hostess and manages the front of the restaurant. The restaurant's name, The Silver Spoon, represents both the quintessence of this mountain area and the name of the town itself in Spanish.

FOOD, SERVICE AND AMBIENCE

The Silver Spoon Restaurant is a period piece, a fine dining establishment "where elegance meets the mountains." It specializes in delectable sauces. I chose the house specialty, the pepper steak. This medium, 8-ounce beef tenderloin was coated on top with black pepper and served with a generous portion of superb, creamy, sweet, delightful and rich raspberry mushroom cream pepper sauce prepared with black raspberry liqueur and French brandy. This same sauce is used on the pepper chicken and linguini dishes. I ordered my steak medium because at The Silver Spoon, medium means you get a hot pink center. Medium-rare comes out with a hot red center. I prefer pink to red. The steak came with linguini, slightly overdone, in a flavorful homemade marinara sauce featuring mushrooms, zucchini and chives. The soup of the day was a hearty vegetable filled with carrots, potatoes, peas, kidney beans, corn, celery, parsley and pepper in a light chicken broth. The salad was a mix of field greens, tomatoes and croutons in a tangy sun-dried-tomato vinaigrette. Their homemade dressings are Parmesan vinaigrette and spicy ranch.

For starters, The Silver Spoon offers cream cheese poppers with the house spicy ranch sauce or the house special, raspberry cocktail sauce; fried appetizers with a Mexican flair and the house spicy ranch sauce; and tiger shrimp seasoned and grilled, wrapped in pepper bacon with a spicy house seasoning or as a shrimp cocktail with raspberry cocktail sauce. The blue-cheese mushroom pepper cream sauce is applied to the beef tenderloin, chicken breast, tiger shrimp and pasta entrées. The smorian (Old English for smothered) beef tenderloin and chicken breast plates are smothered with fresh mushrooms, onions, zucchini, garlic and seasoning. Tiger shrimp are found in several meals either alone, scampi-style, or in combination with rib-eye, filet, Cajun chicken, salmon, or pasta. Vegetarians will be gratified with the vegetarian pasta, similar to a pasta primavera, and the vegetarian spaghetti with the house red sauce consisting of plum tomatoes blended with sautéed mushrooms, onions, garlic and zucchini. Jill prepares all but one of the homemade desserts, including over twenty cheesecakes such as butterscotch-almond, chocolate peanut butter brownie cake, coconut cream pie, lemon torte, amaretto pie and iced mocha mousse. Adam makes the bread pudding with bourbon sauce.

My food was delivered quickly by my server, who was well informed about the menu and the jars of sauces and toppings available for purchase. Background music was a combination of rock, guitar, bossa nova and light jazz. The Cuchara River, whose headwaters are nearby, makes a loop around the restaurant. To reach the entrance of the restaurant you will walk over a covered footbridge. The water below this bridge is the same water that passed by the back of the restaurant moments earlier. The front of the building is a pentagon-shaped, gazebo-style wood-framed structure. The main dining room in the back, overlooking the Cuchara River, has a rock fireplace with a large flowery wreath between a display of golf equipment on the right and a collection of fishing gear on the left. A small bar to the right showcases the restaurant's special sauces. During the summer you can dine on the rock ledge under white canvas umbrellas while you watch and listen to the babbling Cuchara Brook and gaze at the Dakota Wall rock formation.

The front dining room has a host of American Indian and western cowboy paraphernalia, including Navajo Indian masks, kachina dolls, Indian blankets, beaver traps, cowbells and a whip. Accompanying this collection are an original photographic reproduction taken on the Santa Fe Trail in the early 1900s, a watercolor of a young Cheyenne brave and an oil painting of a Lakota Indian war party hunting buffalo. An old English saddle sits on the rafters overhead and a cow skull with horns and a collection of family photos taken in 1890s garb complete the décor.

NUTRITION AND SPECIAL REQUESTS

Silver Spoon cooking features extra-virgin olive oil, sweet cream butter and a lot of wine and brandy. Chef Adam limits salt and does not use MSG. Due to the complexity of the preparation of each entrée and limited kitchen space, special orders cannot be accommodated.

Smorian Beef (or Chicken) Sauce

SERVES 1

Chef Adam serves this sauce over grilled beef tenderloin or chicken breast.

For beef or chicken, use the following

2 ounces unsalted sweet
  cream butter
1 teaspoon minced garlic
2 tablespoons diced yellow
  onion (¼-inch dice)

1 cup sliced mushrooms
  (button or portobello)
⅓ cup diced zucchini
  (¼-inch dice)

For beef, also add the following

¼ teaspoon lemon pepper 　　　3 ounces red table wine
¾ teaspoon Italian seasoning 　　or Burgundy

For chicken, also add the following

½ teaspoon Mrs. Dash original 　3 ounces white table wine
　seasoning blend 　　　　　　　or Chablis
¾ teaspoon dry basil

1. Melt butter in saucepan. Add garlic, vegetables and appropriate seasonings.
2. Sauté on high for 2–3 minutes. Move pan constantly, shaking and stirring.
3. Add wine. Reduce heat to medium. Boil for 3 minutes.
4. Reduce wine. Lower heat to low. Continue cooking and reducing the wine for 4 minutes. Serve over grilled beef tenderloin or chicken breast.

Recipe by Adam Depweg

Wine Recommendations: For beef—Parducci Petite Sirah or Australian Jacob's Creek Shiraz

For chicken—Beringer Chardonnay or Preston Dry Creek Sauvignon Blanc

ꙮ DURANGO ꙮ

DURANGO IS DERIVED *from the Basque word* Urango, *meaning "watering town or place." The "D" was later added by the Spanish. Former territorial governor A. C. Hunt named the town after returning from Durango, Mexico. Durango was the watering station for the stagecoach line and wagon trains.*

Durango reflects three cultures—Native American, Anglo and Hispanic—and is a center for ranching, farming and recreational activities. Once a predominant coal mining community and commercial center, Durango today is known for its Victorian architecture and the Durango and Silverton narrow-gauge railroad.

Zip Code: 81301 **Population:** 13,922 **Elevation:** 6,523 feet

636 MAIN—KEN & SUE'S EAST

636 Main Avenue
Phone: (970) 385-1819
Fax: (970) 385-1801
E-mail: None
Website: None

Directions: From the intersection of Highways 160 and 550 where Highway 160 separates from Highway 550 and heads west, go north on Highway 550 to the first traffic signal and turn right onto College Drive (6th Street). Go 2 blocks and turn left onto Main Avenue. The restaurant is ½ block up on the right.

ESSENTIALS

Cuisine: American
Hours: Seven nights 5 P.M.–10 P.M.
Meals and Prices: Dinner $14–$22 (soup and salad extra)
Nonsmoking: Yes
Take-out: Yes
Alcohol: Full bar, but no blended drinks because of the noise
Credit Cards: All five
Personal Check: Local only
Reservations: Accepted for parties of six or more. For less than six, call thirty minutes in advance and be put on waiting list.
Wheelchair Access: Yes

HISTORY AND BIOGRAPHY

636 Main occupies a building from the 1890s that was once used as a garage and a hardware store. In the 1970s it was a pool hall; in the 1980s, The Cat & The Fiddle Restaurant did business here. In the 1990s, Father Murphy's and The Chop House both served food from the premises. The building was vacant when Ken and Sue Fusco bought it, fixed it up and opened 636 Main in April 2001.

Ken and Sue also own 937 Main—Ken & Sue's Place, reviewed below. Ken got his start in the restaurant business at his family's pizzeria in Ft. Lauderdale, Florida, in the early 1980s. He graduated from the

Culinary Institute of America in Hyde Park, New York, in 1989. He worked at several restaurants in Boca Raton, Florida, in the 1990s and met his wife at one of them, Prezzo Restaurant. In 1998, Ken and Sue came to Colorado and opened 937 Main in April 1998. Ken is the head chef at both restaurants. Sue manages the front of 937 Main.

FOOD, SERVICE AND AMBIENCE

636 Main offers upscale cuisine in a dining room with modern atmosphere and a very pleasant patio. It uses the same method and style of cooking as its sister restaurant at 937 Main but offers different cuisine, with an Asian flavor to many dishes. I like Greek food, so I ordered the mixed greens with Kalamata olives, plum tomatoes, cucumbers and feta cheese in a lemon-thyme vinaigrette. It was a very fresh, good-sized salad with lots of crumbled feta, tomato and cucumbers. For my entrée, I chose the cilantro-crusted halibut with sweet sticky rice and baby bok choy in piquant, sweet and tangy sake-tamari sauce. The halibut was flaky with a firm texture and a crunchy crust, but I always seem to have difficulty tasting cooked cilantro. I prefer the raw, fresh kind. This was also a plentiful plate.

I would recommend preceding your entrée with one of the starters, a satay (meat on a skewer), or a salad. There are several good options: Korean chicken noodle soup, lobster and avocado hand rolls and smoked salmon with sirachi aioli; mahogany-glazed chicken, tempura shrimp, or grilled sirloin satays with various dipping sauces; and chopped Asian salad and two others with lemon-pecorino dressing and cilantro-lime vinaigrette, just to name a few. Headlining the entrées are lobster-mascarpone stuffed spinach ravioli, basil-marinated chicken atop fazzoletti and maple-mustard glazed New York strip accompanied by a tasty side dish like blistered asparagus, crispy spinach or lobster-Yukon smashers. Topping their list of desserts is molten chocolate cake with homemade coconut ice cream. This dessert should be ordered with dinner, as it takes eighteen minutes to bake. Their other sweet delights are toasted pound cake, banana foster crème caramel and homemade ice cream from the Durango Creamery.

Servers were dressed in black shirts and jeans and were very polite— I got a lot of "yes sirs" and "no sirs." I sat on the patio and listened to recordings of Frank Sinatra and Big-Band swing music. The patio is an enclosed yet spacious area with a vine-covered rock wall, tables under three canopies and an area in the center encompassed by a two-foot brick wall. Walkways under black-iron arches lead to this area, which has two tables under canvas umbrellas. A variety of ferns grow on the red brick terrace. The interior of the restaurant has a modern look with a sloping plaster wall and oval-shaped light fixtures hanging on long cords a mere two feet above the tables. The layout is one long dining room, with a bar along the right wall that is flanked with wine racks. The dining room is embellished with frosted-glass and black-iron sconces, black lacquer molding and paintings of flowers in black picture frames.

NUTRITION AND SPECIAL REQUESTS

636 Main accommodates guests with dietary needs and special requests. They have just a few vegetarian items—some appetizers and an udon noodle bowl— on the menu.

Baby Green Salad with Granny Smith Apples, Gorgonzola Cheese, Toasted Walnuts and Fried Onions with Roasted Shallot Vinaigrette

SERVES 1

½ of a Granny Smith apple
3 cups mixed baby greens
½ cup walnuts, toasted
¼ cup Gorgonzola cheese

3 ounces Roasted Shallot
Vinaigrette (recipe follows)
Crispy Fried Onions (recipe follows)

1. Cut around the core of the apple, then thinly slice the apple lengthwise.
2. Place in mixing bowl along with greens, toasted walnuts, Gorgonzola cheese and Vinaigrette.
3. Toss together, then place on plate. Top with Crispy Onions.

Roasted Shallot Vinaigrette

5 shallots
2 cups vegetable oil
1 tablespoon honey

½ cup apple cider
pinch of salt and pepper
1 sprig of thyme

1. Preheat oven to 400 degrees. Place shallots and oil in an oven-safe pan and roast for 30 minutes. Cool.
2. Puree shallots, oil and remaining ingredients in blender or food processor. Makes about 20 ounces.

Crispy Fried Onions

2 cups oil
1 medium white onion, peeled
and thinly sliced

1 cup flour

1. Pour oil into a deep pan and heat on stovetop.
2. Dust the onion slices in flour. When oil is hot, fry the onions until they are golden. Drain; serve hot.

Recipe by Ken Frisco

Wine Recommendations: Petite Sirah or Red Zinfandel

937 MAIN—KEN & SUE'S PLACE

937 Main Avenue
Phone: (970) 259-2616
Fax: (970) 259-2450
E-mail: 937main@frontier.net
Website: None

Directions: From the intersection of Highways 160 and 550 where Highway 160 separates from Highway 550 and heads west, go north on Highway 550 to the first traffic signal and turn right onto College Drive (6th Street). Go 2 blocks and turn left onto Main Avenue. The restaurant is 3½ blocks up on the left.

ESSENTIALS

Cuisine: New American bistro
Hours: Mon.–Fri. 11 A.M.–2:30 P.M. Seven nights 5 P.M.–10 P.M.
Meals and Prices: Lunch $7–$15. Dinner $10–$19 (soup and salad extra).
Nonsmoking: All, including the patio
Take-out: Yes
Alcohol: Full bar
Credit Cards: All five
Personal Check: Local only
Reservations: Accepted for six or more for lunch or dinner
Wheelchair Access: Yes
Other: Service charge of 18% may be added to parties of nine or more

HISTORY AND BIOGRAPHY

937 Main was built in the 1890s and was originally a barbershop. In the 1970s, the Warm Flow (vegetarian) Restaurant occupied the premises. A cigar shop followed the Warm Flow and preceded Grandma Chung's, a Chinese restaurant that lasted for about nine years. The Baja Grill, a short-lived Mexican restaurant, filled the gap before Ken and Sue Fusco opened 937 Main in April 1998.

Ken and Sue also own 636 Main—Ken and Sue's East, reviewed above. They are both from Florida, where they met. Ken is a graduate of the Culinary Institute of America and the head chef at both restaurants. Sue manages the front of 937 Main. Ken was the 2001 president and Sue was the 2001 vice-president of the Durango Chapter of the Colorado Restaurant Association. Ken and Sue are active participants in Durango's cultural and culinary events, and 636 Main is one of the most popular restaurants with locals.

FOOD, SERVICE AND AMBIENCE

Ken and Sue's Place offers fine food in a warm and friendly atmosphere. I enjoyed a very delicious soup-and-sandwich combination the day I lunched there. The soup of the day was artichoke-tomato, with exceptionally ripe tomatoes that tasted like they had just been picked, along with pepper, oregano and lots and lots of flavor. The sandwich I chose was grilled Atlantic salmon on focaccia bread with lemon-caper tartar sauce. It was messy but good. Once you pick up half the sandwich, you do not dare put it down. The bread was too small for the amount of filling, which included lettuce, leaf spinach, tomato, salmon and the savory sauce. The salmon was firm yet flaky. Assorted sliced breads and homemade salty rolls, which I particularly liked because they reminded me of kimmelwick rolls, accompanied the meal.

Starters, side salads and main-plate salads were on both the lunch and dinner menus. Spotlighting the starters and salads were tomato-bisque soup, crab and artichoke spinach dip, spicy shrimp spring roll, sesame-seared rare tuna and a house Caesar salad with homemade croutons. The main-plate salads featured southwestern Cobb with grilled chicken, Chinese chicken, spinach with toasted pistachios and grilled eggplant and crispy calamari with Asian slaw. There were several savory sandwiches, such as grilled eggplant with sun-dried tomato aioli on Kaiser, half-pound burgers, grilled veggie wrap and grilled tuna steak.

The lunch pastas included angel-hair, penne, fusilli and lemon-pepper linguini mixed with oven-dried cherry tomatoes, farm-raised oyster mushrooms, grilled chicken, goat cheese and toasted pine nuts. Daily lunch specials augmented their usual specialties of Asian stir-fry and Thai shrimp with basmati rice. Highlighting their dinner entrées were Aunt Lydia's meatloaf with red wine gravy, herb-seared chicken breast stuffed with goat cheese, pistachio nut–crusted grouper, cedar-planked Atlantic salmon with tomato-cucumber salsa and chipotle and honey-mustard glazed New York strip.

Service was fast and came with a smile. I was in Durango in August, which is a lot like Europe in August—everyone takes their vacations that month. When I arrived at 11:55 A.M., one table was occupied. When I placed my order at 12:02 P.M., six tables were taken. By 12:13 P.M., all eleven tables were full. Evidently everyone in Durango takes the noon hour for lunch, so beware! Big-Band recordings were played for background music. The dining room has a high ceiling with hanging plants and a bar along the right side with wine shelves for the back bar. Enhancing the environment are photographs of the Red Mountain waterfalls and Yankee Boy Basin, blended with acrylic and oil paintings of the Mediterranean and the Cotswold hills in southwest England. The courtyard behind the building has a tent with heaters and is used year-round. An orange brick wall is to the left, a waterfall is in one back corner, and a tree fills the other corner. If you have the time, check out the narrow three-foot-wide alley between 937 Main and the building to the south that was once, supposedly, the passageway to one of Durango's brothels. It is lighted by lamps made of yellow glass and black iron. Ken and Sue's offers fine food in a warm and friendly place.

NUTRITION AND SPECIAL REQUESTS

937 Main is accommodating to guests with special needs. In addition to using a local bakery, the staff makes their own focaccia bread, pastries, salty rolls, stocks, dressings, soups and three homemade desserts.

Chocolate Molten Cake

SERVES 1

1 ounce unsalted butter
2 ounces sweet chocolate
1 teaspoon cocoa powder
2 egg whites
2 teaspoons sugar

shaved chocolate
shredded coconut
coconut or vanilla ice cream
(optional)

1. Preheat oven to 400 degrees. Melt butter and sweet chocolate over a double boiler. Mix in cocoa powder.
2. In a mixing bowl, whip egg whites to a medium peak. Add 2 teaspoons sugar.
3. Combine the butter and chocolate mixture and the egg whites and blend. Place in an 8-ounce baking dish and bake for 12 minutes in preheated oven. Take out of the oven and let cool for 5 minutes.
4. Flip the cake—it will be gooey—upside-down on a serving plate.
5. Garnish with shaved chocolate and shredded coconut. If desired, serve with either coconut or vanilla ice cream.

Recipe by Ken Frisco

Beverage Recommendation: Pear cognac

CHRISTINA'S

3416 North Main
Phone: (970) 382-3844
Fax: (970) 382-3865
E-mail: None
Website: www.durango.com/christinas

Directions: From the intersection of Highways 160 and 550 where Highway 160 continues west by itself, go north on Highway 550 about ½ mile to the intersection of Main Avenue just past 14th Street. Bear left onto Main Avenue and proceed north about 1½ miles to the restaurant, located on the right just past 34th Street.

ESSENTIALS

Cuisine: American and Continental eclectic
Hours: Mon.–Sat. 7 A.M.–9 P.M., Sun. 7 A.M.–8 P.M. Closes one hour later each night from Memorial Day weekend through SEP. Breakfast until 11:30 A.M., lunch 11 A.M.–4 P.M., dinner from 4 P.M.
Meals and Prices: Breakfast $5–$9. Lunch $6–$11. Dinner $6–$18 (Steak entrées include soup or salad. All others extra).
Nonsmoking: Smoking permitted only at bar
Take-out: Yes
Alcohol: Full bar
Credit Cards: MC, VI, AE
Personal Check: Local only
Reservations: Accepted
Wheelchair Access: Yes
Other: Banquet room available for up to fifty people

HISTORY AND BIOGRAPHY

Christina's is in a building originally occupied by the Silver Saddle Saloon in the 1950s. Over the years, a variety of Greek, Mexican and fried-chicken restaurants came to roost on these premises, including Starvin Arvin's in the early 1990s. Current owners and managers Roger and Diane Todar opened Christina's in 1996. Roger has been in the restaurant business since 1971. He managed a chain of Buffum's

Restaurants and owned three restaurants in southern California. Diane started in the restaurant business in 1976 and also worked at Buffum's Restaurants. Head chef Emiliano Narango has been at Christina's since 1996 and in the restaurant business since 1981. He has been with Roger since 1988, first working with him in California. He also cooked at French Hollywood Restaurant and Gourmet Catering in California.

FOOD, SERVICE AND AMBIENCE

I usually skip breakfast when doing research for my book, due to the lack of imagination on most breakfast menus. Not so at Christina's, where you will find plentiful portions of creative dishes. Linda and I enjoyed their generous breakfasts and uncommon Sunday specials. She had the fresh basil, tomato and feta cheese three-egg omelet with the ingredients both inside the omelet and on the side. Two giant home-made biscuits accompanied the dish. I chose the chili verde breakfast burrito, a huge wrap filled and topped with chunks of pork, melted Monterey Jack, cheddar cheese and green onions, all smothered in a spicy green chili. Tasty sides of beans with cheese and a little spice and pico de gallo came with the meal. You will not leave Christina's hungry— you will leave with a to-go box. Other Sun-day special offerings are apple-butter stuffed French toast, a mashed-potato omelet, a crab asparagus omelet with Mornay sauce and a field greens pizza salad. Roger is a lover of food, and it shows in his menus and specials.

Christina's chefs make their own soups and sauces and about forty different salad dressings. At any one time they will have about seven dressings available, such as lemon-blueberry poppyseed, cilantro lime, or Gorgonzola honey-Dijon. They also bake their own bread, including loaves of Kalamata olive, rosemary walnut, sun-dried-tomato Asiago and sunflower-seed wheat.

The extensive breakfast menu features several accompaniments to your eggs, like Italian sausage, charbroiled chicken breast, carne Asada steak, turkey bacon and fish, as well as a wide selection of omelets, pan-cakes, French toast, Greek and Italian skillets, fruit smoothies, yogurt, and steel-cut oats. An equally lengthy lunch menu includes pastas, salads, burgers, melts and sandwiches including chicken and feta, char-broiled and marinated turkey tenderloin, roast beef and portobello mush-room. Starters for dinner include Cajun popcorn shrimp, chicken wings with habanero ranch dressing, and sautéed mushrooms; there's also shrimp Louie, walnut chicken Athena, southwestern chicken Cobb salad, pastas and poultry prepared a variety of ways, steaks, seafood and stir-fries. The menus offer enough choices to satisfy the most fastidious diner.

Service was fast, friendly and efficient. My coffee cup, which empties quickly in the morning, was refilled several times. Christina's has two very attractive dining areas to either side of the red brick entrance. Pastel colors, flower bouquets, potted plants and prints of flowers decorate the restaurant. There are also paintings depicting pastoral settings of country cottages, homes with walkways, streams, lakes, trees and lots of foliage. Injected into this bucolic setting is a prodigious painting of the Durango Train Station and Engine 481. The bar and piano lounge is to the far left of the entrance, and during most evenings in the summer you can listen to live classical, light jazz, or bluegrass music. Christina's excels in providing wide selections, generous servings and value in a pleasing environment.

NUTRITION AND SPECIAL REQUESTS

Roger says they get a lot of requests and accommodate them. They use low-fat milk, canola and olive oils and offer sugar-free syrup.

Pasta Scramble

SERVES 4

This makes a great breakfast or brunch entrée, accompanied by fresh fruit.

8 large eggs, broken
1 cup ricotta cheese
¼ cup grated Romano cheese
    (can substitute pecorino
    or Asiago)
¼ cup grated Parmesan cheese
½ cup heavy cream
½ teaspoon red pepper flakes
½ teaspoon salt
1½ teaspoons chopped fresh
    oregano leaves

1 tablespoon chopped fresh basil
    leaves
1½ teaspoons chopped Italian
    parsley leaves
¼ cup butter
6 ounces mushrooms (about 12),
    sliced
4 Roma tomatoes, chopped
1 cup chopped fresh spinach
1 pound rainbow rotini pasta,
    cooked

1. Mix the first 10 ingredients in a large bowl.
2. For each serving: In an 8-inch egg pan, melt 1 tablespoon butter and sauté 3 sliced mushrooms, 1 Roma tomato and ¼ cup chopped spinach. Add a cup of the egg mixture and a cup of the cooked pasta. Cook over medium heat till the eggs are set.
3. Repeat for the other 3 servings.

Recipe by Roger Todar

Wine Recommendation: Asti Spumanti (Italian sparkling wine)

❧ EDWARDS ❧

LOCATED FOUR MILES *west of Avon, the small town of Edwards was originally named Berry's Ranch after Harrison Berry, the townsite owner. There are two versions of the story behind the town's name change: One is that it was named after Melvin Edwards, Colorado secretary of state in 1883. The other gives credit to a post office inspector named Edwards and to the railroad, which in 1912 changed the name of the station there to its current form.*

Zip Code: 81632 **Population:** 8,257 **Elevation:** 7,226 feet

SATO

0105 Edwards Village Boulevard, D101
Phone: (970) 926-7684
Fax: (970) 926-7680
E-mail: staff@satosushi.com
Website: www.satosushi.com

Directions: Take exit 163 from I-70. Head south for ½ mile to the traffic signal at Highway 6. Continue straight for 750 feet and turn right onto Edwards Village Boulevard. Take the first right into Edwards Village Center. The restaurant is in the second red brick building on the right.

ESSENTIALS

Cuisine: Japanese and sushi with other Asian influences
Hours: Seven days 5 P.M.–10 P.M., Mon.–Fri. 11:30 A.M.–2:30 P.M.
Meals and Prices: Lunch $8–$13. Dinner $11–$25 (soup and salad extra).
Nonsmoking: Yes
Take-out: Yes; carry-out orders may be limited due to restaurant's in-house business.
Alcohol: Full bar
Credit Cards: MC, VI, AE, DS
Personal Check: Local only
Reservations: Accepted for parties of six or more only
Wheelchair Access: Yes
Other: Service charge of 18% added for parties of six or more.

HISTORY AND BIOGRAPHY

Sato, which is Japanese for "village," opened in April 1999 in a new building completed that year. Previously, Sato (known as Sato Zushi) had been located in Vail Village during the 1997–1998 winter season. Molly Vanderbark and Jeff Sandoval have managed Sato since its inception in Edwards. Molly spent two years at the Hong Kong Café, formerly in Vail, before coming to Sato. Jeff has been in the restaurant business since 1987, having previously worked in Milwaukee, Wisconsin, and Las Vegas and Reno, Nevada. This is the first restaurant he has managed in Colorado. Kitchen chef Ryan Rambin and sushi chef Ted Minami have also been with Sato from day one. Ryan is from Louisiana, a graduate of the Culinary Institute of America in New York and spent about five years cooking in Aspen and Vail before coming to Sato. Ted trained in Japan and has worked in Aspen and Vail for seventeen years.

FOOD, SERVICE AND AMBIENCE

Sato offers appetizers, sushi and sashimi, soups, salads, sandwiches and a few other items for lunch. I tried three sushi menu items—raw albacore, Colorado bass and flounder on rice—as well as *tem zaru*—tempura shrimp and asparagus with cold soba, a Japanese buckwheat noodle. This light lunch combined some flavorsome, crispy tempura with the relatively neutral taste of the soba. Tempura dipping sauce, wasabi (the Japanese horseradish paste), and thinly sliced cucumber and green onions accompanied the tempura. Soy sauce, pickled ginger and wasabi came with the firm and fresh sushi.

The sushi (two pieces per order), sashimi (six pieces) and sushi rolls (six pieces) are available with a wide variety of fish, shellfish and vegetables. For appetizers, you can choose from fried calamari, shrimp egg roll, foie gras with sautéed spinach and crab cakes. Miso soup and seaweed or squid salad are on the menu for the next course. Teriyaki pork or barbecued chicken sandwiches, tempura tofu, stir-fry dishes and chicken satay with Thai peanut sauce are the lunch entrées. Dinner entrées include Asian pork baby-back ribs, grilled tandoori chicken, pan-seared duck breast and several more stir-fries. Sato serves some delectable desserts, like tempura-fried vanilla ice cream, three-chocolate terrine, bananas Foster with vanilla ice cream, white chocolate bread pudding and crispy cinnamon wonton with green tea, ginger, or vanilla ice cream. All the desserts are homemade except for the ice cream.

Service was well poised and helpful. This is a one-room, long restaurant with an alcohol bar and sushi bar to the right of the entrance. The other three sides have windows and fern-green walls with dark orange posts. There is no artwork in the restaurant, just frosted white sconces, a red brick arch over one window in the middle of the room, banana and palm trees and exposed ventilation pipes overhead. The overall look is modern and somewhat austere. To compensate, Sato's experienced chefs will provide you with fresh raw fish or cooked Japanese delights for a savory dining experience.

NUTRITION AND SPECIAL REQUESTS

Sato's staff will accommodate special requests if they have the ingredients on hand. However, this can be very difficult on busy nights. Their menu is higher-end and everything is made from scratch. Most of their requests come from the sushi bar.

Miso Soup

SERVES 6

8 cups water
1 tablespoon dashi (dried
    fish broth)
½ cup white miso paste

½–1 cup of each of the following:
    sliced shiitake mushroom,
    finely sliced green onions,
    finely cubed tofu, diced
    wakame (dried seaweed)

1. In a large saucepan over medium heat, mix together the water, dashi and miso paste.
2. When soup is hot, add the remaining ingredients and serve immediately.

Recipe by Ted Minami

Beverage Recommendation: Chilled Sake

(Sato's favorite is Mu, or try something made by Ozeki)

WILD HORSE BISTRO

27 Main Street
Phone: (970) 926-0639
Fax: (970) 926-0616
E-mail: billm@vail.net
Website: www.vail.net/riverwalk.com

Directions: Take Exit 163 from I-70. Head south ½ mile. About 100 feet before the traffic signal at Highway 6, turn left into the Riverwalk Business Center. The Inn at Riverwalk is the first building on the left. The restaurant is in this building and faces south.

ESSENTIALS

Cuisine: Mountain fare
Hours: Mon.–Sat. 11:30 A.M.–10 P.M. Closed Sun. Closed end of APR to early MAY.
Meals and Prices: Lunch $8–$13. Dinner $10–$26 (soup and salad extra).

Nonsmoking: All
Take-out: Yes
Alcohol: Full bar
Credit Cards: MC, VI, AE, DS
Personal Check: Local only
Reservations: Accepted
Wheelchair Access: Yes
Other: Children's menu

HISTORY AND BIOGRAPHY

The Inn at Riverwalk was built in December 1996. Originally, the space now occupied by Wild Horse Bistro was empty condo space. The restaurant opened in March 1998. The Inn is owned by Summit Habitants. Chris and Michael Ryan operate the restaurant. Chris manages and works the front, and Michael is the executive chef. Chris has been in the restaurant business since 1988. She worked at the June Creek Grill in Edwards (now the Grill at Singletree) and managed restaurants in Denver and Boulder, Colorado. Michael has been cooking professionally since 1997. He graduated from culinary school at Indiana University of Pennsylvania in Punxsutawney, Pennsylvania, before working in Colorado at the Hyatt at Beaver Creek. Sous-chef Thomas Leonard, from New Jersey, was fresh out of the Culinary Institute of America in Hyde Park, New York, when he joined the Wild Horse Bistro in January 1999.

FOOD, SERVICE AND AMBIENCE

Wild Horse Bistro is an upscale mountain restaurant using high-quality, fresh ingredients and serving several vegetarian dishes. I had the opportunity to sample their black bean and carrot soup finished with cilantro sour cream. It was a delightfully delicious blend of flavors with a creamy texture, a little peppery and spicy. My sandwich selection was also vegetarian, the mozzarella sandwich with roasted mushrooms, Roma tomatoes, roasted red bell peppers, fresh basil and balsamic glaze on sun-dried tomato bread. All of the ingredients tasted fresh, especially the basil. The bread was fresh and soft with a crispy crust. This was an excellent, scrumptious vegetarian dish, even if it was a little messy (the mushrooms tended to fall out of the sandwich). This was also a good-sized lunch: a large sandwich with a big serving of thinly cut, slightly salted French fries on a sizable plate. I have had smaller dinner entrées. A small cup of tart coleslaw and a pickle slice completed the meal.

Wild Horse offers several tempting appetizers, soups and salads for lunch and dinner, including artichoke Asiago spinach dip with toasted pita chips, lemon-pepper fried calamari, vegetable spring roll, tempura shrimp, grilled chicken satay, crispy polenta and chicken and sausage gumbo. For sandwiches, you can select a shaved turkey and melted Swiss, a Reuben or a Creole mustard-grilled chicken breast. They offer a wrap with tomato, bacon and Brie and another with tempura softshell crab. Another lunch option is to order a plate of chicken-fried steak or meatloaf. The dinner entrées present an array of possibilities from vegetarian to a carnivore's favorite meat. Wild game was not on the menu, but I did have my choice of Asiago-crusted chicken breast, seared sesame-crusted tuna, grilled jerk pork loin, grilled rib-eye, and roasted mushroom, Roma tomato, fresh basil, spinach and garlic tossed in black-pepper linguini. A selection of Vail Mountain Roasters teas, and after-dinner cordials and ports, are offered. Decadent desserts are also on the menu and include Chocolate Intemperance, pecan bread pudding and homemade pecan pie.

I had to wait a bit to get my order taken and to receive my food, as I visited during a very busy lunch hour. Otherwise, service was very efficient. Old rock tunes were playing through the speakers, and the dining room got noisy when filled to near capacity. This is a one-room restaurant with a glass window separating the exterior and an interior entrance from the inn. The bar and dining room are separated by columns. The booths have southwestern-style cushions in dark reds, browns and oranges. A black-and-white autographed photo of illustrator Joe Beeler and framed covers of two books illustrated by Beeler (*Hash Knife Cowboy—Recollections of Mark Hughs*, by Stella Hughs; and *Cattle, Horses, Sky and Grass—Cowboy Poetry of the Late Twentieth Century*) are displayed. Beeler's drawings of cattle rustlers and horses, ropes, chaps, saddles, hatchets and wooden axes also garnish the rest of the restaurant. Wild Horse Bistro is friendly, distinctive and an excellent value.

The staff at Wild Horse Bistro use fresh ingredients, offer low-calorie dressings, and will do anything possible to accommodate special requests.

Roasted Vegetable and Fresh Herb Risotto

SERVES 2

1 red bell pepper	3 cups chicken stock, kept warm
1 red onion	1 cup shredded Asiago cheese
1 small white onion	1 tablespoon chopped garlic
5 small button mushrooms	½ cup heavy cream
1 carrot	1 tablespoon chopped fresh
cooking oil	rosemary
salt and pepper	1 tablespoon chopped fresh thyme
1 cup Italian arborio rice	

1. Preheat oven to 350 degrees. Dice vegetables and roast with a little oil, salt and pepper in preheated oven until brown around the edges.
2. Heat medium pot with just enough oil to coat the pan (about 2 tablespoons).
3. To make the risotto, add rice and cook, stirring, until a nutty aroma is present. Add 1 cup of chicken stock. Let rice absorb stock.
3. Add another cup of stock, stirring occasionally, and repeat until stock is gone. Add Asiago cheese, reserving 1 tablespoon for later.
4. In a sauté pan, heat a little oil and chopped garlic. Add a handful of the roasted veggies and sauté for about 1–2 minutes.
5. Add the cooked risotto. Mix thoroughly and add the reserved tablespoon of Asiago cheese, cream and salt and pepper to taste. Cover pan so that the cream will be absorbed, stirring occasionally.
6. Garnish with chopped herbs. Serve.

Recipe by Michael Ryan

Wine Recommendation: Wildhorse Chardonnay

❧ EMPIRE ❧

LOCATED BESIDE THE *west fork of Clear Creek, Empire was named after New York, the "Empire State," the original home of the men who founded the town. It is an old gold and silver mining area, with several old mines, including Hartford, the Gold Dust, Gold Fissure, Atlantic, Empire City Mine, the Mint and McKinley.*

Zip Code: 80438 **Population:** 355 **Elevation:** 8,614 feet

THE PECK HOUSE

83 Sunny Avenue
Phone: (303) 569-9870
Fax (303) 569-2743
E-mail: info@peckhouse.com
Website: thepeckhouse.com

Directions: Take exit 232 from I-70 west of Idaho Springs and head north on Highway 40 for 2 miles into Empire. Turn right on Main Street (there is no street sign, but Jenny's Restaurant is on the left corner). Go 1 block and turn left. The restaurant is on the right.

ESSENTIALS

Cuisine: Continental and Colorado
Hours: Sun.–Thu. 3 P.M.–9 P.M., Fri.–Sat. 4 P.M.–10 P.M.
Meals and Prices: Dinner $17–$28 (includes starch, vegetable and salad)
Nonsmoking: Smoking permitted only at bar or on patio
Take-out: Yes
Alcohol: Full bar
Credit Cards: All five
Personal Check: Yes, with ID
Reservations: Strongly recommended on holidays, suggested otherwise

Wheelchair Access: Yes, from a path on the side of the building leading up to the porch and entrance

Other: Available for group lunch or brunch for twenty people minimum with advance notice. Eleven rooms available in the lodge.

HISTORY AND BIOGRAPHY

Built in 1862 by wealthy, adventurous Chicago merchant James Peck as a four-room home for his family, The Peck House is Colorado's oldest hotel still in operation. Peck converted the residence to a hotel in 1872 to accommodate travelers, investors, prospectors and visiting mining executives. The existing kitchen, bar and reception area occupy the original dwelling. P. T. Barnum, Ulysses S. Grant and General William T. Sherman are three names that appear in the Peck House registry. The Peck House became a stagecoach stop for stages running over Berthoud Pass and was headquarters for miners, prospectors, tourists and sportsmen. Using power generated from its own waterwheel, The Peck House was the first building in Empire with electric lights. The property remained in the Peck family until 1945, when it was sold to Joseph Emerson Smith, who in turn sold it to the two granddaughters of Adolph Coors, founder of Coors Brewery in Golden, and Henry Colbran, one of the founders of the Colorado Midland Railroad. The granddaughters renamed it The Hotel Splendide, but in 1972 the hotel's name reverted back to The Peck House.

In March 1981, Gary and Sally St. Clair took over operation of the inn and restaurant. Gary has been in the restaurant business since 1958; he formerly owned Carlson's in Greeley, Colorado, and was associated with the Marriott Corporation. Sally handles reservations and the front of the house. Gary is the chef and controls the back of the house. The Peck House was rated three stars by AAA and is listed on the National Register of Historic Places.

FOOD, SERVICE AND AMBIENCE

I have dined here on three occasions. The first time was for Sunday brunch, which, unfortunately, is no longer served. However, it was too good not to mention. I delved into a prosciutto, cream cheese and asparagus omelet that was incredible (a word that does not come to mind too often when I think of an omelet). It was served with fried potatoes, fresh strawberries and raspberries, a plate of homemade breakfast breads and coffee cakes and champagne. My second visit was for New Year's Day dinner, when I was with one of my tour groups. For this holiday dinner, I relished a plate of tender veal medallions sautéed in butter, wine and garlic and covered with lightly sautéed vegetables— fresh mushrooms, bell peppers, onion, celery and tomato. This was a dish for individuals who do not like a rich, thick sauce. These were two exquisite meals, each in its own way.

The other diners in my group enjoyed a tender New York strip with little fat, a superb duck in raspberry sauce and the dish that got the highest praise, a flaky and moist baked salmon filet in butter, brown sugar and lime juice. Accompanying the meal were homemade soft dinner rolls with a light, crisp crust and salad greens with creamy Dijon dressing. All of the meals featured top-quality ingredients, expertly brought together.

On my third dining experience, I experimented with Mrs. Peck's beef and oyster pie, an historic recipe from the past, while Linda selected a more conventional chicken Marsala. For starters, we shared the pâté à la maison, a duet of champagne-poached salmon with curry and chutney combined with duck and black winter truffles. Completing the plate were homemade honey mustard, capers, red onion and homemade pickles. The pâté was rich, piquant, creamy and smooth. All the flavors blended well. For a salad, I chose the field greens, homemade marinated mushrooms, red onion, leeks, tomatoes and green pepper in a tangy homemade curry chutney dressing. Linda selected the flavorful spinach, hot bacon and mandarin-orange salad in a balsamic-base, sweet-and-sour hot bacon dressing. Other homemade dressings are Roquefort, creamy Dijon and sweet Italian.

My entrée contained choice tidbits of beef, oysters, mushrooms and a secret sauce baked in a deep dish (like French onion soup comes in) under a square-shaped puff pastry. The pastry was very flaky and crumbly. After attempting to place chunks of beef, oyster and mushroom on top of the pastry, I gave up and simply crumbled the pastry into the deep dish like croutons. The beef, oysters and secret sauce provided a trio of pungent and biting flavors all working together. This is a dish for someone who favors intense tastes. Sally said some of her customers come here just for this robust dish. My advice is, unless you are in that "mild only" category, give it a go. You will not be disappointed, and it may just become one of your favorites. One thing is for sure: You will not find Mrs. Peck's pie on the menu of any other Colorado restaurant.

Linda's chicken Marsala was a moist, breaded, boneless breast served on fettuccine with a savory, reduced Marsala wine sauce, fresh mushrooms and a hint of garlic. Both of our dishes came with a colorful array of orange honey-mint carrots, steamed green beans tossed with oil and salt and yellow angel-hair pasta with saffron.

Chef St. Clair's Colorado and Continental cuisine also offers choice New York strip or beef tenderloin au poivre; steak béarnaise; lamb Dijon; fresh rainbow trout stuffed with wild rice, artichoke and baby spinach; shrimp Sarah; trout almandine; boneless chicken breast sautéed in wine, butter and spices with fresh sour cream sauce; brace of quail; and medallions of venison sautéed in a Cabernet and brandy sauce. For an appetizer, you can decide between fresh sautéed mushrooms, baked French onion soup, escargots bourguignonne, shrimp cocktail, smoked salmon, or a combination seafood appetizer. A cognac or other after-dinner drink will go well with one of the delectable homemade desserts, such as the torte Elizabeth, a concoction of pound cake, fruit fillings, Grand Marnier, dark Ghirardelli chocolate and crushed walnuts; hot fudge cake; turtle sundae; a daily baked cheesecake, which was lemon the last time I was here; apple strudel; or raspberry Romanoff, consisting of cream, French vanilla ice cream, Kirschwasser and B&B (Benedictine and Brandy).

The service at The Peck House is splendid. Staff are professional, knowledgeable, attentive and well-spoken—always there to warm the coffee, fill the water and see to your every need. They take great care of their customers. Softly playing classical music serenades your elegant dining experience while you gaze through a window at a splendid and majestic view of the Empire Mountain Valley that stretches to Georgetown. The best view, though, is from the front porch, restored to its 1880 character with white paint and red trim. A pair of stuffed deer heads with racks form bookends over the white-brick gas fireplace mantel, further decorated with a wreath. Nineteenth-century work implements—a mining pick, ice saw and branding iron—give the dining room a homestead feeling. Colored lithographs of the period by J. Bien depict Russell Gulch in Gilpin County; the Chief, Squaw and Papoose

Mountain Peaks as seen from Idaho Springs; Blake Street in Denver; and Pikes Peak and Colorado City. Anne Eberle, Sally's cousin, displays her watercolors: mixed florals, day lilies, a landscape and a bountiful basket. The tables are set with silk flowers and pink cloths. The left wall at the entrance of the dining room exhibits black-and-white photographs of Mrs. Peck on the front porch in 1882; her granddaughter Gracie Peck, who died of tuberculosis at the age of twelve; Big Chief Mill; and the town of Empire. Old photos and paintings of The Peck House also adorn this wall. The bar in front of the dining room offers stupendous views of the Empire Valley through picture windows in the back bar. If I were inclined to spend the evening sitting at a bar drinking, this would be my choice. Across from the bar is a small gift area. Victorian grandeur and gold-mining ruggedness, combined with shining service and a luscious cuisine, characterize The Peck House.

NUTRITION AND SPECIAL REQUESTS

The staff at The Peck House will assist guests with special needs or food allergies. Although no vegetarian entrées are on the menu, the staff can prepare a Mediterranean fettuccine for vegetarians. Quail and trout are the leanest entrées on the menu. Butter and cream are used in their cooking, but olive oil can be substituted in some dishes upon request. The Peck House is, though, a place where people come to celebrate, not to diet.

Loin of Lamb with Plum Sauce

SERVES 8

The plum sauce may be served with any grilled red meat but is particularly good with lamb.

8 lamb loins, "eye" part if available (lamb chops may be substituted)
8 ripe dark plums, pitted and sliced thin

½ cup sugar
¼ cup Port wine
1 teaspoon crushed dried mint

1. Grill the lamb loins to medium-rare. If using the eye of the loin, there is no fat on this cut, so do not overcook.
2. Meanwhile, make the plum sauce: Place sliced plums, sugar, Port wine and dried mint in a saucepan and simmer over medium heat until thick and bubbly.
3. Arrange grilled lamb on serving plates. Cover with the sauce. Serve.

Recipe by Gary St. Clair

Wine Recommendation: California Stonestreet Merlot

ESTES PARK

FORMERLY KNOWN AS *Estes Park Village, the town was named after the first white people to settle the area, Joel and Patsy Estes. Joel discovered this valley on a gold-hunting expedition in 1858, brought his family to a homestead claim in 1859, built a cabin on Fish Creek and stayed until the severe winters convinced him to leave in 1866. In the 1870s an Irish nobleman, Lord Dunraven, paid itinerants, drunks and derelicts from Denver's lower downtown district to purchase homesteads in the valley. He would then purchase the five-acre lots from them in an attempt to gain control and maintain it as a private hunting preserve. He built a 6,000-acre empire before his neighbors challenged his deeds and forced him to return to England. After the turn of the century, F. O. Stanley used his invention, the Stanley Steamer, to bring guests up the canyon into Estes Park. He later built his own hotel in 1909. Enos Mills was instrumental in creating Rocky Mountain National Park in 1915, which today can be entered through Estes Park.*

Zip Code: 80517 **Population:** 5,413 **Elevation:** 7,522 feet

CASCADES AT THE STANLEY HOTEL ———————

333 Wonderview Avenue
Phone: (970) 577-4001
Fax: None for restaurant
E-mail: None for restaurant
Website: www.stanleyhotel.com

Directions: From the intersection of Highways 34 and 36, where Saint Vrain Avenue meets Big Thompson and East Elkhorn Avenues, go north on Wonderview Avenue for 0.2 mile. Turn right at the sign for the Stanley Hotel. Go to the yield sign and turn right. Go another 0.2 mile and turn left. Take the first right and follow the signs for the Cascades Restaurant. Park behind the hotel at the column archway. If you reach the dirt road, you have gone too far.

ESSENTIALS

Cuisine: Western fare
Hours: Seven days 7 A.M.–9 P.M. (10 P.M. on Fri. and Sat.)
Meals and Prices: Breakfast $7–$8. Lunch $8–$13. Dinner: $14–$21 (soup and salad extra).
Nonsmoking: Smoking permitted only in lounge
Take-out: No
Alcohol: Full bar
Credit Cards: All five
Personal Check: Local only
Reservations: Recommended for parties of eight or more, otherwise not accepted.
Wheelchair Access: Yes, by ramp
Other: Service charge of 18% may be added to parties of twelve or more. During the summer and on holidays, the MacGregor Room is used to serve Sunday brunch.

HISTORY AND BIOGRAPHY

Cascades is in the historic Stanley Hotel, opened in 1909 by inventor F. O. Stanley. The restaurant opened in June 2000 in a space previously occupied by the Dunraven Restaurant and Lounge and, before that, the

Lariat Lounge. Before Cascades opened for business, the back wall of the space was knocked out, French doors were added, and a courtyard was created. The outside dining area now includes man-made waterfalls (for which the restaurant was named), a pond and a fire pit.

The present owner of the hotel and Cascades is John Cullen, formerly part owner with Grand Heritage Hotels. Cascades manager Taña Torres was hired in July 2001. She previously managed banquets and catering and worked at a country club, all in Ft. Collins, Colorado. Executive chef and food and beverage director Marc Grandmaison joined Cascades in September 2000. He has been in the restaurant business since 1968, including five years as an apprentice under two European chefs and six years on staff at the Stanley's sister hotel, the Providence Biltmore in Rhode Island.

Science-fiction writer Stephen King got the inspiration for his third novel, *The Shining,* while visiting the Stanley Hotel in 1973. The Dunraven, now Cascades, was used during the filming of the movie *Dumb and Dumber.*

FOOD, SERVICE AND AMBIENCE

I stopped into Cascades for lunch and had a delightful Thai peanut, pesto, shrimp and noodle salad. This was a blend of mixed organic greens, crispy noodles and sesame soy vinaigrette with sliced tomatoes and cucumbers around the perimeter of the plate. Five large, tail-on shrimp covered with sweet Thai peanut sauce contrasted fabulously with the sour vinaigrette. This is a must for salad or Asian food lovers. Cascades serves many excellent lunch salads, including chilled Mediterranean tuna and Alaskan crab. For an appetizer, try the smoked salmon, caramelized onion tart, or marinated quail. The soup selections include mashed corn and shrimp chowder and cream of wild mushroom with sherry. If you crave a sandwich, choose from the jerked turkey burger, garden burger, sautéed softshell crab and grilled basil-pesto chicken breast. The vodka-dill salmon and Asian-spiced flank steak are satisfying and filling lunchtime entrées.

Highlights of the breakfast menu are omelets, croissants, eggs Benedict, fresh fruit plates, bagels with smoked salmon, buttermilk pancakes, Belgian waffles, French toast and a variety of breakfast cocktails. Among the more notable dinner appetizers are tomato and artichoke bisque, spinach and artichoke dip, crisp calamari and Asian crab cakes. Ahi tuna with baby spinach, gari (pickled ginger root) and wontons headline the dinner salads. Pistachio- and mushroom-crusted salmon, flame-grilled shrimp, wild mushroom lasagna and Colorado spiced rib-eye steak are a sampling of Cascades' dinner entrées.

Service was friendly and came with a smile. The dining room is a large, open, single room with a bar along the interior wall. Elegant Doric columns divide the room into two sections. The walls are decorated with kerosene lamp-shaped sconces and pictures of birds of North America: the dowitcher, woodpecker, blue jay, duck and finch. Fresh flowers are set at the tables, which are covered with lime-green and white linens. The copper-plated ceiling is reminiscent of the era when the Stanley was built. Glass doors lead to veranda dining with a fire pit for cooking and the aforementioned rock waterfalls. Dining at Cascades combines historical atmosphere and a natural outlook with fine food and a touch of class.

NUTRITION AND SPECIAL REQUESTS

All entrées are made to order, and the staff accommodates dietary needs. The menu offers a limited selection of vegetarian items, including salads, a few soups and appetizers and cheese lasagna.

Thai Chicken Pasta

SERVES 2

You can substitute shrimp for the chicken or use the sauce and vegetables over salads or grilled fish.

1 boneless, skinless chicken breast
sesame oil
Thai Sauce (recipe follows)
pea pods, 8 to 10 per portion

julienned carrots, ½ ounce per portion
bean sprouts, optional
pasta (any may be used), cooked according to directions

1. Make the Thai Sauce as directed below.
2. Remove cartilage and fat from chicken breast and cut in half lengthwise. Heat sauté pan and coat with sesame oil. Sear chicken to medium done.
3. Add pureed Thai Sauce and let simmer on low heat for 8 to 10 minutes while pasta is cooking.
4. Add vegetables and remove from heat.
5. When pasta is done, drain, then toss with Sauce, reserving chicken and vegetables to garnish by placing over top of pasta.

Thai Sauce

1 tablespoon creamy peanut butter	⅛ teaspoon minced fresh ginger root
1 teaspoon soy sauce	2 teaspoons hoisin sauce
¼ teaspoon minced fresh garlic	Sriracha chili sauce to taste
	½ cup chicken stock

Place all ingredients in blender or food processor and puree. Sauce may be adjusted with more or less chicken stock to reach your desired consistency.

Recipe by Marc Grandmaison

Wine Recommendation: Pinot Grigio Ecco Domani

GRUMPY GRINGO

1560 Big Thompson Avenue
Phone: (970) 586-7705
Fax: (970) 685-3433
E-mail: eat@grumpygringo.com
Website: www.grumpygringo.com

Directions: From the intersection of Highways 34 and 36, where East Elk Horn Avenue turns into Big Thompson Avenue, go east on Big Thompson Avenue (Highway 36) for 1.3 miles. The restaurant is on the right.

ESSENTIALS

Cuisine: Mexican

Hours: JUN to mid-SEP: Seven days 11 A.M.–10 P.M. Mid-SEP to JUN: Sun.–Thu. 11 A.M.–8 P.M., Fri.–Sat. 11 A.M.–9 P.M.

Meals and Prices: Lunch and dinner $5–$20 (soup and salad extra)

Nonsmoking: Smoking permitted only in bar

Take-out: Yes

Alcohol: Full bar

Credit Cards: MC, VI, AE, DI

Personal Check: In-state only with ID

Reservations: Only accepted for parties of seven or more

Wheelchair Access: Yes

Other: Service charge of 18% and no separate checks for parties of seven or more. Children's menu. Banquet room available for large groups or families, private parties, wedding rehearsal dinners and meetings.

HISTORY AND BIOGRAPHY

The Grumpy Gringo occupies a building constructed in 1954 by Bill McConnell and Mary Kelly. They opened a frontier-style, western family restaurant called The Range. In the 1980s, they sold the restaurant to a couple named Barnett, who added the bar area and rock fireplace when they operated the Prospector's Pick Restaurant. A few other restaurants later held the space, along with Roth's Family Restaurant, which opened in the mid-1980s and closed in October 1994. After that, the building remained vacant for two years while new owners Monte and Carole House completely gutted and remodeled it. The Grumpy Gringo opened for business in June 1996.

This is Monte and Carole's first restaurant venture. They did their homework, seeking the assistance of several people in the Mexican restaurant business in Denver. Their hard work and attention to detail paid off, as they have one of the most successful restaurants in Estes Park. Managing the restaurant are Catherine (CJ) Jensen and Michelle Mathewson. CJ has been in the restaurant, hotel and food and beverage business since 1980, working in the Denver area. She joined Grumpy Gringo in the summer of 1997. Michelle has been with the restaurant since September 1997. Kitchen manager Robert Wise joined the Gringo team in fall 1997. He had been working in Denver restaurants since 1989.

I ordered one of Grumpy's specialties, the rellenos plate, opting for the traditional, fluffy coated rellenos made with egg batter and the vegetarian sauce. They were stuffed with Monterey Jack cheese and quite good. Completing the plate were Spanish rice, refried beans with Monterey Jack and cheddar cheese melted on top, chopped lettuce and diced tomatoes. A crispy version of the rellenos is also available, prepared with an eggroll shell and chopped jalapeños added to the filling. One complementary serving of warm red, white and blue corn tortilla chips and salsa comes with the meal. The salsa is thick with diced tomatoes, onion, jalapeño peppers and cilantro.

To go with your entrée, Grumpy's offers a half-dozen sauces to choose from, including hot green with chiles and pork, mild green, chili con queso with cheese added, enchilada with mild red chiles and a semi-hot white sauce with cream and jalapeños. As for the entrées themselves, you have your choice of build-your-own burritos, combo plates, fajitas, enchiladas, chimichangas, tacos and flautas. Items can also be ordered à la carte and on the side. Huevos rancheros and a breakfast burrito are on the menu for those desiring breakfast. For heartier appetites, a variety of appetizers are available: Chili con queso, chicken strips and a Mexican pu pu platter with tacos, chile rellenos, potato skins and nachos are some of the best. Rounding out the menu are deep-fried ice cream, sopaipillas, flan, ice cream and a Chocolate Delight for dessert. There's even a gringo menu for guests who crave something other than Mexican food.

When it came to service, I felt like I was in a post office that actually keeps its promise. As the menu attested, my meal was served in "five minutes or less," and my server was attentive.

From the outside, the Grumpy Gringo resembles a Spanish-style adobe structure with a stucco front wall, a courtyard behind it, and vegas connecting the front wall to the main building. Inside, the place is immaculate, with plain white, coarse-textured walls. The few wall decorations toward the front of the restaurant include a clay sun god and Kokopeli figures made from metal, fired with a torch and painted. Shelves on top of the interior wall dividers display artificial red poppies, Mexican clay pots, a big blue clay fish that reminded me of a parrot fish and a blue clay duck. Seating is on hardwood seats with cushioned backs in southwestern colors and patterns. Arched windows on one side of the dining room and rectangular windows on the other side separate walls with no paintings, decorations, or wall coverings. The bar and lounge to the right of the entrance features a stone fireplace. Mexican accordion music played in the dining room.

In the summer, diners can enjoy patio dining at tables with parasols. The banquet room, also knows as the Sombrero Room, has three large, colorful, flashy sombreros with sequins. It also sports more Kokopeli artworks from Chimayo, New Mexico, and Sonoma, Arizona, as well as arch-shaped niches and a cactus decorated with green lights.

The sign in the parking lot is used for a weekly phrase or saying. The week that I visited the sign read "panza llena corazon contento," which means "full stomach, happy heart." It's an apt comment for the Grumpy Gringo.

NUTRITION AND SPECIAL REQUESTS

The Grumpy Gringo has a few menu items for people with special nutrition requirements. They are more flexible with making substitutions in the fall, winter and spring than during the busy summer months.

Margarita Pie

MAKES ONE PIE; SERVES 6–8

1 envelope unflavored gelatin	1 drop green food coloring
½ cup sweet and sour mix	⅓ cup sugar
½ cup sugar	1½ cups whipped cream
⅛ teaspoon salt	1 cooked pie shell
3 eggs, separated	garnish: additional whipped
¼ cup tequila	cream and slices of lime
¼ cup triple sec	

1. In saucepan, add gelatin to sweet and sour mix. Stir.
2. Add ½ cup sugar, salt and egg yolks. Cook over low heat, stirring, until gelatin dissolves. Do not boil.

3. Remove from heat. Add tequila and triple sec and stir until mixture starts to mound.
4. Add drop of green food coloring. Let gelatin mixture cool.
5. Separately, beat egg whites until stiff. Fold ⅓ cup of sugar into egg whites. Add whipped cream.
6. Fold cooled gelatin mixture into egg-white mixture.
7. Pour everything into cooked pie shell. Refrigerate.
8. Serve cut pie slices with a dollop of whipped cream and a slice of lime on top.

Recipe by Carole House

Beverage Recommendation: Your favorite coffee or cappuccino

ORLANDO'S STEAK HOUSE

132 East Elkhorn Avenue
Phone: (970) 586-6121
Fax: (970) 577-0402
E-mail: None
Website: None

Directions: From the intersection of Highways 34 and 36, where East Elkhorn Avenue turns into Big Thompson Avenue, go west on East Elkhorn Avenue. The restaurant is on the left, ½ block past the second traffic signal. Look for the sign for the Wheel Bar and enter there. Go straight past the bar to the stairs at the end of the room and up the stairs to the restaurant.

NOTE: *I recommend parking in the public parking lot on the north side of East Elkhorn Avenue just 500 feet west of the intersection of Highways 34 and 36. From this intersection, the parking lot is just past the Weststar Bank parking lot and just before the first signal. From the parking lot, the restaurant is across the street and two blocks to the west.*

ESSENTIALS

Cuisine: Steak and seafood

Hours: Mid-MAY to SEP: Seven nights 5 P.M.–10 P.M. OCT to mid-MAY: Thu.–Mon. 5 P.M.–10 P.M. Closed Tue. and Wed.

Meals and Prices: Dinner $11–28 (includes soup or salad)

Nonsmoking: No

Take-out: No

Alcohol: Full bar

Credit Cards: MC, VI, AE, DI

Personal Check: In-state accepted; out-of-state with ID

Reservations: Recommended, especially on weekends

Wheelchair Access: The staff can carry a person in a wheelchair up the stairs, about a dozen steps.

HISTORY AND BIOGRAPHY

Orlando's Steak House, above the "world-famous" Wheel Bar, is in a building included on the Estes Park Historic Walking Tour. Constructed in 1915 as the Josephine Hotel and Café Josephine for Josephine Hupp, it went through several owners between 1920 and 1945 before Orlando Michael Nagl purchased the building. He started Mike's Beer Parlor, a poolroom and tavern. In 1956, a fire destroyed the top floor, eliminating one of the few overhangs on Elkhorn Avenue. In 1974, Mike opened Orlando's and turned the restaurant over to his son Steve and his wife Gay in 1977. They still manage the restaurant. The head chefs are Brian Lupo and Don Slocum, who joined the restaurant in 1999. Both chefs have been in the restaurant business since 1996. Brian worked previously at the Wapiti Bar and Grill in Estes Park. Don is from Seattle.

FOOD, SERVICE AND AMBIENCE

Orlando's offers a very limited selection of high-quality items: filet mignon, New York strip sirloin, herbed chicken cooked in wine and mushrooms and served over linguini, cold-water lobster tail, a lobster and filet combo and daily specials. I ordered the surf and turf, a swordfish and filet mignon special. It came with a cup of hot soup—vegetable-beef with wide egg noodles. My medium-rare 6-ounce filet was more rare than medium, so my server quickly returned it to the grill. It was a very tender, succulent, "melt-in-your-mouth" piece of meat. The swordfish, sautéed in white wine and butter and served with avocado butter, was a firm and flavorsome but small 3–4-ounce serving. A small baked potato and mini loaf of sourdough bread with cracked wheat completed the meal.

Dessert selections included pecan and caramel Granny-Smith apple pies, strawberry and turtle cheesecakes and quadruple chocolate mousse cake.

The lone server for the dining room was busy with five tables yet managed to keep my water refilled. Big-band instrumental music from the 1940s and 1950s played quietly. Steve and his son Ty contributed to the dining room décor. Ty, a photographer, has several of his black-and-white outdoor photographs from Rocky Mountain National Park and Moab, Utah, hanging on the walls. Steve, who used to be a casino executive in Las Vegas, added his own gambling touches, including posters of playing cards, the Riviera Hotel and Casino, and a blackjack table. Red brick columns divide the white plaster exterior wall; the interior wall is all red brick. Dining is on burgundy tablecloths with white cloth napkins and candles. A lounge and patio below the restaurant are used for parties and overflow guests on busy nights. For a bit of nostalgia and history with excellent steak or seafood, visit Orlando's above the Wheel Bar.

NUTRITION AND SPECIAL REQUESTS

There is nothing for the vegetarian on the menu. However, the staff will make adjustments, like substituting oil for butter, where possible.

Mahimahi with Avocado Butter

SERVES 4

2 pounds mahimahi filets, skin on, 8-ounce portions	1 cup white wine
flour for dredging	juice from 1 lemon
¾ cup melted butter	¼ cup chopped parsley
2 tablespoons minced garlic	4 lemon wedges
	Avocado Butter (recipe follows)

Avocado Butter

½ pound (2 sticks) butter, softened
1 large ripe avocado, mashed
1 tablespoon minced garlic
Tabasco sauce to taste

dash of Worcestershire sauce
1 teaspoon Lawry's Seasoned Salt
½ lemon juice

Combine all ingredients and stir until smooth.

1. Coat filets with flour.
2. Melt butter in saucepan.
3. Over medium to high heat, fry filets in butter until golden brown (6–7 minutes).
4. Carefully turn filets; add garlic and slowly add wine.
5. Squeeze lemon over filets. Cook uncovered until wine is reduced to a creamy sauce.
6. Place on plate, drizzle sauce over filets. Garnish with parsley and lemon wedge. Serve with Avocado Butter and rice pilaf or baked potato.

Recipe by Brian Lupo

Wine Recommendation: California Concannon Sauvignon Blanc

THE OTHER SIDE

900 Moraine Avenue
Phone: (970) 586-2171
Fax: (970) 586-8547
E-mail: None
Website: None

Directions: From the intersection of Highways 34 and 36, go west on East Elkhorn Avenue to the third traffic signal and turn left onto Moraine Avenue (Highway 36). Bear right after 0.2 mile and continue on Moraine Avenue for 1.3 miles. Turn left at the signal for Mary Lake Road. The restaurant is on the left, on the corner of Moraine and Mary Lake Avenues.

ESSENTIALS

Cuisine: Traditional Western American

Hours: Mid-MAY to mid-OCT: **Dining room:** Mon.–Sat. 11 A.M.–
2 P.M., Sun.–Thu. 5 P.M.–9:30 P.M., Fri.–Sat. 5 P.M.–10 P.M. **Café:**
Seven days 7:30 A.M.–9 P.M. Mid-OCT to mid-MAY: **Dining room:**
Mon.–Sat. 11 A.M.–2 P.M., Sun. 9 A.M.–2 P.M. Seven days 5 P.M.–8:30
P.M. **Café:** Sun.–Thu. 11 A.M.–5 P.M., Fri.–Sat. 11 A.M.–8.P.M.

Meals and Prices: Breakfast $5–$8. Lunch $6–$18. Dinner $12–$25
(includes soup or salad).

Nonsmoking: Smoking permitted only in the lounge

Take-out: Yes

Alcohol: Full bar

Credit Cards: All five

Personal Check: Yes, with ID

Reservations: Accepted

Wheelchair Access: Yes, by a ramp through the side door

Other: Service charge of 18% may be added to parties of eight or more.

HISTORY AND BIOGRAPHY

The Other Side Restaurant has been the only occupant of its building,
constructed in 1978. The owners at that time, John and Pat
Webiermeier, also owned the Covered Wagon Room, a restaurant and
gift shop at National Park Village North on Fall River Road near the
entrance to Rocky Mountain National Park. Whenever one of them
would come from the Covered Wagon to this place they would say, "I'm
going to 'the other side'"—hence the name, The Other Side.

The current owner of The Other Side is Scott Webiermeier, John
and Pat's son. His sister, Kasey, operates the gift shop above the restaurant. John McMillan started in the restaurant business at The Other
Side in 1990 and is the manager. Assistant manager Kendis Bratrud has
been working in restaurants since 1985, including summers at Ed's
Cantina in Estes Park, and has been at The Other Side since 1994. Chef
Mark Tasker also got his start in restaurants at The Other Side in 1990.

FOOD, SERVICE AND AMBIENCE

The Other Side serves good, made-to-order food at reasonable prices. I decided to go vegetarian and ordered the portobello mushroom burger for lunch. It had a definite charbroiled taste with melted provolone and herbs, lettuce and tomato slice on the side and French fries. The burger and fries were not too big or small, just modest size. Other sandwich selections include the Hidden Valley, another vegetarian choice with lots of veggies on a croissant; turkey and avocado; a slow-roasted beef; and a grilled chicken breast. Also on the lunch menu are burgers, a garden burger, baked French onion soup, salads, appetizers like tempura-battered mushrooms and Santa Fe egg rolls and entrées such as Yankee pot roast and rainbow trout.

The Other Side offers a variety of breakfast items, including omelets, pancakes, waffles, French toast, skillets, steak, rainbow trout, huevos rancheros and a Moraine Benedict with tomato and avocado instead of ham and dill hollandaise. The Sunday brunch buffet in the winter serves made-to-order omelets, salads, fruits, sweet rolls, hand-carved roast beef and ham, homemade soups, desserts and two hot lunch entrées with champagne. Arrive for dinner and you will be deliberating over appetizers and entrées featuring land and sea, house specialties and pastas. For starters there are roasted red pepper–stuffed artichokes, baked Brie in a puff pastry and garlic sherry mushrooms. Filet mignon, elk strip loin and Colorado buffalo steak highlight the broiler items. Spotlighting the sea are Rocky Mountain trout prepared four different ways, shrimp scampi, lobster tail and king crab legs. The focal points of the house specialties are the prime rib, cashew chicken, veal Marsala and drunken pork in a walnut-raisin sauce. Pasta lovers can pick penne with homemade Alfredo sauce or with chicken, cordon bleu style. Pies headline the list of desserts—key lime, Snickers and Reese's peanut butter cup—along with a chocolate-strawberry bash with vanilla icing.

Service was cordial and timely. This is an attractive restaurant with a view of a pond and its inhabitants: mallards, wood ducks, geese and the beavers who built a lodge there. The hills beyond the pond are home to muskrat, elk and deer. The restaurant boasts a high vaulted ceiling; a gas-burning rock fireplace; and wildlife paintings of eagles, moose, bears and wolves in mountain settings. The Other Side could also have been named for the mirror image of the natural, western setting that it provides.

NUTRITION AND SPECIAL REQUESTS

The Other Side makes everything from scratch and can adjust recipes to meet specific nutritional needs. The staff is open to substitutions and requests. There are vegetarian omelets on the breakfast menu, vegetarian sandwiches on the lunch menu and vegetarian pasta dishes on the dinner menu.

Drunken Pork

SERVES 5–6

1½ pounds pork medallions
flour to dredge pork, up to 2 cups
3 ounces cooking oil
1 cup sliced mushrooms
1 medium yellow onion, julienned
1 large tomato, diced

¾ cup packed brown sugar
½ cup raisins
¾ cup walnuts (halves or pieces will do)
1 tablespoon ground cinnamon
1½ cups pale dry sherry

1. Lightly flour each cutlet.
2. Heat oil in sauté pan or skillet over medium heat to smoke point (when oil first begins to smoke).
3. Lay pieces in oil without overlapping. Add the mushrooms, onion, tomato, brown sugar, raisins, walnuts and cinnamon all at the same time.
4. Cook until pork is brown on the bottom, about 1–2 minutes.
5. Flip pork. (It is not necessary to ensure that the pork touches the bottom of the pan; in fact, it is better to lay them on top of the sauce mixture so that once sherry is added, it will reduce with the spices.)
6. Add the sherry all at once. Reduce sherry until the sauce thickens to preferred consistency. Stir ingredients while reducing.
7. Lay cutlets on plate and spoon sauce evenly over each dish. Serve.

Recipe by Scott Webiermeier

Wine Recommendation: Pinot Grigio

SILVERADO AT THE LAKE SHORE LODGE ———

1700 Big Thompson Avenue
Phone: (970) 577-6422
Fax: (970) 577-6420
E-mail: None
Website: www.estesvalleyresorts.com

Directions: From the intersection of Highways 34 and 36, where East Elkhorn Avenue turns into Big Thompson Avenue, go east on Big Thompson Avenue (Highway 36) for 1.5 miles. Turn right at the tall sign for The Coffee Cup and the hard-to-see, short, six-foot-tall sign for "Silverado Restaurant, Lake Shore Lodge, Conference Center and 1700 Big Thompson Avenue." Go 200 feet and bear to the right. The green-roofed lodge next to the lake is 500 feet back.

ESSENTIALS

Cuisine: Western bistro
Hours: Year-round: Seven days 11 A.M.–2 P.M. JUN–SEP: Breakfast buffet seven days 7 A.M.–11 A.M. Dinner 5 P.M.–10 P.M. OCT–MAY: Breakfast Mon.–Fri. 7 A.M.–10:30 A.M. Breakfast buffet Sat. 7 A.M.–11 AA.M., Sun. 7 A.M.–12 noon. Dinner Sun.–Thu. 5 P.M.–9 P.M., Fri.–Sat. 5 P.M.–10 P.M.
Meals and Prices: Breakfast $5–$9. Breakfast buffet $8. Lunch $6–$11. Dinner $13–$23 (soup and salad extra).
Nonsmoking: Smoking permitted only on deck outside
Take-out: Yes
Alcohol: Full bar
Credit Cards: All five
Personal Check: Yes, with ID
Reservations: Strongly recommended, especially in summer
Wheelchair Access: Yes
Other: Children's menu. Bar menu. Banquet facilities available for up to 200 people in three separate dining rooms and the mezzanine upstairs.

HISTORY AND BIOGRAPHY

The Lake Shore Lodge and its restaurant, the Silverado, are new. They opened in May 2000, replacing the town's drive-in theater. The owners are Mick and Ola Stanger and their daughter, Sharon Seeley. They also own the Best Western next door and the Park Theater and Aspen Lodge in Estes Park.

Amy Rissler has been the Silverado's manager since October 2000. She has been in the restaurant business off and on since 1970, doing everything from handling banquets to bartending. She worked for five years at the Holiday Inn in Estes Park. Rodney Trieber, the food and beverage director, and John Bunting, the managing chef, have both been with the Silverado since it opened. Rodney has been in the restaurant business since 1980 and has a year of culinary school experience plus a degree in finance and restaurant management. He owned his own restaurant in Fort Collins for seven years and worked at the Holiday Inn in Estes Park for four years before coming to the Silverado. John has been working in restaurants since the age of thirteen and graduated from the Academy of Culinary Arts in New Jersey in 1995. His previous positions include lead cook at the Palace Arms Restaurant in the Brown Palace in Denver, and executive chef at Cuchina Leone in the Cherry Creek section of Denver and the New Sheridan Chop House in Telluride, Colorado.

FOOD, SERVICE AND AMBIENCE

My dinner began with a complimentary shrimp cocktail appetizer: four superb jumbo prawns with cocktail sauce and organic greens in a balsamic vinaigrette dressing. This appetizer is offered year-round on Sunday through Thursday evenings only. The second course, broccoli cheese soup, was rich and thick, with a strong cheese flavor and velvety texture with lots of broccoli and a little chopped carrot. It was served very hot and was filling. For the main course, I chose the chicken Wellington: a very tender chicken breast stuffed with creamy smooth Boursin cheese, wrapped in a lightly browned puff pastry and served on roasted garlic sauce. Side vegetables consisted of broccoli heads, julienne carrots and red pepper strips. A sprig of thyme added the finishing touch. Two warm dinner rolls accompanied the meal.

The breakfast menu offers eggs, omelets, a green chili frittata, a breakfast burrito, steak and eggs, pancakes, French toast, Belgian waffle and a continental breakfast. The breakfast buffet has a fruit display, a pastry display, many everyday items and daily additions or substitutions like cheese blintzes on Tuesdays or French toast substituted for pancakes on Saturdays. For lunch you can order soup, one of the four "C" salads—Caesar, chef's, Cobb, or chicken; pasta with smoked salmon or grilled chicken; sandwiches such as grilled portobello, roast beef and Reuben; or a burger. Starting dinner off right is easy with choices like crab cakes, duck liver pâté, baked Brie and wilted spinach salad. Highlighting the entrées are chicken piccata, prime rib, a filet, New York strip, rack of lamb and wild mushroom strudel. For a sweet finale, there are several delightful desserts to choose from: pumpkin-ginger torte, very berry tart, New York cheesecakes, chocolate decadence cake with four layers and a Granny dumpling—a Granny Smith apple filled with butter and spices, wrapped in pastry and finished to order.

My server was a gentleman, a professional waiter and writer I had met in 1995 at the Dunraven Inn in Estes Park. His name is Randy St. John, and I wrote about his exceptional service in my third edition. Soft, lightly played instrumental music added to diners' enjoyment. A piano bar and lounge are adjacent to the restaurant, but there was no pianist the evening I visited.

The menu promises "Fine Food with a View," and what a view it is. The entire south side of the restaurant is a continuous series of massive ceiling-to-floor windows overlooking Lakes Estes with Longs Peak in full sight. There is not a bad seat in the house for taking in this spectacular scenery. If they only served mediocre food—and it is much, much better than that—Silverado would still be a worthwhile visit. The restaurant itself has a high vaulted ceiling with pine beams and columns, ceiling fans and brass chandeliers. Dining is at tables with burgundy cloths and napkins. Accentuating the room is a sizable western painting over the kitchen showing a cowboy resting with his horse. Silverado has it all: excellent food, exceptional service and an extraordinary panorama.

Chef Bunting will accommodate, as best he can, dietary restrictions or requests for substitutions. Vegetarian selections are available on all menus.

Scallops Milano

SERVES 1

1 ounce olive oil
6 sea scallops
salt and pepper
2 ounces all-purpose flour, sifted
1 tablespoon fresh garlic, minced
3 ounces domestic mushrooms,
    sliced

2 ounces pancetta, cooked and
    chopped fine
1 ounce white wine
3 ounces chicken stock
1 tablespoon butter
3 ounces linguini, cooked
1 ounce diced tomato

1. Heat oil in a sauté pan.
2. Season the scallops with salt and pepper and coat in flour, shaking off the excess.
3. Sear the scallops on one side; turn over and add the garlic, mushrooms and pancetta.
4. When the garlic is lightly browned, deglaze with the wine and add the chicken stock.
5. Let reduce for 2 minutes and remove from heat; swirl in the butter and add salt and pepper to taste.
6. Drain the cooked linguini and place in a serving bowl; arrange the scallops over the pasta and pour the remaining ingredients over the scallops. Garnish with the diced tomato. Serve.

Recipe by John Bunting

Wine Recommendation: California Cline Cotes Oakley Vin Blanc

SWEET BASILICO CAFÉ ————————————

401 East Elkhorn Avenue
Phone: (970) 586-3899
Fax: None
E-mail: None

Directions: The restaurant is located on the northwest corner of Highways 34 and 36. Enter from East Elkhorn Avenue.

ESSENTIALS

Cuisine: Italian
Hours: Memorial Day to SEP: Seven days 11 A.M.–10 P.M. OCT to Memorial Day: Mon., Tue., Thu., Fri. 11 A.M.–2:30 P.M. and 4:30 P.M.–9 P.M. Sat.–Sun. 11:30 A.M.–9 P.M. Closed Wed.
Meals and Prices: Lunch $5–$7. Dinner $7–$15 (includes soup or salad).
Nonsmoking: All
Take-out: Yes
Alcohol: Domestic and microbrew beer and wine
Credit Cards: MC, VI, AE, DI
Personal Check: In-state only with ID
Reservations: Highly recommended, especially in summer
Wheelchair Access: Yes

HISTORY AND BIOGRAPHY

Sweet Basilico Café occupies one end of a small building that was previously used by the Filly Billy sandwich shop. Raul and Shawn Perez opened Sweet Basilico in 1998. This is their first restaurant in Colorado. They have been in the restaurant business since 1979, owning restaurants in Dallas, Texas, and Portland, Oregon. Raul does the cooking. Shawn works the front of the restaurant.

FOOD, SERVICE AND AMBIENCE

Sweet Basilico is a cozy place that is sure to warm your belly and heart. I selected the Tre de Pasta Fantasioso, which allowed me to sample three entrées: lasagna Bolognese, filled with ground beef and topped with a lot of creamy ricotta and mozzarella; cannelloni, a light, fluffy, spongy, baked pasta crêpe filled with beef, spinach, spices and herbs; and mostaccioli with Alfredo sauce. The pastas were perfectly cooked al dente, tender yet a little firm. This was a tidy trio of Italian delights.

The lunch menu features salads, sandwiches on focaccia or fresh-baked Italian bread, pastas with a variety of sauces and specialties like lasagna Florentine, fettuccine Alfredo, eggplant or shrimp parmigiana and manicotti. The dinner menu includes the pastas and most of the lunch specialties plus pizzas, chicken, veal and seafood dishes. Sweet Basilico offers tiramisu, cannoli, cheesecake plain or with strawberries and lemon-blueberry torte from a bakery in Fort Collins. I tried the last, a lemon cake topped with blueberry compote and bordered with whipped cream. If lemon meringue pie is one of your favorites, as it is for me, or if you just like lemons and blueberries, you should try this.

Service was fast, efficient and very pleasant. This is a small but charming, one-room restaurant with only nine tightly fit tables seating thirty people. A trellis at the front of the dining room and a post within the dining room are adorned with artificial grapevines. The décor is attractive, with plastic table covers depicting fruit and framed posters and pictures of mint, rosemary, olives and the chef. Dining is available on the rooftop in summer.

NUTRITION AND SPECIAL REQUESTS

With the exception of dessert, everything at Sweet Basilico—including sauces, dressings and breads—is made from scratch and made to order. The menu advertises that "We can accommodate any special dietary needs."

Chicken Marco Polo

4 boneless, skinless chicken
breasts (5 ounces each)
1 cup flour
4 tablespoons butter
½ tablespoon salt
black pepper to taste

½ teaspoon mashed fresh garlic
1 tablespoon lemon
1 cup button mushrooms
1 cup artichoke hearts
1 cup white wine

1. Dip chicken in flour, coating both sides.
2. Sauté chicken breasts in butter, 2 minutes each side.
3. Add remaining ingredients, except wine.
4. When chicken is cooked, after about 5 minutes, add wine. Cook for 2 more minutes and serve.

Recipe by Raul Perez

Wine Recommendation: Any Chardonnay

TWIN OWLS STEAKHOUSE AT THE BLACK CANYON INN

800 MacGregor Avenue
Phone: (970) 586-9344
Fax: (970) 577-9184
E-mail: blackcanyonweddings@prodigy.net
Website: None

Directions: From the intersection of Highways 34 and 36, where East Elkhorn Avenue turns into Big Thompson Avenue, go north on Highway 34 (Wonderview Avenue) for 0.4 mile. Turn right onto MacGregor Avenue. Go 0.4 mile and turn right at the sign for the Black Canyon Inn. Go 0.1 mile and turn left into the restaurant parking lot.

ESSENTIALS

Cuisine: Continental and Colorado

Hours: Mid-MAY to SEP: Seven days 5 P.M.–10 P.M. OCT to mid-MAY: Wed.–Sun. 5 P.M.–close (8 P.M.–9 P.M. weekdays, 9 P.M.–10 P.M. weekends)

Meals and Prices: Dinner $12–$25 (includes soup or salad)

Nonsmoking: All including bar

Take-out: Yes

Alcohol: Full bar

Credit Cards: All five

Personal Check: In-state only with ID

Reservations: Recommended, especially on weekends

Wheelchair Access: Yes, they have a ramp and wide doorways

Other: Service charge of 18% added to parties of eight or more and parties requesting separate checks. Banquet facility and conference center available for special events and weddings.

HISTORY AND BIOGRAPHY

The Twin Owls Steakhouse is in a building erected by Charles Chapman for the Wayne Stacey family in 1929. In 1965, Dr. Curry Meyers bought this building and a two-bedroom guest house and developed it as the Meyers 3M Guest Ranch. He remodeled the main building's interior into a restaurant. The 3M Guest Ranch and restaurant was renamed the Black Canyon Inn for its location and views of the Black Canyon.

In June 1999, Jim Sloan purchased the property and changed the name of the restaurant to the Twin Owls Steakhouse. The restaurant is managed by the Edward Grueff family, who also own the Estes Park Brewery. Edward's son, Eddie, manages and tends bar. Edward's son-in-law, Jimmy Edwards, also manages. Darren Redford has been the head chef since March 2000. He has been in the restaurant business since 1981, obtaining most of his experience in his hometown of Phoenix, Arizona, and at McKinzie's Chop House in Colorado Springs, Colorado.

FOOD, SERVICE AND AMBIENCE

During the off-season, October to mid-May, the Twin Oaks Steakhouse makes an offer to diners that I have rarely seen in Colorado: A complimentary appetizer is included with dinner. The evening I visited, it was a tasty plate of herbed smoked chicken pâté, gravlax (cured raw salmon), sliced red onion, capers and an assortment of flat breads and crackers. French onion soup with lots of onions, croutons and melted Swiss was served piping hot before my entrée. I went with one of the specials: two lamb loin chops and a pork chop, charbroiled with a rosemary demi-glace made with burgundy and Merlot. The medium-sized pork chop was well done and firm. The two small lamb loins were cooked medium, as I ordered, and tender. Combining the demi-glace with the garlic mashed potatoes that filled the center of the plate made for a savory starch. A medley of sautéed broccoli, red and green peppers, yellow squash, zucchini, carrots and green beans completed the dish. Warm rolls came with the meal.

If you miss the complimentary appetizer, you can order one off their menu, including baked Brie en croûte, sweet corn crab cakes with basil pesto sauce and red pepper coulis, or fresh Gulf shrimp served with a cilantro lime glaze. For a light meal, choose the king salmon salad or Caesar salad with grilled chicken or shrimp. Colorado-style entrées include Rocky Mountain trout basted with lemon-herb butter or breaded in cornmeal and marinated Wapiti loin chops served over a Colorado forest mushroom sauce. The Continental selections feature chicken Florentine, beef bourguignonne and Danish baby-back ribs smoked in-house and served with homemade barbecue sauce. The Twin Owls' specialty is filet mignon MacGregor served with béarnaise sauce and topped with pistachios and blue-cheese crumbs. For dessert, the Twin Owls prepares its own bread pudding with a caramel glaze and crème brûlée. It also serves cheesecakes and Chocolate Decadence.

I arrived early and had my choice of seating, so I selected a table with a view at the far end of the restaurant. My server was courteous and pleasant. Frank Sinatra songs played in the main dining room, which is made of rough-cut logs and decorated with black-and-white photographs of Estes Park circa 1930 and small white Christmas lights. The best seats in the house are by the rock fireplace and where I sat, over-looking a wall of huge boulders, Ponderosa pine trees, the Black Canyon and Twin Owls Peaks. The overall atmosphere is rustic, warm and friendly.

Additional seating for private parties or on busy nights is found in dining rooms above and adjacent to the bar and lounge, both of which have their own fireplaces.

NUTRITION AND SPECIAL REQUESTS

Twin Owls primarily serves meats and fish; just one vegetarian entrée, the vegetable primavera, is on the menu. The staff will make substitutions and honor special requests if they have the ingredients on hand.

Filet Mignon MacGregor

SERVES 4–6

1 teaspoon black peppercorns

1 whole, peeled shallot, diced

4–5 sprigs fresh tarragon, minced

6 ounces red wine, divided

4 ounces red wine vinegar, divided

3 egg yolks

¼ fresh lemon, juiced

8 ounces (1 cup) clarified butter

salt and pepper

4–6 beef tenderloin filets,
    8 ounces each

3 ounces raw pistachios

4 ounces blue cheese

4 sprigs fresh thyme, or 1 pinch
    dry thyme

Béarnaise Sauce

1. Place whole black peppercorns in blender and pulse to crack peppercorns.
2. In a sauté pan, place shallot, cracked black peppercorns, tarragon, 3 ounces red wine and 2 ounces red wine vinegar. Set pan over low heat and allow liquid to reduce until almost completely absorbed. Let stand and cool.
3. In a stainless steel bowl, place egg yolks and remaining red wine and red wine vinegar. Add lemon juice. Whip over double boiler at low to medium heat. Egg yolks should increase in volume and thickness.
4. Continue to whip until mixture reaches ribbon stage. Remove steel bowl from double boiler and place on a wet towel. (This is to keep the bowl from turning during the next step.)
5. Slowly add and stir in clarified butter.

6. Add shallot, peppercorn and tarragon reduction from your sauté pan. Season with salt and pepper.

Filet Preparation

Season meat with salt and pepper. Broil or pan-sear filets to your specifications. Cover with béarnaise and top with pistachios and blue cheese. Garnish with thyme sprigs.

Recipe by Darren Redford

Wine Recommendation: Black Opal Merlot

THE WOODLANDS RESTAURANT

165 Virginia Drive
Phone: (970) 577-7752
Fax: None
E-mail: None
Website: None

Directions: From the intersection of Highways 34 and 36, where East Elkhorn Avenue turns into Big Thompson Avenue, go west on East Elkhorn Avenue for 0.2 mile and turn right at the second traffic signal onto Virginia Drive. Go 200 feet and turn right, staying on Virginia Drive. The restaurant is one block up on the left in the Court Yard Shops. Go to the end of this building and turn left into the first driveway. Follow the road up a hill. There is parking behind the Court Yard Shops. (Note: This parking lot is a town secret, so do not tell anyone! Shhhhh.)

ESSENTIALS

Cuisine: Intercontinental
Hours: JUN–OCT: Tue.–Sun. 11 A.M.–9 P.M. Closed Mon. Thanksgiving to MAY: Wed.–Sat. 11 A.M.–9 P.M. Closed Sun.–Tue. Closed NOV until Thanksgiving.
Meals and Prices: Lunch $7–$10. Dinner $13–$23 (includes soup or salad).

Nonsmoking: All

Take-out: Yes

Alcohol: Full bar

Credit Cards: MC, VI, AE, DS

Personal Check: Yes, with ID

Reservations: Accepted. Recommended on weekends and holidays.

Wheelchair Access: Yes, from the parking lot behind the Court Yard Shops

Other: Children's menu. Available for banquets and private parties.

HISTORY AND BIOGRAPHY

The Woodlands Restaurant is part of the Court Yard Shops, which were designed by Greg Steiner in 1978. He opened The Gazebo Restaurant, which was sold to Mino Ray in 1981. In 1992, Mino moved The Gazebo to a new location, and the property remained empty for about a year. In 1993 the Cow Poke Café moved in for a five-year stay, after which the property was vacant for a year. In May 1999, Norman and Theresa Schaible opened The Woodlands Restaurant. They both manage the restaurant. Norman cooks and Theresa works the front of the restaurant. Norman has been in the restaurant business since 1975, and Theresa since 1980. They both worked at La Casa in Estes Park for five years and at Andria's in Lyons, Colorado, for seven years. They also helped to open and operate Andria's in Estes Park for two years.

FOOD, SERVICE AND AMBIENCE

I started my meal with a bowl of tomato garden soup, a delicious and savory combination of chunks of tomato, pieces of onion, herbs and a sprinkle of Parmesan cheese. I ordered one of the evening specials, the half Cornish game hen stuffed with snow crab meat, onion, herbs, bread crumbs and three cheeses: cream, Parmesan and asadero, which is made by the Amish in Mexico. The hen was baked until the skin was golden brown, and the stuffing was generous. As good as the hen was, I think it could have been improved with a sauce, perhaps with a white cream or cheese. It was accompanied by fluffy lemon wild rice and fresh and tender asparagus spears with béarnaise sauce.

Appetizers, soups, salads, sandwiches and burgers highlight the lunch menu. You can choose from red-hot jalapeño poppers, focaccia pizza fingers, a fresh fruit and cheese plate, chef's or spinach salad, a Monte Cristo or French dip sandwich, turkey and avocado club, or a vegetarian burger or sandwich, just to name a few. Dinner appetizers include most of the lunch appetizers plus shrimp cocktail and fried bay scallops. The dinner entrées showcase steaks and other beef, pork, chicken, veal, wild game and pasta. Some of the more notable selections are beef tenderloin medallions with Jack Daniel's sauce; barbecued baby-back pork ribs; Rocky Mountain red trout; pheasant; elk; veal or eggplant Parmesan; and shrimp, scallop and avocado fettuccini. Flavored coffees, root beer floats, ice cream and sundaes complete the menu and your meal.

Theresa was my server, and she was very pleasant and courteous. Dining at the Woodlands is on two levels: One, reached from the parking lot, has a dining room with paintings inspired by Rocky Mountain National Park, a gas fireplace, a colorful mural full of fall colors and hills and an adjacent enclosed patio with a grand view of downtown Estes Park, Longs Peak and the surrounding mountains. It has a small loft upstairs that you can visit to get an even better view of the scenery. Downstairs is the bar, a second dining room and an open patio that overlooks the man-made stream that is filled with trout in the summer. It is a very pleasing, natural setting in the warmer months. No matter which level of the Woodlands Restaurant you dine on, you will relish some fine cuisine in a pure, unspoiled setting.

NUTRITION AND SPECIAL REQUESTS

No salt is used in any of the Woodlands' cooking. The lunch menu lists a couple of vegetarian dishes, and the staff will accommodate special dietary requests and substitutions where possible. Most items are made from scratch using quality foods. No processed foods are used.

Jack Daniel's Sauce

*This zesty sauce is wonderful with tender cuts of venison, buffalo or beef.
It works well over hamburgers on an outdoor grill.*

¼ cup minced green onions

2 cloves garlic, pressed

½ cup sliced fresh mushrooms

2 tablespoons crushed peppercorns

4 tablespoons unsalted butter,
   divided

2 cups beef stock

¾ cup white wine

½ cup Jack Daniel's bourbon
   whiskey

½ cup heavy cream

1½ tablespoons flour

1. Lightly sauté green onions, garlic, mushrooms and peppercorns in 2 tablespoons of butter. Add beef stock, white wine and bourbon and bring to a boil.
2. Reduce heat to medium and cook until volume of sauce is reduced by about half. Add heavy cream and continue to cook on medium for about 10 minutes.
3. Mix remaining butter with flour to make a roux.
4. Whisk roux into sauce until sauce is consistently smooth.

Recipe by Norman Schaible

❧ EVERGREEN ❧

FIRST CALLED THE POST, *after Amos F. Post, son-in-law of Thomas Bergen, who settled nearby Bergen Park, Evergreen was given its current name by D. P. Wilmot in honor of the dense forests of evergreen trees in the area. Ute Indians used to camp along nearby Soda Creek. Evergreen has enjoyed a variety of residents, including trappers, traders, gold miners, ranchers and lumberjacks.*

Zip Code: 80439 **Population:** 9,216 **Elevation:** 7,040 feet

THUY HOA

28080 Douglas Park Road
Phone: (303) 674-5421
Fax: None
E-mail: None
Website: None

Directions: From I-70 heading west take Exit 252; heading east take Exit 251 (The El Rancho/Evergreen Exit). Follow Highway 74 south for 8 miles into Evergreen. The highway will narrow from four lanes to two lanes and go down a hill past Evergreen Lake before reaching the traffic signal for Highway 73. From this intersection, go straight for 0.1 mile and make a left onto Douglas Park Road. The restaurant is 1 block up the hill on the left. Parking is just beyond the restaurant on the left past the chain fence or on the right if you make a sharp right turn. You can also park in the parking lot on Highway 74 across from Douglas Park Road.

ESSENTIALS

Cuisine: Vietnamese
Hours: Tue.–Sat. 11 A.M.–2 P.M., Sun. and Tue.–Thu. 5 P.M.–9 P.M., Fri.–Sat. 5 P.M.–10 P.M. Closed Mon.

Meals and Prices: Lunch $7–$8. Dinner $11–$18 (includes rice; soup extra).
Nonsmoking: All
Take-out: Yes, but may be restricted at times
Alcohol: Full bar
Credit Cards: MC, VI, AE, DI
Personal Check: In-state only with ID
Reservations: Highly recommended on Fri or Sat. Recommended rest of week.
Wheelchair Access: Yes
Other: Live entertainment four or five nights a week including weekends, beginning at 7 P.M.

HISTORY AND BIOGRAPHY

Thuy Hoa (which means "bouquet of flowers" in Vietnamese and is pronounced "Twee Wah") is in a building that originated as a church in 1905. Between 1967 and 1971 it was the Bijou Movie Theater. From 1979 to 1984 it was a video arcade, and from 1995 to 1997 it was the Coal Mine Chinese Restaurant. The building was vacant when Hoa Spitale and her family opened Thuy Hoa in February 1998.

Hoa had the first Vietnamese restaurant in Denver, from 1979 to 1982, on Montview Boulevard. She was the original owner of the Thuy Hoa Inn, which opened on Federal Boulevard in Denver in 1982. She sold that restaurant in 1990, then opened Chez Thuy Hoa in downtown Denver in 1992. Hoa is also the head chef of the Evergreen restaurant. Her son, Harry Wallace, is the manager. Harry has been working in his mother's restaurants since 1985, waiting tables in the Federal Boulevard restaurant and at Hoa's restaurant in Bergen Park from 1987 to 1990. From 1996 to 1998, he helped manage the downtown Denver restaurant and since January 2000 has managed Thuy Hoa of Evergreen.

FOOD, SERVICE AND AMBIENCE

Linda and I shared an appetizer of Vietnamese egg rolls with ground pork. Proper assembly requires that you use a lettuce leaf like a taco shell, filling it with fresh mint, fresh cilantro, cucumber slices, bean sprouts and rice noodles. Correctly done, you will simultaneously eat and spill. It's messy but delicious.

For her entrée, Linda chose the Saigon noodle bowl featuring a combination of chicken breast with a good grill flavor, shrimp, rice noodles, salad with peanuts down below and the house sauce, all served in a deep bowl with an egg roll. The house sauce consists of fish extract, fish sauce, lemon, vinegar, pepper and sugar. I ordered the shrimp and scallops with fresh sliced tomatoes and garlic sauce. This selection came with green onions, red onion and carrots, but I could not detect the garlic. The scallops were soft. The shrimp were a little firm, with better texture and more flavor than the scallops.

Thuy Hoa has a lengthy dinner menu of over 100 items including seafood, vegetarian and grilled appetizers; combination soups for two or more; seafood specialties; exotic dishes like ginger duck, stuffed Cornish hen, lamb lemongrass, frog legs in garlic pepper sauce and five-spice grilled quail; and chicken, pork and beef dishes.

The lunch menu includes several appetizers, including spring rolls, softshell crab, grilled meats or shrimp, seafood such as crab or mussels and vegetarian stuffed grape leaves, curry, lo mein and chow mein. Combination soups are cooked-to-order and include asparagus and crabmeat soup and wonton egg noodle soup topped with shrimp and duck. You can also have your favorite meat or seafood with steamed rice or in a Saigon noodle bowl. A variety of fried rice dishes completes the lunch menu.

Service was fast, perhaps a little too fast. We were served our entrées when we were just halfway through our appetizer. The staff was very attentive and very quick on the water refills. We listened to solo instrumental piano music while we dined. The dining room features antique doors, stone walls, a high ceiling, alternating vertical segments of ceiling-to-floor windows and tan stucco walls and a bell tower in the front corner. Enhancing the architecture are large gold Japanese fans with designs of flowers and birds of paradise, pictures of black spotted gold peacocks, a brass statue of the "good luck sun god," and pots with Asian patterns. There is a baby grand piano at the entrance to the dining area. The bar to your left as you enter the building was built in Germany in the 1880s and shipped to Cripple Creek, Colorado, in

1897 before arriving at Thuy Hoa more than a century later. A patio is available for dining during summer.

NUTRITION AND SPECIAL REQUESTS

Everything on the menu is made from scratch. Items can be eliminated or substituted if the chef thinks it will taste good. Thuy Hoa offers several vegetarian appetizers and lunch specials, a papaya salad, two vegetarian soups and vegetarian fried rice.

Vegetarian Egg Rolls

MAKES 12 EGG ROLLS, FOR 4 SERVINGS

2 cups crumbled tofu
2 cups finely chopped jicama
2 tablespoons finely chopped
    green onion
½ cup shredded carrots
½ cup finely diced black
    mushrooms
½ cup bean strips (clear, thin,
    bean thread noodles,
    available in Asian markets)

1 teaspoon salt
1 teaspoon pepper
3 tablespoons sugar
12 sheets of rice paper
oil for frying
lettuce

1. Combine all ingredients except rice paper and lettuce. Divide into 12 equal portions.
2. Place mixture on rice papers; fold in edges and roll.
3. Fry in your preferred oil until golden brown.
4. Drain on paper towel and serve with lettuce.

Recipe by Hoa Spitale

FLORENCE

Florence and the surrounding area was once home to Ute Indians. Much later, French and Spanish trappers and explorers passed through the surrounding foothills. The town, originally named Frazerville, was founded in 1860 in honor of "Uncle Joe" Frazer, who developed coal mines on nearby Coal Creek. The name was changed to Florence in 1872 in honor of Senator James A. McCandless's youngest daughter. Oil was discovered near Florence in 1862, and James McCandless was the first to refine oil here, in the first oilfield west of Pennsylvania. The oil was hauled to Denver and sold for wagon grease. In 1872, McCandless donated a townsite and had the first town plat made. By 1901, three oil refining companies operated in Florence.

Zip Code: 81226 **Population:** 3,653 **Elevation:** 5,187 feet

ROLLIN RICH'S STEAKHOUSE

727 East Main Street
Phone: (719) 784-1984
Fax: (719) 784-1985
E-mail: None
Website: None

Directions: From the intersection of Highways 50 and 115 in Penrose, 27 miles west of Pueblo and 11 miles east of Cañon City, go south on Highway 115 for 5 miles into the town of Florence. The restaurant is on the right on Highway 115 (East Main Street) on the northeast corner of Robinson Avenue. It is ¼ mile before the intersection of Highways 115 and 67. Parking could be a problem on a busy summer night. You may have to park on the street.

ESSENTIALS

Cuisine: Steak and seafood

Hours: Mon.–Sat. 7 A.M.–9 P.M., Sun. 7 A.M.–2 P.M.

Meals and Prices: Breakfast, lunch and dinner $6–$30 (includes soup or salad).

Nonsmoking: Yes

Take-out: Yes

Alcohol: Full bar

Credit Cards: MC, VI, AE

Personal Check: Yes, with ID

Reservations: Accepted; recommended for parties of six or more

Wheelchair Access: Yes, to smoking area only

Other: Banquet room available for private parties, wedding receptions and professional meetings.

HISTORY AND BIOGRAPHY

The building used by Rollin Rich's Steakhouse was originally a house and restaurant belonging to the Morelli family from 1982 to 1991. This was followed by Bernardino's Restaurant, owned by the DiRito family, from 1991 until 1997. Next came Nordwall's Family Restaurant, serving steak, seafood and pasta from 1997 to 1999. The Ore House passed through these walls for a couple of months in 1999. The building stood vacant for a year before Richard, Pat and Kathy Owens opened Rollin Rich's in September 2000. This is their first restaurant. Kathy manages the front of the restaurant and helps out as hostess and waitress. Chef Paul Jaques (pronounced "Hawk-iss") was trained by Richard after spending a year in different restaurants in the community.

FOOD, SERVICE AND AMBIENCE

A bowl of warm, savory baked potato soup preceded my steak entrée. It consisted of a milky cream base with potato and bacon pieces topped with shredded Parmesan cheese. The top sirloin was pink inside, medium-rare, as ordered. This was a decent enough steak, broiled, but with no charbroiled taste that I could detect. It came with a baked potato and roll but no vegetables. You can opt for French fries or mashed potatoes instead of baked potato with your T-bone, filet mignon, rib-eye, New York or Kansas City strip, or chicken-fried steak. If steak is not your thing, Rollin Rich offers lobster, crab legs, shrimp, orange roughy, chicken four different ways, spaghetti and pasta prima-vera. For a lighter appetite, grilled chicken, open-face steak sandwiches, and burgers are offered. Chocolate and raspberry tortes for dessert complete the menu.

Service during my visit was quick. I had no wait at all through any part of my meal. As you enter the restaurant take note of the comical paintings of cowpokes and their cows on the red brick wall behind the mauve-colored couches. A tall red-brick gas-burning fireplace reaching up to the vaulted ceiling gives prominence to the front dining room. There is an intriguing blown-up photograph of Cary Grant and Grace Kelly driving a convertible on the French Riviera taken from the 1955 movie *To Catch a Thief*. Mixed in with the movie memorabilia are nature paintings displaying wolves howling at the winter wind, a busy bee and a damsel fly, as well as a painting of the Royal Gorge Bridge as seen from the river.

The back dining room features a red slate fireplace and black-and-white sketches of gondolas in a canal. Downstairs is a private room resembling a mine shaft with natural wood walls, a red brick fireplace, miners' axes and long saws. More Hollywood nostalgia is present, with enlarged photos of James Dean and Marilyn Monroe. The owners plan to add Dean Martin, Frank Sinatra and Elvis Presley, whose photos may be there by the time you visit.

NUTRITION AND SPECIAL REQUESTS

Rollin Rich's is primarily a steakhouse, so steak, seafood and chicken take center stage. However, spaghetti and pasta primavera are available for vegetarians, and the staff has no problem making substitutions where possible.

Baked Potato Soup

SERVES 6

2 ounces olive oil
2 cups diced celery
1 onion, diced
1 cup nondairy creamer
1 quart milk

5 baked potatoes, peeled and
    cubed
1 pint heavy cream
5 slices crispy chopped bacon
salt and pepper

1. Sauté celery and onions in olive oil.
2. Mix nondairy creamer with milk and whip.
3. Combine all ingredients in a large pot and simmer for 2 hours. Adjust salt and pepper to taste. Serve hot.

Recipe by Paul Jaques

❧ FORT MORGAN ❧

THIS FORMER MILITARY *post went by the names of Camp Tyler and Fort Wardwell before being named after Colonel Christopher A. Morgan in 1866. The town became an agricultural center about forty years later when the Northwestern Sugar Company built a factory north of town.*

Zip Code: 80424 **Population:** 11,034 **Elevation:** 4,338 feet

CABLES ITALIAN GRILLE

431 Main Street
Phone: (970) 867-6144
Fax: (970) 867-5038

E-mail: cables@twol.com
Website: www.cablesitaliangrille.com

Directions: Take exit 80 from I-76. Go south on Highway 52 (Main Street) for 0.8 mile. The restaurant is 1 block past Highway 34, on the right, at the intersection with Bijou Avenue.

ESSENTIALS

Cuisine: Italian American
Hours: Seven days 11 A.M.–10 P.M.
Meals and Prices: Lunch and dinner $6–$18 (includes soup or salad)
Nonsmoking: Yes
Take-out: Yes
Alcohol: Yes
Credit Cards: All five
Personal Check: Yes
Reservations: Encouraged but not necessary
Wheelchair Access: Yes
Other: Children's menu. Free delivery in Fort Morgan area.

HISTORY AND BIOGRAPHY

Cables is in a building constructed in 1916 as a garage. It stayed a garage for eighty-one years, until Cables Italian Grille opened in January 1997. The restaurant is named after the cable spools used for tables. The owner, manager and head chef of the restaurant is Mick Peters. Mick has been in the restaurant business since 1975 and was a chef at the Greeley Country Club for thirteen years. His wife, Tonya, handles the books and takes care of the back of the restaurant.

FOOD, SERVICE AND AMBIENCE

Cables Italian Grille has one of the more impressive arrays of homemade pastas and sauces that I have seen in Colorado, but let's begin with the soup. I am not a big minestrone fan, but Cables' version I definitely favored. It has a beef broth and is very thick with chunks of beef, wide egg noodles, finely chopped carrots and onion, tomato pieces, kidney beans, black pepper and other spices. It has a distinctive Southwest flavor to it as well. To get a taste of their different pastas, I went with the spaghetti, ravioli and lasagna combination and substituted marinara sauce for the rich, herb-filled tomato sauce. The homemade, spaetzle-like spaghetti noodles, close to a half-pound I'd say, were thick and chewy. The three tender, fresh, homemade ravioli filled with ricotta cheese were smooth and delicious. The homemade lasagna consisted of five delectable layers of noodles filled with shredded beef and cheeses. The dish came with a meatball. My only complaint was with myself for not requesting more of the savory marinara sauce, made with green peppers, green onions, garlic and herbs. If you love Italian food and appreciate homemade pastas and sauces, then you should definitely come to Cables.

Linda was counting her Weight Watchers points and elected the lemon-pepper chicken salad with blue cheese dressing on the side. This was Cables' large Italian salad featuring lemon-pepper chicken breast tenderloins, black olives, shaved carrot and cabbage, tomato, croutons and pepperoncini. Linda found the chicken to be on the dry side. My advice: Leave your Weight Watchers book at home when you come here, and order what Cables does best, your favorite pasta with your favorite sauce.

Cables' full menu is extensive and covers appetizers, sandwiches, salads, pizzas, burgers, Italian meat dishes, stromboli, calzones, cannoli, steak, fish and even American fare—hand-battered buttermilk fried chicken, fish and chips with freshly breaded catfish loins, a grilled home-style meatloaf sandwich and Rocky Mountain oysters. For those in a hurry there is a "ten-minute ticker" menu of quick-serve lunch items like pasta, pizza slice, a half sandwich, soup, or salad. "Cables Capers" is a collection of appetizers including pepperoni pizza flares (pepperoni and mozzarella rolled in fresh dough), Italian poppers, tangy Buffalo-style or blackened Cajun chicken wings, Italian nachos (with mozzarella, Italian sausage and pepperoni in addition to the standard ingredients) and beer-battered mushrooms.

The salad selections include Caesar, pasta, chef's, mixed Italian, buffalo chicken and focaccia, the latter made with herb-and-garlic-crusted focaccia bread. A barrage of burgers are available, each made with a half-pound of ground Black Angus. The choices are Italian (pepperoni and provolone), mushroom-bacon-Swiss, Hawaiian (pineapple), Border (green chili), smokehouse (barbecue sauce), black and bleu (cracked black pepper and blue cheese) and the meatloaf burger. Fresh center-cut Black Angus steaks and pork chops are also on the menu. The sandwiches, headlined by homemade meatball, are stacked with ingredients such as freshly sliced Italian and American meats, cheeses and vegetables on homemade Italian rolls. The stromboli, calzones and cannolis also use these same fresh ingredients in Cables' homemade dough.

The pizzas come in three sizes with a tangy red sauce and eighteen toppings to choose from, including cappocollo, chicken and artichoke, all on Neapolitan thin crust or Sicilian thick crust. Cables' northern Italian house specialties are highlighted by veal or chicken parmigiana, New York steak Florentine, broiled pesto chicken, shrimp aioli in a garlic olive oil and pomodoro pesto shrimp in a sun-dried tomato pesto sauce. You can create your own homemade pasta and sauce combination from a variety of pastas—spaghetti, fettuccini, angel-hair, linguini, farfalle, and mostaccioli—mixed with tomato, marinara, Bolognese (homemade Italian sausage and seasoned ground beef), Alfredo (rich Romano cheese), olive oil and garlic, pesto, or sun-dried-tomato pesto sauce. In addition to these choices, you also have the pasta specialties— lasagna, manicotti, ravioli and tortellini—as options.

Service during my visit was fast: less than five minutes for the soup, less than five minutes for the entrée. Our server was uninformed about the soup but did substitute the marinara sauce for the tomato sauce. The restaurant sports a glass wall along the entire front, a high ceiling with exposed ventilation pipes, two dining areas separated by a bar in the middle, red brick walls on the sides and a plaster back wall with grape vines painted on it. Linda and I sat at a cable spool adorned with a lit candle in a red glass jar inside a large metal can with holes. There were only a few décor items, but they were appropriate or comical: a poster of a gigantic tomato set in a chair with the caption "Tomato. Something unusual is going on here," a map of Italian vineyards, and a photo of the building's original owner with the caption, "Ace Gillett's Garage—Most Modern Garage in the West, Ft. Morgan. 1918." In the dining room to the left, there is a gas-burning fireplace with baseball trophies and awards on the mantel.

NUTRITION AND SPECIAL REQUESTS

Cables' tomato and marinara sauces are virtually fat-free and cholesterol-free. No oil is used in making the pizza crust. The restaurant uses fresh products and minimal canned goods. Everything is made on the premises. With its extensive menu, Cables receives few special requests, but Mick will try to accommodate guests.

Marinara Sauce

MAKES 4–5 CUPS

2 ripe tomatoes, peeled and seeded
12 green onions
1 red bell pepper
1 green pepper
2 cloves garlic

1 teaspoon dried fennel seeds
2 tablespoons fresh basil
2 teaspoons sea salt
1 cup water
1 cup white Sangiovese wine

1. Finely dice all vegetables.
2. Combine all ingredients over low heat and simmer for 3 hours.
3. Blend all ingredients in Robot Coupe or food processor and return to pot to rewarm. Enjoy over fresh pasta.

Recipe by Mick Peters

❧ FRASER ❧

FORMERLY KNOWN AS *Easton for George Easton, who laid out the townsite, the town was later called Frazier, for Reuben Frazier, an early settler. Postal authorities later adopted the simpler spelling. Today, Fraser attracts both Nordic and downhill skiers to the area. Fraser's experimental forest is a favorite holiday spot for those interested in chopping down their own Christmas tree for a small park fee. An historical attraction is the Cozens Ranch House Restoration, a museum that includes an actual ranch, house, stage stop and post office dating to 1876.*

Zip Code: 80442 **Population:** 910 **Elevation:** 8,550 feet

THE MEADOW VIEW RESTAURANT
AT HIGH MOUNTAIN LODGE

425 County Road 5001
Phone: (970) 726-5958
Fax: (970) 726-9796
E-mail: info@himtnlodge.com
Website: www.himtnlodge.com

Directions: Take exit 232 from I-70 and proceed north over Berthoud
Pass for 31 miles to the town of Fraser. At the traffic signal with Safeway
on the right and Alco on the left, turn left onto Elk Creek Road. Go 0.3
mile (you are now on a gravel-and-dirt road) and turn right onto Fraser
Parkway. Go 0.75 mile and turn left onto CR73 (St. Louis Creek Road).
Go 0.8 mile and turn right onto County Road 50-South. Stay on this road
for 2 miles. At the sign for High Mountain Lodge on the right, make a
sharp 170-degree turn to the right. Go 0.3 mile and make a sharp
170-degree turn to the left (that should balance out your wheels).
Go 0.1 mile and park at the first building on the left. Take the stairway
up to the restaurant.

ESSENTIALS

Cuisine: Eclectic
Hours: Mid-NOV to mid-APR: Seven nights 6 P.M.–9:30 P.M., Sun.
    7 A.M.–1 P.M. Mid-APR to end of APR and JUN to mid-NOV:
    Wed.–Sat. 6 P.M.–9:30 P.M., Sun. 9 A.M.–2 P.M. Closed MAY.
Meals and Prices: Dinner $15–$25 à la carte (soup and salad extra);
    $30–$46 five-course prix fixe. Sun. brunch $8–$14.
Nonsmoking: Smoking permitted only on deck
Take-out: No
Alcohol: Full bar
Credit Cards: MC, VI, AE, DS
Personal Check: Yes, with driver's license
Reservations: ALWAYS REQUIRED
Wheelchair Access: Yes, by ramp
Other: Catering. Available for private parties, family reunions, weddings
    and receptions.

HISTORY AND BIOGRAPHY

The High Mountain Lodge was originally Parrington's at Tally Ho, built in 1973 by Englishman Ed Parrington. He sold it in the late 1980s to a couple who sold it to the current owners, Blaine Gulbranson and Katie Bogle, in August 1998. From 1973 until 1998, the area now used by the Meadow View Restaurant was a private dining area for lodge guests only. Blaine and Katie did extensive remodeling of the kitchen and opened the restaurant to the public while still providing dinner for lodge guests.

Katie's background includes owning her own catering business in Phoenix, Arizona, in the mid-1980s and working in the hospitality business with hotels and United Airlines. She works in the kitchen, takes reservations and handles public relations. Blaine is the mechanic and engineer who maintains the physical operation of the complex.

FOOD, SERVICE AND AMBIENCE

High-end dining with a view to match is what you will find at The Meadow View Restaurant. The Meadow View serves five-course dinners that include your choice of two appetizers, two soups, two salads, five entrées and three desserts. Alternatively, if you are not up to a five-course meal, you can order à la carte, as I did. I chose the Greek salad, which was also one of the entrée choices that evening, and coconut-encrusted marlin. The salad consisted of mixed field greens, ample crumbled feta cheese and Kalamata olives and sliced red onion in an herb vinaigrette made with thyme, celery seed, rosemary and basil. The marlin was seared, which left it rare in the center; ask your server to cook it a little more when ordering if you prefer it cooked through. This was a firm, thick piece of fish sweetened by the coconut crust and sweet chili sauce. Couscous was offered on the side. It was a little dry but tasty and crunchy, enhanced by saffron, basil, garlic and olive oil. The vegetables, also pan-seared and with a delicious flavor, included caramelized red onions, cherry tomatoes, zucchini and sliced chanterelle mushrooms. White rolls, crusty on the outside, soft on the inside, were served with dinner.

The menu changes nightly. Appetizers may include shrimp or duck wontons, poached or seared scallops, truffle pâté, goat cheese crostini, or smoked trout. Expect to see cold homemade soups in the summer, such as gazpacho, chilled raspberry Riesling, or chilled cucumber and roasted pepper. Likewise, hot homemade soups such as rabbit stew, steak and potato, squash or lobster bisque and chicken chili will warm you in winter. The salad selections, which come with homemade dressings, include mixed greens, spinach, green bean and wasabi-cucumber. Entrées feature fowl, beef, wild game, fish and vegetarian or salad dishes. Examples of what you can expect are grilled rib-eye with red wine jus, roasted half duckling atop peach sauce, three-cheese and pine nut ravioli with garlic cream sauce and pan-seared antelope with chipotle sauce. Highlighting the homemade desserts are chocolate or raspberry crème brûlée, plain chocolate swirl or caramel pecan cheesecake, peach cobbler, key lime pie and a chocolate bombe.

Sunday brunch gives you the option of electing the buffet, with chicken and pasta salads, fresh fruits, homemade pastries and a selection of yogurts, or ordering a menu item. All brunch orders include a glass of champagne, mimosa, or Bloody Mary. The menu changes weekly. Depending on the week, you can pick French toast cobbler, caramel French toast, Belgian waffle, banana-nut or gingerbread pancakes, eggs Benedict, filet of salmon, or ratatouille crêpes.

Service was pleasant and informative. The only faux pas that I noticed was the serving of the bread after the salad instead of before. Otherwise, I was treated royally. Spanish violin and guitar music played in the dining room, which has a definite equestrian theme. A mélange of small wood, ceramic, crystal, metal, clay, glass and bronze sculptures of horses, seahorses and unicorns decorate the top of the wall rail encircling the dining room. Complementing these small figures are other artworks of horses. If you enter from the deck, which offers five tables with green umbrellas and a fire pit, you will walk through a small three-stool bar and lounge with a fireplace and piano. The windows face the trees and four man-made ponds, with picturesque views of the meadow and mountains beyond.

NUTRITION AND SPECIAL REQUESTS

The Meadow View will accommodate nutritional and dietary needs during dinner. For breakfast, the restaurant alternates protein dishes one day with carbohydrate dishes the next in an attempt to create a balanced diet that meets high-altitude bodily requirements. Fresh fruit is served with each breakfast.

Grilled Caribou Chops with Cranberry Relish

SERVES 1

The Cranberry Relish makes about 3 cups, enough for 12 servings. It can be refrigerated for up to 2 weeks or frozen for at least 1 month.

3 10- to 12-ounce, well-trimmed, bone-in caribou chops
½ cup red wine vinegar
½ cup balsamic vinegar
1 pound fresh cranberries
juice from 2 fresh oranges (medium size)

½ cup extra–fine sugar
¼ cup Dry Sack sherry
¼ cup finely minced Vidalia onions
½ cup chopped pecans
pinch fresh nutmeg
finely chopped fresh thyme and sprig of fresh thyme

1. Mix together red wine vinegar and balsamic vinegar to make marinade. Trim caribou well; place in pan and cover with marinade. Set aside.
2. Make the Cranberry Relish: Place cranberries, orange juice, sugar, sherry and onions in a medium-sized saucepan. Bring to a boil, reduce heat and let simmer until thick—about 2 hours. Stir in pecans and nutmeg. Remove from heat, but keep warm.
3. Press chopped thyme into the chops and grill according to taste.
4. Place chops on plate with long bones pointing upward, using each other for prop. Spoon ¼ cup of Relish carefully across meat of chops. Garnish with sprig of fresh thyme. Serve.

Recipe by Katie Bogle

Wine Recommendation: California Renwood Zinfandel

&‰ FRISCO ‰&

Swedish immigrant Henry A. Recen built Frisco's first log cabin in 1871. In 1875, Indian scout Henry Learned named the townsite Frisco City after the short form of San Francisco. In its early days, Frisco was known for its dance halls and saloons. Today it is the center of Summit County with easy access to several surrounding ski areas.

Zip Code: 80443 **Population:** 6,478 **Elevation:** 9,050 feet

BACKCOUNTRY BREWERY

720 Main Street
Phone: (970) 668-beer (2337)
Fax: (970) 668-3266
E-mail: ascbeerman@cs.com
Website: www.backcountrybrewery.com

Directions: Take exit 203 from I-70. Go south on Highway 9 for 1 mile to the signal for Main Street. Continue straight for 100 feet and take the first right into the parking lot. The restaurant is on the right. Enter from the southwest side of the building. Go up the stairs to the left following the paw-print path and geological survey maps.

ESSENTIALS

Cuisine: American comfort
Hours: Seven days 11 A.M.–10 P.M.
Meals and Prices: Lunch $7–$15. Dinner $10–$17 (soup and salad bar extra).
Nonsmoking: Smoking permitted only on patio and in bar downstairs
Take-out: Yes
Alcohol: Full bar
Credit Cards: MC, VI

Personal Check: Summit County only with ID

Reservations: No

Wheelchair Access: Yes, by elevator. The restaurant also has an area of refuge, a fireproof room for the handicapped in case of a fire, with a metal stairway leading down from the roof.

Other: Service charge of 17% added to parties of six or more. No split checks for parties of six or more.

HISTORY AND BIOGRAPHY

The Backcountry Brewery was built and opened in 1996. This is brewmaster and owner Anthony S. Caestia's first restaurant venture, and it is the only brewery in Frisco. General manager Molly Headley started waiting tables at the Backcountry in 1998, then moved on to manager and finally general manager. She previously worked at Ge Jo's in Frisco from 1992 to 1998. Backcountry does not have a head chef. Rather, they use a team of qualified cooks.

FOOD, SERVICE AND AMBIENCE

My rib-eye steak with Montreal seasonings was a flavorsome, melt-in-your-mouth 12-ounce piece of meat. This was an excellent steak with fat, which I usually trim, worth eating. The garlic mashed potatoes were lumpy, with skins and white-cream country gravy. They were very authentic-tasting. I also got to try the Backcountry's thin-cut, seasoned French fries. They were tasty, but I still preferred the mashed potatoes. The second side dish was sautéed vegetables: a combination of green peppers, green beans, carrots, onions and zucchini mixed with flavorful seasonings in an oil-mustard glaze. The Backcountry makes good use of seasonings.

Lunch offers grilled burgers, buffalo and chicken breast, which you can customize by choosing your own toppings. Wraps and sandwiches on focaccia bread, French bread hoagies and Kaiser rolls are also featured. Pasta specialties like roasted red pepper pesto, campfire favorites such as cowboy fried steak and South-of-the-Border entrées appear on both the lunch and dinner menus. The gem of the menu, though, in my opinion, is their list of "Backcountry legends." Take for example the New York choice cut, stuffed with roasted garlic and crumbly blue cheese, then topped with a black peppercorn demi-glace, or the slow-roasted prime rib rubbed with a blend of seasonings. Other highlights from this list include ruby-red trout finished with a honey-pecan mustard glaze, pork loin set over an amber pear glaze and chicken breast marinated overnight, blackened, grilled and topped with melted Monterey Jack cheese and fresh pico de gallo.

Be sure to save room for one of the fresh ales and lagers produced in this very location. Backcountry won a gold medal at the prestigious Great American Beer Festival in October 2000 for its Telemark I.P.A. (India Pale Ale). In addition to the four beers that Backcountry brews year around, there is also a changing selection of two or three specialty beers on tap. Your server will be happy to assist you in making your selection.

Service during my visit was friendly and courteous, although my server brought my plate with French fries instead of the baked potato that I had ordered; she then brought me a baked potato, thus allowing me to try both. (Those kinds of mistakes I can live with!)

The Backcountry Brewery has the best views of two worlds: Windows on the east side of the restaurant face Lake Dillon and the marina, while the deck on the opposite side of the building holds breathtaking views of the Tenmile–Mosquito Range to the west. Enhancing the décor are paintings of wild animals in wilderness settings by Pagosa Springs, Colorado, artist Lori Salisbury—wolves howling at the moon; harsh winter scenes with ghostly figures of bears, wolves and Indians; eagles soaring high; elk dueling; buffalo grazing; and a moose in solitude. While dining, one hears a combination of sounds from the open kitchen blended with light rock music in the background. Several of the brewery's large stainless-steel kettles are visible from the floor below to well above the second floor.

NUTRITION AND SPECIAL REQUESTS

The Backcountry Brewery offers fat-free salad dressings; a garden burger consisting of grains, mushrooms, onion and cheeses; a vegetable sandwich on focaccia bread; and a veggie wrap for vegetarian and diet-conscious patrons. They will accommodate substitutions if they have the ingredients.

Ruby-Red Trout with Honey-Pecan Mustard Glaze

The brewery serves this dish with rice pilaf and sautéed vegetables.

5 8- to 10-ounce ruby-red trout filets	Honey-Pecan Mustard Glaze (recipe follows)

1. Preheat a gas or charcoal grill. Spray fish with Pam or other aerosol oil coating.
2. Place fish on preheated grill; cook 4 minutes on each side or until done.
3. Place trout on serving dish and top with 3 ounces of Honey-Pecan Mustard Glaze (or desired amount, heated or cold) on trout. Serve.

Honey-Pecan Mustard Glaze

1 cup honey	¾ teaspoon dill
½ cup whole-grain mustard	¾ teaspoon Cajun seasoning
¼ cup chopped pecans	1 bay leaf
¼ cup lemon juice	

Mix all ingredients together in saucepan and heat until warmed. (It also tastes fine cold.) Makes about 1 pint for 5 servings of trout.

Recipe by Anthony S. Caestia

Wine Recommendation: Woodbridge Chardonnay

✒ GEORGETOWN ✒

GEORGETOWN WAS NAMED *after George Griffith, who, with his brother David, discovered gold here in 1859. Despite the discovery, silver mining became the true source of the town's wealth in the 1870s and 1880s. Georgetown, which became known as the "Silver Queen of the Rockies," and nearby Silver Plume, 2.1 miles away and 638 feet higher, became centers of Colorado's mining boom. To overcome the 6-percent grade between the two towns, Union Pacific engineer Robert Blickensderfer designed a circuitous route covering 4.47 miles but with only a 3.5-percent grade. Today, this stretch of railroad track is known as the Georgetown Loop and is open to the public. With the establishment of the gold standard in 1893, the value of silver plummeted and Georgetown dwindled. In 1966, the Georgetown/Silver Plume Mining Area was declared a National Historic Landmark District.*

Zip Code: 80444 **Population:** 1,088 **Elevation:** 8,512 feet

PANDA CITY

1510 Argentine Street
Phone: (303) 569-0288
Fax: (303) 569-3788
E-mail: None
Website: None

Directions: Take exit 228 off I-70 and go south to the stop sign. Turn left onto Argentine Street. The restaurant is 100 feet down on the right in the Empress Building.

ESSENTIALS

Cuisine: Chinese
Hours: Seven days 11 A.M.–9:30 P.M.
Meals and Prices: Lunch and Dinner $6–$14 (includes steamed or fried rice; soup extra).

Nonsmoking: Yes
Take-out: Yes
Alcohol: Beer and wine
Credit Cards: MC, VI, DS
Personal Check: In-state only
Reservations: Accepted
Wheelchair Access: Yes
Other: Catering. Hot and spicy items marked on menu.

HISTORY AND BIOGRAPHY

Panda City is in the Empress Building, which was constructed in 1980. Prior to Panda City, The Miner Bar and Restaurant, a hairdresser, a masseuse and a realty company occupied the premises. Panda City opened in November 2000 after the space had been vacant for five years.

Owner and manager Terry Duong comes from England, where he owned fish-and-chips and Chinese to-go restaurants. He has been in the restaurant business since 1983. He came to Colorado in 1999 and now owns Panda City restaurants in Gypsum, Edwards and Avon.

FOOD, SERVICE AND AMBIENCE

For lunch, I went hot and sour on the soup and sweet and sour on my combination special. The soup had the right consistency and spiciness, was dark with more pork flavor than most, and had tofu with the proper texture. The combo platter came with fried rice, a crispy egg roll stuffed with cabbage and the usual condiments of sweet-and-sour sauce and hot mustard. The entrée consisted of fried chicken, shrimp and pork with chunks of onion, pineapple, green pepper and sliced carrot. This was an ample portion for lunch, very filling, good-tasting and relatively healthy. (Note: Hot tea is not included with the meal but can be purchased for $1.00. Also, don't expect a fortune cookie with the bill—Panda City doesn't stock them.)

Panda City offers thirty-two lunch specials in all, including eight chicken dishes, five beef, three pork, five shrimp, four chow mein, two lo mein, moo goo gai pan, mixed vegetables and a combination Kung Pao. There are 123 entrées on the dinner menu, plus two family dinner combinations including soup, appetizers, fried rice and choice of main course. The house specialties feature crispy duck, walnut shrimp and Mongolian lamb. In addition to soups and appetizers, Panda City presents beef, pork, poultry, vegetable, seafood, moo shu, egg foo yung, chow mein, lo mein, pan-fried noodles and fried rice. Many come with hot and spicy selections.

The food was served quickly, and I was even offered extra rice. I was the only customer and the music was turned off when I arrived. The dining room was enhanced with large, brightly colored glossy prints of scenes from China: sailing vessels, Panda bears, fish, horses, birds of prey, swans and a peasant and cow. These huge pictures make the dining room seem spacious and bring it to life.

NUTRITION AND SPECIAL REQUESTS

Panda City will accommodate customer requests for something different if they have the item(s) in the kitchen. MSG is added to many dishes, though customers may request that it not be used on their order. A half-dozen vegetable dishes are on the menu, in addition to vegetable lo mein and vegetable pan-fried noodles.

Hot and Sour Soup

SERVES 4

¼ pound tofu, cut into thin strips
¼ pound shredded cooked pork
¼ pound bamboo shoots, cut into thin strips
¼ pound Chinese mushrooms
1 quart of water
4 teaspoons monosodium glutamate (MSG, such as Accent seasoning)

4 teaspoons soy sauce
1 teaspoon white pepper
1 teaspoon chili oil
2 teaspoons cornstarch
4 teaspoons white vinegar
2 eggs, blended

1. Put first 9 ingredients in a medium saucepan. Bring to a boil.
2. Add cornstarch, white vinegar and eggs. Stir and serve.

Recipe by Terry Duong

TASSO'S BISTRO

1025 Rose Street
Phone: (303) 569-3336
Fax: (303) 569-5413
E-mail: tassobistro@yahoo.com
Website: None

Directions: Take exit 228 from I-70. From the end of the exit go south to the stop sign and turn right onto Argentine Street. Go 0.3 mile and turn left onto 11th Street. Go over the bridge. The restaurant is on the right, on the corner of 11th Street and Rose Street.

ESSENTIALS

Cuisine: Continental with a Mediterranean flair
Hours: Sun. 10 A.M.–3 P.M., and 4 P.M.–9 P.M., Mon.–Fri. 11 A.M.–3 P.M., Mon.–Thu. 5 P.M.–10 P.M., Fri. 5 P.M.–11 P.M., Sat. 11 A.M.–11 P.M.
Meals and Prices: Brunch and lunch $7–$15. Dinner $13–$24 (soup and salad extra).
Nonsmoking: Smoking at bar only
Take-out: Yes
Alcohol: Full bar
Credit Cards: MC, VI
Personal Check: Yes, with ID
Reservations: Suggested
Wheelchair Access: Yes
Other: Available for catering, parties and events

HISTORY AND BIOGRAPHY

Tasso's Bistro occupies a corner of Georgetown that was originally filled by a small, modest, one-story house built in the 1890s. In 1966, Frank and Lil Fugita remodeled the building, adding an alpine flavor, and opened Fugita's, an American restaurant with Japanese influence. It was succeeded by a series of restaurants including the Snow Goose and Gabriel's in the 1970s and the Whipple Tree in the 1980s. The Renaissance opened its doors in the early 1990s. It was replaced by 1025 Rose in 1999 before Tasso's Bistro established itself in October 2000.

Owners Tasso and Kim Maras have been in the restaurant business since 1978 and 1980, respectively. They met at the University Club in Los Gatos, California, wherein lies Tasso's claim to fame. Doris Day was a frequent diner there, and whenever she came to the restaurant she would insist that Tasso prepare her meal. Tasso has worked at several restaurants in Colorado, including the Tivoli Deer in Kittredge, El Rancho Restaurant in El Rancho and Valente's in Wheat Ridge. Kim worked at the Sheep Herders' Lodge in Sacramento, California, and at the Quail Lodge in Carmel Valley, California. Tasso is the head chef. Kim is the president and works the front of the restaurant. Stavros, Tasso's father, is the friendly gentleman who also helps out.

FOOD, SERVICE AND AMBIENCE

I found Tasso's Bistro to be a friendly restaurant serving exquisitely prepared and presented Mediterranean meals. Linda and I tried a couple of Tasso's soups, an appetizer and two entrées. My avgolemono soup had an even balance of lemon, rice and egg with chicken broth. It was served lukewarm, but that was quickly remedied. Linda's New England clam chowder was thick with lots of clams. The crab cakes appetizer was light, delicious and flavorful: Dungeness snow crab lightly breaded with tasty scallion aioli, that strong garlic mayonnaise. It was served with crisp fried leeks on top.

Both of our entrées were very colorful and neatly presented. Chef Tasso's dishes are a delight to the eye and the taste buds. Linda's moussaka, a Greek favorite consisting of layers of eggplant, potatoes, ground lamb and beef topped with béchamel sauce and Asiago cheese, came with a bright array of zucchini, yellow squash and carrots. My rainbow trout stuffed with cream cheese, spinach and capers and wrapped in pancetta bacon was served on a plate artfully drizzled with sauce charon, a demi-glace with mushrooms and tomatoes. Both plates were sprinkled with paprika and parsley for finishing touches, and both the traditional moussaka and the more creative stuffed trout showed a superb combination of ingredients.

Brunch, served with a cup of fruit and a mimosa, offers some imaginative, out-of-the-ordinary entrées like stroganoff or ratatouille crêpes; oysters and creamed spinach–stuffed brioche; and stuffed chicken breast, roasted red pepper and Swiss cheese atop basil cream sauce. Lunch choices include salads, sandwiches and smaller versions of some of the dinner entrées plus braised lamb shank, a gyros plate and sea-food pasta. Highlighting the dinner entrées are tenderloin of beef, baked lobster, prime rib, veal medallions and rack of lamb.

Elton John songs and light rock music played softly in the background while a wood-burning stove warmed the room. Brightly colored paintings of Georgetown and Guanella Pass by Colorado Springs artist Marvya Zvonkovich and a black-and-white photo of Aphrodite's Baths in Greece decorated the rose- and cream-colored walls. Strings of white and baby-blue lights hung from the ceiling beams. A belly dancer performs on Saturday evenings beginning at 7:30 P.M. Creekside dining on the patio can be enjoyed in the warmer months.

NUTRITION AND SPECIAL REQUESTS

Tasso has some vegetarian items on the menu, like the grilled veggie sandwich. He prefers to be given advance notice of any special requests so that he can prepare ahead of time.

Moussaka

SERVES 4–6

This classic Greek dish seems very complex to make, but really it's not. Though it does take some time, it is well worth the effort.

olive oil

flour

3 eggplants, skinned, sliced
    ½-inch thick

3 large potatoes, peeled, sliced
    ¼-inch thick

1½ pounds ground beef

1½ pounds ground lamb,
    optional—if not using,
    double the ground beef

1 medium yellow onion, diced

¼ cup chopped garlic

1 cup tomato paste

2 tablespoons oregano

1 tablespoon dill weed

½ tablespoon marjoram

2 tablespoons ground cinnamon

2 tablespoons sugar

1 bay leaf

1 tablespoon each salt and white
    pepper

Béchamel Sauce (recipe follows)

2 cups grated Parmesan cheese,
    divided

1. In a large sauté pan, heat a ½-inch coating of olive oil.
2. Lightly flour eggplant and cook until golden brown on both sides. Take out and set aside.
3. In same pan, cook potatoes until golden brown on both sides and also set aside. Drain oil from pan.
4. Put ground beef (and lamb, if using) in pan; brown and drain off fat.
5. Add remaining ingredients and simmer. You will need to add a little water to thin down the tomato paste. As it simmers, it will rethicken. Don't let it get too dry. You can always add a little more water.
6. Make Béchamel Sauce and set aside.
7. To assemble: Preheat oven to 350 degrees. In a large, well-greased baking dish, add 1 layer of eggplant overlapping to cover entire bottom of pan. Lightly season with salt, pepper and Parmesan cheese.
8. Add layer of potato and lightly season with salt, pepper and cheese.
9. Add meat mixture and level out with spoon; lightly season with salt, pepper and cheese.
10. Add the prepared Béchamel Sauce and level out with spoon. Season with salt, pepper and remaining cheese.
11. Bake in preheated 350-degree oven for 45 minutes, until top is golden brown. Remove from oven and let cool for 20 minutes. Slice and serve.

Béchamel Sauce

½ gallon milk	½ pound (2 sticks) butter
1 teaspoon nutmeg	1 cup flour
1 bay leaf	3 eggs
salt and white pepper to taste	

1. In a large saucepan, add milk, nutmeg, bay leaf, salt and pepper. Bring to a simmer.
2. At the same time in a medium saucepan, melt butter. When melted, add flour and mix well with a wire whip. This is the roux.
3. When milk is hot, add roux mix (flour and butter) to it and mix

with the wire whip as it cooks, until it gets thick. Add eggs and mix well. Remove from heat.

Recipe by Tasso Maras

Wine Recommendation: Camelot Syrah

❧ GLEN HAVEN ❧

THE PRESBYTERIAN ASSEMBLY *Association purchased the land now known as Glen Haven as a summer resort. It was settled by Orren S. Knapp in 1897 and established in 1903. Glen Haven was named by Presbyterian missionary William H. Schureman for its peaceful surroundings. The community resides at the foot of Devil's Gulch, a term the missionary felt was blasphemous, a few miles outside of Estes Park.*

Zip Code: 80532 **Population:** 150* **Elevation:** 7,430 feet

THE INN OF GLEN HAVEN

7468 County Road 43 (Devil's Gulch Road)
Phone: (970) 586-3897
Fax: (970) 586-3707
E-mail: None
Website: www.innofglenhaven.com

Directions: *From I-25 north of Denver,* take exit 257 and go west on Highway 34 for 20.8 miles into the town of Drake. Turn right onto County Road 43 (Devil's Gulch Road) and go 8 miles into Glen Haven. The restaurant is on the left; parking is on the right. *From the intersection of Highways 34 and 36 in Estes Park,* where East Elk Horn Avenue turns into Big Thompson Avenue, go north on Highway 34 (Wonderview Avenue)

---

*Population estimate from Tom Sellers, owner of The Inn of Glen Haven

for 0.4 mile. Turn right onto MacGregor Avenue. Go 7.2 miles. MacGregor Avenue turns into Devil's Gulch Road. The restaurant is on the right; parking is on the left.

ESSENTIALS

Cuisine: English gourmet

Hours: Memorial Day through SEP: Wed.–Mon. 5:30 P.M.– 9 P.M. Closed Tue. OCT through NOV: Fri.–Sat. 5:30 P.M.–9 P.M. Closed Dec. 1–23 for private parties. DEC 26–JAN 5: 1 to 2 seatings each evening for the Twelve Days of Christmas. JAN 6 to mid-MAR and MAY: Fri.–Sat. 5:30 P.M.–9 P.M. Closed mid-MAR through APR.

Meals and Prices: Dinner $17–$30 (includes soup or salad)

Nonsmoking: Smoking in pub only

Take-out: In rare situations, but not as a general rule

Alcohol: Full bar

Credit Cards: MC, VI

Personal Check: Yes

Reservations: Strongly recommended

Wheelchair Access: Yes

Other: Minimum charge per person $16.75. Reserved tables only held for fifteen minutes. One check per table. Service charge of 18% added to parties of 5–7. Service charge of 20% added to parties of eight or more. Available for out-of-the-ordinary business meetings or an elegant wedding reception.

HISTORY AND BIOGRAPHY

The Inn of Glen Haven was originally the Knapps Store and Homestead Ranch. It was sold in the 1940s and passed through several owners while being rumored to be a bordello. In 1965, Bill and Doris Wells purchased the property from the Rogers Family. They were followed by Ted and Karen Hanes in 1978. In 1989, current owners and managers Tom and Sheila Sellers bought the inn. This is their first restaurant. Tom tends bar, and Sheila assists head chef James Commuso. James has been in the restaurant business since 1985 and is from Chicago, Illinois, where he graduated from the Johnson & Wales Culinary Art School. He worked at the inn for three summers part-time before becoming the inn's full-time head chef in December 2000.

FOOD, SERVICE AND AMBIENCE

The Inn of Glen Haven creates dishes with a wonderful blend of flavors and uses sauces that are the ideal accompaniment. All of their stocks are made from scratch. Both my soup and entrée were excellent examples of this. The tomato beet soup with cumin and croutons was creamy, with a dollop of butter and a mint leaf in the middle of the bowl. The cumin and mint were marvelous spice and herb enhancements to liven up the tomato and beet, a great combination in itself. The citrus-ginger sauce was the perfect complement to my tender salmon entrée. Accompaniments were wild rice augmented with fennel, sunflower seeds, walnuts and piñon seeds; and a colorful array of asparagus spears, carrots and green, red, gold and orange bell peppers. Olive bread and poppyseed rolls were also served.

For an appetizer, you can choose simmered artichoke hearts, Brie with fresh fruit, or escargot. Beef, chicken, pork, pasta and seafood are available as entrées. Steak Escoffier, a 10-ounce beef tenderloin laced with fresh herbs, is the house specialty. Also offered are a tenderloin mignon with creamy brandy and green peppercorn sauce, a chicken breast du jour, pork tenderloin, forest mushroom pasta, halibut, trout and daily specials. All of their desserts are homemade, so leave room for Kahlúa cheesecake with chocolate sauce, lemon syllabub with champagne and whipped cream, orange-chocolate mousse, or crème brûlée with caramel sauce and fresh fruit.

Each year, the inn celebrates the Twelve Days of Christmas with twelve feast days from December 26 to January 5 following the Old English Church Calendar. Old English dinners are a specialty of the inn. They include a whole roast suckling pig; special roasts of fowl, beef and lamb; headcheese; pastries; pies; and flaming plum pudding. The inn is a fine setting for an Old English Christmas gathering with family and friends.

My servers were well-dressed professionals, knowledgeable about the menu and their position. An Enya recording was playing when I arrived for dinner. At 7 P.M., a piano player took over with some sad, romantic songs including very slow, deliberate renditions of "Knights in White Satin" and "Somewhere My Love."

The historic Inn of Glen Haven has been faithfully restored to reflect its original charm and the romantic atmosphere of an intimate English country inn. As you enter through big wooden doors, you will first step into the parlor with its huge stone fireplace. To the left is the splendiferous dining room filled with antiques. The wallpaper is a pastel-colored rose pattern. The shelves over the windows and on the room dividers are set with decorator plates, teapots and cups, water pitchers, brass pots and candle holders. Decking the walls are wreaths, large mirrors in gold frames, old photographs of people and white candles in brass holders. The tables are set with white linen and napkins, oil lamps and fresh carnations. Overhead is a log beam ceiling. Further embellishments include stained glass, antique lamps, sheer white curtains and a turn-of-the-nineteenth-century Penny Farthing bicycle.

In the back right corner of the parlor are the piano and a hallway leading to a small English-style pub with a short bar, two tables, a couch and a bookshelf. Beyond the pub is a hidden wine cellar with wall murals by Estes Park artist Bill Wells, antique chairs and lamps, a pellet stove, a knight's armor, arches, artificial grapevines and black-and-white photos of Rome. You will have to find the entrance to the wine cellar yourself. However, I will tell you the secret is in one of the books on the bookshelf. Forget the Concorde. Visit the Inn of Glen Haven instead.

NUTRITION AND SPECIAL REQUESTS

The inn uses oil in place of butter for cooking most of the entrées, except the Steak Escoffier. Substitutions are difficult, says the staff, as specific sauces are intended to accompany certain meats.

Beef Wellington

4 center-cut beef tenderloins,
    8 ounces each
kosher salt
fresh cracked pepper (crack whole
    peppercorns by pulsing in
    blender or using hand chopper)

4 ounces Stilton cheese
2 sheets frozen puff pastry, thawed
    according to package
    directions
2 egg yolks and splash of water

1. Season tenderloins with salt and cracked pepper. Sear all sides in hot cast-iron skillet. Remove from heat. (An alternative method is to use one 2-pound tenderloin for the whole process and sear it to seal the juices inside, then bake it at 375 degrees until done to preference— 145 degrees internal temperature is medium-rare—and cut it into fourths.)

2. Crumble Stilton cheese and place a quarter of it atop each tenderloin.

3. Preheat oven to 375 degrees. Roll puff pastry thin, to approximately ½ of the original thickness. Cut each sheet of pastry into thirds vertically and in half horizontally. Sandwich each piece of beef and blue cheese with two pieces of puff pastry and press edges to seal. (Note: You will have four pieces left over.) Transfer to baking pan.

4. Whip eggs and water together to create an egg wash. Using pastry brush, top the pastry with egg wash. Bake tenderloins in preheated oven until golden brown on top. The beef will be medium-rare to medium.

5. Remove tenderloins from oven. Cut each in half and serve atop a simple brown demi-glace infused with green peppercorns, brandy, sour cream and heavy cream.

Recipe by James Commuso

Wine Recommendation: Australian Black Opal Petite Sirah

GLENWOOD
⁓ SPRINGS ⁓

GLENWOOD SPRINGS, HOME *of the world's largest hot springs pool, was originally called Defiance for the defiant attitude of the miners toward the Indians who controlled the hot springs. The name was changed to Glenwood Hot Springs in 1883 after Glenwood, Iowa, and the mineral springs in the area. It was later shortened to Glenwood Springs. The Ute Indians were the first people to use the mineral hot springs. Later visitors included Doc Holliday, Kit Carson, Buffalo Bill Cody, President Theodore Roosevelt and the actor Tom Mix. Doc Holliday is buried in a cemetery in Glenwood Springs.*

Zip Code: 81601 **Population:** 7,736 **Elevation:** 5,763 feet

JUICY LUCY'S STEAKHOUSE

308 7th Avenue
Phone: (970) 945-4619
Fax: (970) 928-7793
E-mail: None
Website: None

Directions: Take exit 116 from I-70. Go to the traffic signal north of I-70 and turn right onto 6th Street (Highways 6 and 24). Go to the next signal, turn right and go over the bridge. At the first signal, turn right onto 8th Street. Go 1 block and turn right onto Colorado Avenue. Go to the stop sign and turn right onto 7th Avenue. The restaurant is 1¼ blocks down on the right.

ESSENTIALS

Cuisine: Aged steak and fresh seafood
Hours: Sun.–Thu. 11 A.M.–9:30 P.M., Fri.–Sat. 11 A.M.–10 P.M.

Meals and Prices: Lunch $6–$10. Dinner $12–$28 (soup and salad extra).
Nonsmoking: All
Take-out: Yes
Alcohol: Full bar
Credit Cards: MC, VI
Personal Check: In-state only with driver's license
Reservations: Not accepted
Wheelchair Access: Yes

HISTORY AND BIOGRAPHY

Juicy Lucy's Steakhouse opened in July 1999 in a 100-year-old building. In the 1930s, Café Tessadri's occupied the premises. In the 1970s and 1980s a cowboy bar named the Lariat Club did business here, followed by the Defiance Station Bar in the early 1990s. The restaurant is owned, managed and operated by David and Cece Zumwinkle and their partner, Tom Milder. David and Cece owned and operated two restaurants in Vermont before coming to Colorado. David worked as a chef at the Redstone Inn in Redstone, Colorado, and was executive chef at the Ute City Bank in Aspen, Colorado. Cece was the dining room manager and bookkeeper at their restaurants in Vermont and repeats those duties at Lucy's. Tom has been in the restaurant business since 1971 and was sous-chef at the Ute City Bank in Aspen. He worked briefly with Wolfgang Puck at the Grand Champions Club in Aspen. David and Tom share cooking duties at Lucy's, named after David and Cece's daughter. "Juicy" was added to the name simply because it's a good adjective for a steakhouse.

FOOD, SERVICE AND AMBIENCE

Juicy Lucy's has modest-sized servings that are, with the exception of the T-bone steak, moderately priced. Linda, not a big meat-eater, went light and ordered the calamari rings appetizer and a Caesar salad. The calamari was some of the better squid that we have tasted in Colorado. They were, as the menu promised, "tender tentacles" and "righteous rings" seasoned with paprika and served with a pickle relish and paprika tartar sauce. The Caesar salad came with anchovies, "the way Caesar salad should be," according to Linda. I ordered the T-bone, a nicely charred, 1¼-inch-thick steak with lots of pink juicy meat and a fair amount of fat that added to the flavor. (Juicy Lucy's lives up to its name!) The steak came with a baked potato.

Juicy Lucy's only uses Sterling beef, the top 20 percent of choice and prime. It is steam pasteurized before delivery, then aged for 28 days by Lucy's. Other steak selections include filet mignon, porterhouse, top sirloin and New York sirloin. Pork, lamb, elk and rotisserie chicken are alternative choices for meat lovers. Fresh fish is another option, delivered four times a week by three Colorado Front Range distributors. You may see basil-crusted sea bass, halibut, red snapper, ahi, mahimahi, grouper or Rocky Mountain trout featured as the fish of the day.

Our server was very pleasant but failed to check back on our meal once the restaurant got busy. Music from the 1950s was playing during our meal. The restaurant is situated across the street from the Amtrak train station and below the pedestrian and vehicular bridges over I-70. Linda and I sat at one of the two front window tables and watched the train pull out of the station shortly after 6 P.M. The restaurant is decorated with rectangular mirrors along the right and left walls, an old photo of Aspen and a longhorn coatrack at the entrance. The back bar is trimmed with a pair of Texas longhorns and an old sign from one of the former owners, Café Tessadri's. The rear wall sports several paintings that add some local flavor: one of Glenwood Springs, one of a cowboy taking a bath and one of a cowboy making biscuits.

NUTRITION AND SPECIAL REQUESTS

Juicy Lucy's is a steak and seafood house, not a heart-healthy restaurant, but it does serve grilled vegetable kebabs and a grilled vegetarian sandwich. The staff will prepare combinations of entrées on request—for example half shrimp, half steak—then price the dish accordingly.

Seventh Street Salad with Honey-Glazed Walnuts and Honey-Poppyseed Vinaigrette

SERVES 1

2–3 cups spring mix of wild greens, washed and dried
½ cup sliced strawberries
½ cup crumbled Gorgonzola cheese

3 ounces Honey-Glazed Walnuts (recipe follows)
4 ounces Honey-Poppyseed Vinaigrette (recipe follows)

1. Place wild greens in large salad bowl.
2. Add remaining ingredients.
3. Toss and serve.

Honey-Glazed Walnuts

½ cup sugar
¼ cup water
¼ cup honey

¼ teaspoon ground coriander
1 pound walnut halves

1. Preheat oven to 350 degrees. Combine first four ingredients in a bowl. Add walnuts and toss.
2. Spray medium-sized cooking pan liberally with nonstick spray, or brush lightly with oil.
3. Spread walnut mixture on pan and bake in preheated oven for 5 minutes, or until light brown. WATCH CLOSELY! Do not allow walnuts to burn!
4. Remove walnuts from pan and place on another oiled pan to prevent the walnuts from sticking to the hot pan. Let cool for ½ to 1 hour.
5. Break apart walnut mixture like candy. Makes about 2½ cups.

Honey-Poppyseed Vinaigrette

½ cup champagne vinegar
½ cup honey
¼ cup poppyseeds

½ tablespoon chopped shallots
1½ cups olive oil

Mix all ingredients together. Makes about 24 ounces.

Recipe by David Zumwinkle

RENDEZ-VOUS RESTAURANT

817½ Grand Avenue
Phone: (970) 945-6644
Fax: (970) 945-6633
E-mail: None
Website: None

Directions: Take exit 116 from I-70. Go to the traffic signal north of I-70 and turn right onto 6th Street (Highways 6 and 24). Go to the next signal, turn right and go over the bridge. The restaurant is on the right, ½ block past the first signal.

ESSENTIALS

Cuisine: French
Hours: Mon.–Sat. 11:30 A.M.–3 P.M. and 5:30 P.M.–10 P.M. Closed Sun.
Meals and Prices: Lunch $6–$10. Dinner $9–$19 (soup and salad extra).
Nonsmoking: All
Take-out: Yes
Alcohol: Full bar
Credit Cards: MC, VI
Personal Check: Yes, with ID
Reservations: Recommended on weekends. Accepted otherwise.
Wheelchair Access: Yes, including bathrooms.
Other: Service charge of 15% may be added for parties of six or more. Available for large parties and banquets. Catering available. Live music on Fri. and Sat.

HISTORY AND BIOGRAPHY

Rendez-vous is in a building dating back to the nineteenth century. It was formerly used as a clothing store and briefly, for less than one year, as the Daffodil Deli. The building was renovated in 1998, and Rendez-vous opened in January 1999.

Owner, manager and chef John Barbier grew up in restaurants. His father operated a restaurant in the Loire Valley, south of Paris. John graduated from the Versailles Restaurant School in France and worked at the Little Nell in Aspen, Colorado, as well as at Café Bernard, Primavera and Basalt Bistro, all in Basalt.

FOOD, SERVICE AND AMBIENCE

I began my meal with an appetizer of the cassolette of calamari Mediterranean. The appetizer arrived in a small, round casserole dish, sautéed with spices and vegetables and accompanied by a red-pepper coulis consisting of tomato, basil, garlic, green and red peppers, rosemary and red wine mixed with green onions and dried tomatoes. A salad of mixed greens and fresh French bread with olive oil were served on the side. I prefer the simpler Greek-style calamari to this Italian version, whose sauce distracted from the flavor of the calamari.

The evening special written on the sidewalk chalkboard menu first attracted me to this restaurant. It was ostrich steak from the Ynez Valley in California, near Santa Barbara. Of course, I had to order it. The ostrich was a grilled, 9- to 10-ounce, densely textured steak with very little fat. It had not much beef taste, no game flavor and, I thought, a kind of sausage taste. To me, it did not rank up there with kangaroo but was much better than bone-filled iguana and worth a try. The ostrich was topped with green onions, tomatoes and a brown peppercorn sauce. The dish came with scalloped potatoes with sour cream, crispy on the edges, and green beans and carrots.

Other fine appetizers on the menu included escargot au Roquefort, a pâté du jour and roulade, rolled smoked salmon filled with cream cheese. The salads featured Niçoise, chèvre chaud (warm goat cheese), Caesar, tuna and chicken. Among the sandwiches offered are ham-and-cheese and grilled chicken breast, along with vegetable, smoked salmon and prosciutto, salami and Brie panini. Entrées include pasta with meat sauce, pasta with vegetable sauce, stuffed puff pastries, New York steak, trout almandine, sautéed rabbit and grilled duck in a light raspberry sauce.

It was hard to get anyone's attention when I first arrived at the restaurant, but once I did, the service was very pleasant and courteous. The music was French and instrumental, mostly accordion. The dining room contains three large wine barrels, two of which are decorated with artificial grapevines and function as water fountains. The third one, in the middle of the dining room, holds a statue of a waiter serving wine. Posters of edible flowers and tomatoes enhance the pastel yellow walls. More artificial grapevines are used in an overhead trellis. White lace curtains augment the front windows, and Toulouse-Lautrec posters embellish the back wall, giving the room a genuine French feel.

NUTRITION AND SPECIAL REQUESTS

Vegetarian items are offered in each section of the menu. Rendez-vous will do its best to accommodate special requests.

Breaded Veal au Citron

SERVES 4

This dish should be started the day before you plan to serve it, to allow the veal to marinate properly. Chef Barbier serves this with sweet peas and carrots.

1 lemon, juiced	4 veal cutlets, about 8 ounces
1 tablespoon honey	each
1 sprig fresh thyme	2 tablespoons butter
1 sprig fresh rosemary	1 cup fresh bread crumbs
1 teaspoon crushed garlic	1 ounce fresh parsley, chopped fine
1 cup white table wine	salt and pepper to taste
¼ to ½ teaspoon crushed red	additional lemon juice for
pepper (to taste)	finishing

1. Mix first 7 ingredients to make marinade. Pour over the veal cutlets and marinate overnight in refrigerator, or for at least 4 hours.
2. Heat butter in large frying pan. Mix bread crumbs with parsley, salt and pepper. Dip both sides of veal in seasoned bread crumbs.
3. Sauté breaded cutlets in pan until coating turns light brown. Preheat oven to 400 degrees.
4. Move browned cutlets to ovenproof pan. Place in preheated oven for 10 to 15 minutes. Don't overcook, or you will dry out the veal.

5. Remove veal from oven. Sprinkle lemon juice evenly over all four pieces. Serve.

Recipe by John Barbier

Wine Recommendations: French Fleurie Beaujolais or a Monterey Merlot

❧ GOLDEN ❧

SECOND CAPITAL OF *the Colorado Territory from 1862 to 1867 (Colorado City was the first), Golden was originally called Golden City and named after pioneer Thomas L. Golden. He, along with fellow settlers James Saunders and George W. Jackson, established a temporary camp near the mouth of Clear Creek Canyon in 1858. The building used for the Colorado Territorial Capitol is still located on the corner of Washington Avenue and 12th Street. Now it is home to the Old Capitol Grill, reviewed below. Once a railroad center associated with metal production industries, today Golden is a tourist town and the county seat of Jefferson County. It is also home to the Coors Brewery, established in 1872 by Adolph Coors Sr.; the Colorado School of Mines, founded in 1874; and the Hakushika Sake USA brewery, which opened in 1992.*

Zip Code: 80401 **Population:** 17,159 **Elevation:** 5,674 feet

HILL TOP CAFÉ

1518 Washington Avenue
Phone: (303) 279-8151
Fax: (303) 278-7744
E-mail: foodcrazy@home.com
Website: None

Directions: *From central Denver,* take 6th Avenue (Highway 6) west past I-70 and Colfax Avenue (Highway 40). Turn right at the traffic signal at 19th Street in Golden. Drive 6 blocks and turn left onto Washington

Avenue. The restaurant is 3 blocks down on the left on the corner of 16th Street and Washington Avenue. *From north Denver,* take I-70 to exit 265 and go west on Highway 58 to the Washington Avenue exit. Go south (left) on Washington Avenue for 8 blocks. The restaurant is on the right. *From Boulder,* go south on Highway 93 into Golden and turn left onto Highway 58. Exit onto Washington Avenue and go south (right) for 8 blocks. The restaurant is on the right.

ESSENTIALS

Cuisine: Contemporary bistro
Hours: Mon.–Fri. 11 A.M.–2:30 P.M., Mon.–Thu. 5 P.M.–9 P.M., Fri.–Sat. 5 P.M.–10 P.M. Closed Sun.
Meals and Prices: Lunch $7–$10. Dinner $11–$17 (soups and salads extra).
Nonsmoking: All, including outside
Take-out: Yes
Alcohol: Full bar
Credit Cards: All five
Personal Check: Yes, with driver's license and phone number
Reservations: Recommended for lunch or dinner. Recommended one week in advance for weekend dinner.
Wheelchair Access: Yes, by a walkway from the alley

HISTORY AND BIOGRAPHY

The Hill Top Café is in a building constructed in 1900. It was originally the William Boatwright house. In the 1920s and 1930s the house was occupied by an attorney general. In the 1960s it was a fraternity house for the Colorado School of Mines. By the late 1970s, the property was converted into The Hill Top House Restaurant. From 1994 to 2000, The Hampdens Restaurant occupied the premises. In July 2000, J. Allen Adams opened the Hill Top Café.

J. Allen has been in the restaurant business since 1972. Prior to coming to Colorado in 1982, he worked in restaurants in Connecticut, Vermont and New York City, cooking and learning the front of the house. His career in Colorado developed through many stages: kitchen manager at Old Chicago in Boulder; general manager at Old Chicago in

Lakewood; director of operations at the Breckenridge Brewery; and general manager, partner and eventually regional manager with Concepts Restaurants. With Concepts, he worked at the Hotel Boulderado in Boulder, the Realto Café in Denver and the Table Mountain Inn in Golden.

Head chef Ian Kleinman started cooking early in life, at the age of eight in 1984, learning from his father, a chef in Breckenridge, Colorado. Ian worked at The Village, the Gold Pan and the Breckenridge Hilton, all in Breckenridge. After moving to Denver, he was sous-chef at the Rattlesnake in Cherry Creek, the Augusta Restaurant in the Westin Hotel and at the Realto Café. He has developed over sixty soups for the Hill Top, each with a different base.

FOOD, SERVICE AND AMBIENCE

Ian's fabulous plate presentations had me wondering if he had started his career as an architect before deciding on the culinary profession. Both Linda's ginger-seared chicken and apple skewers and my top sirloin were stupendous vertical masterpieces requiring precision balancing from both the creator and the server. These are works not only of artistic design but of structural conception. Linda's tower consisted of two chicken-and-apple skewers standing at 60-degree angles from a sweet half-apple base, flat side down, topped with homemade linguini. The half-apple base made the linguini topping more rounded. The chicken was firm, and the linguini was the "al dente of all al dentes." How else can I put it? Linda and I both thought it was cooked to perfection. That, plus being homemade, meant it was just about the best we had ever eaten. But even better was the black-colored, sweet soy butter made with molasses and tossed with the linguini. We plan to start mixing molasses with soy sauce in our own cooking really soon.

The foundation of my top sirloin monolith was a red-skin potato fried in sherry and cut in half, with a layer of grilled spinach tucked in between. The chive-and-garlic–marinated top sirloin sat atop this, with a combination of butter, chives and onion crowning the edifice. A pencil-thin strand of fried capellini was speared straight upright through the entire chef d'oeuvre. The sherry-fried potato was crisp and browned on the outside, soft on the inside. The steak was very flavorful, with an excellent charbroiled taste, and was cooked to the very minimum of medium-rare. One second sooner and it would have been rare, which was perfectly fine with me. The opposite side of the plate was drizzled with about a tablespoon of roast beet emulsion and three mushrooms, leaving a lot of empty space on the plate.

Preceding our entrées, we were served yummy homemade lemon-and-blueberry bread with a dish of tantalizing and slightly spicy balsamic vinaigrette composed of extra-virgin olive oil, red pepper flakes, Parmesan cheese and basil. I ordered the green salad with a very sweet, cool and delicious citrus vinaigrette. Linda had the creamy, smooth and flavorsome roasted zucchini and oregano soup, an excellent combination.

For first flavors, you might start your meal with phyllo-wrapped almond chicken, lump crabmeat grilled wonton, or a tempura-fried squash blossom. The savory salads include grilled sirloin strips and savoy spinach, tempura chicken and apples and masa-fried calamari. The Hill Top's grilled cracker-crust pizza comes with some unusual toppings, such as capers, sunflower pesto, mango, sweet red pepper walnut paste, smoked salmon, herb cream cheese and fennel. Highlighting the delicatessen sandwiches are a house panini with vegetables, smoked cheeses and baby greens; a shrimp salad on sourdough with avocado; and smoked turkey, apple and peppered bacon on grilled focaccia. Noodle dishes like seared gnocchi and penne pasta are available for lunch or dinner. Other entrées featured on the dinner menu are hoisin-grilled pork tenderloin, grilled portobello mushroom with eggplant and asparagus, wild escolar wrapped in banana leaf and artichoke-encrusted, seared wild salmon.

Service was provided by friendly, attentive, well-spoken attendants who were very knowledgeable about the menu, wines, specials and desserts. Instrumental jazz played lightly and pleasantly in the background. The Hill Top has two dining rooms inside, a covered terrace and a courtyard with tables and umbrellas. Beyond the entrance foyer and host stand is the first dining room, enhanced by a red-rock fireplace with candles burning inside; a series of G. S. Pomm paintings of doorways and windows, titled "Doorways to Gardens"; authentic grapevines; and black-iron sconces with lit candles. The second dining room is adorned with a wine cabinet and a painting of the Napa Valley in California. The hall leading to the terrace has another vineyard picture, this one of Tuscany in Italy. The terrace, used in summer and winter, has a slanted roof with a yellow-and-white canvas cover. Behind the building is a lawn and walkway to the courtyard, an open outdoor dining area trimmed with maroon umbrellas.

I highly recommend this restaurant for lovers of fine food and exceptional service in a relaxed, comfortable environment. Anyone in the architectural, structural design, or construction fields with an appreciation for stupendous vertical food presentations should visit also.

NUTRITION AND SPECIAL REQUESTS

The staff at the Hill Top Café talk to their guests about special dietary needs and allergies and walk them though the menu to select appropriate items. The kitchen will make "off-the-cuff items" on request.

Chive-and-Garlic–Marinated Top Sirloin with Sherry-Honey–Fried Potatoes, Beet Emulsion and Hill Top Compound Butter

SERVES 6

The beet emulsion, sherry honey and compound butter in this dish should all be prepared prior to grilling the steaks.
Also, you will need a deep fryer for the potatoes. Although this recipe seems involved, the preparation actually goes quite quickly.

6 top sirloin steaks, 7 ounces each	6 new potatoes, 3 ounces each, parboiled
	6 ounces spinach, cleaned

Garlic Marinade

2 cups canola oil	½ teaspoon salt
1 ounce chives, minced	1 ounce garlic, peeled and crushed
½ teaspoon black pepper	pinch of paprika

Beet Emulsion

1 medium beet　　　　　　　　　½ cup oil
1 teaspoon balsamic vinegar

Sherry Honey

½ cup honey　　　　　　　　　　1 teaspoon minced garlic
2 tablespoons dry sherry　　　　　pinch crushed red pepper
1 teaspoon salt

Compound Butter

½ cup (1 stick) unsalted butter　　2 tablespoons roasted chopped
1 tablespoon Dijon mustard　　　　garlic
1 ounce Asiago cheese　　　　　　2 tablespoons balsamic vinegar
1 ounce minced green onions

1. Roast the spinach: Place washed and dried spinach on oiled baking sheet or pie pan. Toss to lightly coat the leaves in oil. Roast in hot oven until spinach begins to wilt, about 30 seconds.
2. Make the Garlic Marinade: Place all ingredients for garlic marinade in blender. Pulse or puree for 5 minutes, until completely emulsified and all flavors are infused. In a mixing bowl, place the cleaned steaks. Pour marinade over and place in refrigerator. Steak should marinate for at least 3 hours.
3. To make Beet Emulsion, preheat oven to 400 degrees. Roast beet in oven with a small amount of oil for 10 minutes or until tender. Remove and place in blender or food processor with balsamic vinegar and ½ cup oil. Pulse or puree until emulsified, about 5–10 minutes. Place in refrigerator until you are ready to use it.
4. Make the Sherry Honey: Mix all ingredients for the Sherry Honey in a bowl and keep at room temperature.
5. Make the Compound Butter: Soften the stick of butter in the microwave for 10 seconds, then mix all ingredients together in a bowl with a wire whisk. Place butter in refrigerator until needed.
6. Heat deep fryer to 400 degrees. Preheat grill for steaks.
7. When the grill is hot, place the sirloins on the grill. Cut both the

ends off the potatoes and then cut them in half. When the steaks have almost reached their proper internal temperature (depending on how you like them cooked), place the potatoes in the fryer and fry until golden brown. Take them out and place them in a bowl.

8. Pour Sherry Honey over the potatoes. Place one potato half on each plate. Put a small amount of the roasted spinach on top of the potato, then top with a second potato half. Position the grilled steak on top of the potato tower.

9. Place a tablespoon of the Compound Butter on steak and drizzle some of the Beet Emulsion on the plate with a spoon. Repeat with remaining potatoes and steaks. Serve.

Recipe by Ian Kleinman

Wine Recommendation: 1998 Napa Valley Marcolina Cabernet Sauvignon

OLD CAPITOL GRILL

1122 Washington Avenue
Phone: (303) 279-6390
Fax: (303) 279-7055
E-mail: None
Website: None

Directions: *From central Denver,* take 6th Avenue (Highway 6) west past I-70 and Colfax Avenue (Highway 40). Turn right at the traffic signal at 19th Street in Golden. Drive 6 blocks and turn left onto Washington Avenue. The restaurant is 7 blocks down on the left on the corner of 12th Street and Washington Avenue. *From north Denver,* take I-70 to exit 265 and go west on Highway 58 to the Washington Avenue exit. Go south (left) on Washington Avenue for 4 blocks. The restaurant is on the right. *From Boulder,* go south on Highway 93 into Golden and turn left onto Highway 58. Exit onto Washington Avenue and go south (right) for 4 blocks. The restaurant is on the right.

ESSENTIALS

Cuisine: Traditional American
Hours: Sun.–Thu. 11 A.M.–8:30 P.M., Fri.– Sat. 11 A.M.–9:30 P.M.
Meals and Prices: Lunch $6–$8. Dinner $8–$18 (state dinners include soup or salad; territorial meals do not).
Nonsmoking: Yes
Take-out: Yes
Alcohol: Full bar
Credit Cards: MC, VI, AE
Personal Check: Accepted with ID
Reservations: Accepted
Wheelchair Access: Yes
Other: Service charge of 15% for parties of six or more. There is no split plate fee.

HISTORY AND BIOGRAPHY

The Old Capitol Grill is in two historically significant Colorado structures. The main building, on the south side and known as the Mercantile Building or Loveland Building, was originally constructed of wood in 1860 by W. A. Loveland. It was rebuilt in 1863 with brick and served as Loveland's Pioneer Store, Golden's first merchandise store. The second story of the building was constructed as a meeting hall used by the territorial legislature in 1866 and 1867 when Golden was the capital of the Colorado Territory. The Colorado School of Mines held some of its first sessions here with Loveland as one of its first trustees. The Colorado Central Railway, another one of Loveland's ventures, located some of its first offices in this building.

From 1868 to 1941, the main level of the building was used as a mercantile, dry goods store and grocery. In 1884, Nicholas Koenig, whose name can be seen on the old wall safe, bought out all other partners. His commercial enterprise stayed in the Koenig family for fifty-seven years. In the early 1900s, the names of Golden's men enlisted in the armed services were painted on the side of the building. From 1941 to 1971, the building remained in use as the Golden Mercantile, making a total of 108 continuous years in the same commercial use. In 1971 the building was converted into a restaurant appropriately named The Mercantile.

The second structure, on the north side, was built by Adolph Coors in 1906. It was used as a distribution center and as a saloon owned by Charles Sitterle featuring Coors products. Both structures were remodeled by the Silverheels Restaurant in 1992–1993. The exterior and facade were restored to their circa-1920 appearance, and the interior was designed to represent our American West heritage.

In July 1997 new owner Brian Hunt opened the Old Capitol Grill. He is from Phoenix, Arizona, and has been in the restaurant business since 1978. He spent eight years helping to open TGIF restaurants throughout the country and eleven years opening Claim Jumper restaurants in California and Colorado. David Maka is the general manager. He is from Michigan and has been working in restaurants since 1986. The kitchen is run by Brian and a team of chefs.

FOOD, SERVICE AND AMBIENCE

The Old Capitol Grill provides a truly American dining experience in an historic setting. I stopped in for lunch and ordered the half rack of baby-back ribs with a broccoli wedge and Texas toast. The kitchen staff marinates the ribs in their own sauce for 10 to 12 hours before sending them to their own smoker. The meaty ribs, six of them, were cooked in Hickory Range bottled barbecue sauce to which a few spices had been added. The well-done ribs were cooked in accordance with the restaurant's menu, which states, "Thoroughly cooked foods from animal origin reduce the risk of food-borne illness." The broccoli wedge had been steamed in a plastic bag in the microwave and was crisp. The ribs came with just the sauce that was cooked on them, so I requested extra barbecue sauce on the side, which came at no extra charge. A sweet whole orange on a cabbage leaf garnished the dish.

Old Capitol Grill's lunch and dinner menu begins with appetizers such as nachos, fried onions, Buffalo wings and artichoke dip. Highlighting the soups, salads and sandwiches are clam chowder and onion soup, Far East and Caesar salads, burgers and meatloaf and barbecued beef and pastrami sandwiches. Showcasing the dinner entrées are sizzling steaks, spit-roasted chicken, a selection of Mexican fare, fish and chips and blackened chicken pasta.

My server was appropriately dressed all in black with a cowboy belt, black handlebar moustache and goatee. The restaurant has a distinctively western look. The print on the booth cushions depicts a ranch with Indian pottery and rugs, chili peppers and cowboy boots. Paintings of Mt. Cohen, the cliffs of the Upper Colorado River and Wyoming Territory in 1882 adorn the eggshell-colored walls, as do paintings by Thomas Moran showing cowboys and horses. The door-ways are arched and painted green, and the safe from the Koenig Mercantile Company is set into one wall. Patio dining on both the 12th Street and Washing-ton Avenue sides of the restaurant is available, weather permitting.

NUTRITION AND SPECIAL REQUESTS

The management says they can make any reasonable amendments to the menu items and they are flexible with substitutions. Much of the food is deep-fried, though, and nutrition is not an overriding concern.

Creamy Mushroom Pepper Sauce (a.k.a. Chicken Enchilada Sauce)

MAKES ENOUGH FOR 4 SERVINGS

Old Capitol Grill uses this sauce on both the
Ranch Chicken Burro and Trailside Chicken.

1 onion, chopped	½ tablespoon chili powder
2 teaspoons chopped garlic	½ tablespoon black pepper
1 ounce diced Ortega chilies	3 cups cream of mushroom
½ teaspoon diced jalapeños	soup (do not use condensed)
½ teaspoon ground cumin	water

1. Sauté onions, garlic, Ortega chilies and jalapeños along with all the spices.
2. Add cream of mushroom soup and water as needed for desired consistency. Stir to blend, and heat until hot. Serve.

Recipe by Brian Hunt

❧ GRANBY ❧

NAMED FOR GRANBY HILLYER, *a Denver attorney, Granby is located near the confluence of the Colorado and Fraser Rivers and is known as "the dude ranch of Colorado." Six famous guest ranches are all within a half-hour drive of Granby. Nearby Granby Reservoir is the second-largest reservoir in Colorado.*

Zip Code: 80446 **Population:** 1,525 **Elevation:** 7,939 feet

PAUL'S CREEKSIDE GRILL

62927 Highway 40, in The Inn at Silver Creek
Phone: (970) 887-2484
Fax: (970) 887-2475
E-mail: pcgs2@yahoo.com
Website: www.paulscreekside.com

Directions: From the intersection in Fraser where Highway 40 crosses Elk Creek Road (going west) and Meadowridge (going east; look for the Safeway), go north on Highway 40 for 13 miles. Turn right at the sign for Sol Vista Golf and Ski Ranch. Go ¼ mile and turn left just before the pedestrian bridge. Park in the lower parking lot (the upper one is limited to fifteen-minute parking) and walk up to the entrance of The Inn at Silver Creek. Enter and walk up the stairs to the lobby. Turn right and walk past the two stuffed bears, but "do not touch or antagonize them." Take the stairs down to the next level and turn right. The restaurant is twenty feet down on the right.

ESSENTIALS

Cuisine: California-style bistro
Hours: Memorial Day weekend to Labor Day and mid-DEC to MAR: Seven nights 5:30 P.M.–9 P.M., Sat. 7:30 A.M.–10 A.M., Sun 7:30 A.M.–1 P.M. APR, SEP, OCT and Thanksgiving to mid-DEC: Seven nights 5:30 P.M.–9 P.M. Closed MAY to Memorial Day weekend and NOV to Thanksgiving.

Meals and Prices: Breakfast buffet $6–$7. Dinner $10–$19 (soup and salad extra).
Nonsmoking: All
Take-out: Yes
Alcohol: Full bar
Credit Cards: MC, VI, AE, DS
Personal Check: Local only with ID
Reservations: Recommended for dinner
Wheelchair Access: Yes, by elevator
Other: Children's menu. One check per table. Service charge of 17% added for parties of six or more. Gift certificates available.

HISTORY AND BIOGRAPHY

The Inn at Silver Creek was built in 1982. The original restaurant in Paul's location went through a variety of images and looks before closing in 1990. This space then remained vacant until Paul's Creekside Grill opened in May 1997. The restaurant is owned by the Home Owners Association at The Inn at Silver Creek. Paul Streiter and his wife and business partner, Angela Rey, lease the restaurant's space. Paul is the general manager. A graduate of the Culinary Institute of America (CIA) in Hyde Park, New York, he worked as an apprentice chef at the Waldorf Astoria Hotel in New York City for one year and in Paris for two winters. He was also the executive chef at the Grand Lake Lodge from 1989 to 1990. He assists the chef with the menu's design, but he does not cook. That responsibility falls to executive chef Rick Person, also a CIA graduate, who has been cooking since 1992 in the Caribbean and Florida and at Paul's since 1998.

FOOD, SERVICE AND AMBIENCE

I ordered the special, roast beef open-faced on white bread with mashed potatoes and brown gravy. Chips and salsa came with the meal. The corn chips were crisp, light and flaky, just the kind I like, but the salsa was a tomato puree with garlic—not my kind of salsa. The thin, shaved slices of lean, well-done roast beef were quite good. The real horseradish, not the creamy stuff, served on the side had a pleasingly harsh taste. I like that. The mashed potatoes also had good flavor and a few lumps.

The weekend all-you-can-eat breakfast buffet offers Belgian waffles, scrambled eggs, hash browns, meats, biscuits and gravy, fresh muffins, granola, yogurt and fruit. For a dinner appetizer or light meal, you can choose from crispy tiger coconut shrimp with spicy black-bean papaya sauce, three-cheese melt onion soup, pan-seared crab cake, baby spinach salad, Cobb salad, or a 10-ounce cheddar burger. Highlighting Paul's entrées are Thai noodles with shrimp, tofu and peanuts in a light chili sauce; half rack of pork ribs coated in Szechuan barbecue sauce; grilled 10-ounce New York strip; fettuccini with grilled chicken and asparagus; beef and shrimp fajitas; salmon baked on a cedar plank with strawberry–red onion chutney; and mushroom-spinach ravioli. Key lime pie and cheesecakes are offered for dessert.

Service was fast and courteous. My food was served in about five minutes. Paul's is a children-friendly, family-oriented restaurant. Crayons, pictures for the children to color and puzzles are available for the kids. Slow, quiet rock music played in this spacious, three-story-high dining room.

Harry the ficus is the center attraction, filling the center of the dining room. He has been with Paul since the restaurant opened. Amy Buffet caricature paintings of the waiter in tux, black bow tie, white apron and towel, carrying champagne glasses, and of the chef dressed in white carrying a chicken, adorn the gold, yellow and white rough-textured walls. Parisian street café scenes and a Toulouse-Lautrec poster also enhance the setting. Potted plants and bottles of pickled red peppers and kumquats are set on the wall dividers.

Looking up, you can see chandeliers hanging from wood beams, the lobby on the story above and philodendron vines making their way through the railing. Looking out the windows and glass doors, you will see patio dining adjacent to the hot tubs and pools. An adjacent dining area called the Remington Room is used for private parties, special events and overflow. It features a rock fireplace and John Rume artworks in bright colors depicting golfers and cowboys. Whether you bring the whole family or just yourself, you will enjoy an upscale dining experience either indoors or poolside.

Paul says they are very accommodating with special requests and will do things like substitute steamed vegetables for sautéed, or use no oil. They have three lighter-fare items and two entrées on the menu for vegetarians.

Braised Lamb Shank

SERVES 4–6

Paul's Creekside Grill serves this with a mushroom risotto and squash ratatouille.

½ teaspoon fennel seed
1 teaspoon coriander seed
½ cup flour
1 tablespoon Madras curry powder
4–6 lamb shanks (about 1 pound each)
¼ cup canola or corn oil
¼ pound carrots, chopped
¼ pound celery, chopped
½ pound onion, chopped
4 Roma tomatoes, chopped

¾ cup domestic or portobello mushrooms, chopped
2 tablespoons minced garlic
1 stalk lemongrass, beaten and chopped
⅓ cup soy sauce
1½ tablespoons grated or chopped ginger root
2½ quarts water
salt and pepper to taste
basil and mint chiffonade for garnish (optional)

1. Mix fennel seed, coriander, flour and curry powder in small bowl. Roll lamb shanks in this mixture, coating roughly on all sides. Shake off excess.
2. On stovetop, heat oil in a roasting pan until pan is very hot, almost to smoking point. Sear shanks on all sides until golden brown.
3. Remove shanks from pan. Add all the chopped vegetables, garlic and lemongrass.
4. Cook veggies until lightly caramelized, about 10–12 minutes, stirring frequently. Add soy sauce and ginger.
5. Return shanks to pan. Add water until it covers the meat.
6. Cover pan and simmer on stovetop 2½ to 3 hours, until meat becomes tender.

7. Remove shanks from liquid. Strain liquid, then place in saucepan and reduce over medium heat. Add salt and pepper to taste.
8. Serve 1–2 shanks per person, topped with the reduction sauce and garnished with basil and mint chiffonade (raw or sautéed).

Recipe by Rick Person

Wine Recommendation: 1998 David Bruce Pinot Noir

⤫ GRAND LAKE ⤫

GRAND LAKE IS *situated on the north shore of the largest natural body of water in Colorado, after which the town got its name, and on the headwaters of the mighty Colorado River. It was founded as a mining settlement but is today a popular summer resort, serving as the west entrance to Rocky Mountain National Park. In the winter, Grand Lake is a mecca for snowmobile enthusiasts.*

Zip Code: 80447 **Population:** 447 **Elevation:** 8,380 feet

CAROLINE'S CUISINE

9921 Highway 34 (No. 27)
Phone: (970) 627-9404
Fax: (970) 627-9424
E-mail: caroline@rkymtnhigh.com
Website: www.sodaspringsranch.com

Directions: From I-70, take exit 232. Proceed north on Highway 40 for 46 miles to Granby. At the west end of town, turn right onto Highway 34. Go 10 miles. Just when you get to mile marker 10, turn left into Soda Springs Ranch. Then take another immediate left and go 0.1 mile up to the octagonal-shaped restaurant.

ESSENTIALS

Cuisine: Contemporary bistro
Hours: JUN–SEP: Seven days 5 P.M.–9 P.M. (9:30 P.M. on Fri.–Sat.).
OCT–MAY: Wed.–Sun. 5 P.M.–9 P.M. (9:30 P.M. on Fri.–Sat.).
Closed Mon.–Tue. Closed mid-APR to mid-MAY and end of OCT
to early NOV.
Meals and Prices: Dinner $7–$25 (soup and salad extra)
Nonsmoking: Smoking permitted only on the patio and in the bar
Take-out: Yes
Alcohol: Full bar
Credit Cards: All five
Personal Check: In-state with ID
Reservations: Suggested
Other: Children's menu. No separate checks. Service charge of 15%
added to parties of six or more. $3 per plate charge for split entrées.
Private party room available for special anniversary or birthday.

HISTORY AND BIOGRAPHY

Caroline's Cuisine is located on the Soda Springs Ranch Resort, built in
1982. The original restaurant was called the Soda Springs Ranch
Restaurant. Caroline and Jean-Claude Cavalera reopened it as Caroline's
Cuisine in October 1991. Caroline, who has been a chef since 1981, is
a graduate of Culinary Institute of America in Hyde Park. She cooked
at Callaway Gardens in Georgia from 1984 to 1986 and was sous-chef
at the Ritz–Carlton in Laguna Beach, California, from 1986 to 1989.
Jean-Claude, who has a culinary degree from France, began cooking in
1973 in Nice and went to the Savoy Restaurant in London in 1975. He
cooked at La Chaumière in Washington, D.C., from 1979 to 1983,
opened the Intercontinental in San Diego in 1983–1984, and was executive sous-chef at the Ritz–Carlton in Laguna Beach from 1984 to 1989
and executive chef at the Ritz–Carlton in Boston from 1989 until 1991.
Caroline manages the kitchen and will prepare your fabulous dinner.
Jean-Claude manages the front and will be your most gracious host.

Caroline changes the menu seasonally (in summer and winter). Jean-Claude says their regular customers like the menu changes because it's almost like coming to a new restaurant. Popular, often-requested items are returned to the menu. While you may not see the exact offerings on the menu that I discuss here, you can expect similar creative contemporary cuisine. On my first visit to Caroline's, I ordered the roasted half-chicken with sautéed mushrooms, bacon and pearl onions. On my second visit, I chose a roasted red-pepper tapa appetizer and the duck confit entrée. The tapa—three half-slices of red pepper served next to two slices of French bread with a tomato spread toasted on top, chopped tomatoes and a tapénade of crushed Niçoise olives, garlic and olive oil—was light and scrumptious. Definitely give this one a try, as it will stimulate your appetite without filling it. The duck, served with a not-too-sweet dried cherry sauce, was tender to the degree of being soft. According to Jean-Claude, it's the confit style of cooking that gives the duck this texture. The duck is rubbed with rock salt and herbs (thyme, rosemary and garlic) and allowed to sit overnight. The salt and herbs are washed off the next day. The duck is then cooked in some of its fat at 200 degrees for four hours. The result was the most mouth-watering, succulent duck I've ever eaten!

You can start your dining experience at Caroline's Cuisine with escargot, carpaccio, baked artichoke dip with crispy pita chips, smoked salmon with capers, frog legs with fried okra, or fried Brie. The soup and salad selections include gumbo, blackened chicken over Caesar salad, grilled chicken salad and Niçoise shrimp salad. All entrées are served with bread and an alouette (called Boursin in France) of cream cheese with fresh garlic, thyme and chives. This was very tasty and very filling as well. Among the other entrées you may enjoy are grilled rib-eye steak, Pacific rock shrimp over linguini with a corn cream sauce, steak Diane, grilled sea bass over a red bell pepper coulis and seared scallops served over couscous. Options for a lighter appetite feature vegetarian and meat lovers' pizzas, steak and prime rib sandwiches and hamburgers. You can complete your meal with cappuccino or espresso to complement desserts such as chocolate lava, apple tart, cheesecake, and marinated strawberries over ice cream.

Service was pleasant and very attentive on both my visits. The music was a combination of French, Italian, classical and jazz. At the entrance, you will find a small waiting area with a couch, chairs and a piano under green umbrellas with an artificial grapevine. Straight ahead is a small dining area that was decorated with still-life paintings by Efren and artworks of waiters with mustaches in tuxedos by Amy Buffet when I visited. The art changes monthly. The bar and lounge to the left of the entrance are enhanced by a gas stove in front of a rock wall, old wooden snowshoes, a stained-glass artwork of a macaw and a knight's shield, sword and ax. The main dining room in the back is trimmed with a wine rack on the wall and a sign reading "Tourists treated same as Home Folks." The private dining area upstairs can hold a party of up to twenty people. The deck off the lounge is lighted with oil lamps. Also adjacent to the lounge is a wine room displaying 150 different wines. This odd, octagonal building has picturesque views of the rolling hillside. Plan to spend a little extra time here to view the current art exhibit, chat with your host, and revel in an enchanting dining experience.

NUTRITION AND SPECIAL REQUESTS

Caroline's always has vegetarian entrées. They receive a lot of special requests for sauce on the side and are willing to accommodate when they can. All of their pasta is made from scratch.

Escargot

SERVES 1

1 cup sliced mushrooms
½ teaspoon chopped garlic
½ teaspoon chopped shallots
8–10 snails, out of shell
⅛ cup white wine

3 ounces butter, plus additional
   for sautéing mushrooms
½ teaspoon chopped herbs,
   fresh—thyme, chives, oregano,
   sage
pinch of salt

1. Sauté mushrooms in small amount of butter until tender.
2. Add garlic, shallots and escargot. Sauté until garlic is tender.

3. Add white wine and bring to a boil.
4. Add the 3 ounces of butter, shaking the pan while butter melts. It is very important to shake the pan as the butter melts in order to keep the butter emulsified.
5. Add herbs and salt to taste. Serve in casserole dish.

Recipe by Caroline Cavalera

Wine Recommendation: Clos du Bois Sauvignon Blanc

❧ GUFFEY ❧

GUFFEY, AN EARLY *gold-mining camp, was originally called Idaville and then Freshwater before it was named for J. K. Guffey, a pioneer settler.*

Zip Code: 80820 **Population:** 33* **Elevation:** 8,600 feet

PEACEFUL HENRY'S

1245 Cañon Street
Phone and Fax: (719) 689-6475
E-mail: None
Website: None

Directions: Take exit 101 from I-25 in Pueblo and go west 38 miles to Cañon City. Continue west on Highway 50 for 10 more miles, going past the entrance to the Royal Gorge. Turn right onto Highway 9 and go 21 miles to a fork in the road. Take the right fork onto County Road 121. The restaurant is 1.2 miles up on the left.

---

*Population figure from Bruce Buffington, owner of Peaceful Henry's, who says he can name all the residents.

ESSENTIALS

Cuisine: Fine dining in casual rustic atmosphere
Hours: Fri.–Sat. 5 P.M.–9 P.M., Sat. 8 A.M.–11 A.M., Sun. 9 A.M.–1 P.M.
Meals and Prices: Breakfast $5–$8. Dinner $11–$17 (includes salad).
Nonsmoking: Yes
Take-out: Yes
Alcohol: Full bar
Credit Cards: MC, VI, AE
Personal Check: In-state only with ID
Reservations: Strongly recommended
Wheelchair Access: Yes, by ramp
Other: Children's menu

HISTORY AND BIOGRAPHY

Peaceful Henry's is in a pinewood log structure built in 1992 for Delphinium's Café. When Delphinium's closed in 1997, the building stood vacant until Bruce and DeeAnn Buffington opened Peaceful Henry's in January 2001.

The restaurant is named for former Guffey resident Henry Reed. Henry came to Guffey during World War II and lived with his cat in a one-room log cabin heated by an old propane stove. He would spend his days sitting in a chair in front of his cabin, whittling wood and going to the General Store for a strawberry ice-cream cone. One cold evening in late May 1993, his propane stove failed, the flame went out, and Henry and his cat died of gas poisoning.

Bruce has been in the food and beverage business since 1977. He was the beverage manager for the Imperial Hotel in Cripple Creek, Colorado, from 1992 to 1995. In 1993, Bruce opened the General Store and Liquor Store in Guffey, and in 1998 he added a saloon. His dog Shanda, a golden retriever, has been the mayor of Guffey since 1993. Dee started in the restaurant business in 1996 at the Double Eagle Casino in Cripple Creek and worked there until 1998. Bruce and Dee also manage the restaurant. Their partner, Richard Mandel, took all of the photos in the restaurant. Chef and Guffey native Isaac Schechter has been in the restaurant business since 1995, previously with Delphinium's and with Peaceful Henry's since it opened. Breakfast cook

Jeff McClain has been cooking for twenty years, was a head cook in the Army, and has also been with Henry's from the beginning.

FOOD, SERVICE AND AMBIENCE

I arrived at Peaceful Henry's hungry. I began by ordering the oysters on the half shell. They were from Galveston, Texas, and were eight of the most mouth-watering oysters that I ever ate. They slid right down the ol' palate with practically no grit. (I think I detected one small piece.) Accompanying the oysters were the usual lemon and a homemade cocktail sauce with shallots.

I followed the oysters with a bowl of New England clam chowder, Friday's soup du jour. It was topped with shallots, creamy but not very thick, with potato, bacon and clam pieces that were chewy yet tender. In place of regular bread, two Italian bread twists were served with a flavorful, thick marinara sauce with just the right spices.

My entrée was the crab cakes Baltimore. They were two pancakes filled with lump crabmeat, similar in appearance to potato pancakes, crunchy on the outside and very tender on the inside. They came with more homemade cocktail sauce. Simply scrumptious! The mashed potatoes were lumpy with garlic and red skins and had a scoop of brown gravy with chopped shallots in the middle. They were just like Mom used to serve, except for the shallots. Lumpy food is good. The vegetables were green beans, broccoli and—one I had never tasted—baby yellow carrots from the Caribbean. I at first thought these were squash. Parmesan cheese was melted on top of the vegetables.

Other fine appetizers to choose from include a classic shrimp cocktail, a vegetarian mushroom mélange pizza, a quesadilla with veggies and bacon, Thai chicken spring rolls and French onion soup. The entrées included pasta Prince William with linguini and vegetables in a rich Alfredo sauce, tournedos with peppercorn sauce, pork tenderloin medallions, both a steak and chicken daily special and a fresh catch of the day. The portions are large and filling, but try to leave room for a delectable dessert like tiramisu, seven-layer cake or caramel-apple cheesecake.

Henry's offers three-egg omelets, buttermilk pancakes, eggs Benedict, sausage and biscuits and French toast for breakfast.

Service was attentive and amiable. I had a nice chat with Bruce, who was working the bar. Live entertainment began at 7 P.M. with a guitar-playing singer. This is a sizable log cabin with a very high, arched ceiling and two log vegas running the length of the main dining room. To the back of the dining room are the bar and kitchen, a fishnet and small white lights. The walls are trimmed with Richard Mandel's color photos taken in Arches National Park and Monument Valley in Utah and in western Colorado. There is also a fine collection of black-and-white scenes of winter wildernesses and sparkling springs. Tall glass doors lead from the dining room to a wooden deck with tables under umbrellas for cool, relaxing summer evening dining. Friendly people, exceptional food, live music and an entertaining atmosphere all add up to a good time at Peaceful Henry's. Henry Reed would be proud!

NUTRITION AND SPECIAL REQUESTS

Peaceful Henry's serves a vegetarian appetizer and a vegetarian pasta dish for dinner. They accommodate some substitutions.

Pork Tenderloin Medallions in Sherry, Soy and Sweet and Sour Sauce

SERVES 8

Peaceful Henry's serves this over cooked linguini or rice.

6 pounds pork tenderloins, trimmed	1 cup sweet and sour sauce (store-bought, or make your own)
4 cups sherry, your choice	cornstarch
½ cup soy sauce	

1. Slice pork ¾-inch thick.
2. Combine sherry, soy sauce and sweet and sour sauce and use half of the resulting sauce to marinate pork for at least 6 hours.
3. Sauté pork until cooked through. Add remaining sauce. If necessary, thicken sauce with a little cornstarch. Serve.

Recipe by Bruce Buffington

Wine Recommendation: Australia Rosemount Chardonnay

✺ GUNNISON ✺

GUNNISON WAS NAMED *after Captain John W. Gunnison, who led a surveying team through the area in search of a railroad route to the west. He and most of his company were killed by Ute Indians in Utah in the fall of 1853. Today, the Pioneer Museum on Highway 50 displays many of the artifacts and buildings representing Gunnison's ranching heritage, as well as a narrow-gauge railroad engine, boxcar and caboose.*

Zip Code: 81230 **Population:** 5,409 **Elevation:** 7,703 feet

KATIE'S COOKERY

112 South Main Street
Phone: (970) 641-1958
Fax: None
E-mail: cookery@snowcap.net
Website: None

Directions: Entering Gunnison on Highway 50 from either the west or east, turn south onto Highway 135 (Main Street) in the center of town. The restaurant is about 100 feet from Highway 50 on the left.

ESSENTIALS

Cuisine: Down-home cooking
Hours: Mon.–Thu. 10:30 A.M.–10 P.M., Fri.–Sat. 10:30 A.M.–12 midnight. Sun. 5 P.M.–9 P.M. Closed first Sun. of each month unless there is a holiday. Then, closed second Sun.
Meals and Prices: Lunch $3–$8. Dinner $7–$10 (includes soup or salad and two sides).
Nonsmoking: Smoking permitted only on patio
Take-out: Yes
Alcohol: Full bar

Credit Cards: MC, VI

Personal Check: Local only

Reservations: Accepted

Wheelchair Access: Yes

Other: Shared plate charge $.50. Service charge of 15% added for parties of six or more.

HISTORY AND BIOGRAPHY

Katie's Cookery is in a Mediterranean villa-style house built in 1938. The home had two owners until the 1970s, when the Gunnison County Department of Public Health moved in and operated for twenty years. In the 1990s, the former house was converted into office space, and a travel agency occupied the premises. In 1997, Susie Pike leased the property and opened a used children's clothing store. A year later she changed the business into The Tea House Restaurant, which lasted until November 2000. In May 2001, Katie Hynes, Amanda Vincent and Daryl Braga opened Katie's Cookery.

As girls, Katie and her sister Emily would play "restaurant" and dreamed of having a real restaurant of their own one day. In June 1999, as a college project for her business class, Katie opened a sandwich and ice-cream shop in a 1947-era, 14- by 7-foot trailer. Emily was her helper. In March 2000, Emily and her fiancée, Stuart Willard, lost their lives in a tragic car accident. The fountain and garden in front of the restaurant are a memorial to Emily and Stuart. Katie attributes the early success of the restaurant to her sister's spirit.

Katie began working in restaurants in Seattle, Washington, before going to work at The Tea House and running Katie's Cookery in the trailer, which operated during the summers of 1999 and 2000. She handles the kitchen. Amanda managed a coffee shop in Seattle and helped Katie in her trailer in 2000. She controls the front of the house and schedules employees. Daryl has worked in restaurants in California and Connecticut. He operates the bar and takes care of payroll and finances.

FOOD, SERVICE AND AMBIENCE

Katie's Cookery is new, spirited, friendly, lively and a great place for both vegetarians and carnivores, people and dogs. They specialize in homemade soups, pies, cookies, sauces and dressings. They are also honest! I stopped here for lunch and ordered a cup of soup and a sandwich. My server brought me a bowl. Katie, whom I had not yet met, happened to walk by, and I pointed out that I had received a bowl of soup when I only ordered a cup. She informed me that the bowl actually held eight ounces and was therefore one cup in measurement. "A cup is a cup," as she told me, at Katie's Cookery. I must have visited over 900 restaurants in the past ten years where this was not the case!

The soup that day was Katie's beer-cheese: big slices of carrot, potato and onion in a chicken base with cheddar, Swiss and dill. It was hearty, warm and good. My sandwich accompaniment was the Grecian grill, a lightly toasted fresh French roll with Swiss cheese, red pepper, artichoke hearts, red onion, black olives and cucumber with a side of garlic-feta vinaigrette. This vegetarian delight could be supplemented with turkey or ham, but I kept it vegetarian. The vinaigrette contained two of my favorite ingredients, but I found the sandwich held up just fine on its own if it was dry.

Katie's Cookery features a different homemade soup each day of the week. On Monday, it is rosemary mushroom; on Friday, country corn chowder; and on Sunday, beef stew. No less than nine salads are listed on the menu, including green pea with water chestnuts and sunflower seeds in a tangy sour-cream dressing, sesame teriyaki with grilled chicken or tofu and fajita salad served with a warm tortilla, sour cream and salsa. All of the dressings are homemade and a fresh biscuit and honey butter are served with any soup or salad.

Highlighting the specialty sandwiches, all served with a pickle and bag of chips, are bratwurst, Polish sausage, hot dogs, veggie dogs, the Cookery cucumber, hot meatball, a monster club and the Californian with ham, avocado and Swiss. You can create your own half-pound, charbroiled burger by adding toppings from the list of two dozen additional fixin's such as sauerkraut, red peppers, artichoke hearts and avocado. They also offer a veggie burger and other specialty burgers.

Your choices for a dinner appetizer are baked artichoke dip, spinach dip, herb-stuffed mushrooms and nachos. Headlining the main courses are boneless barbecued pork ribs with homemade barbecue or jerk-style sauce, grilled sweet-and-sour chicken breast, homemade meatballs with sweet-and-sour or marinara sauce and stir-fried vegetables. You get to select two of the following sides with your entrée: tortellini, Katie's mashed potatoes, fruit salad, roasted vegetables, small green-pea salad and the cook's daily choice. If you brought your favorite canine, you can treat him or her to homemade dog biscuits with peanut butter, barbecue, chicken or beef flavorings. For dessert, try one of Katie's delicious homemade pies, like pumpkin, peach, apple or berry; homemade peach or berry cobblers; or homemade Dutch-apple crisp. They also serve (non-homemade) New York and brownie cheesecakes and Midnight Madness ice cream (white chocolate ice cream with fudge, caramel swirls and chunks of chocolate brownie).

Service during my visit was provided by a team of college and post-college young people with a lot of energy and love for what they are doing. They played a combination of lively jazz with percussion and vocals mixed with moderate to hard rock music, but only quietly in the background. The four rooms of the restaurant are painted in solid bright colors. Blue is used at the entrance, where you can get dog treats, ice cream, T-shirts, biscuits and cookies at a small counter. The bar, undersized and with no seating, is in this room. The front dining room, where I sat, is painted bright yellow with bay windows and a brown brick fireplace and mirror overhead matching the fireplace in size. White sconces and photographs of Emily and her fiancée, Stuart Willard, hang on the walls. The middle dining room is painted red, and the back room is green. They both display changing artworks by local artists as well as by some of the restaurant staff. Seating is on wooden chairs with turquoise cushion seats at wood tables.

The building has a tile roof made of abalone, Spanish arches in front of a porch, tables under umbrellas on the driveway in front of the garage and a courtyard in the rear. A wall mural on the side of the courtyard depicts a window, a flowerpot, flowers and a grapevine. On select Friday and Saturday evenings, live music is played in the corner of the courtyard. Some of the kitchen's fresh herbs come from a small garden in the back.

NUTRITION AND SPECIAL REQUESTS

When asked, Katie told me that nutrition and special requests are "my main thing." Not only is she willing to accommodate special requests, she actually encourages it. The following proclamations on the menu verify Katie's statement: "If you have any food allergies or special requests, just let us know"; "Get creative and we'll make your concoction come to life"; and "If we have it we'll serve it." The staff receives many special requests and can "pretty much handle them all." No milk or cream is used in their cream sauces. Instead, the sauces are thickened with flour and butter. The marinara, salsa, teriyaki, peanut sauce, spinach dip and artichoke dip are all homemade. Katie's Cookery received the People's Choice Award for Best Vegetarian Restaurant in Gunnison County in 2001, their first year of operation.

Thai Peanut Sauce

MAKES 1 CUP

2 ounces soy sauce

2 ounces peanut butter

2 ounces red wine vinegar

2 ounces sesame oil

¼ teaspoon cayenne pepper
    (use more for spicier sauce)

1 clove garlic, crushed

¼ teaspoon red pepper, crushed
    (use more for spicier sauce)

½ teaspoon Thai seasoning

Blend all ingredients in a food processor. Use on stir-fried vegetables, meat, pork, beef, chicken, or shrimp. Serve with rice or noodles.

Recipe by Katie Hynes

❧ HAXTUN ❧

THE EASTERN PLAINS *hamlet of Haxtun was established when the Burlington Railroad built a line in 1888. The town is named after a railroad contractor.*

Zip Code: 80731 **Population:** 982 **Elevation:** 4,039 feet

HAXTUN INN RESTAURANT ———————————

101 South Colorado
Phone: (970) 774-4900
Fax: (970) 774-4902
E-mail: carole@kci.com
Website: None

Directions: Take exit 125 from I-76 at Sterling. Go east on Highway 6 for 30.2 miles into the town of Haxtun. As you approach Haxtun, you will see a tall white water tower with "Haxtun" on it. The restaurant is across the street from this landmark. Turn left at the "business district" sign; this is actually South Colorado. Go 0.3 mile. The restaurant is on the left, on the corner of Colorado and Strohm Street.

ESSENTIALS

Cuisine: Steak, seafood and burgers

Hours: Wed.–Sat. 11 A.M.–1:30 P.M.,Wed.–Thu. 5 P.M.–8:30 P.M., Fri.– Sat. 5 P.M.–9 P.M., Sun. 10 A.M..–2 P.M., 5 P.M.–8 P.M. Closed Mon.–Tue.

Meals and Prices: Sun. brunch buffet $10 (seniors and children discount). Lunch $5–$10. Dinner $10–$27 (includes starch, vegetable and soup or salad).

Nonsmoking: Yes

Take-out: Yes

Alcohol: Full bar

Credit Cards: All five

Personal Check: In-state only with ID

Reservations: Accepted for parties over six

Wheelchair Access: Yes, through a side entrance ramp

Other: Banquet room available for private parties, business meetings, rehearsal dinners, wedding receptions and class reunions. Three suites for accommodations. Gift certificates.

HISTORY AND BIOGRAPHY

The Haxtun Inn was originally called the Shirley Hotel and Restaurant when it was built in 1919. A butcher shop and ice house stood where the lounge is today. The hotel upstairs was abandoned from 1945 until

1995, when the rooms were given extensive remodeling. In March 2000, current owners and managers Fred and Carole Borra opened the three-room inn and restaurant. Fred has been in the restaurant business since 1963. He owned the Village Coffee Shop in Boulder, Colorado; a 24-hour coffee shop in Ohio; and Springers Restaurant in Longmont, Colorado. He also opened the Brokers Restaurants in Denver and Boulder and, with Carole, two restaurants on St. Thomas in the Virgin Islands. Fred did the remodeling of the restaurant and is the head chef. Carole works the front of the restaurant and handles the books, just as she did at Springers. Their daughter, Brenda Farnsworth, is a server, and their son-in-law, Wil, is a cook at the restaurant.

FOOD, SERVICE AND AMBIENCE

The Haxtun Inn is one of the very few historical, elegant, fine dining establishments in eastern Colorado. Linda and I made the drive east for dinner. I selected one of the Haxtun Inn's more popular items, the London broil, with twice-baked potato and New England clam chowder. The chowder had very tender pieces of clam, bacon bits (which gave it a salty taste) and potato. The London broil consisted of 6 ounces of beef medallions, pink on the inside and charred on the outside, with good texture and taste. The twice-baked potato was topped with Monterey Jack and cheddar cheeses and came with the skin and lumps, as it should. The vegetable of the day was sautéed asparagus spears with a dollop of melted cheddar cheese on top and button mushrooms. Linda ordered the roasted half-chicken, a sizeable portion of very moist, seasoned meat. She went to the salad bar, a small cart with about twenty items and four dressings. Her meal came with a large baked potato and the vegetable du jour.

If you like Rocky Mountain oysters, you can get them as an appetizer, an entrée or in a sandwich at the Haxtun Inn. Other appetizers include buffalo wings, onion rings and shrimp cocktail. Several types of steaks are offered: chops, chicken-fried, teriyaki flank, sirloin, New York, rib-eye, filet mignon, porterhouse, buffalo and steak Oscar (two filets topped with fresh asparagus, king crab meat and hollandaise). The lengthy menu also provides shrimp dishes, fish, beef or buffalo burgers, salads, fajitas, seafood pasta, smothered burritos, smoked pork chops, chicken fettuccine and chicken cordon bleu. Smaller appetites may be satisfied by one of the sandwiches—chicken breast, San Francisco turkey, Reuben, fish, French dip, steak and cheese, or chicken Philly.

Highlights of the all-you-can-eat Sunday brunch are the soup and salad bar; breakfast station, including omelets freshly prepared by Fred while you watch; a waffle station with many hot toppings; a meat-carving station hosting slow-roasted baron of beef and a second roast of the day (turkey, pork, or ham) carved by Wil; a lunch station with a variety of entrées, potatoes, gravies and hot fresh vegetables; and a dessert station.

The front desk of the hotel is used to check in both room and dinner guests. After a couple ahead of us checked into a room, we were seated in the lounge—this because the regular dining room had been reserved that evening for a private birthday party. The lounge is pleasantly decorated with Victorian furnishings and western artwork. Paintings of cowboys and horses on the plateau and the skull and horns of a sheep complement the white-textured walls splashed with flesh-colored paint and the white-lace curtains with red frill borders. Stained glass separates the lounge from the bar in the back. Romantic orchestra music played throughout the lounge. The elegant dining room also has white-lace curtains and is sparsely trimmed with decorator plates, a wreath, ceramic vases and books. Carole was our cheerful, friendly, efficient and informative server.

NUTRITION AND SPECIAL REQUESTS

Although Carole informed me that they have only had one identified vegetarian in the restaurant in a year and a half, they will gladly accommodate special requests if at all possible. Vegetarians can order a stir-fry dish or a meatless burrito in addition to enjoying the salad bar and many items at Sunday brunch.

Watergate Salad

MAKES 4–6 ONE-CUP SERVINGS

2 3.4-ounce packages Jell-O instant pistachio pudding (dry)	1 11-ounce can mandarin oranges
	1 cup mini-marshmallows
1 8-ounce can crushed pineapple (do not drain)	dash of nutmeg (if desired)
	1 8-ounce tub Cool Whip

1. Pour the dry packages of pistachio pudding into a mixing bowl. Add crushed pineapple, mandarin oranges, and juice. Mix all together until creamy.
2. Add the mini-marshmallows and blend. Add the dash of nutmeg (optional).
3. Fold the tub of Cool Whip into the mixed ingredients. Refrigerate for several hours before serving.

Recipe by Fred Borra

❧ HESPERUS ☙

HESPERUS, LATIN FOR *the evening star that shines in the West, was settled in 1882 by John A. Porter when the Hesperus Coal Mine opened. Located a few miles west of Durango, it was named by the Rio Grande Southern Railroad for Hesperus Mountain northwest of town.*

Zip Code: 81326 **Population:** 75* **Elevation:** 8,200 feet

KENNEBEC CAFÉ & BAKERY

4 County Road 124
Phone: (970) 247-5674
Fax: (970) 385-5897
E-mail: kennebeccafe@aol.com
Website: None

Directions: From the intersection of Highways 160 and 550 in Durango, where Highway 160 separates from Highway 550 heading west, go west on Highway 160 for 11.2 miles. The restaurant is on the right, on the corner of County Road 124.

*Population figure from the U.S. Post Office in Hesperus.

ESSENTIALS

Cuisine: Mediterranean with Spanish flair
Hours: Tue.–Sun. 6:30 A.M.–3 P.M. and 5 P.M.–9:30 P.M. Closed Mon.
Meals and Prices: Breakfast $4–$7. Lunch $6–$9. Dinner $13–$22 (includes salad).
Nonsmoking: All
Take-out: Yes
Alcohol: Full bar
Credit Cards: MC, VI
Personal Check: Local only
Reservations: Recommended for dinner or parties of ten or more for breakfast or lunch during the week; not accepted for weekend breakfast or lunch.
Wheelchair Access: Yes, including restrooms
Other: Catering available for wedding or rehearsal dinners, family reunions, holiday events or business gatherings

HISTORY AND BIOGRAPHY

The restaurant is named after nearby Kennebec Pass and a local mining family in the 1800s. The former occupants of this site were Chip's Place and the Canyon Motel, both built in the 1940s by Don Demerest. Actors Shirley Maclaine, David Niven, and the rest of the cast stayed at the Canyon Motel while shooting the Indian scene in the movie *Around the World in 80 Days.* Kennebec Café co-owners Barbara Helmer and Miguel Carrillo demolished the old restaurant and built a new, very attractive, clean-looking restaurant in its place. It opened in March 2000.

Barbara is a pastry chef by trade. She has owned her own catering business, Anything Goes Cuisine Catering, since 1982. She started The Upper Crust Bakery in Durango in 1982, then sold the business to Carver's in 1985. She worked as a pastry chef at Durango's Palace Restaurant from 1985 to 1991 and as a baker at the town's Season's Restaurant between 1995 and 1996. Miguel started in the restaurant business in 1987 at Café Zinc and Kachina's in Laguna Beach, California, and Bistro 201 in Newport Beach, California. He came to Durango in 1991 and cooked at Francisco's for five years while working in Barbara's catering business. Adrian Helmer, Barbara's daughter, grew up working with her mother in restaurants and catering. She has been at Kennebec since it opened, helping with the restaurant's operations.

FOOD, SERVICE AND AMBIENCE

Kennebec Café serves a Mediterranean-Mexican mix. I dodged both (not intentionally) and requested the grilled rib-eye for lunch. The steak was medium-rare, as ordered, thin, but still a sizeable 8–10 ounces, with some fat and an exceptional charbroiled taste. It was served open-face on sourdough bread. Six large cornmeal-battered onion rings were set on top of the steak. They provided a hearty crunch when bitten into and held together well. The chipotle mayonnaise on the side was mild, not hot, and an excellent flavor-enhancer for the steak. The house pasta salad for that day was orzo with chopped red onion, red pepper, parsley and cucumber. Served cold with tomato and pickle slices and a lettuce leaf, it was a wonderful substitute for rice.

The breakfast menu offers some common items like a breakfast burrito, oatmeal, eggs any style and corned beef hash, as well as some special dishes such as potato pancakes with homemade applesauce, homemade granola, apple-nut pancakes and brioche French toast in a rich custard batter. The omelets are made with some anomalous ingredients: Havarti cheese, artichoke, feta cheese, crab and spinach.

A Caesar salad with homemade dressing, grilled tomatillo chicken with a pumpkin-seed dressing and grilled salmon with a lemon-caper dressing are three salads available for lunch or dinner. If you crave a sandwich, try the torta Mexicana, a medley of Mexican foods in a *bolillo,* or a hard roll. The burgers are grilled to order and feature certified Angus beef; there's also a homemade veggie burger and a turkey burger. The artichoke is served baked and stuffed for lunch and crisp-fried for dinner. The Mediterranean mix consisting of chicken souvlaki, dolmades, hummus, tabbouleh and pita bread is also a dual meal delight. Highlights of the dinner entrées are seared sea scallops in a lemon vinaigrette, grilled prime rib steak with red wine sauce, grilled lamb chops in a Dijon marinade and pan-roasted Gulf shrimp. For a sweet ending to your dining experience you have the option of tiramisu, lemon mousse cake topped with shaved white chocolate, sour-cream apple pie with fresh homemade whipped cream, or chocolate cake with mascarpone cheese, chocolate ganache and raspberry coulis.

Service was attentive and courteous. Kennebec really does have a spic-and-span look and feel. There are many appealing facets to the architecture and quality characteristics about the décor. A big bouquet of flowers graced the front counter and fresh roses were at each table. The tables in the front dining room are made of polished granite in assorted shades of black, white and orange. They are set on a travertine floor. The more refined back dining room has Formica and mahogany tables with mahogany-stained chairs. Vertical windows alternate with the walls facing north and west, providing pleasing views of the trees and surrounding hills. Grab a table with a window view and you can see Parrot Peak and Kennebec Pass. An alcove in the far right corner of the restaurant holds a single table for eight. Overhead is a circular soffit ceiling with corbel arches. Alabaster sconces and dried flowers are set in the niches. Archways at the entrance lead to a limestone patio with cream umbrellas protecting black metal tables. The Kennebec Café & Bakery offers unexpectedly pleasant dining. Do not pass it by when you are in the southwestern part of the state.

NUTRITION AND SPECIAL REQUESTS

Kennebec Café & Bakery uses olive oil and clarified butter in its cooking. All breads and pastries are made in-house. They try their best to accommodate special requests depending on the volume of business.

Huevos Kennebec

SERVES 1 OR MORE

corn tortillas
oil to coat a pan
cooked black beans
eggs

Green Chile–Tomatillo Sauce
(recipe follows)
queso fresco (Mexican cheese)
Pico de Gallo (recipe follows)

Green Chile–Tomatillo Sauce

1¼ pounds tomatillos, husked
½ bunch of green onions,
    coarsely chopped
2 ounces jalapeños, stems
    removed, chopped
2 cloves garlic
1½ teaspoons fresh oregano,
    stems removed

1½ teaspoons fresh thyme
½ gallon water
2 teaspoons white pepper
2 teaspoons ground cumin
salt to taste
butter
flour

1. Combine first 7 ingredients in a large pot and bring to a boil. Reduce heat to a simmer and cook 20 minutes.
2. Remove from heat and puree in small batches in blender or food processor. Return to the pot and add the white pepper, cumin and salt. Return to stovetop and heat to slow boil.
3. Meanwhile, make a roux by slowly cooking together equal parts of butter and flour in a saucepan, until a golden color is obtained. Whisk ¼ cup roux into hot sauce. Makes about 2 quarts. Refrigerates and freezes well.

Pico de Gallo

3 tomatoes, diced
1 white onion, diced
½ bunch cilantro, chopped
3 jalapeños, seeds and ribs
    removed, minced

juice from 2 fresh limes
1 tablespoon dried oregano
2 teaspoons black pepper
salt to taste

Combine all ingredients in bowl. Makes 4 cups.

To assemble Huevos Kennebec

1. Heat corn tortillas in hot oil for 30 seconds. Use 2 6-inch tortillas per serving. Blot dry on paper towels.
2. Top with your favorite warmed black beans.
3. Top with 2 eggs, cooked any style, hot Tomatillo Sauce, queso fresco and fresh Pico de Gallo. Serve.

Recipe by Barbara Helmer

❧ IRWIN ❧

THE TOWN OF *Irwin, located a few miles west of Crested Butte, was named after Dick Irwin, an early prospector. Irwin was once home to more than 5,000 residents during the mining boom of the 1880s and was visited by President Grant.*

Zip Code: 81224 **Population:** 25* **Elevation:** 10,700 feet

IRWIN LODGE RESTAURANT

111 Clara Load
Phone: (970) 349-9800
Fax: (970) 349-9801
E-mail: irwin@crested butte.com
Website: www.goirwin.com

Directions: From the intersection of Highways 50 and 135 in Gunnison, go north on Highway 135 for 28 miles to the town of Crested Butte. Go 1 block past the first stop sign and turn left onto Whiterock Avenue. Continue on this road through town, at which point it becomes Kebler Pass Road and eventually turns to a gravel surface. Drive 6.4 miles on this road, until you come to a small sign for Irwin Lake Campground. You will need to veer right (going left will take you over Kebler Pass) and go 3.3 miles to the rectangular-shaped, pinewood log arch and the sign overhead for "Irwin Lodge." Pass under the arch and go 1.2 miles to the back of the lodge. Walk around the building to the entrance to the lodge and restaurant and breathtaking views.

NOTE: During winter the lodge and restaurant are only accessible by prearranged snowmobile or snowcat taxi. Call the restaurant in advance.

ESSENTIALS

Cuisine: Fine American

---

*Population estimate from Irwin Lodge owner Molly Eldridge.

Hours: Mid-NOV to mid-APR: Seven days 7 A.M.–10 A.M., 11 A.M.–4 P.M. and 5 P.M.–9 P.M. Early JUN to mid-OCT: Sun.–Fri. 7 A.M.–10 A.M., 11 A.M.–4 P.M. and 5 P.M.–9 P.M. Closed Sat. for weddings and banquets. Closed mid-OCT to mid-NOV and mid-APR to early JUN.

Meals and Prices: Breakfast $4–$7. Lunch $8–$10. Dinner $16–$30 (includes soup or salad).

Nonsmoking: Smoking permitted only on the porch

Take-out: No (not many requests)

Alcohol: Full bar

Credit Cards: MC, VI, AE, DS

Personal Check: Yes, with ID

Reservations: Recommended for dinner, not necessary for breakfast or lunch

Wheelchair Access: No

Other: Children's menu. Available for business meetings, corporate retreats, conferences, special events, and weddings. No phones.

HISTORY AND BIOGRAPHY

In 1974, a Texas oilman named Dan Thurman built the Irwin Lodge as a private hunting facility for the benefit of his employees. It is situated on 2,200 acres of land known as the Clara Load. In the mid-1980s, Thurman sold the lodge and surrounding property to a group of Chicago families that gradually dwindled to one family. The last remaining family went bankrupt and was bought out by one of the fathers. He sold everything to another couple who owned the property for a few years—and ran the lodge—before selling in 1997 to the Irwin Ten, a group of shareholders from Colorado and California. Two of the ten are on-site operating owners. They are Don Trischett, who works as night manager, and Molly Eldridge, who handles reservations.

Christopher Vann is manager of the lodge and dining room. He has been in the hotel, restaurant and food service businesses since 1986, working for ten years in San Antonio, Texas, before coming to Colorado in 1996. He started at the Irwin Lodge in April 2001. Head chef Jeff Blackwell has been cooking in restaurants since 1985. He spent seven years at the Green Hill Country Club in Quantico, Maryland, working his way up from line cook to executive chef. From 1992 to 1997 he was sous-chef at the Atlantic Hotel, also in Maryland. In 1997, he came to Colorado as executive sous-chef for Gourmet Alternative, a Denver catering business, and later worked at Beaver Run in Breckenridge, Colorado. He joined Irwin Lodge in May 2001.

The Irwin Lodge is the highest commercial resort and the largest snowcat powder lodge and ski operation in North America.

FOOD, SERVICE AND AMBIENCE

The Irwin Lodge Restaurant has one of the three best views of any restaurant in this book. (The Pine Creek Cookhouse in Ashcroft and Facing West in Lake City are the other two.) I drove up here from Gunnison for lunch on a pleasant, sunny summer day that turned to rain later. The chipotle-bacon dressing on my salad was creamy and spicy, but not hot, with bits of bacon, and very good. The marinara sauce on the al dente penne pasta had chunks of tomato in a moderately thick sauce. For lunch appetizers, you can choose from buffalo wings, hand-cut French fries, soup, nachos, or chips and salsa. A garden, Caesar, or chef's salad is also available along with burgers and sandwiches, including a salmon BLT, buffalo chicken and smoked turkey.

The breakfast menu features buttermilk and fruit pancakes, French toast with bananas Foster, a daily omelet, breakfast burrito, fresh fruit salad and fried-egg sandwich. The selection of dinner appetizers includes pan-seared sea scallops, jumbo shrimp and pork tenderloin satay. Highlighting the dinner entrées are elk or grilled pork tenderloin, pan-seared duck breast, grilled lamb loin, shrimp and scallop pasta and penne pasta primavera.

Service was friendly and informative. Weather permitting, you should dine on the patio with a tin roof and spectacular views of Lake Irwin, the Anthracite Mountain Range and Ohio Pass. From up here you can see Ruby, Owen and Purple Peaks to the right and, off in the distance, Beckwith Peak. The lodge itself is a 24,000-square-foot cedar log structure with twenty-one rooms and one master suite. The indoor dining area, part of an 8,000-square-foot common area highlighted by a massive fieldstone fireplace, is adorned with photos of skiers, wildflowers, Irwin Lake, the Irwin Lodge and, my favorite, four Irish setters posed in front of a sign reading "Caution: Snowcats may be encountered at any time." Seating is on wooden chairs at wood tables. No music was playing during my visit. Adding to the ambience are framed reviews of the lodge from newspapers and magazines. I think even Bette Davis would agree that "it's a bumpy ride" to the Irwin Lodge Restaurant, but well worth it.

NUTRITION AND SPECIAL REQUESTS

The Irwin Lodge does not get many special requests but will accommodate people with allergics. They have no problem making substitutions for items like sauces and cheeses. The menu lists one vegetarian appetizer, a garden burger and one vegetable entrée. At this remote location, the staff makes use of diesel generators and coal-fired heating, and they treat their own spring water.

Grilled Eggplant and Roasted Red-Pepper Salad

SERVES 1

1 red bell pepper	1 ounce Boursin cheese, crumbled
1 small eggplant	2 ounces spring greens
olive oil	Dijon-Thyme Vinaigrette (recipe
salt and pepper	follows)

1. Roast the whole red pepper on a hot grill until charred on all sides.
2. Put red pepper into a small container with a plastic lid. Let it steam itself for 30 minutes, then peel the skin off.
3. Slice 3, ½-inch-thick slices off the eggplant. Brush with olive oil, salt and pepper.
4. Grill eggplant slices on hot grill for 1–2 minutes. Turn 45 degrees and grill for 1–2 minutes longer.
5. Turn eggplant over and grill for 1–2 minutes. Turn 45 degrees once again and grill for 1–2 minutes longer. (This results in a criss-cross pattern on both sides of the eggplant.)
6. Slice red pepper into quarters and place on plate.
7. Layer the eggplant on the pepper slices.
8. Top with crumbled Boursin cheese. Finish with nest of spring greens. Drizzle with Dijon-Thyme Vinaigrette (recipe below).

Dijon-Thyme Vinaigrette

4 ounces white wine vinegar

8 ounces canola oil

2 sprigs fresh thyme, leafed

2 ounces Dijon mustard

salt and pepper to taste

1 ounce sugar

1 teaspoon vanilla extract

Mix all ingredients together. Makes 1 pint.

Recipe by Jeff Blackwell

❧ KEYSTONE ❧

KEYSTONE'S HISTORY IS *both rich and mysterious. Originally called Jackstraw Flats, Keystone served as an early transportation center before fading into obscurity. As early as 1810, mountain trappers discovered gold and silver in the creeks and rivers but managed to keep them a secret until 1859 to protect their peaceful beaver ponds. John C. Fremont, guided by Kit Carson, led the first government survey and mapping expedition through Summit County in 1843. The first reported silver strike in Colorado was in 1863 near Saints John, 10 miles up the Montezuma Canyon from Keystone Village. The famous Comstock Lode was uncovered there in 1865. In the 1880s, Old Keystone was a railhead for the Snake River mining towns of Montezuma, Argentina, Chihuahua and Saints John. As late as the 1930s, the Erickson and Ida Belle mines on Keystone Mountain produced profitable ore. Remains of Old Keystone can still be found at the Keystone Equestrian Center and Center for Continuing Education. Ralston Purina opened Keystone Ski Resort in November 1970.*

Vail Resorts Incorporated purchased Keystone Resort in 1997. Reservations can be made at any of the six restaurants by calling (970) 496-4FUN(4386) or (800) 354-4FUN(4385). The website for all the restaurants is www.Keystoneresort.com. There is no fax or e-mail address for the six restaurants.

Zip Code: 80435 **Population:** 825 **Elevation:** 9,547 feet

ALPENGLOW STUBE

Top of North Peak in the Outpost Lodge

Phone, fax, e-mail and website: See Keystone introduction at the beginning of this chapter.

Directions: Take exit 205 from I-70. Proceed in a southeasterly direction on Highway 6 for 7.8 miles (1¼ miles past the Keystone Lodge). Turn right onto Montezuma Road. Go 0.1 mile. Continue straight to park in close-in parking (fee) or turn left to park in outlying parking (free). Look for the solid-colored flags (not banners), which will direct you to the walkway leading to the first of two covered gondola rides. The first one takes about fifteen minutes, the second about twenty minutes. There is a short walk between gondolas and between the second gondola and the restaurant. The gondola rides are free.

ESSENTIALS

Cuisine: Contemporary Colorado

Hours: Mid-JUN to Labor Day and Thanksgiving to mid-DEC: Wed.–Sat. 5:30 P.M.–8:45 P.M. Closed Sun.–Tue. Mid-DEC to mid-APR: Seven days 11 A.M.–2 P.M., Mon.–Sat. 5:30 P.M.–8:45 P.M. Closed mid-APR to mid-JUN and Labor Day to Thanksgiving.

Meals and Prices: Lunch buffet $24. Sun. brunch $29. Dinner: 6 courses $80, 7 courses $92.

Nonsmoking: Smoking permitted only on patio

Take-out: No (Imagine trying!)

Alcohol: Full bar

Credit Cards: All five

Personal Check: No

Reservations: Required for dinner. Accepted for lunch and Sunday brunch.

Wheelchair Access: Yes! You can transport an individual in a wheelchair up both gondolas and into the restaurant.

Other: Surcharge of 4.7% in addition to applicable state and local taxes added to bill.

HISTORY AND BIOGRAPHY

The Outpost Lodge and Alpenglow Stube (pronounced "stüb á") Restaurant were built in November 1991. At 11,444 feet above sea level, this is the "highest gourmet, AAA Four-Diamond™ and Wine Spectator award-winning restaurant in North America."

General manager Angela Cartwright is from Austria and has been in the restaurant business since 1965. She has prior experience as an executive chef at the Lake Wright Convention Center and Golf Resort in Virginia Beach, Virginia. Angela has been with Keystone Resort since 1991 and has managed the Ski Tip Lodge, Der Fondue Chessel and the Outpost Café. Manager Bryon Scott has been with Keystone Resort since November 2000. He began his food and beverage career as a waiter in San Diego, California, spent two years at the Mission Bay Hilton in San Diego and eventually worked his way up to convention services supervisor. He landed a management position with the Sheraton and Westin on Harbor Island, California, where he stayed for seven years before coming to Colorado.

Executive chef Chris Wyant has been with Keystone since October 1988. Since being appointed chef in December 1994, he has implemented the highly successful "Dégustation Menu" featuring seven unique courses. He is a graduate of the Pennsylvania Institute of Culinary Arts and was an apprentice at the Greenbrier Hotel, a Mobile Five-Star™ property in White Sulphur Springs, West Virginia. He is known for his consommés, terrines and sausages and is a member of the American Culinary Federation certified in nutrition, safety and sanitation.

FOOD, SERVICE AND AMBIENCE

The "Stube" has the most fabulous lunch buffet in Summit County. I ordered the alpine buffet with entrée. The entrée included a bowl of French onion soup, which I found to my liking because it was not too thick—the broth was still a major part of the soup. (It seems the trend for most restaurants lately has been to load up this soup with onions and croutons.) The elaborate buffet featured homemade breads like pesto, sourdough, chili, pumpernickel and focaccia; cheeses such as Monterey Jack, Brie, homemade mozzarella and Roquefort; a selection of salads from asparagus with artichoke hearts and German potato to buffalo mozzarella with tomatoes marinated in balsamic vinegar and crawfish with bell peppers; a complement of strawberry vinaigrette and honey-Dijon dressings to go with the salads; fruits; duck chutney; smoked salmon and trout; goose liver pâté; gravlax; bunderfleisch (cured beef); prosciutto; Genoa salami; and a dessert station. For my entrée, I selected the veal schnitzel, tender medallions with a Pomeroy mustard sauce made with shallots and garlic. While the veal was top-quality, I found this dish to be heavy on the salt. I should mention that I (almost) never use table salt and I may be more salt sensitive that the average person. The dish came with sides of spaetzle and mixed fresh vegetables. Entrées only come with the Sunday brunch buffet. The rest of the week, the buffet includes the chef's carving station.

There are always four entrées on the Sunday brunch menu, which changes weekly. You will find a rotisserie choice like roast pheasant, duck breast, free-range chicken, or Cornish game hen; an item from the wood grill such as rib-eye steak sandwich, pork chops, grilled quail, or pork tenderloin; a seafood selection, possibly baked salmon, grilled shrimp, or sautéed grouper; and a chef's favorite, such as beef medallions or North Carolina barbecued pork.

The six-course dinner starts with Stube pinecones (duck foie gras and roast garlic hummus served with kirschwasser-soaked pumpernickel). This is followed by your elected appetizer of pheasant with roasted-corn relish, tuna tartare, lamb chop, ragout of blue crab, or Napoleon of heirloom tomato. Next is a baby lettuces salad in a champagne vinaigrette or wilted spinach salad in warm bacon vinaigrette. A fresh fruit sorbet will cool and cleanse your palate before the main, fifth, course. The entrées offer something for everyone: roast duck breast from the rotisserie, pan-roasted grouper, duet of veal and lobster, wood-grilled filet mignon, a vegetarian alpine harvest and hardwood-grilled caribou chop and wild game sausage. The Stube presents the perfect ending to your meal with the gratin Stube, a cheese custard with fresh berries and toasted almonds; there are also bread pudding, caramelized apple, espresso chocolate mousse, cinnamon shortbread and hazelnut granita or homemade ice cream from which to choose.

The chef's dégustation is seven uniquely prepared courses. Those partaking in this dining delight will be served one of four different off-the-menu appetizers, soups, sorbets, entrées and desserts as selected by Chef Chris and his staff. This works ideally for parties of four, where each person will get a different item with each course. Unlike the six-course prix fixe menu, a salad is served after the entrée and prior to dessert.

Cheerful is the best way to describe the service here. It is also professional, helpful and very attentive. The gas fireplace with brass pans and a picture of a fox hunt over the mantel provided a warm and cozy atmosphere as I looked out on a frozen, picturesque wonderland filled with tons of snow and blowing wind. Highly appropriate and appealing antler chandeliers hang from the vaulted ceiling, supported by very large ponderosa-pine posts and vegas. With windows all around, there is little space left for wall décor except for one wreath. Mother Nature takes over, however, as you will enjoy one of the most spectacular views found anywhere in Colorado in any season.

NUTRITION AND SPECIAL REQUESTS

Most people who dine here are out to have a good time, splurge and forget about their diets or nutrition. This is a special-occasion restaurant. Having said that, Chef Chris is very willing to cater to dietary or nutritional requirements. If you call ahead, he and his staff will make almost anything anybody requests. Most of the special requests they get are from vegetarians, though there are always vegetarian choices on the menu.

Gratin Stube

SERVES 4

½ pint fresh berries	2 egg yolks
14 ounces heavy cream	1 whole egg
¼ teaspoon ground nutmeg	Sweetened Cream-Cheese Topping
¼ teaspoon salt	(recipe follows)
⅔ teaspoon vanilla extract	slivered or sliced almonds
⅓ cup brown sugar	

1. Fill 4 ramekins with fresh berries. Preheat oven to 275 degrees.
2. Bring cream, nutmeg, salt, vanilla and brown sugar to a boil.

3. In a separate pan or bowl, mix egg yolks and whole egg together to blend.
4. Slowly whip ⅓ of hot cream mixture into eggs. Then slowly pour this back into the remaining mixture.
5. Divide custard among the ramekins, filling almost to the top of each.
6. Place ramekins in baking pan with an inch of water. Bake in pre-heated oven for 1½ hours or until set.
7. Remove custards from oven and water bath and chill in refrigerator for at least 4 hours, preferably overnight.

Sweetened Cream-Cheese Topping

4 ounces cream cheese   ¼ cup powdered sugar
½ teaspoon vanilla extract

1. Cream the cheese with the vanilla.
2. Add the powdered sugar slowly until smooth.
3. Store in refrigerator until needed.

To serve

1. Top each gratin with Cream-Cheese Topping and almonds.
2. Reheat in 300-degree oven until warm throughout, about 5 minutes.
3. Remove from oven and serve.

Recipe by Chris Wyant

Wine Recommendation: Chateau d'Yquem, a French Sauterne

THE BIGHORN STEAKHOUSE ─────────

Keystone Village, Highway 6
Phone, fax, e-mail and website: See Keystone introduction at the beginning of this chapter.

Directions: Take exit 205 from I-70 and continue in a southeasterly direction on Highway 6 for 6 miles. The Keystone Resort is on the right. A parking lot is located on the left directly across from the resort; the entrance is on the left just past the resort. After parking your car, take the underground walkway under Highway 6 to reach the entrance to the resort. Walk straight back through the lobby and take the stairs down to the restaurant.

ESSENTIALS

Cuisine: Steak, chicken and seafood
Hours: DEC–APR: Sun.–Thu. 5 P.M.–10 P.M., Fri.–Sat. 5 P.M.–10:30 P.M. MAY–NOV: Sun.–Thu. 5:30 P.M.–9:30 P.M., Fri.–Sat. 5:30 P.M.–10 P.M.
Meals and Prices: Dinner $18–$31
Nonsmoking: All
Take-out: No
Alcohol: Full bar
Credit Cards: All five
Personal Check: In-state only with ID
Reservations: Not accepted
Wheelchair Access: Yes, by elevator
Other: Children's menu and young adults' menu. A 4.7% surcharge, in addition to applicable state and local taxes, is added to bill.

HISTORY AND BIOGRAPHY

The Bighorn Steakhouse opened in December 1974 and featured a soup and salad bar. In fall 1993 it merged with the Garden Room Restaurant. Two years later, the Bighorn switched to a southwestern menu with a taste of the west in an attempt to offer flavors that more closely matched the tastes of its guests. Today, the Bighorn has returned to the original steakhouse theme with special steak entrées and the salad bar.

The Bighorn is managed by Mary Lou Li Puma, general manager of food and beverage at the Keystone Lodge. She also oversees the Edgewater Café, the Tenderfoot Lounge and the Garden Room. Mary Lou began her management career in 1974 in the Chicago area. She began working at Keystone in 1998 as manager of the Edgewater Café. Mary Lou has a passion for the industry and enjoys working closely with her staff and providing excellent service to resort guests.

Tom Angwin has been executive chef for all Keystone dining establishments since 1999. He studied at the Culinary School of South

Carolina before moving to New York City, where he helped to evolve the menu at Milano's Restaurant. He came to the Keystone Lodge in 1997.

FOOD, SERVICE AND AMBIENCE

I dined at the Bighorn on two occasions. On my first visit, dinner was served with warm wheat bread and the soup and salad bar. The soup of the day was a thick and spicy sirloin steak with mushrooms, white pepper, pimentos and onions. For my entrée, I chose the herb-marinated top sirloin topped with onion hair and served with a brown demi-glace and a baked potato. The onion "hair" was very fine strands of onion rings. The sirloin was extremely tender and lean with no fat or gristle and stood up fine on its own, although the demi-glace was quite good also. This was a top-quality piece of meat.

On my second visit, with Linda, we were brought sourdough and sun-dried-tomato rolls and tried the New England clam chowder, thick with plenty of clam strips and big chunks of potato. The salad bar offered a fine collection of mixed greens, leaf spinach, pasta seafood salad with baby shrimp and mussels, potato and fruit salads, large black olives, artichoke hearts and hard-cooked eggs. The shrimp cocktail featured five large prawns served in a champagne glass on a bed of lettuce with a center of cocktail sauce. The oysters Rockefeller, with spinach and baked hollandaise on top, was a delicious but subdued departure from the more common oysters on the half shell. I found the baked hollandaise to be more palatable than the cream hollandaise that I gave up eating years ago, though I still prefer my oysters raw.

My grilled lamb T-bone, which I ordered medium-rare, came out more rare than medium but had a meaty flavor, sufficient fat and small bones. There were two chops and two barbecue sauces, a tangy, tomato-flavored one and a sweet shallot sauce. The meal included sautéed vegetables and garlic mashed potatoes with skins and pepper and a fresh sprig of rosemary. The combination definitely satisfied my taste buds. Linda ordered the baked shrimp stuffed with crab. She found the crab to be on the dry side but the shrimp to be moist.

The Bighorn specializes in aged, certified, choice, corn-fed beef: prime rib, filet mignon, New York strip, rib-eye, top sirloin and porterhouse. Other specialties include Rocky Mountain trout almandine, garlic-and-herb whole roasted chicken, grilled pork chops and roasted veal chops. Accompaniments such as brandied sautéed mushrooms, creamed spinach and asparagus or broccoli-flavored hollandaise are available. To finish your dining experience, you can select from spiced rum bread pudding, homemade raspberry and white chocolate ice cream, mud pie or fruit cobbler.

Service was friendly and efficient, and the servers were very well-spoken and observant. During my first visit, my server noticed that the burner under the salad bar's hot bacon dressing had gone out and immediately went to the kitchen to bring some hot dressing to my table. Soft jazz played quietly in the background. The booths of this elegant yet casual restaurant are covered in southwestern patterns and colors: rust red, maroon, white, turquoise and brown. The pine walls are accented with black-iron-and-glass sconces. Enhancing the southwestern motif are paintings of mountains, deserts, cowboys and horses, a clay pot in the shape of a bull and a brass sculpture of Indians on horses.

NUTRITION AND SPECIAL REQUESTS

Nondairy creamer, margarine and a variety of low-salt, low-cholesterol and low-sugar items are available upon request. Ask your server about "health-wise" information. The chefs will be happy to accommodate your requests and special dietary concerns.

Veal Marsala with Rosemary Demi-Glace

SERVES 2

2 tablespoons butter, divided
1 pound veal medallions
salt and pepper
1 teaspoon minced garlic
1 teaspoon minced shallots
2 ounces Marsala wine

1 teaspoon fresh, chopped
    rosemary
1½ ounces veal demi-glace
fresh rosemary sprigs for garnish
    (optional)

1. Heat a sauté pan and add 1 tablespoon butter. Let it melt and start to brown. While the butter is melting, generously sprinkle salt and pepper on both sides of the veal medallions.

2. As the butter begins to brown, add the seasoned veal to the pan. Be careful not to let the butter brown too much or it will become bitter.
3. Let veal cook until well caramelized on both sides, approximately 1 to 1½ minutes each side. Remove veal from the pan and set aside.
4. Add second tablespoon of butter along with garlic and shallots. Cook until aroma is noticeable. Pull back from heat, add Marsala and flame.
5. Reduce the Marsala by half; add fresh chopped rosemary and demi-glace. Bring to a light boil.
6. Return the veal to the pan of sauce to reheat.
7. Arrange medallions on serving plates, overlapping each. Spoon sauce over ⅔ of the meat. Garnish each plate with a fresh rosemary sprig (optional). Serve.

Recipe by Tom Angwin

Wine Recommendation: Australia Rosemount Shiraz

EDGEWATER CAFÉ

Keystone Village, Highway 6

Phone, fax, e-mail and website: See Keystone introduction at the beginning of this chapter.

Directions: Take exit 205 from I-70 and continue in a southeasterly direction on Highway 6 for 6 miles. The Keystone Resort is on the right. A parking lot is located on the left directly across from the resort; the entrance is on the left just past the resort. After parking your car, take the underground walkway under Highway 6 to reach the Keystone Resort. When you exit the tunnel you will be outside. Take the stairway down to the left. The restaurant is around to the left.

ESSENTIALS

Cuisine: American bistro
Hours: Seven days 6:30 A.M.–2 P.M.
Meals and Prices: Breakfast and lunch $8–$10
Nonsmoking: All

Take-out: Yes

Alcohol: Beer, wine and limited bar

Credit Cards: All five

Personal Check: In-state only with ID

Reservations: No

Wheelchair Access: Yes

Other: Children's menu. Available for private parties and functions in the evening. Please inform server if you would like separate checks. A 4.7% surcharge, in addition to applicable state and local taxes, is added to bill. Service charge of 15% added to parties of six or more.

HISTORY AND BIOGRAPHY

The building now housing the Edgewater Café and the Keystone Lodge was constructed in 1970. The original restaurant at this location was the Brassierie. It served breakfast and lunch in the space that is now the back of the restaurant. A few years later, the front of the restaurant along with the Lakeside Suites were added to the hotel and conference space. In 1985, the name of the restaurant was changed to Edgewater Café with an emphasis on casual family-style dining in a relaxed atmosphere with affordable prices. Outdoor seating was added in 1990, doubling the size of the restaurant.

General manager Murphy Funkhouser has been in the food and beverage business since 1992. She began her career at the Keystone Resort as the food and beverage training specialist before taking over at the Edgewater in May 2001. Keystone Lodge general manager of food and beverage Mary Lou Li Puma oversees the Edgewater Café as well as the Bighorn Steakhouse, the Tenderfoot Lounge and the Garden Room. Mary Lou began her management career in 1974 in the Chicago area.

Executive chef Tim Koch has been at the Keystone Resort since 1997 and at the Edgewater Café since 1999. His upbringing on a dairy farm in Illinois has influenced his culinary skills. With an appreciation for fresh and seasonal foods, Tim uses local Colorado products such as San Luis potatoes, Palisade peaches and Olathe sweet corn. He is a 2000 graduate of the Colorado Mountain Culinary Institute, where he was voted apprentice of the year by his instructors and classmates.

The Edgewater Café is on-the-waterfront dining with a covered patio on the edge of Keystone Lake. I enjoyed lunch here on two occasions. The Philly steak sandwich was filled with tender and tasty grilled buffalo beef strips, lightly sautéed green peppers, slightly more sautéed onions and melted cheese. A mix of cubed melons was served on the side. The Black Forest chicken Dijon sandwich had tender and moist grilled chicken breast, lean and salty Black Forest ham, Swiss cheese, fresh tomato and lettuce and thinly sliced sautéed onion all on a toasted onion roll. It came with fries. Both sandwiches were tasty and filling.

For breakfast, the Edgewater offers traditional American fare as well as a hearty all-you-can-eat buffet at certain times. Specialties on the breakfast menu included Sante Fe huevos, three-egg omelets, eggs Benedict, a croissant sandwich, a fresh fruit plate, a health nut plate, country biscuits and gravy and Texas-style French toast with cinnamon. Headlining the breakfast buffet are hickory-smoked salmon, fruits, cereals, an omelet station and banana-nut waffles.

The Tuscan table is the highlight of lunch. This buffet presents the flavors of Italy and the Mediterranean with an antipasto platter, home-made soups, pasta dishes, freshly baked breads and garden greens with fresh vegetables and house dressings. The lunch entrées feature Caesar and Cobb salads; wraps such as Thai beef and spinach salad with wild mushrooms; and panini sandwiches including three-cheese, Tuscan chicken and beefeater's. For dessert try the tiramisu, raspberry–white chocolate bread pudding with hot fudge sauce, or a selection of the homemade sorbets or ice creams. During the ski season, the Edgewater is occasionally opened for dinner featuring nightly specials, appetizers, dinner entrées and a soup and salad bar.

I found the service here to be fast and friendly as well as helpful. Windows in the dining room face west for superb views of the moun-tains, Keystone Lake and neighboring shops. The dining room is divided into two areas by a concrete wall with openings. Within the openings are stained-glass and wrought-iron artworks. The walls are decorated with paintings of a lake, the misty Tetons, waterfalls, rivers and rock beds. A multicolored banner runs through the restaurant over-head. The deli area at the entrance has an interesting painting of a door opening to the ocean.

NUTRITION AND SPECIAL REQUESTS

Egg substitutes are available for those watching their cholesterol. The Tuscan table provides several healthful choices. Special requests will be honored where possible.

Venison Stew

MAKES ABOUT 10 8-OUNCE SERVINGS

1 tablespoon confectioners' sugar
⅓ cup flour
2 tablespoons kosher salt
2½ pounds venison stew meat
¼ cup vegetable oil, divided
⅓ pound pearl onions
4 cloves garlic, peeled and chopped
1½ cups dry red wine
3 cups beef stock
1 cup chopped tomatoes with their juice (canned or fresh)
1 bay leaf
4 carrots, quartered lengthwise and cut into ½-inch lengths

1½ pounds potatoes, peeled and cut into ½-inch dice
5 shiitake mushrooms, stemmed and thinly sliced
2 tablespoons brandy
1 10-ounce package of frozen peas, defrosted and drained
3 sprigs fresh thyme, chopped (or 1½ teaspoons dried thyme)
3 sprigs fresh oregano, chopped (or 1½ teaspoons dried oregano)
freshly ground black pepper to taste

1. Combine the confectioners' sugar, flour and salt in a large bowl. Add the venison and toss.
2. Heat 2 tablespoons of oil in a large wide pot over high heat. Working in batches, brown the meat, setting each batch aside in a bowl as it is finished.
3. Add 1 tablespoon oil to the pot. Stir in the onions and garlic and sauté until browning. Stir in the wine and scrape the bottom and sides of the pan with a wooden spoon to release the brown bits, then reduce the wine by half.
4. Stir in the stock and bring to a boil, then add meat, tomatoes and bay leaf. Simmer for 30 minutes. Add carrots and potatoes and simmer for 45 more minutes.
5. While stew is simmering, heat remaining oil in a medium frying

pan over high heat. Stir in mushrooms and cook until they are
seared; deglaze with brandy and reserve.

6. When stew has simmered for the entire 1¼ hours, add the seared
   mushrooms, peas, thyme, oregano and black pepper. Bring back to
   a simmer and serve.

Recipe by Tim Koch

Wine Recommendation: Lyeth Meritage Cabernet Merlot

IDA BELLE'S CANTINA

Keystone Village, Highway 6

Phone, fax, e-mail and website: See Keystone introduction at the
beginning of this chapter.

Directions: Take exit 205 from I-70 and continue in a southeasterly
direction on Highway 6 for 6 miles. The Keystone Resort is on the right.
A parking lot is located on the left directly across from the resort; the
entrance is on the left just past the resort. After parking your car, take the
underground walkway under Highway 6 to reach the Keystone Resort.
When you exit the tunnel you will be outside. Take the stairway down to
the left. The restaurant is around to the left a few doors past the
Edgewater Café.

ESSENTIALS

Cuisine: Mountain Mexican

Hours: Seven days 11 A.M.–10 P.M. Closed mid-APR to mid-MAY and
mid-SEP to mid-OCT.

Meals and Prices: Lunch and Dinner $8–$15

Nonsmoking: Yes

Take-out: Yes

Alcohol: Full bar

Credit Cards: All five

Personal Check: In-state only with ID

Reservations: Not accepted

Wheelchair Access: Yes

Other: Service charge of 15% added to parties of six or more. One check per table. A 4.7% surcharge, in addition to applicable state and local taxes, is added to bill.

HISTORY AND BIOGRAPHY

Ida Belle's Cantina was formerly Bentley's Restaurant, which opened in 1970 along with the Keystone Resort. Ida Belle's took over the space in 1989.

Ida Belle's chef and manager, Tracy Servadio, began his career in his father's steakhouse in 1967, working his way up from the pantry to the kitchen. In 1970 Tracy moved to Maine to open a second restaurant with his father, leaving in 1983 to become kitchen manager at a popular pizzeria in the area. In 1986 Tracy became sous-chef at the Seaman's Club in Portland, Maine. In 1990 he moved to Colorado to explore the mountains and spent four years working in the ski industry at Copper Mountain. He signed on with Ida Belle's in 1994.

FOOD, SERVICE, AND AMBIENCE

I ordered Ida Belle's soft spinach taco and found it to be a tasty alternative to traditional beef or chicken tacos. It consisted of a sun-dried-tomato tortilla stuffed with sautéed spinach, cheese and mild red enchilada sauce, then topped with sour cream. The plate also hosted baked beans, white rice, a delicious corn relish with mild green chilies and diced red peppers and sides of lettuce, diced tomato and sliced black olives. For dessert, I treated myself to a piece of banana-chocolate pie: rich banana-flavored whipped-cream filling on a chocolate crust, topped with chocolate shavings, a stiff dollop of more whipped cream and a banana-shaped, banana-flavored hard candy. Side dollops of whipped cream sprinkled with gold flakes were an elegant garnish.

Highlighting the list of appetizers were chicken wings, tortilla and black bean soups, green or red chile, taquitos, nachos and jalapeño poppers. Ida Belle's offers a variety of flame-broiled burgers, South-of-the-Border chicken breast sandwiches with a chipotle marinade and barbecued baby-back ribs. Topping the Mexican entrées were grilled steak or chicken fajitas, a smothered or bean burrito, beef or chicken hard-shell tacos, taco salad, a California wrap and pork chops smothered in green chile. Their desserts, or "tailins" as they are called here, featured a homemade brownie sundae, homemade apple pie, homemade ice cream, white chocolate cheesecake with raspberry sauce and the Aztec chocolate bombe, a delicious concoction of chocolate mousse and mocha on a chocolate cookie covered with hard chocolate.

The young, amiable waitstaff wore nametags with historical names. You can inquire of your server about the facts regarding the person he or she represents. A combination of blues and rock music permeated the air of this restaurant designed to resemble its namesake, a mine. The entrance looks a lot like a mine shaft, with a wagon wheel and part of a still as accoutrements. There is a huge photo of miners and brewery workers combined with modern-day photos of people dressed in nineteenth-century garb. A miner's lantern, old skis and poles, an old washboard and a "Danger" sign from a mine adorn the wooden walls, posts and beams. A rock fireplace houses an inset television. Warm-weather guests who don't care to dine in a mine shaft can enjoy patio dining on the lake.

NUTRITION AND SPECIAL REQUESTS

Ida Belle's serves a garden salad, a bean and rice burrito and a veggie burger. They will honor special requests whenever possible.

Chihuahua Creek Chicken Enchiladas with Colorado Red Chile Enchilada Sauce

MAKES 8 ENCHILADAS FOR 4 SERVINGS

1 ounce vegetable oil
1 small onion, diced
3 Anaheim green chilies, roasted and diced
1 jalapeño, diced
½ teaspoon ground cumin
1 teaspoon chili powder
½ teaspoon black pepper

½ teaspoon salt
2 tablespoons chopped cilantro
½ pound Jack cheese, shredded
1 pound chicken breast
½ cup vegetable oil
8 6-inch white corn tortillas
Colorado Red Chile Enchilada Sauce (recipe follows)

1. Heat 1 ounce of vegetable oil in sauté pan. Sauté onion and green chilies for 4 minutes. Add jalapeño and spices. Sauté for 2 minutes.

2. Cool mixture and add cheese.
3. Grill the chicken breast, dice and add to chili and onion mixture.
4. Heat remaining ½ cup of vegetable oil in sauté pan. Dip the corn tortillas in the oil one at a time, about 5 seconds on each side. Preheat oven to 350 degrees.
5. Divide the prepared filling among the tortillas and roll up. Place seam-side-down in baking pan.
6. Put enchiladas in preheated oven and bake until heated through and cheese is melted, about 10 minutes. Top with Enchilada Sauce.

Colorado Red Chile Enchilada Sauce

15 ancho chilies	1 teaspoon sugar
15 gaujiulo chilies	1 teaspoon ground cumin
1 ounce olive oil	1 teaspoon dried oregano
1 small onion, diced	1 teaspoon salt
2 cloves garlic, diced	1 ounce flour

1. Soak chilies for ½ hour or until hydrated. Take off stems and puree in food processor.
2. Heat oil in saucepan; add chile puree, onion, garlic, sugar and spices. Cook for 20 minutes, stirring frequently.
3. Mix in flour; cook for 5 minutes.
4. Remove from heat and strain.
5. Retain strained portion for use on enchiladas. (Dispose of the watery part.)

Recipe by Tracy Servadio

Beverage Recommendation: Mango or Strawberry Margarita

KEYSTONE RANCH

Keystone Ranch Road, P.O. Box 38

Phone, fax, e-mail and website: See Keystone introduction at the beginning of this chapter.

Directions: Take Exit 205 from I-70. Go south on Highway 6 for 6.3 miles. Turn right onto West Keystone Road, then make an immediate left at the "T" in the road. Go 0.3 mile and turn right onto Soda Ridge Road. Go

1 mile and turn left at the stop sign onto Keystone Ranch Road. Go
1.3 miles to the entrance to Keystone Ranch. Go 100 feet past the gate
and take the fork to the right. Continue ½ mile to the restaurant.

ESSENTIALS

Cuisine: Upscale Rocky Mountain

Hours: Late OCT to mid-MAY: Thu.–Tue. 5:30 P.M.–8:45 P.M. Closed
Wed. Mid-MAY to late OCT: Seven days 11 A.M. 2 P.M., Mon.–
Sat. 5:30 P.M.–8:45 P.M.

Meals and Prices: Lunch $8–$12. Dinner: Six courses, $72 for adults,
$38 for children under twelve.

Nonsmoking: All. Smoking permitted in the living room or lounge only.

Take-out: No

Alcohol: Full bar

Credit Cards: All five

Personal Check: In-state with driver's license

Reservations: REQUIRED for dinner. Recommended for lunch.

Wheelchair Access: Yes

Other: Available for weddings, receptions, special events, parties and
banquets. A 4.7% surcharge, in addition to applicable state and
local taxes, is added to bill.

HISTORY AND BIOGRAPHY

The Keystone Ranch was originally built as a cattle ranch and lettuce
farm in 1938 and remained a working ranch until 1977, producing veal,
lettuce and dairy products for local consumption. The current living
room was the original ranch house. The fireplace was a wedding present
to newlyweds Bernadine Smith and Howard Reynolds, who ran the
ranch for forty years. During the 1940s and 1950s, the Ranch was host
to wealthy and influential visitors including President Dwight
Eisenhower and other prominent Republicans. The dining room was
added in 1947, the lounge and bar in 1980, the restaurant in 1981 and
the golf course in 1982. As a restaurant, the style of food has progressed
from country fare to "nouvelle cuisine" to an approach that incorporates
predominantly indigenous Rocky Mountain ingredients.

Ron Wolfe has been general manager at Keystone Resort since

November 1997, first at Alpenglow Stube and now at the Ranch. He has worked since 1984 as a manager and maitre d' at the House of Lords in the Sheffield Hotel in Anchorage, Alaska; Regina's Restaurant in San Francisco, California; the Amelia Island Plantation in Florida; the Mauna Kea Beach Resort on Hawaii; and The Broadmoor in Colorado Springs, Colorado. Mark Kimball, a former waiter at Alpenglow Stube, has been the Ranch's maitre d' since fall 2000.

Chef de cuisine David Welch's interest in cooking dates back to his early childhood, when he would watch his grandmother cook. In high school he worked as a dishwasher in Keystone's main kitchen, where he met and was mentored by Keystone's acclaimed French chef, Michel Franch. He landed positions at Silverheels in Silverthorne and Saddle-Ridge in Beaver Creek before becoming sous-chef for the Keystone Ranch and chef de cuisine at the Ski Tip Lodge. He is currently pursuing his certification as an executive chef. David is accompanied by sous-chef Travis Hall from Hawaii. Travis is a graduate of the Pittsburgh Culinary School and has been with David since fall 1998. A team of six rotating apprentices from the Colorado Mountain College also staff the kitchen.

The Keystone Ranch has been the recipient of the AAA Four Diamond Award™ for every year since 1987, the DiRoNA Award for every year since 1990 and the Wine Spectator Award of Excellence for every year since 1996. In 2001, the Ranch was rated the fifth-best restaurant for food for restaurants in Denver and the Mountain Resorts by Zagat and noted for its 3 "E"s: elegance, excellence and expense.

FOOD, SERVICE AND AMBIENCE

Dinner at the Keystone Ranch is a six-course festival beginning with the chef's welcome. I have had the exceptional pleasure of dining here twice. On my first visit, the edible introduction was a pheasant galantine with pistachios and dried cherries on apricot Cumberland sauce made with poppy seeds and strawberry aspic. My second dining experience began equally auspiciously, with pesto-baked chicken salad in a small wonton cup with black-bean tapénade and balsamic reduction. The creative presentations are as appealing to the eye as they are appetizing to the palate. For the first course appetizer, I selected the smoked chicken, chilled and sliced with peppered mango, sliced jicama, nasturtium leaf, fried leek and raspberry and tangerine dressing. It was tangy and sweet. On my second outing I went with arctic caribou and grilled foie gras. The caribou was about a two-inch-thick medium-rare piece served with candied dates, citron and a very mild currant sauce. As for the foie gras, it is difficult to believe that chopped liver can be this good.

The second course was a forest-mushroom soup with red peppers and chives, warm with tasty seasoning. I also tried the wild game soup with barley, a mix of venison and buffalo with finely chopped carrots, onions and chives. One of the third-course salads I tried was a light, fruity and flavorful poached crimson pear marinated in port wine with celery root, coleslaw, walnuts, lettuces, mosh (related to water chestnut), Stilton blue cheese, a nasturtium flower and citrus vinaigrette. The other was composed of baby lettuces, crunchy toasted pepitas, savory Gorgonzola compote and a slightly pungent mustard-seed vinaigrette in an artistic presentation that included a ribbon of pickled beet curled into a bouquet and held together by a stem of pickled carrot. The intermezzo that precedes the main course is a granita, fruit ice, or sorbet that cools and refreshes the taste buds. I partook of sorbets on both occasions: a nectarous guava-rum with blueberry-mint sauce and a mango-ginger with blood-orange coulis. The latter was served frozen. Fortunately, I was sitting at a western-facing window so the setting sun melted the sorbet to where I could eat it.

The fifth course is the entrée. I chose the game bird quorum, a whole roasted quail with crab, sweet-pepper and quinoa stuffing accompanied by a pheasant breast braised in port wine and forest mushrooms and a grilled breast of Muscovy duck marinated in balsamic vinaigrette and Dijon. This was served with littlehead ferns, grilled artichoke, baked Black Forest and shiitake mushrooms, pattypan squash, yucca root (tastes like a crispy potato), timbale of quinoa and barley, "firecracker," (Fresno peppers, honey and chicken stock) and juniper sauce. It was an elaborate presentation for sight and taste. The roast cherrywood loin of pork on my second visit was wrapped in a roll with apples and San Daniele ham. It was prepared well done so that the apples would be sufficiently warmed and was served with thyme fingerling potatoes, blanched and cooked in pork stock and Calvados (a dry apple brandy) natural jus.

Coffee, after dinner-liqueur and/or dessert can be taken at your table, or better yet, in the living room. If this is your first time at the Ranch, I recommend the Grand Marnier soufflé, a perennial favorite. It is served in a crock with warm pistachio crème anglaise on the side.

Being a lover of cherries, I indulged in the sour-cherry clafoutis on my second visit. It consists of a sour-cherry custard and cake filling in a toasted, crisp coconut macaroon cup with white "hair" (crystallized spun sugar threads). Both were luscious endings to memorable evenings.

Service at the Keystone Ranch is sophisticated, professional and knowledgeable. Everyone you come in contact with is well-dressed. The background music may be classical violin or light jazz, selected to blend well with the décor and ambience. The restaurant sports lodgepole pine banisters, steps, railings and vegas, with the original wrought-iron hinges on the doors. Several windows look to the Shadow, Buffalo, Baldy and Geo Mountains. Rust-colored curtains match the cloth table napkins and contrast nicely against white tablecloths. A rock fireplace with dried flower and fern arrangements on the mantel, a picture over the mantel of a log cabin in winter (cozy and cold, it fits right in if you are here in winter) and southwestern artworks add to the mountain charm. The living room where desserts and after-dinner cordials are served is highlighted by thick-cushioned couches, coffee tables, a rock fireplace and four heads of deer with antlers.

NUTRITION AND SPECIAL REQUESTS

The Ranch offers vegetarian options and will accommodate special requests.

Creamy Forest Mushroom Soup

MAKES ABOUT 5 CUPS

1¼ pounds fresh oyster
   mushrooms, chopped
½ medium onion, finely chopped
3 garlic cloves, minced
1 tablespoon olive oil
1 tablespoon porcini (cèpe) powder*
1 teaspoon packed brown sugar
½ cup Sercial Madeira wine

5 cups Mushroom Stock
   (recipe follows)
1 tablespoon sherry vinegar
½ teaspoon minced fresh
   thyme leaves
1 cup heavy cream
salt and pepper
minced chives for garnish

*Available at some specialty foods shops and by mail-order from Marché aux Delices, (888) 547-5471.

1. In a 4- to 5-quart heavy kettle, heat oil over moderately high heat until hot but not smoking and sauté mushrooms, onion and garlic with porcini powder and brown sugar, stirring until the liquid given off by the mushrooms is completely evaporated and mushrooms begin to brown.
2. Add Madeira and boil, stirring occasionally, until liquid is evaporated. Stir in Mushroom Stock, vinegar and thyme and bring to a boil. Stir in cream and salt and pepper to taste and simmer, uncovered, 15 minutes.
3. In a blender, puree soup in batches until smooth (use caution when blending hot liquids), then transfer to a saucepan and reheat over moderately low heat until hot. Serve soup garnished with chives.

Mushroom Stock

2 pounds white mushrooms	2 quarts water
2 onions	1 teaspoon salt

1. Quarter mushrooms and, in a food processor, finely chop in 4 batches, transferring to a 6-quart stockpot or heavy kettle.
2. Finely chop onions and add to mushrooms with water and salt. Simmer mixture, uncovered, 2 hours.
3. Pour stock through a large, fine sieve into a large bowl, pressing hard on solids. Yield should be about 5 cups; if yield is less, add enough water to make 5 cups; if more, boil stock until reduced to 5 cups.

Recipe by David Welch

SKI TIP LODGE ─────────────

764 Montezuma Road

Phone, fax, e-mail and website: See Keystone introduction at the beginning of this chapter.

Directions: Take exit 205 from I-70. Proceed in a southeasterly direction on Highway 6 for 7.8 miles (1½ miles past the Keystone Lodge). Turn right at the sign for Montezuma Road and Keystone Ski Area. Go 0.1 mile and turn left onto Montezuma Road. Go 1 mile. The restaurant is on the right.

ESSENTIALS

Cuisine: Coloradoan with multicultural influences
Hours: Seven nights 5:30 P.M.–8:45 P.M.
Meals and Prices: Four-course dinner $58. Children's menu $32.
Nonsmoking: Smoking permitted only on patio
Take-out: No
Alcohol: Full bar
Credit Cards: All five
Personal Check: In-state with driver's license
Reservations: Required
Wheelchair Access: Yes
Other: Will organize and cater weddings, reunions, parties, or other special occasions. Surcharge of 4.7%, in addition to applicable state and local taxes, is added to bill.

HISTORY AND BIOGRAPHY

A portion of the Ski Tip Lodge was built in the 1880s as a stagecoach stop; it is the area near the restrooms in the current building. Max and Edna Dercum purchased the structure in summer 1942, adding to the building to make it their private residence. Another log wing was added in 1946. As skiing became more popular at Keystone and Arapahoe Basin Ski Areas, the Dercums expanded their home to become Colorado's first skiers' guest ranch. They opened a restaurant in the mid-1950s. In 1982, Keystone Resort took ownership of the property and converted it into a bed and breakfast and restaurant.

General manager Angela Cartwright is from Austria and has been in the restaurant business since 1965. She was executive chef at the Lake Wright Convention Center and Golf Resort on Virginia Beach. Angela has been with Keystone Resorts since 1991 and has managed Alpenglow Stube, Der Fondue Chessel and the Outpost Café. Manager and innkeeper David Wilcox had been with Keystone food and beverage for more than ten years when he was promoted to his current position in September 2000. David began his career at the age of fifteen and has worked in many positions, from prep cook to waiter to host. He helped manage several restaurants during his career, gaining experience in Italian, French and American cuisine.

Executive chef Scott Goeringer has been with Keystone since September 2000, working as sous-chef in the resort's main lodge kitchen before his promotion to the Ski Tip Lodge. Raised in Colorado, he spent years working at his parents' candy shop in Georgetown and at the Fort Restaurant in Morrison, Colorado. Scott attended Denver's Emily Griffith Opportunity School Food Production and Management one-year program, then went to work at the Broadmoor Hotel in Colorado Springs, Colorado.

FOOD, SERVICE AND AMBIENCE

Your four-course dinner begins with a choice of soups followed by a salad or appetizer selection and entrée. The options change nightly. A decision on dessert is left until the completion of your entrée. The evening that I dined here, I chose potato chowder with smoked ham and turkey. The chowder was delightful—thick with parsley, carrots and pimentos. For an appetizer, I picked smoked Rocky Mountain trout with caper mayonnaise and cucumber-tomato-fennel relish. It was very tasty and not too filling. For my entrée, I selected a very lean, roasted Colorado lamb loin, dry-aged two to three weeks and served in rosemary natural jus. This delicious dish came with artichoke hearts marinated in Madeira wine; sweet potato cakes prepared with raisins, freshly grated carrot, walnuts and Granny Smith apples; julienned carrots; grilled tomato marinated in balsamic vinegar; and shiitake mushrooms. All together, it was a stupendous taste sensation! All of the Ski Tip's desserts are homemade. I decided on the chocolate hazelnut terrine—a chocolate pâté served chilled on raspberry sauce with kiwi relish, similar to a chilled chocolate mousse—which was sweet and delectable. My selection won out over apple Granny with walnut and golden raisins, Bing cherry ice cream, baked chocolate crème caramel and litchinut sorbet.

The food here is more homespun than those found at other Keystone Resort restaurants. The warm, homemade breads include a sesame lavosh, zucchini with walnuts and Parmesan-mushroom. All of the sauces, soups and stocks are made in-house. Chef Scott tries to buy ingredients locally as much as possible. Fruits come mainly from places like Palisade, Delta and Rocky Ford, Colorado; vegetables from Pueblo and the Front Range. The trout is either from Colorado or farm-raised in Idaho. The Wyoming pheasant is purchased from a Loveland, Colorado, distributor. The rabbit is from Colorado's Western Slope or Canada. Chef Scott uses Texas boar, New Zealand venison, Colorado and New Zealand lamb and Nebraska buffalo. A beef plant in Sterling, Colorado, dry-ages their tenderloin and filet mignon. The shellfish arrives frozen, but almost all of the other fish arrives fresh, next day (like Pacific salmon), or via second-day air from Honolulu, Hawaii (like coral perch, tuna and mahimahi).

You will find five different entrées on each evening's special menu: red meat, poultry, game, fish and vegetarian. The choices range from beef sirloin, buffalo, ostrich, kangaroo, lamb, quail, pork, elk and venison to calamari, shrimp, Pacific salmon, lobster, caviar and scallops. Examples of the vegetarian dishes are caramelized tomato and goat-cheese tart, lentil and forest-mushroom pie and sesame seed bean curd with soybean salad.

My cheerful and amicable server was resourceful in providing answers to my queries and took me for a tour of the lodge. Windham Hill piano and guitar selections provided soothing music for listening. Look up as you enter the dining room, and you will see a couple of painted Santa Claus figures on ceiling boards used to cover the holes left behind when an old stove was removed. A wood-burning fireplace now stands in the corner. The folksy artwork includes pictures of a fox hunt, a mother dressing her children for winter and a frozen lake with ice skaters. A small walk-in wine cellar is just what you would expect from a lodge dating back to the 1880s. Australian Brenda McDonald, an innkeeper herself in nearby Frisco, decorated the dining room.

You may want to repair and unwind for dessert in either the living room or lounge. The living room has some comfortable cushioned chairs and couches on which to relax while you set your cappuccino and dessert on the coffee table, a seasoned toy chest filled with games. Old wood skis rest overhead on hand-hewn wood beams. At one end of the living room are an immense fireplace, a stuffed ptarmigan and a large wreath. At the opposite end is a row of windows without curtains. The lounge has its own sizeable rock fireplace, adorned with copper pans, an impressive semi-circular hearth and an aged trunk used as a coffee table. A sign from Dillon hangs in the room: "We're doomed to be damned but damned if we're doomed," an early-1960s reference to the pending Dillon Dam. The lounge is adorned with antiques, including a vintage

Emerson piano and a Tyler desk with roll-back top. Between the lounge and private dining room is a small bar, next to which is a painting by Rolf Dercum, son of Max and Edna, of a jolly Swiss fellow who visited the Dercums in the 1940s. Come and see for yourself the numerous displays of antiquity in this historic building and treat yourself to a marvelous meal at the same time.

NUTRITION AND SPECIAL REQUESTS

Chef Goeringer tries to work with guests' dietary needs as much as possible. For example, he stopped putting garlic and wine in stocks until they are used, to accommodate people with those allergies. In addition to daily vegetarian choices, they will try to satisfy vegans as well.

Peach and Pistachio Pithiviers

MAKES 8

To assemble this dish, you first need to make the pistachio frangipane and peach coulis. The lodge serves this dessert warm, with ice cream.

Pistachio Frangipane

1 cup sugar
pinch of salt
1 cup all-purpose flour
3 cups cream

1 vanilla pod, split
3 large eggs, beaten
¾ cup crushed pistachios
4 tablespoons butter, softened

1. Sift together the sugar, salt and flour and place them in a heavy-bottomed pot. Bring the cream and the vanilla bean to a boil in a separate pan.
2. Stir the eggs into the flour mixture and then stir in small amounts of the cream (it is important to add the hot milk slowly, so the eggs do not scramble).
3. Return the mix to the stove and, over low heat, stirring constantly, cook out the flour. This will take 3–5 minutes.
4. Remove from the heat and fold in the pistachios and butter. Frangipane can last for 1 to 2 weeks, if refrigerated.

Peaches and Peach Coulis

8 fresh small peaches	2 teaspoons fresh basil, chopped fine
1 cup sugar	(plus extra for garnish, if desired)

1. Peel peaches. The best way to do this is to blanch the peaches in boiling water for 30–60 seconds and then immediately shock them in ice water. The skins peel and pull away from the flesh easily.
2. Neatly halve and pit four peaches, setting them to the side.
3. Pit the remaining peaches, roughly chop them, mix them with the sugar and bring them to a boil slowly, over low heat.
4. Once the peaches have boiled for 5–10 minutes, puree them and strain.
5. Fold the basil into the sauce and chill.

Pithiviers

8–12 tablespoons Frangipane	3 puff pastry sheets, 10″x15″
(recipe above)	egg wash (egg yolk or egg white
8 peeled peach halves from	mixed with a small amount
coulis preparation	of water or milk)

1. Allow the puff pastry to warm for a few minutes before use.
2. Fill the pitted peach halves with the Frangipane.
3. For each, cut a base of dough about ¼-inch larger than the peach and a top about 1 inch larger than the peach. Brush the bases with egg wash.
4. Place a peach half on each base, filled side down, and then cover with the large piece of puff dough. Seal the "pie" with a round cutter, the same diameter as the peach, but do not cut through.
5. Trim off excess dough to ⅛ inch from the base of the peach.
6. Chill for 1 hour, then brush with egg wash and score the top in a fluted pattern.

Assembly

Preheat oven to 425 degrees. Bake the pithiviers for 8–12 minutes, or until the puff pastry is no longer translucent. Place on serving plate. Garnish with additional peach coulis and fresh basil. Serve warm with your favorite ice cream.

Recipe by Scott Goeringer

LA JUNTA

La Junta was *originally named Otero after Miguel Otero, who established the town in 1875 when the Santa Fe Railroad was built through the area. The name was changed to La Junta, which means "the junction" in Spanish, and refers to the joining of the Santa Fe Railway and the Kansas Pacific Railroad. Two places of local interest are the Koshare Indian Museum and Bent's Old Fort.*

Zip Code: 81050 **Population:** 7,568 **Elevation:** 4,052 feet

MEXICO CITY

1617 Raton Avenue
Phone: (719) 384-9818
Fax: None
E-mail: None
Website: None

Directions: Coming into La Junta on Highway 50 (1st Street in La Junta) from the east, go ¾ mile past the turnoff for Highway 350. Turn right onto Raton Avenue (one block past Colorado Avenue). Go 1.1 miles (16 blocks). The restaurant is on the left.

ESSENTIALS

Cuisine: Mexican
Hours: Mon.–Fri. 11 A.M.–1 P.M., Mon.–Thu. 5 P.M.–8 P.M., Fri.–Sat. 5 P.M.–8:30 P.M. Closed Sun.
Meals and Prices: Lunch $4–$5. Dinner $6.
Nonsmoking: All
Take-out: Yes
Alcohol: Full Bar
Credit Cards: No
Personal Check: In-state only with ID

Reservations: Recommended Fri. and Sat. night. Accepted otherwise.
Wheelchair Access: Yes

HISTORY AND BIOGRAPHY

Mexico City is in a building originally occupied by the Country Club Restaurant in the 1950s, where you could get a T-bone steak or filet mignon dinner for $2.50 and a shrimp cocktail or glass of wine for $.50. In the mid-1970s, El Cid's Mexican Restaurant replaced the Country Club, but it closed in the summer of 1977. Mona Munoz then opened Mexico City in November 1977. Mona had been working as a dishwasher and waitress in her parents' Mexican restaurant in La Junta, El Azteca, since 1976.

FOOD, SERVICE AND AMBIANCE

Mexico City's menu is 95% Mexican also offering burgers and fries. I went with the tamale, enchilada and chile relleno combination with vermicelli. The pork-filled tamale with corn meal coating had good texture: not too hard, not too soft. Goldilocks would have liked it. The chicken enchilada, though, had very little chicken. The chile relleno was the best of the three. A 6-inch-long chili pepper stuffed with cheddar cheese and a crisp deep-fried breading. The vermicelli was in a sauce containing tomato paste, onion, garlic and salt, with cheese, and was not overcooked. However, it had a lot of greasy oil because it was deep-fried in lard. Packaged chips with homemade salsa accompanied the meal. The salsa was a liquid tomato, onion and jalapeño combination.

For an appetizer, you can choose from an avocado dip or salad, nachos, quesadillas or the refried bean and cheese dip. Side dishes include beans, vermicelli, green chili, sopapillas and French fries. The lunch menu features combination and á la carte items such as tostados, tacos, burritos, menudo and posole. The same Mexican fare appears on the dinner menu with chicken flautas and hamburger steaks added.

My server took my food order and served my meal quickly. No music played in this restaurant, which is the only one located in a residential area in Otero County. The main, nonsmoking, dining room has a true Mexican presence with Spanish-arch doorways and entrances; chili peppers and Mexican pots painted on the walls; a string of real chili peppers, a Mexican rug and a miniature sombrero hanging on the wall; an adobe-style fireplace and a poster of a bullfight in Puerto Vallarta. Mona added a personal touch of her own to the faux brick back wall by mounting a stuffed marlin that she caught in Mazatlán. The smoking section to the side is sparsely decorated with only a Tecate rug. There is also a small bar in the back. Mexican is the predominant cuisine in La Junta and the one you should select in this part of the state.

NUTRITION AND SPECIAL REQUESTS

At Mexico City they deep-fry most items in canola oil. The vermicelli is deep-fried in lard. However, you can, and should, request they substitute oil for the lard. The beans are cooked in a pot, not fried. They have some healthful seafood specials like codfish and shrimp. Rice is not on the menu. They receive some special requests, which they will honor, if possible.

Vermicelli

SERVES 6

1 12-ounce package coiled vermicelli
oil for deep frying
1 onion, chopped in blender

1 tablespoon garlic powder
1 tablespoon salt
3 cups of water
1 15-ounce can of tomato sauce

1. Break the vermicelli coils and deep fry in oil until golden. Drain the oil.
2. Add the onion, garlic powder and salt to the vermicelli.
3. Add the water.
4. Simmer for 10 minutes
5. Add the tomato sauce and simmer for 15 minutes longer. Serve.

Recipe by: Mona Munoz

Beverage Recommendation: Dos Equis beer

✎ LAKE CITY ✎

LAKE CITY WAS *named for nearby Lake San Cristobal (Spanish for Saint Christopher), the second-largest natural lake in Colorado. With over seventy-five buildings from the late 1800s, it is Colorado's largest historic district—and the only town in Hinsdale, the least-populated county in Colorado.*

Zip Code: 81235 **Population:** 375 **Elevation:** 8,658 feet

FACING WEST

5200 Snowmass Road
Phone: (970) 944-0400
Fax: (970) 944-0402
E-mail: lisa@facingwestrestaurant.com
Website: www.lisa@facingwestrestaurant.com

Directions: From the post office and visitors center in Lake City, go 4.5 miles north on Highway 149. Turn right at the sign for Lake Fork Hunt and Fish Club and Facing West. Go over the bridge and follow the road for 0.2 mile to a "T" intersection. Turn left and go 0.1 mile. Turn right and go 0.1 mile up to the restaurant.

ESSENTIALS

Cuisine: Savory San Juan fare
Hours: Mother's Day to second Sunday in OCT: Tue.–Sat. 5 P.M.– 9 P.M., Sun. 10 A.M.–2 P.M. Closed Mon. Closed second Mon. in OCT to just before Mother's Day.
Meals and Prices: Dinner $18–28 (includes starch, vegetable and salad). Brunch $15 (champagne extra).
Nonsmoking: Smoking permitted only on deck

Take-out: Yes
Alcohol: Full bar
Credit Cards: MC, VI, AE
Personal Check: Yes, with ID
Reservations: Recommended
Wheelchair Access: Yes, by ramp, and includes deck and bathrooms
Other: Split plate charge $3. No separate checks. Available for private
parties, banquets, weddings and catering.

HISTORY AND BIOGRAPHY

Facing West was originally part of the V. C. Bar and Ranch, built in the
1940s. In 1979, the Lake Fork Hunting and Fishing Club became the
proprietor. They leased the building to several restaurateurs who operated restaurants over the next twenty years, including the Lake Fork
Restaurant and Nola's at Lake Fork, a Mexican bar. In spring 1999, Sam
and Lisa Bracken purchased the building, rebuilt the deck, carpeted,
added antler chandeliers and opened Facing West. Sam has been a cook
in the Denver metro area since 1987. He previously worked in the
kitchens of The Fort Restaurant in Morrison and Moon Dance,
Sostanza and Chives in Denver. Lisa has been waiting tables since 1988
at the Briarwood Inn in Golden, Colorado, where she met Sam, and at
Brasserie Z in Denver. Sam does the cooking at Facing West. Lisa manages the front, working as hostess, waitress and hospitality specialist.

FOOD, SERVICE AND AMBIENCE

I had a hard time deciding which entrée to select, but I finally chose the
headliner, the rosemary-crusted and house-aged prime rib of beef. This
was a succulent, grilled (although it tasted charbroiled), delicious piece
of meat with chopped leeks, some fat and a little gristle. An exceptional
beef needs no accompaniment, so I preferred the flavor of the prime rib
without the creamy horseradish on the side. The dish came with garlic-
herb mashed potatoes with lumps, skins and chives. The vegetable of
the moment was sweet and crunchy glazed carrots cut like fries with
ridges. There was a bite to their texture. The spinach salad with raspberry vinaigrette was served on a 5-inch-diameter plate with bacon bits,

julienne-sliced carrots, jicama and mandarin oranges on the side. The dressings and sauces are all homemade. A miniature loaf of warm bread completed my meal.

For starters, you can order smoked pork ribs with plum barbecue sauce, Rocky Mountain smoked trout spread, or mussels Sarlo. Side dishes of pommes frites, Gorgonzola and sweet basil grits and sun-dried-tomato polenta are available. The list of dinners includes a bit of every-thing: steaks, seafood, Colorado lamb, rabbit, elk and Cornish game hen. Highlights of this list include filet Wellington with a brandy-cream sauce, Rocky Mountain rainbow trout in a piñon-nut crust with a spicy ancho-chili tartar sauce, rabbit served with wild mushrooms and pearl onions and elk served with the house savory blueberry sauce. For dessert, you can go light or heavy with a cheese and fresh fruit plate, peaches flambé prepared tableside, a warm brownie sundae, triple crème brûlée or a flourless chocolate torte.

Highlights of the Sunday brunch are an omelet station with a vari-ety of ingredients, a carving station with hand-carved house-smoked brisket and ham, traditional brunch items, gravlax and desserts.

Lisa, the host, was extremely polite and courteous and worked with a smile. She knows people and hospitality. My server, a well-mannered gentleman, was attentive and well-spoken even with a Czech accent. A medley of musical tunes filled the air during my visit, from light jazz with trumpets and horns to orchestra and violin music. Facing West presents live piano jazz and acoustic guitar entertainment. They also have some creative specials like the "Seafood Experience" and wine dinners. Call or check their website in advance for dates and times.

This is a long, narrow restaurant with a wall of windows facing west (hence the restaurant's name). Most of the tables are next to the window. From here, or from the redwood deck, you get a strikingly picturesque view of the valley below and the San Juan Mountains beyond. This vista provides more than ample ambience. The few paintings on display show brown trout and a Spanish mission house with vegas. The setting is ele-gant, with a piano at one end of the dining room, a wood-burning stove with a circular brick base at the opposite end and tables in between trimmed with fresh flowers and white linen. Facing West has superb cui-sine, warm, friendly people and one of the best panoramas in Colorado.

NUTRITION AND SPECIAL REQUESTS

Facing West will accommodate any special request within reason and within its power. For example, there is a special pasta dish without garlic for patrons allergic to garlic. The dinner menu has limited choices for vegetarians: baked Brie and tomato bruschetta appetizers and grilled vegetable Napoleon. Sunday brunch offers more for vegetarians, including omelets, malted waffles, French toast, fresh vegetables, cheeses, salads, fresh fruits and breads and pastries.

Blue Cheese and Artichoke Grits

MAKES 1½ QUARTS

3 cups milk	½ cup whipping cream
2 cloves garlic, minced	3 large eggs, lightly beaten
1 teaspoon salt	1 14-ounce can artichoke hearts,
1 cup quick-cooking grits	drained and chopped
(not instant!)	2 teaspoons fresh chopped basil
1 cup crumbled blue cheese	¼ teaspoon pepper
⅓ cup butter	

1. Bring milk, garlic and salt to a boil in a medium pot.
2. Lower heat. Gradually stir in grits. Cover and adjust heat to a simmer. Stir occasionally for 10 minutes.* Meanwhile, preheat oven to 325 degrees.
3. Stir in cheese and butter until melted.
4. Stir in whipped cream and rest of ingredients.
5. Pour into lightly greased 1½-quart soufflé dish or individual ramekins.
6. Bake in preheated oven for 1 hour, 10 minutes. Makes 1½ quarts.

*NOTE: *To be safe, rather than covering and reducing heat, stirring occasionally, reduce heat and leave the pot uncovered, then stir constantly so that there is no sticking.*

Recipe by Sam Bracken

❧ LEADVILLE ☙

WHEN SILVER WAS *first struck in Leadville in 1876, the town was called by many names: Agassiz, Boughtown, Carbonate, Cloud City, Harrison and Slabtown. The name Leadville was chosen for the large amount of argentiferous lead ores in the area. In addition to being the "Silver Capital of the World" at one time ($15 million in silver was extracted from the area in 1880, when the town was the second-largest in Colorado with a population of 30,000), gold, lead, zinc, copper and molybdenum deposits have also been mined over the past 120 years.*

Leadville is a historical treasure chest: The Healy House and Dexter Cabin, two original homes restored to nineteenth-century décor and turned into a museum; the Tabor Opera House; the Heritage Museum and Gallery, which includes a diorama of the town's mining history and a Styrofoam replica of the 1896 Ice Palace; and the National Mining Hall of Fame and Museum, which has exhibits dealing with the mining heritage here and throughout the nation, are all found within the town's rambling borders. At 10,152 feet elevation, Leadville is the highest incorporated city in North America. It is a National Historic Landmark District with seventy square blocks of Victorian architecture and a twenty-square-mile mining district.

Zip Code: 80461 **Population:** 2,821 **Elevation:** 10,152 feet

TENNESSEE PASS COOKHOUSE

Ski Cooper at the top of Tennessee Pass
Phone: (719) 486-1850
Fax: None
E-mail and website: www.tennesseepass.com

Directions: *From the Front Range,* take exit 195 (past Frisco and just before Copper Mountain) from I-70 and go south on Highway 91 (over Fremont

Pass) for 22½ miles. Turn right onto Highway 24 and go 9 miles to the Ski Cooper ski area at the top of Tennessee Pass. Turn right and go ½ mile to the Piney Creek Nordic Center. It is the small brown building on the right side of the parking area. This is where you will meet your guide for the 1-mile hike to the restaurant. Allow ½ to ¾ hour for the hike.

From Vail and other towns on the Western Slope, take exit 171 (between Avon and Vail) from I-70 and head south (toward Minturn) on Highway 24. Go 22½ miles to the Ski Cooper ski area and turn left. Go ½ mile to the Piney Creek Nordic Center. Proceed as directed above.

From Leadville, take Highway 24 north out of town and go 9 miles to the Ski Cooper ski area at the top of Tennessee Pass. Turn right and go ½ mile to the Piney Creek Nordic Center. Proceed as directed above.

ESSENTIALS

Cuisine: High-country gourmet

Hours: Thanksgiving to end of APR: Seven nights, meet at Nordic Center at 5:30 P.M. End of JUN through SEP: Thu.–Sun., meet at Nordic Center at 6:30 P.M., Sat.–Sun. 12 noon–1:30 P.M.

Meals and Prices: Lunch $10–$15. Dinner—four-course meal: $55 in winter, $50 in summer.

Nonsmoking: Smoking permitted only on deck

Take-out: No

Alcohol: Beer and wine

Credit Cards: MC, VI

Personal Check: Yes

Reservations: REQUIRED for dinner. Suggested for lunch.

Wheelchair Access: Yes. They will take guests to the restaurant by jeep or snowmobile.

Other: This restaurant is accessible by foot during summer and by snowshoes or cross-country skis during winter. Guests who are unable or unwilling to make the journey on their own can request to be driven to the restaurant by snowmobile or jeep. All dinner entrées must be ordered when you make your reservation. Plan on spending 3–4 hours for dinner. Available for private parties or catering.

HISTORY AND BIOGRAPHY

The Tennessee Pass Cookhouse takes the prize for most "off-the-beaten-path" restaurant in this guide. Not only do you have to venture to the top of one of Colorado's 10,000-foot passes, but you also have to hike about a mile with a 300-foot elevation gain.

The restaurant itself is in a circular, domed building called a yurt and modeled after the Mongolian gair. The yurt sits on a thirty-foot-diameter deck. The deck and yurt were built by owners Ryer Triezenberg and Ty Hall in 1995; the restaurant opened for business in December 1995. Ryer has been working in restaurants since 1981. He was a breakfast chef at the Hotel Lenado Bed & Breakfast in Aspen, Colorado, and then assistant manager at the Pine Creek Cookhouse in Ashcroft from 1987 to 1995. Ryer manages and cooks at the restaurant. His partner, Ty Hall, runs the Piney Creek Nordic Center, where you start your journey to the restaurant, and helps serve at the Cookhouse. Ron Strong assists in the kitchen and has been at the Cookhouse since 1999. He started in the restaurant business in 1987 and previously worked for Creative Caterers in Aspen.

FOOD, SERVICE AND AMBIENCE

I ventured to the Tennessee Pass Cookhouse with about twenty other diners during a spring snowstorm. The one-mile hike to the yurt was on a snow-packed, wide trail. Our return trip was through five or six inches of newly fallen snow.

Dinner at the Cookhouse was an experience in contrasting yet compatible tastes. Chef Ryer's first course was an appetizer plate featuring wild boar sausage with cranberries, a unique mixture combining spices and fruit; Mrs. Dog's sweet, hot mustard, a palatable contradiction in itself; grilled portobello mushrooms offset by fresh strawberries, grapes and pineapples; and pizza topped with goat cheese, pesto, yellow squash and roasted red peppers. The entire plate was sprinkled with fresh chopped basil.

The second course, curry-carrot soup with crumpled rosemary in the middle, continued the trend of mixing spicy with mild—in this case, spicy curry with mild carrot and just a touch of rosemary to make it savory and interesting. The soup was creamy with a grainy consistency.

The green leaf salad came with raspberry vinaigrette and was served with soft and chewy dark Bavarian rolls straight out of the oven. For my entrée, I chose the elk, eight medium-rare, mouth-watering, soft-as-silk medallions with the sharp edge of sage discriminating against the fruity taste of wild blueberries. The meat was accompanied by yams mixed with red potatoes, softened by butter and cream and seasoned with garlic, sage, rosemary, basil, oregano and thyme. A side of mixed sautéed vegetables—snow peas, broccoli and carrots completed the plate.

The other entrées that evening were rack of lamb with rosemary-pistachio pesto, tangerine-teriyaki salmon and a quarter-chicken with wild mushrooms.

Service was pleasant and well-organized. Instrumental jazz music played while we watched the snow fall. In better weather, I was told, I would be able to see Mt. Elbert, Mt. Massive and Mt. Holy Cross from the yurt. On either side of the entrance was a Tibetan greeting, mantras on silk hangings. The yurt was heated by a wood-burning stove. Candles and dried mountain flowers had been placed at each table. The window openings were covered by a wooden trellis and plastic. The wood-framed dome has narrow wood beams stretching from the top of the circular wall to the six-foot-diameter oval glass top in the center, covered with snow. The yurt dining room was embellished with Tibetan rugs; colorful paintings of cross-country skiers, snow cabins, Mongolian gairs and Teng Boche Monastery near Mt. Everest; a photo of Ski Cooper circa 1948; homemade log furniture and a modern piece of art depicting a storm approaching over the mountains. The Tennessee Pass Cookhouse is very cozy and very warm when it is very snowy outside. It is a unique dining experience in Colorado that should not be missed.

NUTRITION AND SPECIAL REQUESTS

The Tennessee Pass Cookhouse does offer vegetarian specials like grilled tofu and vegetarian lasagna. They will also make something special if requested in advance.

Grilled Elk Tenderloin with Wild Blueberry–Sage Sauce

This recipe may also be prepared with red deer in place of the elk.

2 pounds elk tenderloin
½ cup olive oil
1 teaspoon fresh ground cumin
1 teaspoon fresh ground pepper
1 teaspoon garlic powder

½ teaspoon salt
1 tablespoon soy sauce
Wild Blueberry–Sage Sauce
  (recipe follows)

1. Combine olive oil, spices, salt and soy sauce to make marinade. Pour over tenderloin and let marinate a minimum of 2 hours.
2. Preheat grill. Remove meat from marinade. Cook on heated grill until done to taste (the Cookhouse serves it medium-rare), then slice into ¼-inch-thick medallions and arrange in fan shape on each of 4 plates.
3. Drizzle Blueberry Sage Sauce over half of each portion. Serve.

Wild Blueberry–Sage Sauce

3 cups wild blueberries
3 cups port wine
¼ cup chopped fresh sage

3 tablespoons freshly ground,
  roasted peppercorns

Put blueberries in saucepan and cover with port wine. Bring to a simmer. Add sage and pepper. Continue to simmer ½ to 1 hour, until reduced.

Recipe by Ryer Triezenberg

Wine Recommendation: Benzinger Pinot Noir

❧ LOUISVILLE ❧

LOUISVILLE WAS NAMED *after Louis Nawatny, who led the first coal-boring expedition after C. C. Welsh discovered coal in the area in 1877. Nawatny also owned the land on which the original settlement was located and filed the town plat in 1878.*

Zip Code: 80027 **Population:** 18,937 **Elevation:** 5,337 feet

KAREN'S COUNTRY KITCHEN

700 Main Street
Phone: (303) 666-8020
Fax: (303) 666-4908
E-mail: None
Website: None

Directions: Take the Broomfield/Lafayette exit from the Denver-Boulder Turnpike (Highway 36) and go north 4 miles on Wadsworth Parkway (Highway 287). Turn left onto Highway 42. Go 2¼ miles and turn left onto Pine Street. Go ¼ mile. The restaurant is on the right at the corner of Pine and Main Streets.

ESSENTIALS

Cuisine: Healthful country
Hours: Mon.–Fri. 6:30 A.M.–2:30 P.M., Sat.–Sun. 7:30 A.M.–2:30 P.M.
Meals and Prices: Breakfast $5–$9. Lunch $5–$6.
Nonsmoking: All
Take-out: Yes
Alcohol: Full bar
Credit Cards: MC, VI, AE, DS
Personal Check: Yes, with ID
Reservations: Not accepted
Wheelchair Access: Yes, through a side entrance

Other: Children's menu. Homestyle bakery and gift shop on premises. Service charge of 15% added to parties of six or more. Available for outside catering.

HISTORY AND BIOGRAPHY

Karen's Country Kitchen occupies two buildings, dating back to the 1890s, and is listed on the National Historic Register. The original shop on the corner was Louisville's first bank. In June 1974, Karen Mulholland started a gift shop and bakery on the site and was soon serving sandwiches for lunch. When waiting lines started to form for the bakery's six small tables, she found old doors on her father's farm that could double as tables for the restaurant and as counters for jewelry displays. In 1979, Karen expanded into Selma's Bakery shop next door, a building that started as the town's first post office. The two structures still stand much as they were when originally built a century ago.

In December 1995, Buddy and Amy Chick purchased the restaurant from Karen. They sold the restaurant in August 2001 to Jackson Loos (pronounced "Lows") and Mark Bickler. Jackson is a graduate of the California Culinary Academy in San Francisco and has been in the restaurant business since 1989. He is a former instructor at Westlake Culinary Institute in Los Angeles and cooked at the Saddlepeak Lodge in Malibu, California, before coming to Colorado in 1995. He was executive chef for two years at the Redfish New Orleans Brewhouse in Boulder, Colorado, and executive chef at Panzano in the Hotel Monoco in Denver for two years. Before taking over Karen's, he was part owner and executive chef of Café Louis in Boulder. Mark has owned and managed restaurants in Boulder since 1980. He currently owns the Boulder Café.

FOOD, SERVICE AND AMBIENCE

Linda and two friends joined me for one of Karen's fabulous Sunday breakfasts. A combination of natural talent, experience, qualified people, the freshest ingredients available, prize-winning recipes and an on-site bakery where all baked goods are made from scratch are a few of the reasons why Karen's has become one of the most popular dining spots in the Denver-Boulder area, especially for breakfast.

I couldn't remember when, if ever, I had ordered steak and eggs for breakfast, so I chose the Country Special—a hearty, half-inch-thick, lean, tasty, charbroiled sirloin with hash browns, eggs and Texas toast. Linda had the Jogger—fresh, homemade, crunchy granola topped with yogurt and served with thick, whole-wheat, homemade bread. Our friend Sandi selected the heavenly cheese crêpes filled with sour cream and cream cheese whipped together and topped with strawberry preserves. Our friend Ron elected to go with Jay's Special (named after Karen's produce man)—a delectable "scramlette" with fresh, crunchy broccoli, sautéed spinach, onions and mushrooms, cheddar cheese and sour cream. We all found our meals to be delicious and well-prepared with the freshest ingredients.

The scramlettes—scrambled eggs with your choice of ingredients like spinach, artichoke hearts, avocado, chorizo, turkey and herbed or jalapeño cheese—are a highlight of the breakfast menu. You can also order a country breakfast, with thick-sliced bacon, grilled ham steak, country link sausages, grilled turkey breast, or charbroiled turkey sausage; or choose between breakfast sandwiches, French toast made with their own bread, buttermilk pancakes with just the perfect amount of whole wheat flour—enough for flavor but not so much as to make them heavy, corned beef hash and a breakfast burrito.

Homemade freshness doesn't stop with breakfast. Lunch offers appetizers of baked artichoke dip, chicken fingers and thin onion rings; charbroiled chicken Caesar salad; fresh fruit plate; homemade French onion soup; a veggie club or veggie burger; deli-style sandwiches on homemade breads with homemade side salads (potato, pasta or coleslaw) and burgers.

We waited 15–20 minutes to get a table and about a half hour to get our meals after ordering. This is a very popular place, so expect to wait on weekends—it's well worth it. Our server and all the other servers were very busy. They had no time for chit-chat but performed their jobs effectively and efficiently. This quaint restaurant features several small rooms and little booths with picnic tables, trellis dividers and roofs, hanging baskets, minute pictures of columbines and roses, remnant-cloth napkins, wreaths of dried leaves and dried chili peppers, a brass figure full of holes, stuffed animals and wood carvings. We dined in a cozy booth, one of many, next to a gazebo with a single table and a frosted-glass stencil of an antique car. Further embellishing this charming décor are Victorian-period paintings, a picture of a Parisian store front, tin walls with three-dimensional flower patterns and a small bar (the original store had all tin walls and ceilings). When you dine at Karen's, you'll feel like you stepped back in time to a simpler era, but the food and service are some of the best that you'll find in any current-day country restaurant.

NUTRITION AND SPECIAL REQUESTS

Karen's receives many special requests and will accommodate them within reason. The menu notes "happy heart" substitutions. Jay's special scramble, for example, can be made with egg substitute, yogurt in place of the sour cream and easy on the cheese. Egg whites and dry toast are a couple of other options.

Cheese Crêpes

SERVES 6

Batter

2 egg yolks	½ cup flour
⅔ cup skim milk	6 egg whites

Combine all crêpe ingredients in mixing bowl. Fold batter until well mixed. Let sit for 10 minutes.

Filling

1 cup cream cheese	¼ cup ricotta cheese
1 cup sour cream	1 tablespoon sugar

Combine all filling ingredients in mixing bowl and fold until well mixed.

Topping

2 cups fresh or frozen berries of your choice	¼ cup sugar

Heat berries with sugar in small pan until topping thickens.

Assembly

1. Heat a crêpe pan or similar shallow saucepan over medium heat. Add a bit of butter and swirl it around the pan to melt. Pour in a small amount of batter (about ¼ cup) and tilt the pan to disperse the batter evenly. Cook until the crêpe is golden brown. To remove, tip pan upside-down over a plate. Repeat with remaining batter. Separate cooked crêpes with paper or cloth toweling to keep them from sticking together. Makes 12 crêpes.
2. Once all crêpes have been cooked, spread each with a portion of the cheese filling and roll up, leaving ends open.
3. Add a little clarified butter to a sauté pan (just enough to coat). Sear crêpes in hot pan.
4. Remove to plate and spoon some topping over crêpes. Serve hot.

Recipe by Jackson Loos

Beverage Recommendation: Mimosa

❧ LYONS ☙

LYONS WAS NAMED *after Mrs. Carrie Lyons, pioneer editor of the weekly* Lyons News, *published in 1890–1891. The Lyons family was also instrumental in quarrying the superior sandstone used in many buildings at the University of Colorado campus. Geographically, Lyons is the eastern gateway to the Rocky Mountains, with Highways 7 and 36 leading west to Estes Park and Rocky Mountain National Park.*

Zip Code: 80540 **Population:** 1,585 **Elevation:** 5,360 feet

OSKAR BLUES

303 Main Street
Phone: (303) 823-6685

Fax: (303) 823-3033
E-mail: dale@oskarblues.com
Website: www.oskarblues.com
Directions: From Boulder, go north on Highway 36 for 14 miles. Turn left at the signal where the road comes to a "T" with Highway 66. You will still be on Highway 36. Go 1.4 miles to where the road divides, becomes one-way and bends to the left. From this point, the restaurant is one block down on the left.

ESSENTIALS

Cuisine: Cajun
Hours: Seven days 11 A.M.–10 P.M.
Meals and Prices: Lunch and dinner $6–$18 (soup and salad extra).
Nonsmoking: Yes
Take-out: Yes
Alcohol: Full bar
Credit Cards: All five
Personal Check: Local only with ID
Reservations: Accepted
Wheelchair Access: No
Other: Local and national blues and jazz acts Fri. and Sat. evenings; jam sessions on Tue., Wed. and Thu.

HISTORY AND BIOGRAPHY

Oskar Blues, Lyon's oldest (actually first and only) brew pub, was built in 1995 but remained vacant until April 1997, when Dale Katechis ("Ka-téch-is"), remodeled, added equipment and opened the restaurant. The downstairs, where live jazz is played Tuesday through Sunday, was completed in June 1998. The name Oskar Blues combines the names of two of Dale's friends who he met on a bicycle tour. Oskar is from Sweden; Blue (a nickname) is from Australia. Dale thought, correctly, it would be a good name for a Cajun blues brew pub. He also owns the Redfish New Orleans Brewhouse in Boulder, Colorado.

Dale grew up in the restaurant business, helping in his mother's restaurant and doing catering work in Florence, Alabama. He bartended, waited tables and worked in kitchens before coming to

Colorado in 1993. He managed the Old Chicago Restaurant in Boulder and helped to open the chain's restaurant in Longmont. His brother, Chris, came to Colorado in April 2001 to be chef at Oskar Blues. He has been managing and cooking in restaurants in Huntsville, Alabama, since 1985.

FOOD, SERVICE AND AMBIENCE

Oskar Blues specializes in dishes "from da Bayou." Submitted for your approval are red beans and rice, blackened redfish, shrimp Creole, jambalaya, shrimp étouffée, Cajun crawfish fettuccine, seafood gumbo, crab cakes and catfish. I went with the last, ordering the platter. The farm-raised catfish filets were bite-sized, lightly breaded, fried and both crunchy and meaty. The coleslaw had big and small pieces of cabbage with carrot and was not the sweet variety. The fries were thin but good, and the spicy dipping sauce was not hot but had a tasty tang.

For an appetizer, try Oskar's artichoke and spinach dip, onion rings, buffalo wings, or Texas toothpicks (thin-cut onions and jalapeño peppers, lightly battered and seasoned with cayenne and black peppers). The salad selection includes Caesar, spinach and grilled-chicken chef's. Among the signature sandwiches are turkey Reuben, portobello mushroom and jerk-seasoned chicken breast. There are a half-dozen burgers to choose from, along with seared pork chops, baby-back ribs, portobello cavatappi (a short spiral pasta) and filet mignon. There's also pizza with andouille sausage, crawfish, shrimp and a variety of more traditional toppings. Headlining their list of homemade desserts is Reverend Sandi's stout cake, a coffee and spice cake made with their own brewed stout. Other delectables are the flourless chocolate walnut truffle torte, pecan pie and strawberry-rhubarb cobbler. The Oskar Blues brewery list completes the menu.

This is a casual place, and the servers were fittingly dressed in T-shirts. My server operated at varying speeds: fast with the water, slow returning to take my order, quick with the food, delayed in picking up my credit card with the check. The music playing in the dining room was, as you'd expect, blues. The dining area is elaborately decorated with photographs, many of them autographed, of famous musicians—Elvis, Janis Joplin and Jimi Hendrix, to name a few. At the entrance to the dining room is a 3-D figure of Elvis Presley. One side of the divided dining room leads to balcony dining. There is a bar upstairs in the restaurant and another downstairs with a stage and dance floor.

NUTRITION AND SPECIAL REQUESTS

Oskar Blues can accommodate special requests if they are not extremely busy. They have vegetarian items offered on the menu, and anything can be special-ordered.

Jambalaya

SERVES 4–6

2 tablespoons butter	8 cups chicken stock
1 cup diced yellow onion	2 tablespoons kosher salt
1 cup diced celery	2 tablespoons white pepper
¾ cup diced green bell pepper	2 tablespoons dry mustard
1 teaspoon minced garlic	1 tablespoon plus 1 teaspoon
2 andouille sausage links, chopped	cayenne
1 cup pulled, cooked chicken meat	2 tablespoons filét powder
1 tablespoon jambalaya seasoning	1 tablespoon ground cumin
4 cups converted rice	1 tablespoon black pepper
4 bay leaves	1 tablespoon fresh thyme

1. Melt butter in large pot over medium heat and sauté yellow onion, celery, bell pepper and garlic until translucent.
2. Add the andouille sausage, chicken and jambalaya seasoning. Sauté for an additional 5 minutes.
3. Add rice and stir well.
4. Add bay leaves and stock. Raise flame to high and bring to a boil. Add the salt and spices. Reduce heat to low, cover and allow to simmer for 20–25 minutes. Serve.

Recipe by Shirley "Ya Ya"* Katechis

Wine Recommendation: Heritage Shiraz, Australian

Beer Recommendation: Dale's Pale Ale, a full-bodied, highly hopped pale ale from Oskar Blues

---

*Greek for "Granny"

～ MANITOU SPRINGS ～

FOUNDED BY *Dr. William Bell, an English physician, Manitou Springs was originally called Villa La Font, or Fountain Village. The town was later renamed Manitou, an Algonquin Indian name meaning "spirit." In 1935 the name was changed to Manitou Springs in reference to the area's numerous natural mineral springs. Today, the town of Manitou Springs is on the National Historic District Register.*

Zip Code: 80829 **Population:** 4,980 **Elevation:** 6,320 feet

THE CLIFF HOUSE DINING ROOM

306 Cañon Avenue
Phone: (888) 212-7000 or (719) 785-2415
Fax: (719) 685-3913
E-mail: information@thecliffhouse.com
Website: www.thecliffhouse.com

Directions: Take exit 141 from I-25 in Colorado Springs and head west on Highway 24. Go 4 miles and take the Manitou Springs exit for Manitou Avenue. At the end of the exit, go right (continuing west) onto Manitou Avenue. Go 1.1 miles. Make a sharp right turn onto Cañon Avenue. There is a clock tower and church on the far right corner. The restaurant is 1½ blocks down on the right where they have valet parking. Public parking for $2 is 1 block down (from Manitou Avenue) on the left.

ESSENTIALS

Cuisine: New American
Hours: Seven days, breakfast 6:30 A.M.–9 A.M., lunch 10:30 A.M.–2:30 P.M., dinner 5:30 P.M.–9 P.M.
Meals and Prices: Breakfast $7–$16. Lunch $8–$22. Dinner $18–$36 (soup and salad extra).
Nonsmoking: Permitted only on verandah

Take-out: Yes
Alcohol: Full bar
Credit Cards: MC, VI, AE, DC
Personal Check: In-state with ID
Reservations: Highly recommended
Wheelchair Access: Yes

HISTORY AND BIOGRAPHY

The Cliff House, originally established as The Inn in 1873, was a hotel along the stagecoach line to Leadville, Colorado. When Edward E. Nichols purchased the property in 1876, he changed the name to The Cliff House. The Nichols family operated the hotel for the next seventy-two years, enlarging the hotel to be an elegant year-around resort with over 200 rooms. During that time, The Cliff House entertained many famous guests including Thomas Edison, Henry Ford, Harvey Firestone, P. T. Barnum, F. W. Woolworth and Teddy Roosevelt. After the Nichols family sold the hotel in 1948, The Cliff House went through many owners and changes. It became an apartment house, served as quarters for the military in the late 1950s and 1960s and had one wing torn down to make room for a parking lot. Shortly after James S. Morley purchased the Inn and Restaurant in 1979, the property suffered a fire in 1982. The Cliff House stood vacant until a $10 million renovation project was started in 1997. The Cliff House with the dining room reopened in July 1999.

Food and beverage director Julius R. Watson has been at The Cliff House since it reopened. He is one of four certified sommeliers at the restaurant. He has been in the restaurant business since 1981 and previously worked at a four-star country club in Joplin, Missouri, and the Broadmoor Hotel and Corbett's Restaurant in Colorado Springs. Assistant director of food and beverage Wade Sawaya also came to the Cliff House in July 1999 after working at the Sunbird Restaurant and Peterson Air Force Base in Colorado Springs. He started in the restaurant business in 1986 in Yuba City, California, and came to Colorado in 1992. Chef Jordan Wagman started at The Cliff House in July 2000. He is a 1995 graduate of the Art Institute of Fort Lauderdale, Florida, and has cooked at restaurants in Toronto, Canada, and Newport Beach, California.

The Cliff House received the prestigious Wine Spectator Award of Excellence in 2000 and 2001.

FOOD, SERVICE AND AMBIENCE

Our dinners began with the "Chef's Welcome," consisting of a shiitake mushroom with fresh basil and a sherry-basil vinaigrette. It was a tasty couple of morsels to awaken the taste buds. I order the wilted baby spinach salad, a mound of wilted spinach with crispy and flavorful pancetta bits and three tomato slices on the side. The salad was sweetened by three dollops of ricotta cheese, sweet onion and cracked pepper–maple syrup dressing. Yum!

For my entrée, I chose the blue corn-crusted ruby trout, a very flavorsome dish sweetened by roasted sweet-corn relish, made spicy with sun-dried-pepper aioli and given a crunch from toasted pepitas. Avocado-cilantro butter enhanced the taste even further. French-style green beans were served on the side. Linda's selection was the vegetarian dish, grilled summer vegetables. The portobello mushroom was, she said, "the best" she had ever tasted. It was smooth, mild, tender and sweet with a velvet texture. The accompanying vegetables were a seasoned half-slice of carrot with top intact, red pepper, yellow squash, corn, smoked tomatoes and bean sprouts. The dish also came with wild-mushroom risotto and strong-tasting, pilsner-battered white onion rings.

Our friend Elaine elected to go with the pan-roasted Atlantic salmon. The herb–goat cheese went marvelously with the salmon. Cracked pepper–balsamic strawberries and tangerine aioli also augmented the flavors. We all agreed that dining at The Cliff House was a treat for the taste buds!

For a tempting appetizer, you might try the pan-blackened diver scallops, pepper-seared foie gras, or the grilled Maine lobster medallions. The salad choices included hearts of romaine Caesar, butterfly lettuce and ruby red grapefruit with honey–poppy seed dressing and heirloom tomato with toasted pine nuts in an aged balsamic vinegar. Some of the other savory dinner entrées were charred, marinated Black Angus tenderloin, coarse Dijon-crusted lamb rack, jumbo lump blue crab cakes and garlic-rubbed veal chop. The decadent desserts featured warm apple-walnut pie, chocolate icebox cake with Grand Marnier strawberries, orange tea crème brûlée and triple-chocolate mousse cake.

For breakfast, The Cliff House serves a continental buffet offering cereals, granola, yogurt, fresh fruit, pastries, juice and coffee. You can also order an egg specialty or house specialties like old-fashioned buttermilk pancakes with caramel apples and real Vermont maple syrup, or smoked salmon on grilled flatbread.

Interesting lunch starters include spicy peanut chicken with lettuce, cucumbers and a sweet chili ponzu dipping sauce; baby spinach–artichoke fondue, and caramelized five-onion soup. Highlights among the sandwiches and entrées are smoked turkey tortilla wrap, buffalo burger, grilled pastrami, house-smoked chicken fettuccine, wild mushroom fusilli and cashew beef tips.

Service was exceptional, provided by sharp-looking, well-dressed servers wearing black shirts with textured olive-green vests and gold-and-black ties. Expert service means not only being taken care of by very attentive people, but by people who know how to be attentive at the right moments. Such was the case at The Cliff House. From the four sommeliers the restaurant furnishes for your wine selection to the bus service removing plates and replacing silverware, the service is superb.

We all sat comfortably in our shoulder-high chairs with arm rests as we listened to relaxing classical piano music. The very elegant, Victorian-style dining room is augmented with stained-glass windows, copper-and-glass chandeliers, a red-rock fireplace with a big wreath, a wine cabinet and landscape oil paintings. Outside dining is provided on the verandah in front of the hotel. The solarium, a small private dining room between the main dining room and verandah, seats twelve guests and contains two wine cabinets with glass doors inset in the wall. Once lost and forgotten, this charmingly refined and resurrected structure should be appreciated and experienced by all.

NUTRITION AND SPECIAL REQUESTS

Servers and chefs will work with customers' dietary needs. The restaurant will cater to vegetarians and create new dishes when necessary.

Cranberry-Glazed Pork Tenderloin with Shallot Confit and Potato Gnocchi

SERVES 8

2 pounds russet potatoes
2 pounds all-purpose flour
3 ounces Parmesan cheese
2 eggs
salt and pepper
10 shallots, peeled

1 cup canola oil, divided
your favorite fresh herbs
2 pounds pork tenderloin
6 ounces dried cranberries
2 ounces good cognac

Gnocchi

1. Boil potatoes in salted water until tender. Remove and cool. Peel or rub off skins.
2. When potatoes have cooled, mash by hand and incorporate flour, Parmesan cheese, eggs and salt and pepper to taste.
3. Transfer mixture from bowl onto a flat work surface. Knead just until mixture comes together. Be careful not to overwork the dough or it will become tough.
4. Let dough rest for 10 minutes. Pinch off little pieces from dough and form into small balls. Cook in salted boiling water. When the gnocchi rise to the top, they are done and ready. Drain.

Shallots

Preheat oven to 300 degrees. Combine 10 whole shallots, canola oil (reserve 1 tablespoon canola oil for the pork) and your favorite fresh herbs in an ovenproof pan and bake until fork-tender, about 15–20 minutes.

Pork and Cranberry Glaze

1. Ask your butcher to remove all of the silver skin from the pork. Place on a plate and generously season with salt and pepper.
2. In a heated ovenproof skillet, add the reserved 1 tablespoon of canola oil and sauté pork until golden brown. Finish in 350-degree oven until internal temperature reads 160 degrees.

3. Take the pork from the skillet and let rest for 10–15 minutes. Meanwhile, put the cranberries and cognac into the skillet (be careful not to have this over an open flame, as the cognac will flame) and cook over medium-high heat until cognac is reduced by half.

Presentation

Place the gnocchi and shallots on the bottom of a serving platter. Thinly slice the pork and present around the plate. Drizzle the cranberry glaze over the pork and garnish with the fresh herbs used in the shallot preparation. Serve.

Recipe by Jordan Wagman

Wine Recommendations: Camelot Vineyards Pinot Noir 1997 or
Hartford Russian River Valley Zinfandel 1997

⚘ MORRISON ⚘

MORRISON WAS NAMED *after pioneer George Morrison, who founded the town in 1859. Located at the base of the foothills just west of Denver, Morrison is best known for the Red Rocks Park Amphitheater.*

Zip Code: 80465 **Population:** 430 **Elevation:** 5,800 feet

DREAM CAFÉ

119 Morrison Road
Phone: (303) 697-1280
Fax, e-mail and website: None

Directions: Take exit 270 from I-70 and go south on C-470 for 4 miles. Take the Morrison Road exit. Turn right (west) at the end of the exit and go ½ mile. The restaurant is on the right on the corner of Morrison Road, 1 block before the traffic signal.

Cuisine: New American

Hours: Sat.–Sun. 8 A.M.–12 P.M., Tue.–Sun. 11 A.M.–3 P.M., Thu.– Sat. 5 P.M.–9 P.M. Closed Mon.

Meals and Prices: Breakfast $5–$7. Lunch $5–$8. Dinner $13–$18 (includes salad).

Nonsmoking: All

Take-out: Yes

Alcohol: Beer and wine

Credit Cards: MC, VI, AE

Personal Check: Yes, with ID

Reservations: Recommended for dinner and for parties of six or more for breakfast or lunch

Wheelchair Access: Yes, including bathrooms. There is an outside ramp to the restaurant.

Other: Available for private parties and special functions, Mon.–Wed. evening by reservation. Catering available.

HISTORY AND BIOGRAPHY

Dream Café, which opened in 1996, was originally a house built in 1871. Owner and manager Mossimo Gigli took over Dream Café in October 2000. He hails from a restaurant family in Naples, Italy, and has been in the restaurant business since 1982. He came to the United States in 1989 via London and Holland. From 1993 to 2000 he owned Geppetto's Restaurant in Littleton, Colorado. Chefs Donna Deneke and Jim Carlson are both graduates of the Colorado Institute of Art Culinary School. Donna has been in the restaurant business since 1995. She previously worked as a chef for 3½ years at the Denver Athletic Club and did some catering. Jim has been cooking professionally since 1996.

FOOD, SERVICE AND AMBIENCE

Dream Café rotates fifty dinner entrées weekly on its menu, serving a half-dozen different ones each week. Linda and I were here on St. Patrick's Day with our Greek friend, Elaine, and seven of her friends. The ten of us tried all but one of the entrées, including all of the Thai stir-fry dishes, corned beef and cabbage, stuffed veal rotalo and café salmon Oscar. The crab cakes appetizer with cherry tomatoes and creamy lemon dill sauce proved very tasty. I found the white cheddar–broccoli soup to be thin, but flavorsome, with small pieces of broccoli. All entrées are served with rustic bread and salad with homemade dressings. What we liked best about the food were the homemade dressings and sauces, the large portions of shrimp and salmon, the wonderful Gorgonzola polenta, the very lean corned beef and the cabbage with dill. Things the group did not like were the soft veggies, undercooked mashed potatoes, "a little dry" chicken, a vinegary taste and lack of flavor distinction in the vegetarian Thai stir-fry and a sour taste to the roasted red-onion dressing. The veal was both praised for being greaseless and criticized for being tough on the outside. These Greeks are tough critics. Overall, I'd say Dream Café gets a very favorable rating.

The Thai stir-fry featured seasoned fresh vegetables with a homemade spicy sauce and could be ordered vegetarian with portobello mushroom or with chicken, beef or shrimp. The veal was stuffed with mushrooms, garlic and parsley; rolled up and sliced; then served with Gorgonzola polenta and sautéed buttered squash. The corned beef and cabbage was prepared traditionally, with red potatoes and sweet carrots. The salmon was grilled and served with a homemade crab cake, green-onion mashed potatoes, fresh asparagus sauce and a white wine tarragon butter sauce. Other entrées that rotate into service include southwestern pork tenderloin, veal scallopini, paella, stuffed pepper Italiano, grilled swordfish and ruby trout almandine.

Highlighting the breakfast menu are single- and double-shot flavored espressos, panini sandwiches, fresh bagels, omelets, waffles, French toast, scones and a fresh seasonal fruit plate. The panini sandwiches are made with scrambled eggs and a variety of good ingredients like fresh basil or cilantro, Italian salami, feta cheese, grilled eggplant, pineapple and smoked ham. Soups and salads are among the lunch selections along with more panini sandwiches, such as the spicy southwestern with grilled chicken breast, roasted green chili, pepper Jack cheese, chipotle mayo and fresh cilantro. Dream dips, like artichoke cheese pâté with creamy roasted red pepper, are a delightful alternative to a more traditional lunch and include fresh vegetables and chips. For dessert, Dream Café delivers to your table fresh-baked goods made locally: fruit pies, tarts, cakes and cheesecakes, brownies, bars and cookies with premium vanilla ice cream and toppings.

Service was efficient but a bit slow, especially when it came time to get the check. However, we were all having a good time and in no hurry. Dream Café is in a two-story building with dining on both levels. Our group was in the upstairs dining room. The room has slanted ceilings and some water damage to one of the interior walls. Watch your head as you sit down and also as you walk down the stairs. Black-and-white photos of Paria Canyon in Arizona by Joe Temple decorate the upstairs dining room. Downstairs dining is in a narrow room with windows facing the street: a good place to watch traffic and people. The up side to the place is that it is old with character, cozy and quaint. The down side is that it is old with limited space, narrow stairs and tight fits between tables and walls and other tables and chairs and people. Get the picture? Even with a few faults, though, Dream Café is a treasure that should not be missed.

NUTRITION AND SPECIAL REQUESTS

Dream Café offers vegetarian panini sandwiches for breakfast and lunch; vegetarian soups, salads and dips for lunch; and vegetarian Thai stir-fry as a regular dinner entrée. They will make substitutions on slow nights.

Chicken-Stuffed Pepper Italiano with Gorgonzola Polenta

SERVES 4

¼ cup olive oil
4 medium-sized chicken breasts, diced small
1 tablespoon shallots, chopped finely
2 tablespoons chopped garlic
½ cup chopped roasted red peppers
4 cups fresh chopped spinach
2 tablespoons Italian seasoning

1½ cups Italian bread crumbs
1½ cups grated Romano cheese
fresh chopped basil to taste
4 medium-sized red or yellow bell peppers, tops cut off and seeded
marinara or tomato-basil sauce, kept warm

1. Heat olive oil in saucepan and sauté chicken, shallots and garlic for about 5 minutes. Add roasted red pepper. Add chopped spinach. Sauté another 5 minutes. Preheat oven to 350 degrees.
2. Add Italian seasoning, bread crumbs, cheese and fresh chopped basil to chicken mixture.
3. Stuff peppers with chicken mixture. Place in baking pan and bake in preheated oven for 30 minutes.
4. Remove pan from oven. Top each pepper with marinara or tomato-basil sauce. Serve with fresh fettuccini or Gorgonzola Polenta (recipe follows).

Gorgonzola Polenta

2 cups low-salt chicken broth
1 cup water
1 cup polenta

8 ounces Gorgonzola cheese, or to taste
olive oil

1. Bring chicken broth and water to a boil in a pot.
2. Slowly add polenta while stirring constantly. When it gets thick and creamy, add Gorgonzola and continue stirring until smooth and polenta does not taste chewy anymore, about 5–7 minutes.
3. Pour into 9x12-inch pan and refrigerate until firm. Cut pieces into desired shape and sauté in olive oil until golden brown on both sides.

Recipe by Donna Deneke

Wine Recommendation: Chianti or Pinot Noir

❧ NEW CASTLE ☙

PREVIOUSLY KNOWN AS *Grand Butte and Chapman, New Castle was renamed after the famous mining center of Newcastle, England, by the Colorado Fuel & Iron Company after large bituminous coal fields were discovered nearby.*

Zip Code: 81647 **Population:** 1,984 **Elevation:** 5,550 feet

ELK CREEK MINING COMPANY

502 North Main
Phone: (970) 984-0828
Fax: (970) 984-2317
E-mail: None
Website: None

Directions: Take exit 105 from I-70, a few miles west of Glenwood Springs. Go north 0.1 mile to the stop sign. Turn left onto Highway 6. Go 1.1 miles into the town of New Castle. The restaurant is on the right on the corner of 5th Avenue.

ESSENTIALS

Cuisine: Steak and ribs
Hours: Mon.–Fri. 11 A.M.–10 P.M., Sat.–Sun. 9 A.M.–10 P.M.
Meals and Prices: Breakfast $4–$8. Lunch $6–$9. Dinner $11–$20 (includes soup or salad and one side dish).
Nonsmoking: Yes
Take-out: Yes
Alcohol: Full bar
Credit Cards: All five
Personal Check: Yes, with ID
Reservations: Recommended for parties of six or more. Unnecessary otherwise.
Wheelchair Access: Yes
Other: Service charge of 17% added to parties of six or more.

HISTORY AND BIOGRAPHY

The Elk Creek Mining Company occupies a building dating back to 1893. It was originally the Rocky Mountain Stores Company. Sometime after 1914, it became a service station. From the early or mid-1950s until the mid-1980s, the space was used by Tony's Que Club, a 3.2 bar and pool hall. The property stood vacant for a few years until Laloma West, a Mexican restaurant, took over. Laloma was replaced by Mi Restaurante, which lasted until 1998.

Owners "Spike" Howard and John Walker purchased the property in 1998, spent eight months renovating and opened the Elk Creek Mining Company in August 1999. Spike owns the Dos Hombres Restaurant in Grand Junction, and John owns the Dos Hombres Restaurant in Glenwood Springs.

Manager Todd Colosimo has been at Elk Creek since it opened in 1999. Head chef Bruce Imig started at Elk Creek in 2000 after spending 11½ years cooking at the 19th Street Diner and the Daily Bread in nearby Glenwood Springs. He also worked as a chef in Chignik, Alaska, for two years and in Scottsdale and Tempe, Arizona, for 2½ years. He has been cooking since 1981. Line cook John Crooks also came to Elk Creek in 2000 and splits time waiting tables and bartending at Dos Hombres in Glenwood Springs when he is not in New Castle. He has been working in restaurants since 1980 and previously ran a pizzeria in Lake Tahoe, Nevada.

FOOD, SERVICE AND AMBIENCE

The Elk Creek serves a host of American items and southwestern specialties. You can get steaks, ribs, burgers, pasta, hearty game chili, homestyle chicken pot pie, smoked Colorado trout, prime rib, teriyaki yellowfin tuna steak and pork chops with sun-dried cherry compote and apricot glaze. The "pick a pasta" selection lets you choose one of five noodles and add your choice of five sauces.

The Elk Creek's black bean and ham soup was very good, filled with small ham bits and beans, then topped with cheddar and Monterey Jack cheeses. The baby-back ribs had a lot of meat and were quite tasty, with extra Kansas City pit barbecue sauce laced with Jim Beam bourbon. My side of sage-and-walnut stuffing was dry, not bone-dry so you could gag on it, but certainly lacking the moisture one expects in stuffing.

For lunch or a light dinner, the menu offers Caesar salad with a zesty dressing, seafood salad, burgers with ground beef or buffalo meat and a variety of toppings, club Caesar and veggie portobello wraps, and a classic French dip. Heading the list of breakfast favorites are omelets, eggs Benedict, breakfast burrito, huevos rancheros, French toast and Belgian waffle.

Service was fast, friendly and very helpful. Recordings of Madonna and other contemporary pop singers played softly. Contributing to the nineteenth-century mining company motif are a miner's helmet, an 1896 calendar, an 1881 map of Colorado Territory and old maps of the Leadville Mining District, New Castle, Central City and Black Hawk. Hanging from the ceiling and walls are a child's old wooden wagon and a wooden crate box labeled "Hercules Gelatin" filled with "dynamite" attached to a dynamite plunger. Framed receipts circa 1910 from the Rocky Mountain Stores Company and stock certificates from North Butte Mining Company hang in the booths. In the bar you will find stock certificates from the Modern Gold Place Company along with seven televisions to watch sporting events. One item you should not miss is just inside the front door to your left: a photo of Teddy Roosevelt, Wyatt Earp, Doc Holliday, Morgan Earp, Butch Cassidy, the Sundance Kid, Bat Masterson, Judge Roy Bean and other lawmen. You be the judge if it is authentic. For $5 you can get a copy.

NUTRITION AND SPECIAL REQUESTS

The Elk Creek uses corn oil to fry their foods. The cuisine is primarily meat-based, so only a few vegetarian choices—like the veggie portobello wrap and the pasta picks—are offered. The staff get very few special requests but will make anything on request if they have the ingredients.

San Juan Chicken Salad

SERVES 1

Marinated Chicken

4 ounces of boneless, skinless chicken breast, or 1 full side of breast

4 ounces Italian dressing
2 tablespoons olive oil

1. Marinate chicken breast in Italian dressing overnight or for at least 2 hours in refrigerator.
2. Grill chicken in sauté pan with olive oil or roast in 350-degree oven. Cook until brown. Cool, then slice chicken into strips.

Salad

4 cups mixed greens

2 ounces roasted bell peppers, sliced (sweet red or green)

2 ounces Bermuda onion, sliced

2 ounces tomato, diced

2 ounces black olives, diced

2 ounces cheddar and Monterey Jack cheese, diced, plus additional shredded cheese for garnish

4 ounces Spicy Black Bean Relish (recipe follows)

blue corn chips

1. Mix all of the above, except the Relish, and toss.
2. Arrange on platter. Put chicken strips in center and top with Relish.
3. Garnish the plate's rim with blue corn chips.
4. Sprinkle shredded cheddar and Monterey jack cheese on the chips. Serve.

Spicy Black Bean Relish / Pico de Gallo

1 cup picante sauce

1½ cups chopped tomatoes

1 small cucumber, peeled, sliced and diced

1 ounce fresh cilantro, chopped

½ ounce lime juice

1 ounce red onions, minced

¼ teaspoon kosher salt

¼ teaspoon black pepper

24 ounces cooked black beans (drain, if using canned)

Combine all ingredients except beans to make about 24 ounces of pico de gallo. Or mix pico de gallo with an equal amount of your favorite black beans to make Black Bean Relish.

Recipe by Bruce Imig

Beverage Recommendation: Grand Marnier Margarita

~ PAGOSA SPRINGS ~

PAGOSA SPRINGS IS *named from the Ute Indian word* Pagosah, *meaning "healing water." Alleged to be the world's hottest mineral springs, the hot mineral water of the area's springs produces geothermal heating for the town of Pagosa Springs. These hot springs were a favorite camping place of the Utes and, in the early 1870s, a welcome rest and relaxation stop for Anglo travelers and miners. In 1878 the U.S. Army built Fort Lewis across from the hot springs, but three years later it was relocated west to Durango. In the early part of the twentieth century, sheepherding, cattle ranches and lumber were the main industries in this area. You can still find cattle ranches, cowboys and lumber mills, but tourism and sports like skiing and biking are now the major industries.*

Zip Code: 81147 **Population:** 1,591 **Elevation:** 7,105 feet

J. J.'S UPSTREAM RESTAURANT

356 East Highway 160
Phone: (970) 264-9100
Fax: (970) 264-9063
E-mail: None
Website: None

Directions: *Coming from the east on Highway 160,* the restaurant is on the right, 0.1 mile past the junction with Highway 84. *Coming from the west,* the restaurant is on the left, five blocks past the signal for 4th Street in the middle of town.

ESSENTIALS

Cuisine: Seafood, steak and wild game
Hours: Mon. and Wed.–Sat. 11 A.M.–2:30 P.M.; Sun. 9 A.M.–2:30 P.M.; Sun., Mon., Wed., Thu. 4 P.M.–9 P.M.; Fri.–Sat. 4 P.M.–9:30 P.M.

Light fare served 2 P.M.–4:30 P.M. Closed Tue. Closed beginning of NOV to Thanksgiving and Easter to Mother's Day.

Meals and Prices: Sunday brunch $5–$11. Lunch $7–$11. Dinner $15–$23 (includes starch, vegetable and soup or salad).

Nonsmoking: Smoking permitted only on outside patio

Take-out: Yes

Alcohol: Full bar

Credit Cards: All five

Personal Check: Yes

Reservations: Accepted

Wheelchair Access: Yes

Other: Children's menu. Service charge of 18% may be added to tables of six or more. Available for business luncheons, wedding rehearsals and private parties. Live music.

HISTORY AND BIOGRAPHY

J. J.'s Upstream is in a building constructed in 1995. The original business, The Bistro Restaurant, lasted 1½ years. After it closed, the property stood vacant until 1999, when James and Nancy Dickhoff and their financial partners, John and Phyllis Brown, purchased the property. After taking four months to remodel, they opened J. J.'s, named after the first initials of James and John, in June 1999. The restaurant rests on the bank of the San Juan River, hence the name "Upstream."

James has been in the restaurant business since 1976. He was a cook in small sandwich shops and pizzerias in Denver before becoming a sous-chef at The Ranch in Keystone from 1986 until 1989. From 1989 to 1998 he was the food and beverage director of the Copper Mountain Ski Resort. Nancy started working in restaurants in 1977. She was a cook at the Snake River Saloon in Keystone, a line cook at the Sunshine Café in Silverthorne and a sous-chef at Copper Mountain Ski Resort. James and Nancy manage the restaurant. Dave Woodring has been the head chef at J. J.'s since it opened. He has been cooking since 1971 and was certified at Johnson and Wales in 1981. He was a banquet chef at The Commons in Copper Mountain for two years, handling a cafeteria and banquet and catering functions. He also did banquets at Gassey's in Keystone before going to work at the Broadmoor Hotel in Colorado Springs from 1997 until 1999.

J. J.'s Upstream specializes in seafood and a whole lot more. I chose one of the seafood entrées, the Thai Gulf shrimp tempura. The dinner salad came with a sweet and tangy sesame-ginger vinaigrette and was served with sweet poppy seed bread, a French baguette and cracked pepper and sesame Italian breadsticks. J. J.'s bakes its own breads and make its own salad dressings, soups and stocks. The six large Gulf shrimp in a light tempura batter got some kick from the sweet chili Thai plum sauce. If you do not overdo it on the sauce, it is a great flavor-enhancer. The accompanying wild rice with crunchy roasted piñon nuts and the crisp, not overcooked, julienne-sliced vegetables—carrots, asparagus, yellow squash, yellow peppers and zucchini—were small but flavorsome servings.

For an appetizer before dinner, try the curry crab or Asiago artichoke dip, the forest mushroom strudel, nutty cranberry Brie cheese, or smoked eggplant bruschetta. The other seafood entrées were shrimp scampi with Asiago cheese bread crumbs, orange dill salmon, Canadian walleye lightly battered with a buttery flavor and cranberry almond ruby trout. Other entrées included sun-dried cranberry elk, filet mignon with a prosciutto and leek haystack, slow rotisserie-smoked prime rib, portobello chicken Marsala and smoked eggplant and barley cake. Finish your meal with sun-dried cranberry walnut bread pudding, homemade Italian espresso tiramisu mousse or "sweet therapy" chocolate mousse cake.

Sunday brunch offered the following appetizing selections: a butter croissant dipped in orange-almond egg batter; thick apple-smoked bacon; almond-sautéed filet of trout; frittatas with elk sausage, roasted vegetable and portobello mushroom or asparagus, artichoke hearts and chicken; eggs Benedict with king crab meat or smoked ham, artichoke hearts and avocado; and grilled tofu and vegetables with pesto penne pasta. Lunchtime choices include grilled buffalo burger, portobello and fire-roasted vegetables on herb focaccia bun, grilled salmon BLT, artichoke-grilled chicken on a Kaiser roll, London elk broil, Canadian walleye fish and chips and pasta chicken and asparagus.

Service was fast, perhaps a little too fast. Both the salad and entrée came out within ten minutes of my order, and I was halfway through the salad when the entrée arrived. J. J.'s furnishes a main dining room and riverside dining room inside and a covered patio and beach patio separated by the riverwalk bike path outside. The main dining-room furniture, planters and bar to the left of the entrance all came from Racquets, a former restaurant at Copper Mountain. Oil paintings from a local gallery, ceramic clay sculptures of a mermaid and fish and a fireplace decorate the main dining room. The riverside dining room, called the River Room, has pink adobe walls trimmed with artworks of horses, geese, wolves and buffalo; southwestern pieces of art; ceramic sculptures of coral-reef fish; and a carved wooden trout over the fireplace. J. J.'s maintains twenty live palm trees, four of them inside. In late spring you can sometimes see deer, elk, bear or bald eagles along the San Juan River as well as rafters and kayakers. A spotlight on the river at night sometimes illuminates a beaver in action. The covered patio allows dining under green umbrellas and a log-shanty extension of the building's roof. The beach patio below hosts a tiki bar and pleasant views of the San Juan River. Live music is provided by a pianist on Thursday, Friday and Saturday nights from 6 P.M. to 9 P.M. Every Sunday evening a live band plays, usually unplugged rock and roll, jazz, country, or bluegrass.

NUTRITION AND SPECIAL REQUESTS

J. J.'s does not have any heart-healthy items, but its staff will cater to any special request. Vegetarians have several dinner appetizers and Sunday brunch items, but only two sandwiches and two dinner entrées, from which to choose.

Rotisserie-Smoked Pork Loin Chop
with Apple and Dark Cherry Sauce

SERVES 8–10

1 bone-in, crown, center-cut, pork loin roast
   (about 2½ pounds, 8–10 bones, 1 bone with meat per serving)

Seasoning Rub

2 tablespoons coarse kosher salt	2 teaspoons thyme
2 teaspoons ground black pepper	½ teaspoon granulated garlic
1 tablespoon rosemary	¼ cup olive oil

Apple and Dark Cherry Sauce

1 can dark cherries in juice
½ cup cherry brandy
3 cups water
2 teaspoons cornstarch

½ cup granulated sugar
2 tart Granny Smith apples,
   peeled and diced

Sweet Fried Onions

1 sweet yellow onion
1 cup all-purpose flour

oil for deep frying

1. Make the Seasoning Rub: Mix all listed ingredients together and rub onto bone-in pork loin.

2. Smoke with mesquite. (Suggestion: Soak the mesquite log in water over night. Expose the log to flame long enough to start on fire, then shut down the flame and reduce the oxygen. When the log starts to smolder it is ready to add the pork loin to the smoking chamber. Add a sprig of rosemary atop the mesquite log for added flavor.) Smoke the pork loin with mesquite using a backyard smoker or modified barbecue grill, or simply roast. Smoke it until the center of the loin reads 145 degrees on a stemmed thermometer. DO NOT OVERCOOK. Take the pork loin off the smoker and let rest at room temperature for 15–20 minutes before cutting. While pork is smoking, prepare the Sauce and Sweet Fried Onions.

3. Make the Apple and Dark Cherry Sauce: Drain cherries, reserving juice. Combine drained cherry juice with brandy and water in saucepot. Bring to a boil. Add cornstarch (dissolve in small amount of cool water first). Add rough-chopped drained cherries, sugar and diced apples. Simmer for 10 minutes. Keep warm until ready.

4. Make the Sweet Fried Onions: Peel onions and slice into very thin rings. (A small electric meat slicer or Mandoline is very handy for this step.) Dredge onion rings in flour; shake off excess flour in a sieve. Deep-fry small portions at a time in hot oil until light brown (a crockpot deep-fryer works well). Place on baking sheet lined with paper towels.

5. To assemble: Cut pork loin into pork chops. Place 1–2 chops on a serving plate. Ladle sauce over top. Place a small handful of sweet fried onions on top. Serve.

Recipe by James Dickhoff and **Dave Woodring**

Wine Recommendations: Italian Ecco Damani Pinot Grigio 1999 or Italian Pepi Pinot Grigio 2000

❧ PALMER LAKE ❧

PALMER LAKE WAS *one of the earliest resorts in Colorado and used to go by the names Loch Katrina, Palermo and Divide Lake. The post office called it Weissport after its first railway station agent, C. A. Weissport. The town eventually was named in honor of General William J. Palmer of the Denver and Rio Grande Railroad. The spring-fed lake around which the town was built lies at the top of the divide between the South Platte and Arkansas Rivers' drainages. South of town is the sandstone formation called Elephant Rock, which, from a certain angle, does actually resemble a huge elephant.*

Zip Code: 80133 **Population:** 2,179 **Elevation:** 7,240 feet

B & E FILLING STATION

25 Highway 105
Phone: (719) 481-4780
Fax: (719) 481-6133
E-mail: kerri@divide.net
Website: None

Directions: Take exit 161 (the Monument exit, north of Colorado Springs) off I-25. *If you are coming from the south,* cross over I-25 and go north on the frontage road west of I-25. *If you are coming from the north,* follow the exit up to the frontage road and turn right. Follow the signs for Highway 105 and go 2½ miles into Palmer Lake. The restaurant is on the right in the middle of town.

ESSENTIALS

Cuisine: Continental
Hours: Tue.–Sat. 5 P.M.–9 P.M. Closed Sun.–Mon.
Meals and Prices: Dinner $12–$18 (includes salad)
Nonsmoking: All
Take-out: Yes
Alcohol: Full bar
Credit Cards: MC, VI, DS
Personal Check: Accepted
Reservations: Recommended
Wheelchair Access: Yes
Other: Service charge of 18% added for parties of seven or more.

HISTORY AND BIOGRAPHY

The B & E Filling Station was originally a house built in 1947. It remained a house until the Next Door Café took over in 1993. The building was vacant for a year after that establishment closed in 1995. In February 1996, Chris and Kerri Bohler and another couple by the name of Elliott opened the B & E, which stands for Bohler and Elliott. The Elliotts are no longer involved with the restaurant. The foursome's original intention was to lease a former filling station to open their restaurant. Instead, they purchased this former house, but they kept the apt "filling station" in the name.

Chris has been in the restaurant business since 1979, Kerri since 1978. Kerri worked as a waitress and hostess at a truck stop in Oregon before coming to Colorado in 1982. Chris and Kerri met at the now-defunct Husky Anderson Truck Stop in Monument, Colorado. They both went to work at The Villa in Palmer Lake in 1986. Kerri left in 1994, and Chris left a year later. Chris's sister, Laura Hendricks, is a server at the B & E.

Being a lover of Greek food, I could not pass up the Greek chicken dish. I highly recommend this one. It is a delicious mixture of meat, veggies and cheese with a sautéed chicken breast filled with peppers, onions and roasted red bell peppers and baked with red onions, Kalamata olives, olive oil and garlic. My choice of starch was garlic mashed potatoes with gravy and a sprinkling of parsley. Linda had the juicy portobello mushroom caps stuffed with crisp grilled vegetables. Her starch selection was grilled polenta, slow-cooked cornmeal with sun-dried tomatoes, butter and Parmesan. It was a tasty alternative to rice or potato and came served in the shape of a small loaf. Our salads came with a sweet balsamic vinaigrette and a feta-cream dressing.

Everything is made to order at the B & E. For an appetizer, you can try lavosh, blue crab and crawfish cakes, escargot, or steamed Prince Edward Island mussels. Enticing entrées include shrimp, scallops, crab and artichoke hearts in lobster cream sauce over pasta; roasted sliced leg of lamb with lingonberry red-wine sauce; sesame-cashew shrimp; and rotisserie-roasted duck. For dessert you can choose a "killer" cheesecake like Bailey's chocolate, cinnamon-almond amaretto, lingonberry or chocolate Kahlúa; flan; chocolate mousse with strawberries; or a mixed fruit cobbler.

My server was a funny lady. I ordered a glass of wine for myself, and she brought me the whole bottle. When she came back the second time, she had two glasses of wine. Later, she tried to remove my glass with two ounces of wine left in it. I think she really wanted some wine for herself. Despite her wine fetish, she was quite good at checking back on us and keeping our water glasses full. Instrumental jazz played moderately loudly in the two small dining rooms. The pink stucco walls were embellished with pastel watercolors of meadows, mountains, horses and ranch houses. Arched doorways separated the dining rooms and stained glass filled the arched window openings. Paintings of the Broadmoor Hotel and the town of Palmer Lake by Joseph Bohler, Chris's father, also adorn the dining areas. The B & E is more than just a place to fill up. It is a comfortable, relaxed place to indulge your palate in some exceptional, finely prepared food.

The B & E will accommodate special requests if they have the ingredients. Substitutions are easily made on things like creams or sauces.

Greek Chicken

SERVES 1

1 8-ounce butterfly or double-lobe boneless, skinless chicken breast, pounded to ½-inch thickness

1 ounce feta cheese, cut into a long, 3-inch strip

½ roasted red bell pepper

¼ cup fresh spinach, cleaned and stemmed

flour for dredging chicken

⅛ cup extra-virgin olive oil

½ cup red onions, thinly sliced

6 Kalamata olives

¼ cup dry white wine

chopped fresh parsley

1. Place pounded chicken breast on work surface and spread lobes out. Remove any excess fat or skin. Preheat oven to 450 degrees.
2. Place strip of feta inside the ½ roasted red bell pepper and place this on one side of chicken breast.
3. Place spinach on the other lobe or half of chicken breast and fold together. Dredge in flour. Heat olive oil in ovenproof sauté pan. Place chicken breast in pan and brown on one side for 4 minutes, then turn.
4. Add sliced onions and olives. Sauté for 3 minutes, then add white wine.
5. Place in preheated oven for approximately 10–15 minutes, until wine has evaporated and onions have caramelized in pan.
6. Remove from oven. Transfer chicken to serving plate and pour the remaining sauce over chicken. Sprinkle with parsley. Serve.

Recipe by Chris Bohler

Wine Recommendation: Italian Santa Margarita Pinot Grigio

❧ PARKER ❧

FORMERLY CALLED PINE *Grove, Parker was a station on the old Happy Canyon Road from Denver to Colorado Springs. The town was later named after James S. Parker, who served thirty-three years as postmaster. In the early 1860s, he was a stage driver on the Smokey Hill South stage route.*

Zip Code: 80134 **Population:** 23,558* **Elevation:** 5,865 feet

ITALIAN FAMILY

10971 South Parker Road
Phone: (303) 805-4744
Fax: (303) 805-9384
E-mail: None
Website: None

Directions: Take exit 193 from I-25 (just south of Denver) and go west on Lincoln Avenue for 5 miles. Turn right onto Parker Road (Highway 83) and go 1¼ miles to Main Street. Turn right onto Main Street, then take the first left into the Safeway Plaza. The restaurant is on the right between KMart and Safeway.

ESSENTIALS

Cuisine: Italian
Hours: Seven days 11 A.M.–10 P.M.
Meals and Prices: Lunch and Dinner $5–$7 (soup and salad extra). Pizza $12–$16 and up.
Nonsmoking: All
Take-out: Yes
Alcohol: Beer and wine
Credit Cards: MC, VI
Personal Check: Accepted with ID

*Parker is the largest town in this book.

Reservations: Not accepted. First come, first served.
Wheelchair Access: Yes
Other: Free local delivery

HISTORY AND BIOGRAPHY

Italian Family opened in January 2000. Prior to that, Pizza Nizza occupied this location, as it had since 1995 when the building was constructed. Owner Mike Bertinelli has worked in restaurants his entire life. He previously was general manager in restaurants in Denver, Colorado Springs and St. Louis, Missouri. He is also part owner of Jackson's Hole and the Tower Bar and Grill, both in Denver. His son, Chris, is the manager and head chef. This is his first restaurant venture.

FOOD, SERVICE AND AMBIENCE

For my meal at Italian Family, I ordered the Italian Family salad and the portobello ravioli with homemade meatballs. The salad features the standard pepperoni, green peppers, mushrooms, onions, black olives, tomatoes, pepperoncini and shredded mozzarella. Italian dressing with oregano and oil was served on the side. It was okay, but the ravioli stuffed with ground portobello mushroom was better. I received eleven ravioli squares topped with a flavorful, thick and spicy, homemade marinara sauce and accompanied by two soft and chewy garlic-and-butter bread twists. The homemade meatballs, a recipe from owner Mike Bertinelli's mother, were delicious. They were very tender, made with onion and sprinkled with parsley. Most of the items on the menu are Mike's family's recipes.

Other dinner entrées include regular lasagna with sausage, vegetarian lasagna, linguini, tortellini and baked ziti with your choice of homemade sauces: marinara, meat, pesto or Alfredo. Sandwiches such as Italian beef and chicken Parmesan are also on the menu, along with salads, subs and homemade minestrone soup. Pizza is their specialty, by the slice or pie. In addition to the usual toppings, Italian Family offers meatballs, chicken, cotto and Genoa salamis, spinach, Kalamata olives, artichoke hearts, basil, portobello mushrooms, cream cheese, cauliflower and broccoli. Your choices for dessert are cannolis with homemade filling, cheesecakes and tiramisu.

Service at Italian Family is very casual; you place your order at a counter, get your own soft drinks and then wait for the staff to bring your food. My salad arrived quickly, about five minutes after I ordered it, and my entrée followed about five minutes after that. There is no follow-up service after the food is brought out from the kitchen. The young guys who handle the operation appear to be serious and ambitious. Instrumental and vocal jazz along with Italian favorites like Dean Martin singing "That's Amore" played throughout the restaurant.

Italian Family is a long, one-room restaurant with simple, basic décor. White artificial flowers adorn tables covered with red-and-white checkered plastic covers. To the left of the entrance is the deli, where you can order items to take home. The counter where you place your food order is just beyond the deli. There are two televisions, one over the counter, the other at the end of the room. Providing cheer and amusement to the lime-green and dark-green walls are framed posters of Italian beer and people working with and eating spaghetti. One poster depicts a tall clown feeding spaghetti to a midget clown. Other posters show "The spaghetti eater" and "The spaghetti setter." Italian Family is aptly named: a family-friendly restaurant serving family recipes of Italian cuisine.

NUTRITION AND SPECIAL REQUESTS

Special requests such as light sauce or an extra-crispy pizza crust are handled routinely. Vegetarian pizzas, vegetarian lasagna and some other pastas without meat are available.

Meatballs

MAKES 10 MEATBALLS FOR 5 SERVINGS

1½ pounds ground beef	½ teaspoon dried basil
1 small yellow onion	¾ teaspoon granulated garlic
½ cup bread crumbs	¾ teaspoon granulated onion
2 eggs	2 tablespoons parsley
½ cup Parmesan cheese	¼ teaspoon salt or to taste
¼ cup water	¼ teaspoon pepper to taste
⅛ cup milk	½ teaspoon sugar
¼ teaspoon dried oregano	

1. Preheat oven to 400 degrees. Put all ingredients in large mixing bowl and mix thoroughly.
2. Oil a sheet pan and portion meatballs to desired size (e.g., 3–4 ounces).
3. Roll meatballs, place on baking sheet and bake in preheated oven for 15–25 minutes, until golden brown.

Recipe by Josephine Pigg

ᴥ PINEWOOD SPRINGS ᴥ

ORIGINALLY CALLED *Little Elk Park, Pinewood Springs was renamed in about 1960 with the addition of a new development.*

Zip Code: 80540 **Population:** 1,000* **Elevation:** 6,450 feet

LA CHAUMIÈRE

12311 North St. Vrain Drive
Phone: (303) 823-6521
Fax: None
E-mail: vince@peakpeak.com
Website: www.lachaumiere-restaurant.com

Directions: From the intersection of Highways 36 and 7 in the town of Lyons, go northwest on Highway 36 for 8 miles. Pinewood Springs is in a little valley on the highway. The restaurant is on the right.

ESSENTIALS

Cuisine: French and Continental
Hours: Tue.–Sat. 5:30 P.M.–10 P.M., Sun. 2 P.M.–9 P.M. Closed Mon.

---

*Population based on an estimated 300 to 350 households according to La Chaumière owner Vince Williams and an estimated three people per household.

Meals and Prices: Dinner $17–$25 (includes salad). Six-course meal $35.
Nonsmoking: All
Take-out: Yes
Alcohol: Wine, beer and some mixed drinks
Credit Cards: All five
Personal Check: In-state only
Reservations: Highly recommended
Wheelchair Access: Yes
Other: Gift certificates available

HISTORY AND BIOGRAPHY

La Chaumière was originally a hamburger stand and diner called the Old Stagecoach Inn, built in 1965. John Pierre opened La Chaumière in 1974. La Chaumière means "cottage in the mountains" or "thatched roof" in French. Heinze Fricker, a German, was the long-time owner of La Chaumière from 1976 to 2001. In April 2001, current owners Vince and Edie Williams purchased the restaurant, their first. Vince started in the restaurant business in 1974 and graduated from the Culinary Institute of America in Hyde Park, New York, in 1978. Vince and Edie worked together at The Homestead in Hot Springs, Virginia; Bishop's Lodge in Santa Fe, New Mexico; The Teller House in Central City, Colorado; Bandito's Cantina and the Keystone Resort in Keystone, Colorado; and, from 1992 until 2001, The Bayard House Restaurant in Chesapeake City, Maryland. Vince also cooked at the Cottage Grove Village Green Resort in Oregon. Vince is the chef. Edie runs the front of the restaurant and handles the books, beer and wine.

FOOD, SERVICE AND AMBIENCE

La Chaumière offers some very nicely seasoned foods. Linda and I dined here with our good Greek friend, Elaine. We split an appetizer of calamari rings stuffed with crab that were sweet and tasty. Our dinner salads were dressed in a thick orange-colored herb vinaigrette made with sun-dried tomatoes and canola oil.

Linda's entrée choice was the pesto chicken pasta, firm chicken with fresh sautéed cauliflower, broccoli, carrots and gold peppers served with angel-hair pasta. I ordered the sautéed sweetbreads, six very soft and tender medallions with toasted pine nuts in a flavorsome rosemary demi-glace topped with a sprig of fresh rosemary. The plate accompaniments were potatoes, roughly mashed and very tasty mixed with the demi-glace; seasoned and sautéed snow peas, carrots, yellow squash and zucchini; an edible orchid flower center, which I ate; and chopped green, red and yellow peppers and parsley on the rim. Elaine ordered the grilled tuna steak special with wasabi herb butter. It also had a firm texture with flavorsome seasoning. For dessert, we tried the flaming bananas flambé prepared tableside. It consisted of a stick of butter, raw cane sugar, honey, a squeeze of lemon, banana liqueur, 151 Bacardi rum and two bananas. The finished concoction was then poured over vanilla ice cream. Simply sweet and delicious!

La Chaumière's appetizers feature mesquite-smoked turkey, duck liver pâté, escargots á la bourguignonne and smoked salmon from Villa Tatra across the street. La Chaumière also has its own smokehouse. Chef Vince's award-winning Maryland crab soup is the menu highlight. Main course selections include broiled salmon in white wine, filet mignon with red wine, Anaheim pepper stuffed with lump crabmeat and shrimp and tournedos Baltimore: twin petite beef filets, one topped with crab cake, one with shrimp cake. A six-course sampling menu is also available. For dessert, you can decide between crème brûlée, chocolate mousse with raspberry sauce, meringue with strawberries or homemade ice cream or sorbet. You also have the option of enjoying an after-dinner cognac, armagnac, liqueur, or dessert wine.

Edie was our professional and well-spoken server. George Gershwin's "An American in Paris" was fitting musical accompaniment to our dinner.

La Chaumière is a French-style, one-story, country roadside restaurant with a deer park and a beautiful view of the surrounding hillside. The building is accented by a green roof, yellow-and-white striped awnings, three tables with a flagstone wishing well and lovely flower beds of dahlia, petunias, marigolds and gardenias—very French and very pretty.

The dining room continues this French Country café theme with paintings of outdoor French cafés and restaurants, the French countryside and market and a table set with pie and Benedictine. Prints of Claude Monet's "Nympheas" and Van Gogh's "The Café Terrace" complement this milieu. Blue-and-white decorator plates with pictures of orchards and vineyards hanging on the rock fireplace also look good in this environment.

There are three small café-style tables in a small room across from the front of the restaurant. Adjacent to this is a small private room with a bay window facing the highway, where the chef's table is located for small gatherings and private parties. This room is decorated with several Monet prints, a photo of "L'Hospitalite a la Chaumière" and stained-glass art pieces hanging in the windows. La Chaumière is true to itself, presenting authentic French Cuisine in a French-style setting.

NUTRITION AND SPECIAL REQUESTS

The restaurant accommodates many special requests, for example, lightening some of the heavy French sauces. The menu lists only one vegetarian entrée, a platter of fresh, seasonal vegetables, but Chef Vince will gladly make something vegetarian that isn't on the menu, for example, pasta.

Vince's Award-Winning Crab Soup

MAKES 1½ GALLONS; FREEZES WELL

This recipe has won seven first-place awards and three third-place awards since 1993 in both the Judge's and People's Choice categories of the Maryland Soup Cook-Off in Annapolis, Maryland. I am pleased to be the first to obtain approval to publish it.

½ cup finely diced celery (about ¼ inch)

½ cup finely diced carrots

½ cup finely diced onion

¼ cup olive oil

½ cup finely diced potato (about ¼ inch)

½ of a #10 can of diced tomatoes (51 ounces by weight)

3 cups tomato juice

3 cups water

1 ounce Old Bay Seasoning

1 tablespoon chicken base

1 tablespoon crab base

2 tablespoons fresh oregano (or use ½ tablespoon dried oregano)

1 tablespoon fresh thyme (or use ½ tablespoon dried thyme)

2 tablespoons fresh basil (or use ½ tablespoon dried basil)

2 tablespoons chopped fresh parsley

½ pound claw crab meat

½ pound jumbo lump crab meat

1. In a large soup pot, sauté celery, carrots and onion for 3 minutes in olive oil.
2. Add potatoes, diced tomatoes, tomato juice, water, Old Bay Seasoning, bases and herbs. Bring to a boil; turn down heat and simmer until vegetables are tender, about 20–30 minutes.
3. Turn off heat and let soup sit for 5 minutes.
4. Add parsley, fresh claw meat and jumbo lump crab meat. Stir well. Serve hot, or refrigerate or freeze for later use.

Recipe by Vince Williams

Wine Recommendation: French Chartron La Fleur Bordeaux

❧ PONCHA SPRINGS ❧

THE WORD "PONCHA" *means tobacco in an Indian language, and some people believe Poncha Springs got its name after an early settler to the area cultivated tobacco by using hot-springs water from above the town for irrigation. Others say the real spelling of the town is Poncho, which is Spanish for paunch, a reference to the low bend in the mountains near town.*

Zip Code: 81242 **Population:** 466 **Elevation:** 7,465 feet

GRIMO'S

146 Main Street
Phone: (719) 539-2903
Fax: (719) 530-0468
E-mail: None
Website: None

Directions: From the intersection of Highways 50 and 285 in Poncha Springs where Highway 50 continues east, go 300 feet south on Highway 285. The restaurant is on the right.

ESSENTIALS

Cuisine: Italian

Hours: Tue.–Sat. 4 P.M.–9 P.M. Closed Sun.–Mon.

Meals and Prices: Dinner $7–$15 (includes soup and salad).

Nonsmoking: All

Take-out: Yes

Alcohol: Full bar

Credit Cards: MC, VI

Personal Check: No

Reservations: Recommended, especially on Fri. and Sat.

Wheelchair Access: Yes

Other: Children's menu. Service charge of 15% added on groups of six or more. Extra plate charge $1. Catering and private parties available.

HISTORY AND BIOGRAPHY

Grimo's is in a building constructed in 1887 that has been used as a general store, a post office and a pawn shop. The section in the back was added in the 1950s for use as a three-bedroom apartment. Owners Frank and Kitty Grimo opened Grimo's in 1985. Frank worked at two restaurants in Leadville between 1983 and 1985, including the restaurant at the Silver King Hotel. He is also the manager and head chef at Grimo's.

FOOD, SERVICE AND AMBIENCE

Grimo's is a quaint and quiet Italian roadside restaurant serving first-rate Italian dishes in a pleasant environment. A cup of Italian vegetable soup and a small salad are served with dinner. The soup is peppery, with pearl onions, green beans, tomatoes, okra, onion and carrot. I found it to be just a little spicy, with some good vegetable flavors. The salad came with a house Italian dressing and consisted of mixed greens, tomato, black olives and pepperoncini. It was served with slices of Italian bread with herb butter. A house blue cheese, along with French and ranch dressings, are also available.

I have tried three of Grimo's entrées. Their shrimp scampi offers large sautéed shrimp in a rich sauce of lemon, garlic, butter, wine and herbs and is excellent. The veal Marsala consisted of thicker medallions than usual, but they were very good also. The cannelloni was a crêpe filled with spinach, chicken, veal and beef melded with oregano, basil and pepper and topped with a blend of marinara and Alfredo sauces. This was an interesting combination of chopped and tender meats. I particularly liked the smooth texture. The side dishes of spaghetti or fettuccine with marinara sauce, while not large portions, were well prepared and indicated that the pasta entrées would be quite good also. I recommend the homemade cannoli for dessert, a delicious conglomeration of sweet flavors—ricotta cheese, chocolate chips, a hint of Amaretto, coconut and mint—that is soothing to the palate, as well.

For a starter to your meal you can choose from artichoke hearts baked in a Romano and Parmesan cheese sauce, stuffed clams or mushrooms, escargot, toasted ravioli, or, when it is served as a special, calamari Sicilian style. Pastas include manicotti, lasagna, ziti, linguini, and cheese tortellini, each with marinara, Alfredo, Bolognese, or clam au jus sauce. If you prefer meat or seafood to pasta, Grimo's presents filet mignon wrapped in bacon or in a Marsala sauce, rib-eye with Toscana butter sauce, scallops, shrimp or chicken pesto, chicken Tetrazzini and fettuccini Alfredo. They also serve parmigiana made with chicken, eggplant or veal. In addition to the cannoli, there are homemade cheesecake, chocolate mousse and Italian rum layer cake. They also offer tiramisu.

My order was promptly taken, and the food was served fairly quickly; however, there was no follow-up to the service. On one occasion, classical and New Age music was playing; on another, Italian opera played, which seemed more appropriate for this atmosphere. Grimo's is decked in a combination of Italian styles conglomerated with Colorado accents. The front dining room has sliced log walls, a pellet stove, pinewood posts and granite rock doorways decorated with Chianti bottles. The red tablecloths and napkins match the curtains and red brick wall. The back dining room is adorned with pictures of cattle, sheep, rabbits, ducks and geese, along with a pinewood post in the middle of the room trimmed with Chianti bottles. The room is further enhanced by a winter scene painting of mountains with a lake and waterfalls, a framed menu in Italian, a Claude Monet print of "Woman with a Parasol," and small crystal chandeliers.

Grimo's uses canola oil, Puritan oil and very little salt in their cooking. They occasionally get special requests and will do whatever they can to please the customer. Grimo's serves many vegetarian pasta entrées and a couple of vegetarian antipasti.

Chicken Cacciatore

SERVES 4–6

Cacciatore means "hunter" in Italian and indicates the chicken is simmered in well-seasoned tomato sauce, or hunter's style.

2½ to 3 pounds cut-up fryer
  chicken
2 medium onions, sliced
2 cloves garlic, minced
2 tablespoons olive oil
2 teaspoons dried oregano,
  crushed
2 teaspoons basil, preferably
  fresh
1 teaspoon dried rosemary,
  crushed

1 medium green bell pepper,
  cut in 2-inch slices
1 medium red bell pepper,
  cut in 2-inch slices
16 ounces canned pear tomatoes,
  hand squeezed
salt and pepper
½ cup red wine
2–3 ounces of fresh mushrooms,
  sliced

1. Bake or fry chicken pieces until brown. Discard grease.
2. In a saucepan, sauté onions and garlic in olive oil, until onions are glossy. Add all spices, bell peppers, tomatoes and salt and pepper to taste. Add wine. Simmer 30 minutes.
3. Preheat oven to 350 degrees. Put the chicken pieces in a roasting pan. Cover with the sauce and raw mushrooms. Bake in preheated oven for 30–45 minutes, until chicken is tender and about to fall off the bone, stirring occasionally. Serve.

Recipe by Frank Grimo

Wine Recommendation: Burgundy

～ RIDGWAY ～

NAMED FOR *R. M. Ridgway, superintendent of the Mountain Division of the Denver and Rio Grande Railroad, Ridgway was a station for wagon transportation to the mines.*

Zip Code: 81432 **Population:** 713 **Elevation:** 6,985 feet

THE ADOBE INN

251 Liddell Drive
Phone: (970) 626-5939
Fax: (970) 626-5936
E-mail: None
Website: None

Directions: From the intersection of Highways 550 and 62 in Ridgway (between Montrose and Ouray), go west on Highway 62 (Sherman Street) for ¼ mile. Go over the bridge and take the first left onto Liddell Drive. Go 0.1 mile. The restaurant is the brown stucco building on the right with the white sign reading "Lodge and Cantina."

ESSENTIALS

Cuisine: Northern Mexican and New Mexican
Hours: Seven nights 5:30 P.M.–9:30 P.M.
Meals and Prices: Dinner $12–$14 (includes chips and salsa and salad or tostada).
Nonsmoking: All
Take-out: Yes
Alcohol: Full bar
Credit Cards: MC, VI, AE, DS
Personal Check: Accepted
Reservations: Accepted
Wheelchair Access: Yes

Other: Children's menu. Substitutions discouraged. Available for small gatherings.

HISTORY AND BIOGRAPHY

The Adobe Inn was originally The Pueblo Mexican Restaurant, built in 1984. Terre and Joyce Bucknam have owned and managed the Adobe Inn since 1987. They have been in the restaurant business since 1964. Terre worked as a manager at the Forest Inn in Lake Tahoe, Nevada. He and Joyce are former owners of The Back Narrows Inn and Restaurant in Norwood, Colorado, a restaurant featured in my third edition. They began creating their Mexican recipes at the Back Narrows. All of the recipes at the Adobe Inn—which, by the way, does house three rooms for rent—belong to the Bucknams, and their chefs follow these recipes.

FOOD, SERVICE AND AMBIENCE

The Adobe Inn has developed a widespread reputation for outstanding Mexican food, not only domestically but internationally as well. Their mix of ingredients and preparation results in some uncommonly good common dishes. Their beef enchilada, which I tried with the bright-red vegetarian rojo (red chili) sauce, was made with soft flour tortillas and had a distinctive flavor. The chile relleno with the verde (green chili) sauce, uses New Mexico–style pork and a crisp flour tortilla. The chile just melted in my mouth. The bean tostado with mozzarella cheese, frijoles, lettuce, tomato, green onions, guacamole and sour cream on a crunchy, fluffy shell that broke easily with a fork was a splendid suffusion of flavors. The corn casserole side dish prepared with cornmeal, corn and green peppers was very tasty.

The Adobe Inn's specialties include chicken, cheese, shredded beef and/or bean enchiladas; beef and cheese or spiced crab chimichangas; a chicken and cheese flauta; and bean, beef and bean or chicken and bean burritos. They serve four distinguished sauces: Besides the rojo and verde, they have suiza, a chicken broth made with tomatillos and cilantro; and tomato cream, consisting of tomatoes, eggs, cream, cilantro and chilies. Pepper poppers, dips, nachos and chips and salsa can be ordered as an appetizer. Salad, posole, chipotle soup, lime tortilla soup and quesadillas are available for a lighter meal. Four delectable desserts are offered: Kahlúa mousse, cheesecake, ice cream and flan, a traditional Mexican favorite.

Even with all this good fare, I haven't told you the ultimate reason to try Adobe Inn: The restaurant has the best chips and salsa I have tasted in any of my many travels throughout Colorado. Both the corn chips and flour chips are homemade. The corn chips are firm and crispy; the flour chips are soft, airy, bubbly and a little sweet. The salsa is for cilantro lovers, and the serving is generous. If I am within 100 miles of Ridgway, my wife, Linda, makes me stop here for a dozen orders of chips and salsa to bring home. Even if you cannot enjoy a leisurely meal at the Adobe Inn, you should stop by for their chips and salsa.

The waitstaff have eight to ten years' experience each and deliver efficient and professional service. The dining room is adorned with early Mexican and American Indian art. Membra Indian tribe designs, depicting lizards and fish, are imprinted on the sconces. There are several black-and-white photos of Mexican dancers and caballeras on horses and paintings of Mexicans in their villages. Chili ristras, strings of garlic, skulls of steer and buffalo and a large pot filled with straw augment the sierra-red tile floor, the white stucco walls and the adobe arches and fireplace. For a true taste of Mexican cuisine in a South-of-the-Border environment, put The Adobe Inn on your dinner card.

NUTRITION AND SPECIAL REQUESTS

The Adobe Inn deep-fries in peanut oil for greater quality and flavor. They use organic cornmeal in their corn casserole. Whole tomatoes are used in place of canned. Red chilies come from Tumatacari, Arizona, and green chilies are from Albuquerque, New Mexico. Anasazi beans used for the frijoles are from Dove Creek, Colorado. Five of the thirteen dinner entrées are designated for vegetarians but, as Joyce says, "Mexican food is not nonfattening." The menu states "Please—we discourage substitutions," and when the restaurant is very busy, especially in the summer, you may not have your special request fulfilled. Otherwise, the chef will accommodate your request or substitution wherever possible.

Flan

SERVES 8

4 cups milk

peel of one orange

2¾ cups granulated sugar,
    divided

4 large eggs

4 egg yolks

pinch of salt

1. Preheat oven to 300 degrees.
2. In a heavy saucepan, boil the milk and orange peel together until the mixture is reduced by one-quarter. Remove the peel and allow milk to cool.
3. In a mixing bowl, combine ¾ cup of the sugar, the eggs, egg yolks and salt. Add the cooled milk.
4. In a heavy nonstick frying pan, heat the 2 remaining cups of sugar. Stir gently but constantly until the sugar has melted completely and is amber in color.
5. Pour the melted sugar into 8 individual custard cups, coating the bottom of each. Slowly pour the custard mixture over this. Pour 1 inch of boiling water into a shallow baking dish. Carefully set the custard cups in the pan, then place in preheated oven and bake for 40–45 minutes.
6. Remove from the oven and allow to cool. May be refrigerated until ready to serve. To serve, run a knife around the edge of each cup, then turn upside-down over small plate; the flan will slide out with the burnt-sugar topping crowning it.

Recipe by Joyce Bucknam

Beverage Recommendation: Your favorite coffee.

The Adobe Inn serves a cinnamon-flavored Mexican coffee.

❧ SALIDA ❧

Salida, originally called *South Arkansas, was founded by the Denver and Rio Grande Railroad when it reached the location in 1880. Following a recommendation by Governor A. C. Hunt, the post office ordered the name changed in 1881. The governor had recently returned from a trip to Mexico, where he had seen the word* salida *on the exit of public buildings (*salida *is Spanish for "departure" or "exit").*

Zip Code: 81201 **Population:** 5,501 **Elevation:** 4,870 feet

ANTERO GRILL

14770 U.S. Highway 285
Phone: (719) 530-0301
Fax: (719) 530-0584
E-mail: anterogrill@anterogrill.com
Website: www.anterogrill.com

Directions: The restaurant is located on Highway 285 between Salida and Buena Vista, 1 mile north of the intersection of Highways 285 and 291, just south of mile marker 135 and on the east side of the highway.

ESSENTIALS

Cuisine: Modern American cowboy
Hours: Mother's Day through OCT: Tue.–Sat. 11:30 A.M.–2:30 P.M. and 5:30 P.M.–9 P.M., Sun. 12 noon–8 P.M. Closed Mon. NOV to Mother's Day: Tue.–Sat. 11:30 A.M.–2 P.M., Tue.–Thu. 5 P.M.–8 P.M., Fri.–Sat. 5 P.M.–9 P.M. Closed Sun.–Mon.
Meals and Prices: Lunch $5–$7. Dinner $10–$17 (soup and salad extra).
Nonsmoking: Smoking permitted only on the deck
Take-out: Yes
Alcohol: Full bar

Credit Cards: MC, VI
Personal Check: Yes, with driver's license
Reservations: Suggested, especially for dinner
Wheelchair Access: Yes, by ramp
Other: Available for private parties and professional meetings. Specialty weekends scheduled around an ethnic cuisine, like French, Italian, or Caribbean, featuring decorations and special food items. Wine dinners.

HISTORY AND BIOGRAPHY

The Antero Grill occupies a building constructed in 1945. The original business was Snoozy King, a gas station and liquor store. It was followed by a cowboy bar and, in the early 1990s, King Charles English Pub. The Cattle Baron occupied these premises for six months in 1996. The property then stood vacant for two years before Antero Grill opened in July 1998.

Antero Grill is family owned and operated. Owners Mark and Ann Wooley have been in the restaurant business since 1970 in Florida, where they owned four restaurants. Daughter-in-law Edy Wooley waits tables and tends bar. She has been working in restaurants since 1987, first for the Marriott Corporation in California, then as food and beverage director at the Hotel Santa Fe in New Mexico.

Son, co-owner and executive chef, Dave Wooley, a fourth-generation chef and restaurateur, began working in his father's Italian restaurant in 1979 folding pizza boxes. During high school he worked as a line cook at three different restaurants in central Florida. In 1993 he graduated from Walt Disney World's three-year culinary apprenticeship program in Orlando, Florida. He began working as a banquet and brunch chef at the Eldorado Hotel, a four-star establishment in Santa Fe, New Mexico, in 1995. He then took a sous-chef position at The Club Restaurant at the Hotel St. Francis, also in Santa Fe, and was soon promoted to executive chef. Throughout his career he has won numerous awards and published many of his recipes. Antero Grill, the first and only restaurant in Chaffee County to receive a three-diamond rating from AAA, is his first experience in a Colorado restaurant. Dave grows his own herbs, tomatoes, strawberries, beans and baby spinach in the grill's greenhouse.

FOOD, SERVICE AND AMBIENCE

Chef Wooley uses fresh ingredients in developing his creative and excellent presentations. I tried the rock shrimp quesadilla: four fresh, crispy flour tortillas, crisscrossed and overlapped, layered on top of coffee barbecue sauce, drizzled with lime crema and sprinkled with parsley. It all came with roasted vegetables, smoked mozzarella, cheddar and Monterey Jack cheeses, and they did not scrimp on the shrimp. There were fresh tomatoes in the salsa fresca. This was an interesting, unusual and tantalizing combination of tastes. It is for the adventuresome eater, although there is not much threat of danger.

The Antero Grill's modern American cowboy cuisine is the only example of it you will find in this book and, I am almost certain, the only one you will find in Colorado. Headlining the lunch menu are crispy tortilla, smoked garlic Caesar and baby spinach salads; a goat cheese, roasted red pepper and wild mushroom enchilada; maple-roasted butternut squash bisque; and veggie, beef and buffalo burgers served on cornmeal Kaiser rolls. Featured dinner items include homemade game sausage: a blend of buffalo, venison and wild boar, all smoked, with dried blueberries and wilted spinach; penne pasta baked with homemade buffalo chorizo; and wrangler's meatloaf made with green chilies, wild mushrooms and applewood bacon.

Service was a pleasing combination of casual but courteous. Chris Isaac and country-western songs played when I visited. There are two dining rooms separated by a gas fireplace, with a bar in the first dining area. The heavily textured, white stucco walls resembling whipped topping are adorned with pictures of cowboys riding horses, bucking broncos and rustling cattle. Ropes hang from the sconces and the back cushions of the booths have a buffalo print. The western decor is further enhanced by original 1880s photos of cowboys and horses taken in Medford, Oklahoma, including one titled "Cattle Annie and Little Britches, 1881."

NUTRITION AND SPECIAL REQUESTS

Antero Grill can accommodate guests with wheat and dairy allergies and make substitutions. The soups, desserts, breads, muffins and prickly-pear cactus butter are all homemade. In fact, 98 percent of the menu is made from scratch.

Caramelized Asparagus

salt to taste
2 bunches asparagus tips
   (about 2 pounds)
½ yellow onion, julienned

2 tablespoons olive oil
½ cup shaved Parmesan cheese
1 tablespoon freshly cracked
   black pepper

1. Heat cast iron skillet until very hot.
2. Mix salt, asparagus, onion and oil. Cook in skillet until asparagus starts to caramelize on outside (it will begin to release its own juices and become slightly sticky), about 3–4 minutes.
3. Serve warm, topped with shaved cheese and cracked black pepper.

Recipe by Dave Wooley

LAUGHING LADIES

128 West 1st Street
Phone: (719) 539-6209
Fax: (719) 539-7059
E-mail: laughing@amigo.net
Website: www.laughingladies.com

Directions: *From Highways 285 and 291,* northwest of Salida, go 8 miles into Salida on Highway 291, which becomes 1st Avenue. The restaurant will be on the left between F and G Streets. *From Highway 50 in Salida,* go north on F Street. There is a Texaco station on the corner and the Rainbow Motel on the south side. Go 1.1 mile on F Street and turn left onto 1st Street. The restaurant is a half-block down on the right.

ESSENTIALS

Cuisine: Modern American
Hours: Thu.–Mon. 11 A.M.–2:30 P.M. and 5 P.M.–9 P.M., Sun. 8 A.M.–2 P.M. Closed Tue.–Wed.

Meals and Prices: Sun. brunch $6–$7. Lunch $5–$7. Dinner $9–$15 (soup and salad extra).

Nonsmoking: Smoking permitted on garden patio only

Take-out: Yes

Alcohol: Yes

Credit Cards: MC, VI, DS

Personal Check: Yes. ID requested for check numbers under 1200.

Reservations: Recommended throughout the summer and all weekends

Wheelchair Access: Yes

Other: Delivery within a one-block radius

HISTORY AND BIOGRAPHY

Laughing Ladies was named after ladies of the evening, or "sportin' gals," as they were described to me, who would never cross 1st Street in Salida. This was propriety in those days. "Proper" folks would frequent the business establishments on 1st Street, including the location of this restaurant. The alley and the area north of 1st Street was "sportin' gals" territory. A shoe store and tailor shop were the original occupants of this building, constructed in 1905. In 1929 it became Mom's Café; later, it was the Home Café, where John Ash, culinary director at Fetzer Winery in California, learned to cook in the 1950s. From 1958 until 1969, the restaurant was called Joe's Café. This was followed by Luigi's Italian Restaurant, from 1969 to 1978. The space then lay vacant for sixteen years until Laughing Ladies opened in 1994.

Proprietors Jeff Schweitzer and Margie Sohl have owned the restaurant since 1996. Jeff has been in the restaurant business since 1983; his wife, Margie, has worked in restaurants since 1986. Both Jeff and Margie are graduates of the Restaurant School in Philadelphia. Following graduation they moved to Lake Tahoe, Nevada, where Jeff went to work at Harvey's and Harrah's. Margie cooked at Caesar's. Then it was on to the Napa Valley—Mustard's Grill for Jeff, and Auberge du Soleil for Margie. At Laughing Ladies, Margie does the cooking while Jeff handles the front of the house.

FOOD, SERVICE AND AMBIENCE

Linda and I sampled some of the Laughing Ladies' unique and intriguing tastes. The puree of forest-mushroom soup included portobello, button and crimini mushrooms and was made with veal stock, potatoes, onions, cayenne pepper and rosemary. It had no dairy or chicken and was savory and delicious. The goat cheese and roasted squash enchiladas with avocado pico de gallo offered a distinct blend of flavors. The honey-grilled pork chop was blackened on the outside, tender and juicy on the inside and exceptional. It came with Yukon gold potato hash made with heavy cream, spinach and maple-lacquered bacon, a sheer delight: Cooked bacon is cooled in the pan, brushed with maple syrup, then heated to 500 degrees in the oven for two minutes. Chef Margie's cuisine will make your mouth water!

For an appetizer, try the lemon-garlic braised duck with cornmeal cakes, spinach salad with champagne vinaigrette, or grilled polenta and portobello mushrooms. Among the entrées are sage-roasted chicken, snapper and rock shrimp fricassee, garlic-grilled skirt steak with poblano chile pesto and pancetta-wrapped snapper. The delightfully decadent desserts include mocha bread pudding, chocolate truffle torte with Merlot syrup and warm caramel apple tart with vanilla bean crème Anglaise.

Red chili and pico steak Benedict, red chile enchiladas, eggs and brown rice, smoked ham hash and huevos rancheros are spotlights of the Sunday brunch. Salads, sandwiches, appetizers and a burger are offered for lunch. Leading the selection are lemon chicken, Cobb and Chinese chicken salads; grilled chicken with prosciutto, roasted turkey and ham and Gruyère cheese sandwiches; and spicy chicken linguini.

Jeff was our most hospitable, humorous, attentive and informative server. His presence will ensure you a pleasurable evening. Modern American art adorned the red brick walls. Multimedia wood carvings and paintings, iron artworks and an acrylic panel enhanced the setting. This is a place where you can find fine food and have a good time. I think the laughing ladies would have loved this place, and I think you will too.

NUTRITION AND SPECIAL REQUESTS

At Laughing Ladies everything is made to order, substitutions are fine, and special requests are accommodated. Much of their produce, including lettuce, potatoes and onions, comes from Colorado's San Luis Valley. Vegetarians and vegans can select from several dishes.

Rock Shrimp Chile Relleno Appetizer

SERVES 4

1 medium zucchini, diced ⅜-inch

1 medium yellow crookneck squash, diced 3⅜-inch

2 tablespoons olive oil

salt and pepper to taste

2 red bell peppers (or you can use 4 canned roasted pepper halves)

2 tablespoons minced garlic

1 cup rock shrimp, cleaned (70- to 90-count per pound)

½ cup diced tomatoes

2 tablespoons chopped cilantro

¾ cup heavy cream

½ teaspoon salt

1½ tablespoons chipotle paste

field greens

champagne vinaigrette

juice of ½ lemon

⅓ cup Monterey Jack cheese

sour cream

1. Preheat oven to 425 degrees. Toss diced zucchini and crookneck squash with 2 tablespoons olive oil, salt and pepper. Roast in preheated oven for 15 minutes. Meanwhile, char and peel peppers. Remove seeds and cut into halves. (Omit this step if you are using canned roasted red peppers.)

2. Heat a sauté pan and warm olive oil over high heat. Add minced garlic and briefly sauté.

3. Add shrimp, diced tomatoes, ½ cup of the roasted and diced squash and zucchini and cilantro. (Note: you will have squash and zucchini left over.)

4. Stir for 1 minute, then add cream and ½ teaspoon salt and chipotle paste. Cook for 2 minutes over high heat. While shrimp mixture is cooking, compose a small salad on one end of each serving plate. Dress with a simple champagne vinaigrette.

5. Reheat the pepper halves on a grill to get some marks on them, and drape them on the plates so they may be filled.

6. Finish the shrimp with juice of lemon and cheese.

7. Portion the shrimp mixture on top of the pepper halves using a slotted spoon. Fold each pepper half over the shrimp mixture, top with

some of the sauce from the pan and garnish with sour cream streaks across the pepper. Serve hot.

Recipe by Margie Sohl

Wine Recommendations: 1999 Sonoma Cutrer Russian River Ranch Chardonnay or 1998 Beringer Napa Valley Sauvignon Blanc

THE WINDMILL

720 East Highway 50
Phone: (719) 539-3594
Fax: (719) 539-3479
E-mail and website: www.windmillonline.com

Directions: The restaurant is on the north side of Highway 50 on the corner of State Street in Salida, 2 blocks west of McDonald's on the same side of Highway 50 and 1 long block east of Burger King on the opposite side of Highway 50.

ESSENTIALS

Cuisine: Family Tex-Mex
Hours: Seven days 11 A.M.–10 P.M.
Meals and Prices: Lunch $6–$13. Dinner $6–$16 (soup or salad, starch and vegetable included; Tex-Mex entrées include refried beans, Spanish rice and chips and salsa).
Nonsmoking: Yes
Take-out: Yes
Alcohol: Full bar
Credit Cards: All five
Personal Check: Yes, with ID
Reservations: Accepted except in summer
Wheelchair Access: Yes
Other: Children's menu. Service charge of 15% for groups of six or more. Special orders or extra plate $1. Senior discount of 10% available on request on adult menu. No discount on specials.

HISTORY AND BIOGRAPHY

The Windmill Restaurant is in a building that formerly housed a car dealership and repair shop. There actually is a windmill on top of the building. In 1984, Jack Jones and his two sons, Clifton and Clayton, founded the Windmill. The wood, windows and incredible collection of antique signs were added by the Jones boys. In June 2000, Curtis and Theresa Killorn purchased the restaurant. They have, collectively, thirty years of experience in food service and management, including waiting tables at the Windmill, six years by Curtis and one year by Theresa. Mo Luna, who has been cooking at the Windmill since 1991, is head chef. He is from Mexico and returns there regularly to scout new ideas for the restaurant's cuisine.

FOOD, SERVICE AND AMBIENCE

The Windmill serves a large selection of American, Mexican and Tex-Mex dishes. Linda and I tried their hot and spicy wings seasoned "the Cajun way." These were served very meaty, temperature-hot and tasted like they were covered in Frank's sauce (which is used on Buffalo wings) topped with Cajun spices. I think folks from New Orleans would prefer these more than people from Buffalo would. Linda liked her chicken salad, which assembled smoked chicken strips, tomatoes, sprouts and almonds with honey-mustard dressing in an edible bowl. She thought the mix of alfalfa and almonds with honey-mustard dressing was the perfect combination. I ordered the scraps and scraps, which sounds like something I would have fed to one of our corgis, but was actually quite appetizing from a human viewpoint. It was 12 ounces of Kansas City sirloin cut up into chunks, breaded and grilled with garlic seasonings. The steak was tender and juicy, but the accompanying steamed vegetables tasted overcooked. You may want to order one of the other side-dish options: rice, baked potato or French-fried potatoes.

Highlights of the Windmill's multipage menu include roast pork with homemade gravy, jagerschnitzel, hand-breaded onion rings "piled high and enough for two to four people," Rio Grande fajitas (chicken grilled with squash, corn, onion and mushrooms), chicken pasta primavera and catfish coated with cornmeal and fried. Also available are a variety of burgers, sandwiches, nachos, salads, fajitas, Mexican combination plates and steaks. Dessert options include tiramisu, chocolate toffee mousse cake with Kahlúa, chocolate suicide layer cake and New York–style cheesecake.

Our server was more serious than jovial, but accommodating and able. The décor, courtesy of the Jones boys, consists of a multitude of antique advertisers' signs, mostly gasoline- and auto-related, including signs for Red Crown Gasoline, Gulf Standard Oil of Texas products, Rambler Parts & Service, Western Union Telegraph & Cable Office, Colonial Club 5¢ Cigars and a barber's pole with the sign "Look Better, Feel Better." One wall is devoted to the Artists of the Rockies Association and includes mixed-media, acrylic, oil, watercolor and colored-pencil sketches, mostly of wolves and trees. You will also spot an ancient Conoco gas pump, old cans of oil and transmission fluid next to cans of Pabst Blue Ribbon and Hamm Beer, a Power Max gasoline pump, Santa's sleigh with "Meadow Gold Ice Cream" written on the side, and wagon wheels. The Windmill has saved a piece of the American pie from the past. Stop in for a bit of nostalgia and commercial history to go with your Tex-Mex.

NUTRITION AND SPECIAL REQUESTS

The Windmill offers fifteen vegetarian items, two diet plates, grilled chicken and steamed vegetables. They say they never get special requests, possibly because there is a $1 fee.

Grilled Tequila-Lime Chicken

SERVES 4

4 skinless, boneless chicken breasts
1 cup tequila
½ cup lime juice
1 red bell pepper, cut into thin strips
6 jalapeño peppers
2 yellow onions, cut into thin strips
1 garlic clove, mashed
butter
lime wedges, for garnish

1. Allow chicken to marinate in tequila and lime juice overnight or for at least 2 hours. You can either charbroil (which is the preferred method for this recipe) or pan-fry the chicken. Reserve marinade.
2. As the chicken is cooking, fry the peppers, onions and garlic in butter on high heat. Once the vegetables have been fried to just before tenderness, add reserved marinade (or more tequila and lime juice) to make a saucy mixture.
3. Cut chicken into strips. Pour vegetables over the chicken strips. Garnish with lime wedges. Serve.

Recipe by Curtis Killorn

Beverage Recommendations: Lime or regular margarita, or René Junot red wine

❧ SILVER CLIFF ☙

SILVER DEPOSITS WERE *discovered near Silver Cliff in 1877, soon followed by the establishment of rich mines. Established in 1878, the town once aspired to be the state capital.*

Zip Code: 81252 **Population:** 512 **Elevation:** 7,980 feet

YODER'S HIGH COUNTRY RESTAURANT

700 Ohio Street
Phone: (719) 783-2656 or 783-2661
Fax: (719) 783-0328
E-mail: yoders@ris.net
Website: None

Directions: Take exit 98B off I-25 in Pueblo and go west 2 blocks on 4th Street. Turn right on Main Street and go 3 blocks to 4th Street (Highway 96). Turn left onto Highway 96 and stay on Highway 96 for 24 miles to the town of Wetmore. Continue on Highway 96 for 25 miles to the town of Silver Cliff. Turn left on Mill Street. There is a red-brick building on the corner used by Pizza Madness. (If you pass the Silver Cliff town hall and museum, you went too far on Highway 96.) Go 1 block on Mill Street. The restaurant is on the southeast corner of Mill Street and Ohio Street.

ESSENTIALS

Cuisine: Home cooking

Hours: OCT–MAR: Mon.–Fri. 11 A.M.–8 P.M. Closed Sat.–Sun. APR: Mon.–Sat. 11 A.M.–8 P.M. Closed Sun. MAY–SEP: Mon.–Sat. 11 A.M.–8:30 P.M. Closed Sun.

Meals and Prices: Lunch (served all day) $3–$6. Dinner (from 4:30 P.M.) $7–$14 (includes soup and salad bar).

Nonsmoking: All

Take-out: Yes, including bakery items

Alcohol: No

Credit Cards: MC, VI, DS

Personal Check: Yes, with ID

Reservations: Requested for groups of six or more in the evening.

Wheelchair Access: Yes

Other: Service charge of 15% added to parties of seven or more. Children's menu.

HISTORY AND BIOGRAPHY

Yoder's was built in the early 1900s with the adjacent motel. From 1994 to 1997 it was a coffee shop and bakery. The former owners, the Yoders, built the dining room in 1996. Current owners Kevin and Kate Davies have operated Yoder's since September 1997. This is their first restaurant in Colorado. Prior to coming west, Kevin and Kate worked in Kansas, catering on and off since 1980 and managing a country club and a steakhouse. Together they manage and cook at the restaurant. They make their own pies, desserts and soups. They also have their own smoker for smoked brisket, ribs and chicken.

FOOD, SERVICE AND AMBIENCE

Yoder's (doesn't that sound appetizing?) provides good home-cooked food served in a fast and friendly manner. Their chicken dumpling soup had very good flavor and was thick with rice, carrots, celery, parsley and small dumpling pieces. The turkey Manhattan was a hot sandwich with thinly sliced tender turkey piled high inside white bread with mashed potatoes, all covered with a heap of rich, brown gravy.

In addition to regular lunch and dinner menus, Yoder's has daily soup-and-sandwich specials; meal specials like chicken teriyaki, shrimp Alfredo and fish; and a prime rib special. Featured on the lunch menu are hot pork tenderloin or beef sandwiches, sloppy joes, burgers, home-made soups and salads. The dinner delights include char-grilled steaks cooked to order, butterfly shrimp and ham steak with pineapple. For dessert, choose from a variety of homemade pies, cakes and cookies made fresh daily.

There is a small dining area at the entrance with a few tables and the salad bar. Accentuating the main dining room are color photos of Crestone, Lower South Colony Lake and the Grand Tetons; pieces of leather artwork; a pellet stove in front of a corner piled high with rocks; and a pinewood ceiling, posts and beams. A small fenced patio with two tables is just off the front dining area. Come to Yoder's for good "down-home country cooking!"

NUTRITION AND SPECIAL REQUESTS

For the vegetarian, Yoder's offers a fifteen-item salad bar with six dress-ings, including a light ranch and a fat-free Italian, soup and a grilled cheese sandwich. Substitutions are accommodated if the item is in stock, and they will try their best to fulfill special requests.

Black Bean and Buffalo Sausage Soup

MAKES ABOUT 2 QUARTS

1 quart water

1½ teaspoons chicken base

½ teaspoon minced garlic

½ cup chopped celery

¼ cup chopped onions

pinch parsley flakes

pinch oregano flakes or dry oregano

salt and pepper to taste

1 cup chopped tomatoes

½ cup picante sauce

3 cups cooked black beans, drained (rinse them if using canned)

1 cup cooked red or kidney beans, drained (rinse if canned)

½ cup frozen corn

2 to 3 buffalo sausage, Polish-sausage style

grated cheese

tortilla chips

1. Bring water, chicken base, garlic, celery, onion, parsley, oregano and salt and pepper to boil in stock pot.

2. When celery and onions are tender, add the tomatoes, picante sauce, black beans, red or kidney beans and corn. Cook over medium heat, stirring occasionally.

3. Grill the sausage, cut into bite-size pieces and add to the soup. Simmer for 30 minutes.

4. Garnish with grated cheese and serve with tortilla chips.

Recipe by Kevin Davies

✑ SILVERTON ✑

FIRST CALLED *Baker's Park after the first prospector in the area, Charles Baker, Silverton went by several other names, including Reeseville, Quito and Greenville. Baker came to this narrow valley in 1860 when the region was still part of Ute Indian territory. He did find gold, but not much mining activity took place until after the Civil War.*

The name Silverton was chosen in an election in 1875 in reference to the silver mines in the San Juan region. Silver mining and the railroad boosted the population of San Juan County to about 5,000 by 1910. However, as mining declined so did the town's populace. Today, Silverton is a summer tourist town on the northern terminus of the Durango-Silverton narrow-gauge train.

Silverton is situated in San Juan County, which has the distinction of having the highest mean elevation of any county in the United States. Snowfall averages 200 inches a year. Government studies have shown that the air on top of Molas Pass, just south of Silverton, is some of the clearest and cleanest to be found anywhere in the continental United States.

Zip Code: 81433 **Population:** 531 **Elevation:** 9,305 feet

HANDLEBARS

117 13th Street
Phone: MAY–OCT: (970) 387-5395; NOV–APR: (602) 947-5557
Fax: (970) 387-5992
E-mail: handlebars@mindspring.com
Website: located under Silverton Chamber of Commerce

Directions: From the intersection of Highways 550 and 110 (Greene Street), proceed on Greene Street for 7 blocks. The restaurant is in a big blue building on the left at the corner of 13th Street. The restaurant entrance is around the corner on 13th Street, the first door on the left.

ESSENTIALS

Cuisine: High-country burgers and barbecue

Hours: MAY–OCT: Seven days 10:30 A.M.–10 P.M. Closed NOV–APR.

Meals and Prices: Lunch $6–$11. Dinner $9–$23 (includes soup or salad and vegetable or potato).

Nonsmoking: Yes

Take-out: Yes

Alcohol: Full bar

Credit Cards: MC, VI, DS (also marbles, skate keys and first-born)

Personal Check: Silverton only

Reservations: Accepted

Wheelchair Access: Yes

Other: Buck-a-Roos (Children's) menu. People requesting separate checks are dragged through the streets by wild horses, or an 18% service charge is added to each check. I think you have a choice.

HISTORY AND BIOGRAPHY

Handlebars is set in a building constructed in 1881. The front of the building was used as a bank. The side of the building was a hardware store. The back became a bowling alley and bar, and the upstairs was used as a telegraph office. Baker's Park Rendezvous Restaurant, named after Charles Baker and the town's original name, occupied these premises from 1974 until 1988. The building sat vacant for about six months until the current owners opened Handlebars in 1989.

The Boden family owns and operates Handlebars. Ken and his mother, Alyce, are the owners. Ken has worked in restaurants his entire life. He previously owned and operated the Sundial Garden Café in Carefree, Arizona, from 1987 until 1991. Ken's sister Sheri is the manager and previously managed the Sundial. Ken's other sister, Mary, is the hostess. Louise Tapia, the head chef, has been with the restaurant since 1994 and has been Handlebars' cook since 1996.

FOOD, SERVICE AND AMBIENCE

Handlebars' beef ribs were, as the menu promises, "downright tasty," topped with Handlebars' own mild and flavorsome barbecue sauce. The meat just fell off the bone. The meal came with salad, baked potato and roll. I'm told their pork ribs are even better! Other dinner entrées include 12- to 20-ounce steaks, prime rib, baby-back ribs, center-cut pork chops, several chicken dinners, spaghetti and rainbow trout. Buffalo wings, Rocky Mountain oysters and onion rings are served as appetizers. For lunch, you can choose from several selections of salads and sandwiches, buffalo chili, soup of the day and gazpacho. The apple cisp with caramel sauce (see recipe below) is a favorite dessert with guests at Handlebars.

Friendly service extends out to the street at Handlebars. An amiable hostess greeted me on the sidewalk before I even entered the restaurant. That's hospitality! Service was quick also. My meal came out in about fifteen minutes. Despite the Old West saloon setting, Handlebars has a family atmosphere. I observed families sitting at tables right next to the bar with its collage of Polaroid photos of men with handlebar mustaches. Across from the bar is a wood-burning fireplace set in an authentic ore car. Stuffed wild animals are the main theme of this high-ceilinged restaurant; among them are a full-size mounted elk, a grizzly bear, deer, moose, armadillo, raccoon, geese and a duck flying upside-down over the bar. Accompanying the wildlife are a host of horse-riding gear, wooden skis and snowshoes and posters and signs. A couple of my favorite pieces of signage read "Bartenders Fully Licensed" (to dispense advice, I imagine) and "Earth First. We'll mine the rest of the planets later." A permanent greeter at the front door is a short caricature figure of a miner with a beard and handlebar moustache wearing a sombrero and overalls and holding a gold pan.

NUTRITION AND SPECIAL REQUESTS

Handlebars has an extensive menu that will satisfy carnivore and vegetarian alike. For the latter, there are soups, salads, a vegetarian sandwich and a vegetarian burger. They honor special requests.

Apple Crisp with Caramel Sauce

MAKES ONE 9x13-INCH PAN

8 Granny Smith apples, peeled
and cored
1 cup heavy cream
½ cup sugar
¼ cup flour
1 tablespoon ground cinnamon

1 tablespoon freshly squeezed
lemon juice
½ teaspoon kosher salt
Topping (recipe follows)
Caramel Sauce (recipe follows)

1. Butter a 9x13-inch pan. Slice the apples into thin wedges. Toss the apple slices in a large bowl with the cream, sugar, flour, cinnamon, lemon juice and salt. Layer the apples into the prepared pan.
2. Preheat oven to 350 degrees. Make the Ropping (recipe follows). Spread the Ropping over the apple mixture.
3. Bake in preheated oven for 45 minutes to 1 hour, or until the apples are soft and the mixture is bubbling. Serve warm with Caramel Sauce drizzled on top (recipe below).

Topping

1½ cups flour
1 cup packed light brown sugar
2 teaspoons ground cinnamon

¼ teaspoon kosher salt
12 tablespoons unsalted butter

1. Mix the flour, brown sugar, cinnamon and salt in bowl.
2. Cut the cold butter into small pieces and blend it with the dry mixture, using a fork or your hands. The mixture should not be overworked. It will look crumbly.

Caramel Sauce

4 cups sugar
1 cup water

¼ cup unsalted butter
1 to 2 cups heavy cream

1. Combine the sugar and water in a large, wide, heavy saucepan and bring to a boil. Note: Use a pan in which you can see the color of

the sugar as it cooks. Stir as needed to dissolve the sugar. Do not stir again once the mixture begins to simmer. Continue a steady boil to reduce the mixture and bring it to a light brown color. This may take 20–30 minutes.

2. When the light-brown stage is reached, watch carefully as it changes to golden brown. It should be fairly thick. At this time, remove it from the heat and slowly stir the butter into the sugar syrup.

3. Blend in enough cream to make the consistency fairly thick, yet golden brown in color. Serve warm.

Recipe by Ken Boden

Beverage Recommendations: Your favorite coffee or a "Jumper Cable"

(Amaretto, Bailey's Irish Cream, Kahlúa and coffee topped with whipped cream)

❧ SNOWMASS VILLAGE ❧

ORIGINALLY CALLED *Snowmass-at-Aspen and later West Village, Snowmass was named for Snowmass Creek, which it borders. Snowmass Village was established in 1967 as a ski resort.*

Zip Code: 81615 **Population:** 1,822 **Elevation:** 6,880 feet

IL POGGIO

57 Elbert Lane
Phone and Fax: (970) 923-4292
E-mail: None
Website: None

Directions: On Highway 82, heading toward Aspen from Glenwood Springs, go 7 miles past the town of Old Snowmass. Turn right on Brush Creek Road. Take the fork to the left after ¼ mile, continuing on Brush Creek. Go 5 miles to Divide Road, then continue ¼ mile on Brush Creek Road and take the second right. Enter Lower Mall Parking. Park in Lot #6 or the closest available lot. Go across the street from the top of Lot #6.

Take the metal staircase up two flights and walk to the street. You should be at the beginning of Elbert Lane. The restaurant is 100 feet down Elbert Lane on the left across from the Wildwood Lodge.

ESSENTIALS

Cuisine: Italian

Hours: Seven days 5:30 P.M.–10 P.M. Closed mid-APR to mid-JUN and mid-SEP to late NOV.

Meals and Prices: Dinner $14–$33 (salad extra)

Nonsmoking: All

Take-out: Yes

Alcohol: Full bar

Credit Cards: MC, VI

Personal Check: Local only

Reservations: Recommended, especially in winter

Wheelchair Access: Yes. The staff will carry chairs up the few steps in front of the building.

Other: One check per table. Split plate charge of $3.50.

HISTORY AND BIOGRAPHY

Il Poggio is Italian for the top of a little hill. It refers to the terrace of the vineyard where the prime grapes are grown. Il Poggio occupies a building constructed in the late 1960s, the same time Snowmass Village was built. This building has always been used as a restaurant. Shavano's, an American restaurant, and the Pepper Mill both preceded Il Poggio, which opened in June 1989. Current owner and executive chef Chris Blachly took over Il Poggio in June 1990. He completed a three-year apprenticeship with the American Culinary Federation and cooked for six years at the Greenbriar in Boulder, Colorado, and for 2½ years at Charlemagne in Aspen. Manager Ted Greene joined Il Poggio in 1996. He has been in the restaurant business in Aspen since 1983 and previously worked at Syzygy for six years.

FOOD, SERVICE AND AMBIENCE

Il Poggio serves some fine Italian dishes. Its staying power, more than ten years, is a testament to that fact. I began dinner with the insalata spinaci, fresh spinach, pears, pancetta (Italian bacon) and pecorino Toscano cheese with honey-pomegranate dressing. There were some nice-sized pieces of pecorino, one of my favorite cheeses, and the pancetta was crispy, crumbly and very flavorful. The dressing was mostly tart-tasting and a little sweet with the honey and pears. For the entrée, I chose far-falle, the bow-tie pasta, with Kalamata olives, fresh tomatoes, Sicilian salted capers, garlic, basil and parsley. This was served steaming hot. The farfalle was al dente excellente, tender but with a chew. All of the flavors suffused well. This was a superb Greek-style Italian dish, both fresh and salty tasting.

For starters, Il Poggio offers an antipasto salad with salami and pro-sciutto, grilled bread brushed with olive oil and garlic and served with daily accompaniments, broiled shrimp with spicy Calabrian chili glaze and imported Italian air-cured beef. The pastas are available in appetizer or main-course portions and feature fettuccine with shrimp and arti-choke hearts in a pink vodka-cream sauce; rigatoni with duck confit, mushrooms, spinach, pine nuts and roasted pepper; and ravioli with a goat cheese and sweet-potato filling in a hazelnut cream sauce. The secondi selections include grilled Moroccan spiced pork chop, roasted pancetta-wrapped all-natural chicken breast, daily fish specials, beef ten-derloin with grilled portobello mushroom and grilled lamb sirloin mar-inated in mint, rosemary, lime and garlic. You can order a side vegetable of the day, roasted red creamer potatoes, or Italian white beans.

I arrived when the restaurant opened and received prompt, friendly service when placing my order and receiving my food. The front dining room with its bar and windows looking down on the Village Mall is a great people-watching place. If people-watching does not interest you, there is an open kitchen with a stone fireplace where you can watch the chef prepare your meal and everyone else's. You will pass by a wine rack set in the wall as you enter the more upscale-looking back dining room. Posters of espresso, corkscrews, grapes, Chianti and liqueur adorn the mauve-colored walls. There is also an engaging photograph of a stone, rectangular-arched doorway with an iron gate that looks like it was taken in Italy.

Il Poggio will try to accommodate guests' dietary needs. There are several antipasti and pasta vegetarian dishes and one secondi vegetarian plate, the polenta, portobello mushrooms and grilled seasonal vegetables with pomodoro sauce. In addition, other menu items can be prepared for vegetarians on request. They can also eliminate items, like chicken stock, in preparing the food.

Spinach Salad with Honey-Pomegranate Dressing

SERVES 1

This recipe calls for pecorino Toscano, a cheese made in Tuscany, Italy, from sheep's milk. It is not to be confused with the more familiar pecorino Romano.

6 ounces spinach leaves	1–2 ripe pears, peeled, cored
2 ounces pecorino Toscano,	and sliced thin
sliced thin	freshly ground black pepper
2 ounces pancetta, diced, crisped	Honey-Pomegranate Dressing
in a sauté pan and drained	(recipe follows)

Place spinach, cheese, pancetta and pears in a salad bowl. Add fresh ground pepper and as much of the dressing as you like. Toss and serve.

Honey-Pomegranate Dressing

¼ cup honey	½ cup pomegranate vinegar
¼ cup olive oil	salt and pepper to taste

Combine all ingredients in a mixing bowl using a wire whisk. Makes 1 cup.

Recipe by Chris Blachly

THE STONEBRIDGE RESTAURANT

300 Carriage Way
Phone: (970) 923-2420
Fax: None
E-mail: None
Website: None

Directions: On Highway 82, heading toward Aspen from Glenwood Springs, go 7 miles past the town of Old Snowmass. Turn right on Brush Creek Road. Take the fork to the left after ¼ mile, continuing on Brush Creek. Go 5 miles to Divide Road, then continue another ¼ mile on Brush Creek Road and take the second right. Enter Lower Mall Parking. Park in Lot #2 or Lot #1. The restaurant is in the Stonebridge Inn across from the lower half of Lot #2. After you enter the building, go straight back to the bar. The restaurant is to the right of the bar.

ESSENTIALS

Cuisine: American West
Hours: Seven nights 6 P.M.–9:30 P.M. Closed beginning of OCT to end of NOV and end of APR to beginning of JUN.
Meals and Prices: $13–$30 (includes starch and vegetable; salads extra).
Nonsmoking: All
Take-out: Yes
Alcohol: Full bar
Credit Cards: MC, VI, AE, DS
Personal Check: Local (from the Roaring Fork Valley) only
Reservations: Recommended
Wheelchair Access: Yes
Other: No separate checks. Service charge of 18% for parties of six or more. Split plate fee: $2 for salads, $4 for entrées.

HISTORY AND BIOGRAPHY

The Stonebridge Inn was built in the late 1960s, the same time as the village. Prior to 1990, the space currently occupied by the restaurant was used for offices and the front desk. In the early 1990s, the Inn remodeled and opened a pasta bar in this place. The Stonebridge Restaurant opened in 1996. The restaurant is part of the inn, owned by Destination Hotels and Resorts. Manager Annie Windle has been at the Stonebridge Restaurant since 1997 and previously worked at El Rancho Restaurant, west of Denver, from 1994 until 1997. Executive chef Erich Owen came to the Stonebridge in July 2001. He is from Fort Collins, Colorado, and has been cooking since 1991. He is the former owner of Erdinger Hof in Durango, Colorado, now E. O.'s Chop House. He was executive chef for three years at Harmon's in Telluride, Colorado, and sous-chef at Cache Cache in Aspen, Colorado, before coming to the Stonebridge. He also served an apprenticeship in San Francisco, California; Germany; and Austria.

FOOD, SERVICE AND AMBIENCE

The Stonebridge's Colorado cuisine offers several meat and wild game dishes and a couple of vegetarian selections. I ordered a salad with my entrée, going with the tomato, feta and arugula with Kalamata olive vinaigrette followed by the smoked pork tenderloin. The white feta cheese, black dressing, red and yellow pear tomatoes and green arugula made for a very colorful plate presentation. The pear tomatoes were sweeter and had more of a fruit flavor than do cherry tomatoes. The tenderloin was house smoked, topped with a grain mustard and fresh herb crust and served with green peppercorn sauce. Before smoking, the pork is rubbed with molasses, celery salt, whole peppercorns and paprika. The tenderloin was very tender and consisted of seven half-pink, half-brown medallions. It was high-quality and lean with no fat. Potato-leek gratin—thinly sliced potatoes layered with melted Parmesan cheese and strands of leek—accompanied the tenderloin. The vegetables, julienned carrots and asparagus with snow peas, were a sweet dish.

For starters at the Stonebridge you can choose house-cured Muscovy duck and spinach salad, crab and crawfish cakes with an ancho-chili aioli and avocado, smoked salmon served with fresh figs, or rabbit ravioli with cognac-tarragon cream. High points among the entrées are grilled quail marinated with juniper berries and fennel, filet mignon wrapped in applewood-smoked bacon, elk tenderloin grilled and sauced with apricots and morels and Colorado rack of lamb espresso scented with a lavender-vanilla demi-sauce.

My service was quick and efficient. Lively jazz was piped into the dining room with walls of glass on two sides for views of the adjacent patio, neighboring lodges and spruce and fir trees. To the right of the host's stand is a small alcove decorated with a canvas of red, white and green grapes, for private parties. To the host stand's left is a waiting area with a rock fireplace, couches and chairs. Embellishing the dining area are stone pillars, a wine rack behind closed glass doors and paintings of Mesa Verde and a southwestern valley. The chair frames are made of treated natural logs. Overhead is a slanted glass roof with pinewood log beams and a trellis of aspen branches facing the lodge above. The patio is decked with potted flowers, an aspen tree growing though the floor and canvas umbrellas.

NUTRITION AND SPECIAL REQUESTS

The staff will poach or grill fish using a fresh vinaigrette or light oil in lieu of heavy cream or their sauces. They will substitute low-fat new potatoes for rice and serve steamed vegetables. They do not receive many special requests. In addition to salads, the Stonebridge serves an herb-crusted baked Brie appetizer and mushroom risotto and capellini entrées for vegetarians.

Green Peppercorn Demi-Glace

SERVES 4

1½ tablespoons olive oil
1 tablespoon diced shallots
1 teaspoon diced garlic
2 cups brandy
2 cups veal stock

2 teaspoons whole green
    peppercorns
dash of salt and pepper
1 tablespoon honey, optional

1. Heat olive oil in medium saucepan.
2. Sweat shallots and garlic in olive oil. Add brandy and reduce by half.
3. Add veal stock. Reduce by half.
4. Strain sauce. Add peppercorns, salt and pepper. (A little honey may be added to take some of the spice out of the peppercorns.) Serve

over beef, pork tenderloin, New York strip, rib-eye, elk, venison or caribou (any dark red meat). Makes 1 cup.

Recipe by Erich Owen

◈ STEAMBOAT SPRINGS ◈

STEAMBOAT SPRINGS WAS *originally a summer playground for the Ute Indians. The town boasts 150 medicinal springs with a combined flow of 2,000 gallons per minute and temperatures ranging from 58 to 152 degrees. The town derived its name from the peculiar puffing sounds emitted by one of its former springs. To the trappers of the 1880s, it produced a sound that resembled a steamboat chugging. This spring was destroyed during construction of the Moffat Railroad, now the Denver and Rio Grande Railroad, in 1908. Steamboat is located in a big bend in the Yampa River with the springs on the south bank of the river. Today, Steamboat Springs is considered by many to be "Ski Town USA" because of the large number of Olympic and National Ski Team members produced here.*

Zip Code: 80487 on the mountain; 80488 in the town
Population: 9,815 **Elevation:** 6,728 feet

MEDITERRANEAN GRILL & TAPAS LOUNGE

1965 Ski Times Square
Phone: (970) 879-9232
Fax: (970) 879-1297
E-mail: None
Website: www.steamboatresorts.com

Directions: From Highway 40, 1 mile east of the town of Steamboat Springs, exit onto Mt. Werner Road. Go north 0.7 mile, past the traffic signal, and turn left onto Mt. Werner Circle. Go 0.3 mile and turn left onto Ski Times Square. Follow the winding road for 750 feet to the three-way stop. Continue straight 0.1 mile. To your right, you will pass the Torian Plum Condos and Plaza and an alley. The building to your right just past the alley is the Thunderhead Lodge. Drive past the entrance to the lodge to the parking lot. The restaurants are in the lodge.

ESSENTIALS

Cuisine: Mediterranean

Hours: Mediterranean Grill: JUL through SEP and DEC through APR: Seven nights 5:30 P.M.–10 P.M. Closed MAY–JUN and OCT–NOV. Tapas Lounge: JUN to mid-OCT and late NOV to mid-APR: Seven days 3 P.M.–10 P.M. Closed mid-APR through MAY and mid-OCT to late NOV.

Meals and Prices: Mediterranean Grill: Dinner $17–$25 (soup and salad extra). Tapas Lounge: Tapas $5–$8. Light entrées: $6–$16 (soup and salad extra).

Nonsmoking: All nonsmoking in Mediterranean Grill. Smoking permitted anywhere in Tapas Lounge.

Take-out: Yes, for Tapas Lounge only

Alcohol: Full bar in both restaurants

Credit Cards: MC, VI, AE, DS

Personal Check: In-state only with ID

Reservations: Recommended for Mediterranean Grill. Accepted for parties of eight or more only for Tapas Lounge.

Wheelchair Access: Yes

Other: Children's menu. Service charge of 18% on large parties. Groups and special functions welcome.

HISTORY AND BIOGRAPHY

This is a dual review. The Thunderhead Lodge contains two notable restaurants, the Mediterranean Grill downstairs and the Tapas Lounge upstairs. The Thunderhead Lodge was built about 1970. In the 1980s, the Conservatory was the restaurant upstairs. Rocky Osso's, upstairs, and Cipriani's, downstairs, followed the Conservatory and lasted about ten years. Between 1999 and 2001, the Lobster Ranch occupied the upstairs while Monahan's Irish Pub did business downstairs. The current occupants, the Mediterranean Grill & Tapas Lounge, opened in February 2001.

Greg Pace, Chris Delaney, Tony Lawrence and Joey Bowman are the owners of the two restaurants. Greg and Chris are also the managers. Greg has been in the restaurant business since 1989. He previously cooked at the Coos Bay Bistro, managed the Hornet and opened the Painted Bench, all in Denver. Chris spent a year each cooking at Antares and Mattie Silks in Steamboat. Tony and Joey are the chefs. Tony got his start in the business in his parents' hotel and steakhouse in Australia. He did an apprenticeship in Florida and worked for two years at Mattie Silks and seven years at Riggio's, both in Steamboat. Joey started cooking in his mother's cafeteria in Massachusetts. He graduated from the New England Culinary Institute in Montpelier, Vermont, in 1991. Before coming to the Mediterranean Grill, Joey worked as a chef for four years at Cipriani's and as a sous-chef for four years at Antares, both in Steamboat.

FOOD, SERVICE AND AMBIENCE

For a medley of marvelous Mediterranean pleasures for the palate, you owe it to your senses of taste and smell to dine at the Mediterranean Grill & Tapas Lounge. I had a royal tapas feast for lunch at the Tapas Lounge. My personal banquet included seven tapas, a Greek salad, basmati rice, couscous and red grapes just for garnish and to cleanse the palate between bites. Chef Bowman is deep into flavors, and I had the sensational opportunity to try a multitude of them. The Montrachet, herbed goat cheese wrapped in phyllo dough, baked and served with raspberry fruit compote, was sweet, fruity and very rich. It was so good, I could not feel guilty about the calories or fat content. The chorizo sausage came with sweet mustard and grilled peppers and was charred on the outside, pink on the inside. The grilled quail was accompanied by thin, crispy onion rings and a banana-citrus aji, which provided a sweet contrast to the flavorsome charbroiled taste of the quail. The sea scallops were nicely seared, soft, not mushy, with a little chew to them and served with shiitake mushrooms and a red wine reduction. The red wine added a pleasing flavor. The Mojo shrimp were grilled with lime, rum and a chipotle glaze. I know most of the rum burns off when it is cooked, but the combination of flavors was intoxicating and with a little "burn." It was very pleasant. The piquillo was a whole red pepper stuffed with the chef's daily selection of herbed goat cheese, which off-set the pepper's spicy taste. The littleneck clams were stuffed with finely chopped roasted vegetables and had a delicious seafood broth. The Greek salad segment was highlighted by artichoke hearts, red onions, feta cheese, Kalamata olives and field greens in a light herb vinaigrette. The basmati rice and couscous combination had a tasty grainy texture and was excellent. This was, indeed, a celebration for the taste buds!

Many of the tapas presented in the Tapas Lounge are offered as appetizers in the Mediterranean Grill. The following salads can be found on both restaurants' menus: seared tuna, duck confit and green bean and roasted pecan and Gorgonzola. The Tapas Lounge light entrées featured a number of Mediterranean delights that included a grilled Moroccan hamburger; grilled beef, shrimp, chicken, or vegetable served as shish kebabs or in pita bread; grilled chicken shawama with whipped roasted garlic; Portuguese seafood crêpe; roasted vegetable penne pasta tossed with pine nuts; and a daily panini sandwich selection. Among the Mediterranean Grill's list of entrées are Moroccan lamb with a pistachio-nut crust, grilled tenderloin of beef with shiitake mushroom and bacon demi-glace or sauce béarnaise, horseradish-crusted Alaskan halibut, veal loin chop stuffed with duck confit, a chef's daily Latin grill selection and another daily special creation. Topping the desserts are a flourless choco-late cake, Grand Marnier frozen soufflé and a mousse du jour layered with fresh fruit.

I was served by the bartender and one of the owners. Both were very courteous, efficient and knowledgeable about the menu and specials. I listened to Mediterranean music from Spain and Italy while I gourman-dized. The Tapas Lounge has a predominantly Mediterranean décor. Blue and white paintings from Santorini, Greece, adorn the blue, orange and rust-colored walls, supplemented by artwork from South of the Border and a sizeable rock fireplace. This is a favorite après-ski location in the winter. The deck outside offers scenic views of the mountains.

The Mediterranean Grill downstairs is smaller, quieter and more intimate than the Lounge upstairs. There is a small bar with four stools to the right of the entrance. The white tablecloths and peach-colored napkins match the peach-and-white, rough-textured walls. The decor is simple and limited to diamond- and sunflower-shaped mirrors in copper frames; brass, leaf-pattern wall lamps; a tall, rusty-iron candle-holder; and a frosted-glass artwork of a pretty maiden. Tiny alcoves in the arched window frames facing the patio are used to house potted plants. Adjacent to the Mediterranean Grill is a third dining area called the Soda Creek Café, where skiers can get a breakfast buffet before heading to the slopes.

NUTRITION AND SPECIAL REQUESTS

The Mediterranean Grill & Tapas Lounge offer numerous vegetarian menu items. They use high-quality meats, free-range and free of preservatives. All of their greens are very fresh. They use all-natural products, expensive oils and vinegars and the marrow from the bone in their demiglaces. They fill special requests frequently. If they have the product, they will do their best to accommodate.

Paella

SERVES 4–6

Whereas most paellas incorporate rice into the dish, this version does not, so you should cook rice, couscous, or a combination of the two to accompany it.

1½ ounces olive oil
¼ cup diced onion
⅛ cup chopped garlic
¼ cup fresh fennel (or
    1 teaspoon ground fennel
    if fresh not available)
pinch of crushed red pepper flakes
pinch of saffron
3 cups mixed seafood, whatever
    you would like

½ cup diced roasted chicken
    or duck
½ cup chorizo sausage, ground
½ cup diced tomatoes
¼ cup white wine
2 cups chicken stock or fumé
    (fish stock)
salt and pepper

1. Sauté onion, garlic, fennel, crushed red pepper flakes and saffron in olive oil or butter in large pan.

2. Add seafood with the chicken or duck, sausage and tomatoes.
3. Deglaze with white wine and add stock. Reduce by one-half. Season to taste with salt and pepper. Serve over rice or other cooked grain.

Recipe by Tony Lawrence and **Joey Bowman**

Wine Recommendations: Your favorite Pinot Grigio or Chardonnay, depending on whether you want to accent the red or white meats

RIGGIO'S

1106 Lincoln Avenue
Phone: (970) 879-9010
Fax: (970) 879-5198
E-mail: riggios@peoplepc.com
Website: www.riggiosfinefood.com

Directions: Entering downtown Steamboat Springs on Highway 40 (Lincoln Avenue) from Rabbit Ears Pass, go 9 blocks past the hot springs pool on the right. The restaurant is on the right between 11th and 12th Streets.

ESSENTIALS

Cuisine: Italian

Hours: Seven nights 5:30 P.M.–9:30 P.M. or 10 P.M. Closed MAY. JUN to mid-NOV every Wed. night has a special five-course dinner, no menu offered.

Meals and Prices: Entrées $15–$25 (includes starch). Pasta $13–$19. Pizza $9–$10. Soup and salad extra. Five-course Wed. night dinner $17.

Nonsmoking: Smoking permitted only at bar

Take-out: Yes

Alcohol: Full bar

Credit Cards: All five

Personal Check: Local only

Reservations: OCT–APR reservations encouraged. JUN–SEP reservations only accepted for parties of eight or more.

Wheelchair Access: Yes, through a side entrance

Other: Children's menu. Service charge of 18% may be added for parties of six or more. Available for private parties and large groups.

HISTORY AND BIOGRAPHY

Riggio's location was originally a car and truck dealership and garage built in the 1930s. Over the years, the building has been used as a supermarket, a Sears catalog store and a hunting and fishing outdoor shop. Riggio's opened in 1990 at Lincoln Avenue and 7th Street. In 1994 the restaurant moved to its present site.

The owners are Dominick and Karen Riggio. They previously owned The Helm Restaurant (now The Grubstake) in Steamboat from 1988 to 1990. Both were involved in catering with Continental Hosts and Catering, where they met. Dominick is the head chef. Karen is the manager and hostess. She is very friendly and treats her customers like family. Karen's father, Vinnie, loves to cook and helps in the kitchen a few nights a week.

FOOD, SERVICE AND AMBIENCE

Riggio's will treat you with warm Italian hospitality while they serve you their outstanding creations. Wednesday evening is a popular night with the locals at Riggio's. On this one night of the week, the restaurant serves a five-course dinner in place of its regular menu. I just happened to be in Steamboat Springs on a Wednesday night and stumbled upon this great offering. The five courses include soup, choice of antipasto, salad, choice of entrée and dessert. The zuppa was a hot cup of pasta fagioli, a spicy Tuscan specialty of white beans, tomatoes, garlic and macaroni in chicken broth. I prefer this soup to minestrone. I think it has better flavor and a good "Italian" taste. Five slices of warm Italian bread were brought to my table to go with seasoned olive oil. For my antipasto, I chose the funghi, three broiled mushroom caps filled with garlic-and-herb bread stuffing, topped with melted Parmesan and served with a raspberry coulis. The mushrooms were juicy and tasty with a lot of mushroom flavor. Riggio's house salad is sizable, a very good mix of red onion, black olives, shaved carrot, mixed greens, pepperoncini, artichoke hearts, tomatoes and small chunks of cheese in a Gorgonzola vinaigrette. For the entrée, I elected penne puttanesca. It was a large portion of properly prepared penne pasta and vegetables, spicy, but not overspiced. It came with a generous amount of capers, tomatoes and black olives and a few artichoke hearts. There was nothing too spicy about any of the dishes. However, by the fourth course, this had been a lot of food. The accumulation of spices was beginning to add up. The dolci was a welcome cool-down to my gastronomic meltdown: vanilla cake with strawberry filling, chocolate ganache, whipped cream and a mixed berry coulis. This five-course dinner was a superb value.

Riggio's fourfold menu features antipasto, entrées, pizza and pasta. For starters, try the fresh steamed mussels in white wine, grilled Italian sausage, or broccoli sautéed with olive oil, lemon and garlic. The entrées come with pasta or Tuscan roasted potatoes. They include fresh filet of salmon; grilled eggplant layered with fresh spinach; chicken breast sautéed, grilled or breaded; veal scaloppini; New York strip steak; and filet mignon. The pizzas are made from hand-tossed homemade dough, topped with fresh ingredients like basil, goat cheese, roasted red peppers, spinach and garlic and baked in a brick surface oven. They appear to be worth checking out.

Each pasta dish is based on Italian tradition and preparation. Highlighting this section of the menu are portobello mushroom ravioli, large prawns with lobster tail or sea scallops with gemelli or angel-hair pastas, fresh Manila clams over linguini, lasagna filled with seasoned ground veal and fresh spinach and linguini Alfredo topped with grilled shrimp or chicken. For a truly delectable ending to your dinner, try one of the homemade desserts. The selection varies, but some standards are peanut butter pie, chocolate Marquis (a flourless cake), carrot cake, cheesecake, tiramisu, lemon pignoli (pine nuts) and brown butter mixed berry tart.

Service was very efficient, fast and polite. My server was noticeably very busy but was exceptional in performance and attitude. She even took the time to get an answer from the chef for me despite having to attend to a full load of tables. Guitar music played in the restaurant but it was difficult to hear on this very busy and noisy night.

Riggio's has a high open ceiling with ceiling fans, hanging lamps and visible ventilation pipes. The dining area to the left has the bar, a sculpture called "Moonstruck Owl," a serigraph of a half-veiled woman by Iranian artist Hessam and an abstract rock sculpture on aluminum foil by local artist Nancy Howell. The dining room to the right has a huge mural over the front window called "The Renaissance Feast," which should stir anyone's appetite. A photograph of a canyon wall and an abstract cityscape titled "December San Francisco" further enhanced the décor. A stairway in the far right corner leads to dining in a loft. Figure studies hang from the loft's walls and photos of Karen's great-uncle and two grandmothers can be seen as you ascend the stairs. The loft also displays antique maps of Italy and the world, a painting of a Tuscan villa and a mural of a wine rack.

NUTRITION AND SPECIAL REQUESTS

Riggio's has quite a few vegetarian dishes as well as meat-and-potato dishes for variety. The chefs use only olive oil and have no problem with putting sauces on the side, eliminating garlic, or cooking without wine on request. They say they do not get many special requests but will be accommodating when they can.

Vitello Saltimbocca with
Marsala Mushroom Cream Sauce

SERVES 6

1 clove garlic	6 slices prosciutto ham
¼ cup olive oil	6 slices imported fontina cheese
2 pounds fresh spinach, washed	seasoned flour
and dried	Marsala Mushroom Cream Sauce
1 large leek	(recipe follows)
3 pounds boneless veal loin	

1. Sauté garlic clove in olive oil until brown. Add spinach and cook until wilted. Set aside to cool.
2. Peel leek layer by layer and blanch in boiling water. Slice leeks into strips about ⅜-inch wide and set aside.
3. Cut veal into six pieces, about 8 ounces each.

4. On a sturdy surface, lay out plastic wrap, place a piece of veal in the middle of plastic and cover with another piece of plastic. Using a meat mallet, gently pound each veal cutlet into a thin, wide sheet. Final product should be about 4 times the size of the original piece and about ¼-inch thick.

5. Place 1 slice each of prosciutto and fontina cheese in the center of the veal without overhanging the meat. Place a pluck of sautéed spinach in the middle and roll like a burrito, folding ends in and rolling up in a cigar shape. Now, using the leek strips, tie 2 leeks around veal roll, 1 on each end. Repeat the process with remaining pieces of veal.

6. Dredge veal rolls in seasoned flour and brown on all sides in an oiled ovenproof sauté pan over medium-high heat. Preheat oven to 450 degrees.

7. Once veal rolls are sufficiently browned, move them to the preheated oven to finish cooking, about 10 minutes.

8. Slice on bias and serve with Marsala Mushroom Cream Sauce.

Marsala Mushroom Cream Sauce

½ large onion, finely diced	3 cups cream
¼ cup unsalted butter	2 tablespoons fresh chopped
¼ cup Marsala wine	parsley
1 pound mixed mushrooms, sliced	salt and pepper

1. Sauté onion in butter until slight color appears on edges of onions.

2. Deglaze with Marsala wine. Beware: It will flame up!

3. When flame dies out, add mushrooms and cook for about 3 minutes, tossing about in pan.

4. Add heavy cream and bring to a boil. Reduce cream by about ⅓ volume.

5. Add chopped parsley and season to taste with salt and pepper. Serve immediately.

Recipe by Dominick Riggio

Wine Recommendation: Vernaccia di San Gimignano, a Tuscan white wine

❧ TRINIDAD ☙

NAMED AFTER THE *Holy Trinity, Trinidad was originally called Rio de Las Animas and was first settled in 1859. The town began as a supply depot on the Mountain Branch of the Santa Fe Trail between Bent's Old Fort to the northeast and Raton Pass to the south. Later, Trinidad served as a railhead for cattle drives from Texas to New Mexico on the Goodnight Trail. Over the past century, Trinidad has prospered as the center of one of the world's richest coal-mining districts. Many famous western figures played a part in Trinidad's history: Bat Masterson; Wyatt Earp, who drove the stage; Billy the Kid; and Kit Carson, whose statue graces the park that bears his name. Three miles northeast of Trinidad is Drop City, home of a 1960s hippie settlement and the remains of a dome-shaped building made entirely of car parts, mostly fenders and doors. To reach it, take exit 15 from I-25 and head northeast on Highway 239.*

Zip Code: 81082 **Population:** 9,078 **Elevation:** 6,025 feet

WAZUBI'S BLUE CUP COFFEE HOUSE ———

269 North Commercial Street
Phone: (719) 846-8760
Fax: None
E-mail: stonewallgna@ria.net
Website: None

Directions: Take exit 13B from I-25 south of Walsenburg and go east on Main Street (Highway 160) for ½ mile (6 blocks). Turn left at the signal for Commercial Street. Go 0.2 mile (3 blocks). The restaurant is on the left on the corner of Plum Street (no street sign).

ESSENTIALS

Cuisine: Healthful food

Hours: Mon.–Sat. 7 A.M.–7 P.M., Sun. 1 P.M.–5 P.M.

Meals and Prices: Breakfast (all day) $1–$3. Lunch (11:30 A.M.–2 P.M.) $4–$7.

Nonsmoking: All

Take-out: yes

Alcohol: No

Credit Cards: MC, VI, AE, DS

Personal Check: In-state only

Reservations: Not accepted

Wheelchair Access: Yes

HISTORY AND BIOGRAPHY

Wazubi's and the antique store next door were originally the lobby and part of the Bee Hive Hotel, built in the early 1900s. In the 1950s, the hotel became a bar called the Duck Inn. In the 1970s it was replaced by a discotheque. In the 1990s, a bookstore occupied the premises until Dick and Roxy Anderson opened Wazubi's at the end of 1996. The name was the result of a contest they held in town. In April 2001, Karen Krick, who had spent a couple of years cooking in the Trinidad area, became the new owner, manager and chef. This is her first restaurant venture.

FOOD, SERVICE AND AMBIENCE

Wazubi's is a cozy place where you can get pure and healthful foods and beverages. All of the quiches, soups, breads, pies and pastries, except for the cheesecakes, are homemade. I tried the spinach quiche and fruit salad. The quiche, with a homemade crispy, crunchy crust, was nutritious and good. The fruit salad contained kiwi, grapes, peaches, pears and apricots in a sweet fruit glaze. The quiche was accompanied by a tasty cold black-bean salsa with corn, onion and red pepper. All of the ingredients tasted very fresh.

The other lunch items on Wazubi's blackboard menu on the day I stopped in were turkey sandwich with ranch dressing, French onion soup prepared with bread and cheese and two ground beef, soft tacos. The menu changes, so you may find ham quiche, cream of mushroom or potato soup, chicken soft tacos, Asian chicken salad, or homemade green chili when you visit. For breakfast, expect to find a combination of some of the following: blueberry or banana-chocolate chip muffins; cranberry-oat, peach, raspberry, or cream cheese scones; pumpernickel and strawberry bread; bagels; fruit turnovers; cinnamon buns; English muffins; French toast stuffed with cream and ricotta cheeses and topped with blueberry or raspberry syrup; and the xango, a cheesecake pastry roll filled with cream cheese. Their selection of pies includes key lime, lemon meringue and Dutch apple. A java and juice bar will fill your beverage needs.

Wazubi's is semi self-service. You place your order at the counter, then pick up your beverage, silverware and salt and pepper shakers at a cart. The food is brought to your table. Service during my visit was quick. No music was played. The restaurant is a small, comfortable place with cushioned chairs and couches; an upright piano behind a cabinet filled with soaps, lotions, creams and fancy and pretty tea kettles; and one table with an umbrella. The left wall is one huge mural depicting a conglomeration of architectural styles, including a Spanish arch followed by a walkway leading to a house with a gabled porch and columns. Upstairs is Karen's "Mediterranean Bar," featuring sofas, love seats, coffee tables, cushioned chairs and regular tables and chairs. There is another giant wall mural. This one displays a mélange of historical figures from the Four Musketeers and Don Quixote to Huckleberry Finn and Spanish conquistadors. The back wall exhibits a closed fireplace in front of a red-brick external wall.

NUTRITION AND SPECIAL REQUESTS

Wazubi's uses no preservatives and does all baking from scratch. They can "veggetize" anything like sandwiches or quiche. They offer soy milk in their coffee drinks, add herbs to their protein shakes and have fat-free milk and wheat-free items. Their fruit tea is all natural with protein. They can accommodate most special requests.

Spinach Quiche

1 9-inch baked pie shell
6 eggs
1 cup milk
1 cup half-and-half
1 teaspoon salt
1 teaspoon pepper
1 teaspoon onion powder

1 teaspoon garlic powder
2 tablespoons flour
½ cup feta cheese, crumbled
3 to 4 cups fresh spinach, washed,
    dried and chopped
1 cup Swiss cheese, shredded

1. Preheat oven to 400 degrees. Mix the eggs with the milk, half-and-half, spices and flour in a mixing bowl.
2. Place the feta cheese on the bottom of the pie crust. Add the spinach, then the Swiss cheese.
3. Top with the egg and milk mixture. Bake in preheated oven for 40 minutes.
4. Remove from oven. Let stand for a few minutes before cutting. Serve warm.

Recipe by Karen Krick

⁂ VAIL ⁂

THE VALLEY OF *Gore Creek, where Vail now stands, was first settled in the 1880s by silver prospectors. Unsuccessful at silver mining, they developed homesteads instead and raised cattle and grew crops. Vail and Vail Pass to the east were named after Charles D. Vail, Colorado state highway engineer in the 1930s. The town of Vail is relatively new, having been established in 1959 and incorporated in 1966. Vail Ski Resort opened in 1962.*

Zip Code: 81657 **Population:** 4,531 **Elevation:** 8,160 feet

LA BOTTEGA

100 East Meadows Drive, Suite 37
Phone: (970) 476-0280
Fax: (970) 476-0288
E-mail: labottegavail.com
Website: None

Directions: Take exit 176 from I-70. *From the east,* go ¾ of the way around the roundabout at the end of the exit, pass under I-70, go half-way around the next roundabout and exit onto Vail Road. The restaurant is 1 block up on the left on the corner of Vail Road and East Meadow Drive. *Coming off of I-70 from the west,* go ¼ of the way around the roundabout at the end of the exit, exiting onto Vail Road. The restaurant is 1 block up on the left on the corner of Vail Road and East Meadow Drive.

ESSENTIALS

Cuisine: Northern Italian
Hours: Thanksgiving to Easter and JUL–OCT: Seven days 11 A.M.–10 P.M. Easter through MAY: Mon.–Sat. 11 A.M.–9 P.M. Closed JUN and NOV until Thanksgiving.
Meals and Prices: Lunch $5–$14. Dinner $12–$33.
Nonsmoking: All
Take-out: Yes
Alcohol: Full bar
Credit Cards: MC, VI, DS
Personal Check: Local only with ID
Reservations: Recommended for dinner. Not accepted for lunch (first come, first served).
Wheelchair Access: Yes, by ramp
Other: Split plate charge: $1 for appetizers, $1.75 for main course. No separate checks. Discretionary 18% service charge may apply. Catering available.

HISTORY AND BIOGRAPHY

La Bottega is in a building constructed in 1982 for retail. It has been used for a pizzeria, a bagel shop and a gift shop. In November 1997, La

Bottega opened as a deli, selling sandwiches, pastas and entrées. In January 1999, the restaurant expanded by adding a stone oven for pizza. In July 2001, the restaurant renovated and expanded into the store next door, opening up a tapas-style wine bar.

The restaurant is owned by Steve and Elisabetta Virion. Steve is the chef; Elisabetta is the hostess and handles the wines and the restaurant's accounting. Steve has been in the restaurant business since 1976 and has managed or cooked in restaurants in Italy, France, England and Austria, where he met Elisabetta. He was executive chef at Villa Arceno in Tuscany, Italy, prior to coming to Colorado in 1994 and worked as manager and chef at the Vail Village Inn until 1997. Manager Seth Matasas came to La Bottega in July 2001, after managing at Terra Bistro and The Tyrolean, both in Vail. He is from Illinois, worked previously in New Orleans and has extensive wine knowledge.

FOOD, SERVICE AND AMBIENCE

La Bottega is a cozy place providing a fine selection of northern Italian cuisine. La Bottega's varied lunch menu offers specialty sandwiches, stone oven pizzas, salads, subs, steak and Italian sausage sandwiches, bruschetta and panini sandwiches on focaccia or Italian bread. All of the breads and sauces are homemade. I tried the asparagus with tarragon cream soup, light and thin with a swirl of cream on top. I also tried the "TED"—Thanksgiving Every Day—specialty sandwich. It contains thinly sliced, fresh roasted turkey moistened by stuffing, whole cranberry sauce and mayonnaise, all on a sub roll. I found it to be very refreshing. Other specialty sandwiches on the menu are a traditional Reuben on panini grill, chicken salad and a pastrami sub. The salad selections include a Caesar, the Josephine (the house salad with blue cheese crumbles), a Greek salad and an antipasto salad. Homemade turkey or roast beef highlighted the subs. A whole, oven-roasted chicken, "Tuscan style," is available as a to-go item only.

For dinner starters, you can choose from the pizza of the day made with homemade pizza dough; an arugula salad with pancetta; a marinated calamari, rock shrimp and crab salad; or the asparagus soup. The primi pasta dishes feature spaghetti, penne, fettuccini, fusilli, linguini and gemelli (a short, twisted noodle) mixed with an assortment of mussels, chicken, artichokes, shrimp, crab, scallops or sausage. All pastas are made in-house except the penne and spaghetti. There are also stuffed pastas: baked salmon and scallop cannelloni, porcini ravioli and truffle gnocchi with butter and Parmesan cheese. Second courses include filet of beef with Gorgonzola crust, pine nut–breaded lamb chops, roasted Alaskan halibut with black olive crust and cedar-planked salmon. All of the desserts are homemade and include tiramisu, raspberry cheesecake, tartufo chocolate and hazelnut semifreddo, a profiterole (a miniature cream puff filled with a sweet mixture) and crème brûlée.

Service was fast and casual. The food came out in a hurry, but I received no water refill. Across from the entrance is a small bar and, to the left, the deli from the original restaurant. There is seating at the bar and at the window. The artwork is a potpourri of paintings depicting two horses named Bucky and Smitty, a dusty boot, geometric figures in solid bright colors, a scene from an artist's dream and a belly dancer.

NUTRITION AND SPECIAL REQUESTS

La Bottega has an extensive menu. The food is not overly seasoned, and the staff will accommodate special requests such as eliminating cheese, oil, or butter. Vegetarians may choose between a sub sandwich, all three bruschetta, three panini, a specialty sandwich and five pizzas for lunch, as well as several vegetarian appetizers and pasta dishes at dinner.

Lamb Osso Buco Cremolata

SERVES 6

olive oil	2 cups white wine
6 lamb shanks, 16–18 ounces each	36 ounces chopped tomatoes,
salt and pepper	canned in juice
flour to dust	2 garlic cloves, chopped
1 yellow onion, cubed	1 bay leaf
1 carrot, cubed	1 fresh rosemary sprig
2 celery stalks, cubed	Cremolata (recipe follows)

1. Heat ovenproof roasting pan over medium-high heat on stovetop. Add olive oil.

2. Season the lamb shanks with salt and pepper. Dust with flour and brown on all sides.
3. Remove shanks from pan. Add the cubed vegetables and sauté until onions are translucent. Discard extra oil and fat. Preheat oven to 350 degrees.
4. Deglaze the pan with the wine and cook until almost evaporated.
5. Add chopped tomatoes with the juice. Add the spices and the browned lamb shanks. The shanks should be covered with liquid.
6. Cover with foil and braise in a preheated oven for about 3 hours or until fork-tender. Remove from oven.
7. Check and adjust your seasoning and consistency of sauce. Sprinkle with Cremolata. Serve.

Cremolata

2 tablespoons chopped parsley   ½ teaspoon chopped garlic
½ teaspoon lemon zest

Mix together all ingredients in small bowl.

Recipe by Steve Virion

Wine Recommendation: 1997 Italian Tuscano Etrusco, 100 percent Sangiovese

LA TOUR

122 East Meadow Drive
Phone: (970) 476-4403
Fax: (970) 476-6930
E-mail: latour@quest.net
Website: www.latour-vail.com

Directions: Take exit 176 from I-70 and proceed to the roundabout south of I-70. Head east on South Frontage Road for ¼ mile and turn right into the parking garage. Go to the far (west) end of the parking garage and park. Exit the west end of the parking garage and walk down the stairs. The restaurant is directly across from the bottom of the stairs.

ESSENTIALS

Cuisine: Continental French

Hours: Mid-NOV through APR: Seven nights 5:30 P.M.–10 P.M. MAY through SEP: Tue.–Sun. 5:30 P.M.–10 P.M. Closed Mon. mid-JUN through SEP: Tue.–Sun. 4 P.M.–6 P.M. Provençal tapas menu. Closed Mon. Closed OCT to mid-NOV.

Meals and Prices: Dinner $21–$38. Menu dégustation (five-course small tasting portions) $69, with wine $129. Tapas $2–$8.

Nonsmoking: All, including patio

Take-out: Yes

Alcohol: Full bar

Credit Cards: All five

Personal Check: Local only with ID

Reservations: Highly recommended

Wheelchair Access: Yes

Other: Service charge of 18% added to parties of six or more. Split plate charge $2. Available for corporate or private parties.

HISTORY AND BIOGRAPHY

La Tour started in 1967 in the space next door to the current location (now occupied by the Austria House). It was originally called St. Moritz and was owned by Walter and Mary-Claire Moritz. In the early 1980s, the restaurant moved into its current location and changed its name to La Tour. Paul and Lourdes Ferzacca took over La Tour in September 1998. Paul is the owner and executive chef. He is from Chicago and has been in the restaurant business since 1981. He came to Colorado in 1991 and helped to open Two Elk, on top of Vail Mountain and the Game Creek Club. Lourdes, also from Chicago, came to Colorado in 1993 and worked at the Vail Village Inn before La Tour. Chef de cuisine Greg Shule, again from Chicago, worked at the Game Creek Club before joining La Tour in September 1998.

FOOD, SERVICE AND AMBIENCE

La Tour features contemporary French cuisine with a seasonally chang-ing menu offering simple, elegant food. My dinner started with the

"Chef's Welcome," a dish with Spanish olives, onion and red and yellow bell peppers to awaken the taste buds. Next I tried the classic French onion soup, a very hot broth thick with crisp croutons and gooey Swiss and the traditional strong onion flavor. For my entrée, I chose herbes de Provence–crusted Colorado rack of lamb with basil-mint au jus. My plate contained four lamb chops with just enough flavorful fat. They were a bright pink color, just passing from rare to medium-rare and cut easily with a knife. The chops were coated with a delicious crunchy crust of panko—coarse, light Japanese bread crumbs—and herbs. The basil-mint au jus, a demi-glace made with fresh chopped parsley, was a flavorsome accompaniment to the lamb chops. Alongside the chops was a white bean casserole with pancetta, onion, carrot and celery. It sat on a bed of escarole, a mild-flavored variety of endive with broad green leaves and spinach. Two baby carrots with tops still intact completed the colorful, vertical presentation.

Seafood lovers will want to make a first-course selection of mussels, escargot, a crab and mushroom crêpe, sea scallops, or caviar. Second courses include Maine lobster bisque, toasted goat cheese salad with mustard vinaigrette, roasted beet and baby spinach salad with walnut vinaigrette, pâté, filet mignon steak tartare and foie gras. The entrées include several seafood selections along with pasta, chicken, duck, filet mignon, veal loin and venison in a variety of sauces from roasted tomato–white wine broth to bigarade sauce (a classic French brown sauce flavored with oranges and served with duck). For a side addition to your entrée, choose from haricots verts (green string beans) Provençal, potato or sweet-potato puree with fresh chives, sautéed exotic mushrooms, or sautéed winter greens. Those wanting a diverse sampling of authentic French cuisine can select the menu dégustation. The five courses feature caviar, sea scallops, foie gras, hazelnut-crusted venison and flaming crème brûlée. Wine accompaniments for all five courses are also available. La Tour's wine list showcases over 300 varieties, mostly from France and California and has received the prestigious Wine Spectator Award of Excellence for 1998, 1999 and 2000.

An enticing selection of elaborate desserts will provide a sweet finis to your dining experience. Among them are Napoleon, warm apple tart, wild Maine blueberry dropcake and assorted imported French cheeses.

From mid-June through September, a pre-theater menu of provençal tapas is offered on the patio and in the bar. These small appetizers offer fruits, cheeses, vegetables, seafood and meats. They include citrus-cured salmon canapés, imported Brie with strawberries, sautéed chicken with capers and lemon and sautéed spinach with toasted pine nuts.

My server was friendly, good-humored and professional. Bossa nova music and songs in Italian by a female vocalist provided a pleasing background for this elegant restaurant. I sat in the front dining room, which is a great place for people-watching. A row of five tall glass doors provides the opportunity for viewing while a gas, rock fireplace provides ambience and warmth. In warmer weather, the glass doors are opened and patio dining is available adjacent to the street. Chalk etchings from a local studio enhance the coarse-textured beige walls. Indian paintbrush or ironworks by A. W. Montcalm of Eagle, Colorado, and dark-blue water glasses adorn the tables covered with fine white linen. The two dining rooms in the back are divided by rows of open shelves decorated with glass and ceramic vases. A small bar and lounge occupies a space in the back to the right.

NUTRITION AND SPECIAL REQUESTS

The chefs at La Tour will accommodate any feasible special request. Given advance notice, they can be more obliging. In the past, people with allergies have provided the kitchen with a list of their allergies, and the chefs have altered their selections accordingly.

Sautéed Sweetbreads with Caper–Brown Butter Sauce

SERVES 4

This dish is prepared in two stages. Stage 1 can be done up to three days in advance. Store finished sweetbreads in refrigerator and keep cold until ready to prepare the dish.

Stage 1

2 pounds sweetbreads	2 tablespoons canola oil
1 carrot, large dice	1 cup white wine
1 onion, large dice	1 tablespoon white wine vinegar
1 celery stalk, large dice	2 quarts water

Sachet

cheesecloth, enough to wrap
aromatics
4 whole garlic cloves
12 whole black peppercorns

2 whole cloves
2 whole bay leaves
½ bunch parsley stems
5 fresh thyme sprigs

Stage 2

salt to taste
ground white pepper to taste
2 cups flour
4 ounces (½ cup) canola oil
½ pound pearl onions, cleaned
of any skin
1 pound wild mushrooms or any
assortment available, washed
and cut to desired size

2 ounces capers, drained of
their brine
6 ounces butter
juice from 2 fresh lemons
1 tomato, diced
½ ounce fresh chives

Method for Stage 1

1. Assemble the sachet: Place all the herbs and spices inside a square of cheesecloth, gather ends and tie closed with twine. Rinse sweetbreads in cold running water for 15 minutes. Drain.
2. In a large pot over medium heat, sweat the carrot, onion and celery in canola oil until the onion is opaque.
3. Deglaze with white wine and white wine vinegar.
4. Add sweetbreads, sachet and approximately 2 quarts of cold water, or enough to cover sweetbreads by at least 1 inch.
5. Bring to a simmer and skim off any scum that rises to the top. Let sweetbreads simmer for approximately 30 minutes or until completely cooked.
6. Drain off liquid and discard. Let sweetbreads cool on a sheet pan. Once cool to the touch, peel off any membranes or sinew surrounding sweetbreads and discard. At this time, you can store the sweetbreads for up to 3 days in the refrigerator.

Method for Stage 2

1. Preheat oven to 350 degrees. (You will finish cooking the sweetbreads in the oven after sautéing them.)

2. Put a very large sauté pan on medium-high heat and let it get hot. Season sweetbreads with salt and white pepper, then dredge in flour, shaking off any excess.
3. Add canola oil to hot sauté pan, then sweetbreads and pearl onions. Sauté a few minutes.
4. Add mushrooms and let all items sauté and caramelize nicely.
5. Transfer contents to a baking pan and finish cooking in the oven, about 5 minutes. Meanwhile, return the sauté pan to the stove and heat to medium. Add the capers and butter, swirling pan constantly to allow butter to melt and the milk solids to become golden brown.
6. Deglaze the pan with lemon juice; add diced tomato and fresh chives. Taste the sauce and season with salt and pepper.
7. To serve, place several sweetbreads on a plate, along with a serving of onions and mushrooms, and pour sauce over the top. Repeat with remaining sweetbreads, vegetables and sauce.

Recipe by: Chef-Proprietor Paul Ferzacca

Wine Recommendation: French Chassagne-Montrachet 1 er cru Caillerets

by Bachelet-Ramonet

LARKSPUR ————————————————————

458 Vail Valley Drive
Phone: (970) 479-8050
Fax: (970) 479-8052
E-mail: thomas@larkspurvail.com
Website: www.larkspur.com or larkspurvail.com

Directions: Take exit 176 from I-70 and proceed to the roundabout south of I-70. Head east on South Frontage Road for 0.3 mile and turn right onto Vail Valley Drive. Follow this curvy road for 0.3 mile. Just past Mill Creek Circle on the right is a cream-colored building with a sign for the Golden Peak Lodge well hidden in the back. There is $20 valet parking here during the day but free parking in the evening for dinner. About 100 yards past this parking area is a free parking area, also to the right. Park here and head west behind the Golden Peak Lodge. The restaurant is 100 feet past the parking lot, just past the rear entrance for the lodge.

ESSENTIALS

Cuisine: American classic with French soul

Hours: Mid-NOV to mid-APR: Seven days 11:30 A.M.–9:30 P.M. JUN to Labor Day: Seven days 5:30 P.M.–9:30 P.M., Sun. 11 A.M.–2:30 P.M. Labor Day to late OCT: Seven nights 5:30 P.M.–9:30 P.M. Closed mid-APR through MAY and late OCT to mid-NOV.

Meals and Prices: Brunch $7–$15. Lunch $8–$12. Dinner $25–$32 (soup and salad extra). Chef's Tasting Menu, 5–7 courses, $125.

Nonsmoking: All

Take-out: Yes

Alcohol: Full bar

Credit Cards: MC, VI, AE

Personal Check: Yes, with ID

Reservations: Highly recommended for dinner and parties of six or more.

Wheelchair Access: Yes

Other: Adjacent market offers gourmet boutique food items. Private dining room for up to forty people available for private parties and functions.

HISTORY AND BIOGRAPHY

Larkspur is located in the Golden Peak Lodge, which opened in spring 1997. The original business that occupied these premises was Bella Riva, an Italian restaurant. It closed in spring 1999. The new owners, Vail Resorts, and their tenant, executive chef Thomas Salamunovich, spent the summer of 1999 remodeling and opened Larkspur in December 1999.

Chef Salamunovich is a 1984 graduate of the California Culinary Academy. Between 1986 and 1993, he was a line chef at Stars Restaurant and executive sous-chef at Postrio Restaurant, both in San Francisco. From 1993 until 1999, he was executive chef at Sweet Basil and, during that time, executive chef at Zino Ristorante, both in Vail. His wife, Nancy Sweeney, is Larkspur's art consultant. General manager Adam Baker and beverage director John "Mick" Terhaar have both been with Larkspur since its inception. Adam spent six years managing the restaurants in the Sonnenalp Resort in Vail. Mick has been in the restaurant business since 1982. He spent three years at the Hotel Boulderado and nine years at the Red Lion Inn, both in Boulder, before becoming beverage director at Sweet Basil in Vail.

FOOD, SERVICE AND AMBIENCE

Chef Salamunovich has developed interesting twists to some classic dishes. For lunch, I ordered the seared tuna and salmon bacon club with La Bottega–inspired chopped vegetable salad. The sandwich consists of thinly sliced salmon, quarter-inch cut seared tuna raw on the inside, sliced tomatoes, bacon and mixed wild greens on a French baguette. This is an improved club sandwich for lovers of seafood. The salad contains chopped cucumber, lettuce, celery, Kalamata olives, tomato, red onion and red pepper sprinkled with Parmesan cheese in a light vinaigrette. This sandwich-and-salad combination was unusual, light and very good.

Besides sandwiches with homemade breads, Larkspur offers homemade soups, appetizers, salads, pizza, burgers and entrées for lunch. Highlights of this menu are roasted five-onion soup, warm soybeans, Atlantic salmon Niçoise salad, rock shrimp and wild mushroom pizza and bowtie pasta with wild mushrooms, chicken sausage, goat cheese and hazelnuts.

Chef Salamunovich's inventiveness is even more prominent, I think, on Larkspur's Sunday brunch menu. For example, common French toast is infused with orange and comes with orange supremes (trimmed orange wedges) and pistachios. A simple steak and eggs entrée is conjoined with wild mushrooms and herb hollandaise. Corned beef hash is replaced with duck confit hash to accompany poached farm eggs with asparagus and red-pepper hollandaise. Homemade delights like pastries, Danish and granola with vanilla yogurt and mango also add to Larkspur's brunch experience.

Appetizing dinner starters when I visited were Iranian caviar, duck spring roll, caramelized day boat scallops with vanilla bean vinaigrette and mango and tempura shrimp with curried couscous. More recipe turns are apparent in the main courses: double-cut pork chop with roasted butternut risotto, crab and scallop ravioli with golden beets,

Colorado lamb shank with porcini gnocchi and crispy Long Island duck Diane, to name a few. Larkspur provides 350 wine selections from around the world, with the focus on California and France. To help you choose the right wine with your meal, the restaurant employs four certified sommeliers. Green, Oolong, black and herbal teas from around the world provide a soothing end to your meal. If you crave something sweeter, try a homemade dessert, such as Asian pear crêpes, warm Valrhona chocolate cake with pistachio ice cream, gingerbread or a quartet of homemade sorbets.

Service during my visit was handled in a very professional manner. Slow jazz tunes played during lunch. Elegant simplicity best describes Larkspur's atmosphere, with in-house flower arrangements on each table and color prints of the larkspur flower hanging on the warm mustard-yellow and fern-green walls. The modern décor includes bell-shaped sconces, hanging ceiling lights, white tablecloths at dinner, a wall of carved wooden hummingbirds and a gas fireplace. The restaurant is divided into two dining rooms, with the outside room displaying a bar along the interior wall and glass doors along the exterior leading to a patio with rock columns, where you can dine facing Vail's ski slopes. The interior dining room hosts contemporary art and an open kitchen in the back. Enhancing the surroundings are baskets, giant acorns, bamboo stalks, candles, cattails and hand-painted Italian silk.

NUTRITION AND SPECIAL REQUESTS

Larkspur has a few lunch items for vegetarians, but usually only one vegetarian dinner entrée. There are entrées without garlic for people allergic to garlic. If an item is on the menu, it can usually be modified to meet a patron's nutritional or dietary needs.

Fruitwood-Grilled Quail on Lavender Skewers with Mesclun-Herb Salad, Peach Fritters, Stone Fruit–Viognier Sauce and Nasturtium Confetti

SERVES 4

8 boneless quail, marinated in
olive oil
8 lavender spears
2 peaches, skinned and sliced
into wedges
1 cup mixed, picked herbs—
basil, chervil, chives and
tarragon

4 ounces mesclun mix
3 ounces Vinaigrette (recipe follows)
2 cups Fritter Batter (recipe follows)
2 cups Stone Fruit–Viognier Sauce
(recipe follows)
oil for frying fritters
½ cup nasturtium flowers, julienne
sliced

1. Make the vinaigrette, Fritter Batter and Stone Fruit–Viognier Sauce.
2. Put 2 quails side by side and run 2 lavender skewers into each quail. Grill to medium doneness over a hot fruitwood fire (apple or peach). While the quail is cooking, dredge the peach wedges into the Fritter Batter and fry until golden brown. Dress the herbs and mesclun with the Vinaigrette.
3. On a 12-inch plate, ladle 4 ounces sauce around the diameter. Place mixed salad in the middle. Lay grilled quail on top and place peach fritters around the salad. Garnish with a scattering of julienned nasturtium flowers. Serve.

Vinaigrette

½ ounce champagne vinegar
½ ounce apple cider vinegar

2 ounces olive oil
1 shallot, finely diced

Mix all together; add salt to taste.

Fritter Batter

1½ cups water
1 cup flour

1 tablespoon baking powder
pinch each of salt and cinnamon

Mix all together until batter is smooth.

Stone Fruit–Vognier Sauce

½ bottle Viognier wine
4 shallots, roughly chopped
1 bay leaf
1 cup orange juice
6 fresh apricots, pitted

1 peach, pitted
1 tablespoon honey
1 tablespoon Dijon mustard
dash of lemon juice

1. Pour wine, shallots and bay leaf into a saucepan and heat, stirring occasionally, until wine is reduced by half.
2. Add orange juice, apricots, and peach. Simmer until fruit is soft and there is no remaining alcohol, roughly 15 minutes.
3. Blend and add remaining ingredients. Strain through a fine sieve. Adjust seasoning.

Recipe by Thomas Salamunovich

Wine Recommendation: Jade Mountain "La Provençale" 1998

(a California Syrah and Grenache mix)

RUSSELL'S

228 Bridge Street
Phone: (970) 476-6700
Fax: (970) 476-0081
E-mail: None
Website: None

Directions: Take exit 176 from I-70 and proceed to the roundabout south of I-70. Head east on South Frontage Road for ¼ mile and turn right into the parking garage. Try to park about halfway down the garage. After you park, if you exit on foot at about the middle of the garage, you will come out onto East Meadow Drive at a covered bridge. Walk across this bridge; the restaurant will be to your immediate left.

ESSENTIALS

Cuisine: Steak and seafood
Hours: Seven nights 5:30 P.M.–10 P.M. Closed mid-APR to early JUN and one weekend of OCT.

Meals and Prices: Dinner $21–$37 (includes starch and vegetables, soup and salad extra).

Nonsmoking: All

Take-out: Yes

Alcohol: Full bar

Credit Cards: MC, VI, AE

Personal Check: Yes, with ID

Reservations: Recommended

Wheelchair Access: Yes; the staff will carry patrons in wheelchairs up the steps.

Other: One check per table. Service charge of 18% added to parties of six or more.

HISTORY AND BIOGRAPHY

Russell's opened in 1989 in the building previously occupied by the Ore House. The building was constructed in the late 1960s. The owners are Ron Riley and Michael Staughton. Ron has been in the restaurant business since 1966, working in Aspen and Vail. Michael started in the mid-1970s in Vail. Together they also owned Los Amigos in Vail. Manager Mick Warth has been with Russell's since it opened, in the restaurant business since 1965 and with the Red Lion in Vail for nine years. Executive chef Markus Gutter, from Switzerland, has been with the restaurant since 1995. He has been cooking in restaurants since 1964 and is a graduate of the Culinary School of Switzerland.

FOOD, SERVICE AND AMBIENCE

I was more in the mood for seafood than steak, so I ordered a fish special, blackened ahi tuna in roasted red-pepper sauce. The fish was seared on the outside, rare on the inside. Russell's chefs purposely undercook their seafood, so you need to specify if you want it medium or well done. Otherwise, you will get a seared piece of sushi. The tuna was tender and broke easily with a fork. The sauce had a great flavor and was only mildly spicy. The rice with saffron that accompanied the tuna was light and fluffy. A side of green beans and carrots, a sprig of rosemary and a miniature loaf of warm, soft white bread also came with my order.

The other seafood specials on the evening I visited were salmon with champagne-dill-Chardonnay sauce and sea bass with lemon-tarragon sauce. For an appetizer, you can choose from lightly blackened tuna sashimi, spicy homemade sausage in puff pastry, Norwegian smoked salmon, grilled scallops, escargots and jumbo shrimp. The salad selections include tomato basil, Caesar, field greens with endive in a walnut vinaigrette and spinach. A soup of the day is also offered. The regular seafood menu choices are Rocky Mountain trout and Alaskan king crab legs. Russell's serves certified Angus beef, and indeed, the menu focuses on beef, with entrées such as marinated steak teriyaki, dry aged center-cut New York strip or rib-eye with green peppercorn sauce, filet mignon with béarnaise, slow-roasted prime rib and baby-back ribs. Wiener schnitzel and chicken morel also are offered. To finish your meal, elect one of the following desserts: crème caramel, New York cheesecake, mud pie, chocolate mousse, goldbrick sundae with chocolate and walnuts or a raspberry sorbet.

My service was quick and efficient. I listened to light jazz as I viewed people on Bridge Street. With a creekside view on the other side of Russell's, you have your choice between observing nature or people. The semi-casual dining room is split in two with a bar in the middle and an open kitchen in the back. Color photos of bighorn sheep, a snowshoer and his trail and snowcapped mountains decorate the walls. Lamps with periwinkle-blue shades hang from the ceiling over white tablecloths and napkins.

NUTRITION AND SPECIAL REQUESTS

Russell's is more of a steakhouse than a seafood restaurant, though two or three seafood specials are offered daily. There are no vegetarian appetizers or entrées on the menu. Special requests will be honored whenever possible and time permitting.

Steak Diane

SERVES 4–6

1 tablespoon butter

3 teaspoons finely chopped shallots

½ teaspoon finely chopped garlic

1 jigger (1 ounce) brandy

2 jiggers (2 ounces) red wine

2 teaspoons Grey Poupon mustard

2 cups prepared brown gravy

½ cup heavy cream

chopped chives

salt and pepper

4–6 filet mignons, 8 ounces each

1. Melt butter in saucepan; add chopped shallots and garlic and sauté till golden brown.
2. Add brandy and red wine. Cook until reduced.
3. Add mustard and brown gravy. Simmer for 7–8 minutes.
4. Stir in cream and sprinkle with chopped chives. Makes about 3 cups sauce. Meanwhile, prepare the filets: Sprinkle filets with salt and pepper and grill to desired doneness (recommended medium-rare).
5. To serve, ladle 4–6 ounces of sauce on plate. Place a filet on top of sauce. Repeat with remaining filets and sauce.

Recipe by Markus Gutter

Wine Recommendation: St. Emillion Red Bordeaux

≈ WINTER PARK ≈

WINTER PARK WAS *originally a construction camp for the Moffat Tunnel, whose west portal is located here. Appropriately, the town was named West Portal. Skiing dates back as far as 1925 when there was a 25-cent rope tow. Several years and two fires later, the world's first double chair lift was completed in 1947. The town's name was changed to Winter Park with the assistance of then Denver Mayor Benjamin F. Stapleton and many sports enthusiasts. They were trying to publicize the town as one of the finest winter sports centers in the country. Today, Winter Park is home to a ski clinic for the disabled and hosts the Special Olympics.*

Zip Code: 80482 **Population:** 662 **Elevation:** 9,040 feet

MAMA FALZITTO'S

1128 Winter Park Drive
Phone: (970) 726-9049
Fax: (970) 726-5923
E-mail: mamafalzittos@winterparkweb.com
Website: None

Directions: Take exit 232 from I-70. Proceed north on Highway 40 for 25 miles, over Berthoud Pass, to the entrance to Winter Park Resort on the left. Continue straight on Highway 40 for 0.8 mile past this entrance. Turn left onto Old Town Drive and go 0.2 mile. Turn right onto Winter Park Drive and go 0.6 mile. The restaurant is on the right.

ESSENTIALS

Cuisine: Country Italian
Hours: Tue.–Sat. 5 P.M.–9 P.M. Closed Sun.–Mon.
Meals and Prices: Dinner $8–$16 (includes soup or salad).
Nonsmoking: Smoking permitted only in bar, lounge and patio.

Take-out: Yes
Alcohol: Full bar
Credit Cards: MC, VI, AE, DS
Personal Check: Yes, with ID
Reservations: Accepted
Wheelchair Access: Yes, including bathrooms
Other: Children's menu. Available for specialty parties, banquets, reunions, rehearsal dinners and private events. Catering available.

HISTORY AND BIOGRAPHY

Mama Falzitto's occupies a building constructed in the 1890s as a stage-coach stop. In 1925, Adolph's German Restaurant started doing business here. It went through several owners. From 1973 until 1999 Don Waldron was the owner. In January 2000, Mama Falzitto's was opened by Sue "Mama" Falzitto and Tom Agnew. Sue has been in the food and beverage business since 1975. She worked as a choreographer for a dinner theater in Longmont, Colorado, as a banquet waitress at the Black Bear Inn in Lyons, Colorado, and as food and beverage director for the Glenmoor Country Club in Denver and the Boulder Country Club. Tom has also been in the restaurant business since 1975 and has owned fifteen restaurants throughout his career, in Los Angeles; Atlanta, Georgia; Dallas, Texas; and in Niwot and Trinidad, Colorado. Sue manages the front of the house. Tom is the chef.

FOOD, SERVICE AND AMBIENCE

Mama Falzitto's offers both common and unique Italian dishes. For starters, I tried the tomato clam soup with roasted garlic. It was served very hot, with a strong tomato taste, several small bits of clam and pieces of carrot, onion and celery. The warm butter and garlic French bread that accompanied the soup had a crispy brown crust and soft interior. For my entrée, I chose a new item on the menu and one that I had never seen before, calamari steak, a house specialty. The steak was sautéed, served over spaghetti with a mild, homemade marinara sauce and topped with shrimp scampi. The shrimp were breaded with lots of chopped garlic. Both the calamari, about a 5- to 6-ounce filet, and the shrimp were tender. Calamari lovers should not miss this one. It is also available as an appetizer. The marinara sauce contains much chopped onion and a few spices. A side of sautéed button mushrooms and zucchini also boasted a lot of garlic. As my server, Mama Falzitto, said, "Garlic is the flavor of the kitchen." At Mama Falzitto's you will not leave hungry. This was a plateful.

For an appetizer, Mama will bring to your table a mini pizza, a baked Brie wheel with habanero-raspberry sauce, or a shrimp cocktail with homemade garlic cocktail sauce. Homemade dressings top their salad of fresh seasoned greens. Mama's entrées feature spaghetti in a classic meat sauce, stuffed ravioli with marinara sauce, shrimp scampi and chicken or veal with marinara, Marsala mushroom, or homemade Alfredo sauce. Steak Marsala and a surf-and-turf combo are the other house specialties. Highlights among the desserts are Boston cream pie, New York cheesecake, tiramisu and a homemade apple dumpling created by placing a cored apple inside a puff pastry and adding cinnamon sauce.

As a server, Susan Falzitto was fast and friendly with a big sense of humor. For background music, I listened to a combination of opera and modern songs sung in Italian. I sat in the smaller, quieter and more intimate front dining room facing the road in Old Town Winter Park. The untreated, charred walls of this friendly room are decorated with a wreath of wine corks, a framed poster of St. Francis Vineyard in Sonoma Valley, California, and a picture of a formally attired waiter holding a bottle of champagne and wine glasses. (I have seen this painting in several Grand County restaurants.) A black metal stove in front of a rock column adds a nice touch, as does the one long white candle burning at each table.

The walls of the main dining room display posters of vineyards from France; Sonoma Valley, California; and a wine auction, Texas style. The long wood bar at the entrance is from the hotel in the ghost town of Arrow, up the Moffit Road nearby. Behind the bar are two large mirrors, and at its end is a small wine rack. The lounge is trimmed with a poster of spices and herbs. Off the bar and lounge is a big deck with tables and red-and-white umbrellas. Mama Falzitto's is people-friendly and presents some fine Italian foods. Just the way you would expect things to be in the Italian countryside.

Mama Falzitto's offers a few appetizers, salads and two entrées, pasta marinara and ravioli, for vegetarians. They will honor substitutions, like olive oil for marinara sauce or chicken breast grilled instead of breaded. Sue says they do not get many special requests.

Veal Piccata

SERVES 6

6 veal scallops, 5 ounces each
salt and pepper
½ cup milk
1 egg, beaten to blend
1 cup seasoned bread crumbs
3 tablespoons extra-virgin olive
    oil, plus extra for sautéing veal
6 peeled garlic cloves, finely
    chopped

½ cup capers
½ cup quality white wine
juice from one lemon
1 cup chicken stock or canned
    broth
4 tablespoons unsalted butter
your favorite pasta
your favorite marinara sauce

1. Pound veal scallops to an even thickness. Season with salt and pepper.
2. Combine milk and egg in shallow bowl. Dredge seasoned veal in milk-and-egg mixture. Coat with bread crumbs. Set aside.
3. Make the piccata sauce: In a large sauté pan, heat olive oil until it is very hot. Add chopped garlic.
4. When the garlic starts to brown, after about 4 minutes, add capers.
5. Deglaze mixture with white wine. Add lemon juice and chicken broth. Reduce liquid by two-thirds.
6. Turn off heat and add butter. Reserve sauce.
7. In a separate pan, heat enough olive oil to sauté veal. Sauté breaded veal scallops about 4 minutes on each side.
8. Place sautéed veal on plate and top with reserved piccata sauce. Serve with your favorite pasta and marinara sauce.

Recipe by Tom Agnew

Wine Recommendation: Antinori Chianti Classico Reserva

WOODLAND PARK

FORMERLY KNOWN AS *Summit Park (because it is near the top of Pikes Peak, about 20 miles northwest of Colorado Springs) and Manitou Park, Woodland Park was renamed for the abundance of pine and spruce trees in the area.*

Zip Code: 80866 **Population:** 6,515 **Elevation:** 8,437 feet

AUSTIN'S

228 East Highway 24
Phone: (719) 687-1022
Fax, e-mail and website: None

Directions: *From Colorado Springs on Highway 24 (Ute Pass),* the restaurant is ¼ mile past McDonald's, on the right. *From the intersection of Highways 24 and 67 in Woodland Park,* go east ½ mile on Highway 24. The restaurant is in the pink building 1 block past Fairview, the second traffic signal, on the left.

ESSENTIALS

Cuisine: American
Hours: APR–DEC: Mon.–Sat. 11 P.M..–10 P.M., Sun. 10 A.M.–10 P.M.
JAN–MAR: Mon.–Sat. 11 A.M.–9 P.M., Sun. 10 A.M.–8 P.M.
Meals and Prices: Breakfast $4–$6. Sun. brunch $5–$9. Lunch $5–$7. Dinner $7–$23 (includes soup or salad with starch and vegetables).
Nonsmoking: Yes
Take-out: Yes
Alcohol: Full bar
Credit Cards: MC, VI, AE, DS
Personal Check: Yes
Reservations: Accepted. Canceled if 15–20 minutes late.

Wheelchair Access: Yes
Other: Catering available

HISTORY AND BIOGRAPHY

Austin's occupies a building constructed in the late 1940s. The original establishment was the Brown Craft Restaurant. When I-25 was built in the 1960s, a house that had to be moved for the new interstate was relocated at the back of this location and became the Brown Craft kitchen. The Brown Craft lasted until the early 1970s and was followed by a string of unsuccessful restaurants until Dave and Shelly Maki purchased the property and opened Austin's in February 1997. They named the restaurant after their first son, who was born on the same day the Makis signed the closing papers on the restaurant property.

Shelly has been in the restaurant business since 1973 and Dave since 1976. Together they have traveled from St. Thomas in the Virgin Islands to Alaska to Summit County in Colorado. Both have worked as bar managers. Dave managed The Ritz in Colorado Springs and was a chef at Silverheels in Silverthorne, Colorado, from 1990 to 1993 while Shelly worked as a floor manager. Dave is the head chef at Austin's, and Shelly manages the restaurant.

FOOD, SERVICE AND AMBIENCE

Austin's serves dishes using fresh vegetables, light batters, flavorful ingredients and seasoned sauces. Linda and I tried their Caesar salad, spinach and cheese enchiladas and fish and chips for lunch. Their version of a Caesar salad contains some extra ingredients—red onion, cucumber, black olives, carrot sticks and feta cheese. The enchiladas were prepared in a light batter and featured black olives, sour cream, citrus lime, cumin, coriander, lettuce, diced tomato and a lively chili rojo sauce. Black beans mixed with lime and cheese and rice topped with celery and carrot accompanied the enchiladas. The lightly battered fish was South African capansis, similar to cod but with a nicer texture and better flavor, served with crisp, large fries.

For dinner, Austin's offers appetizers of Maryland crab cakes, calamari and hot spinach and artichoke-heart dip. Highlighting the main courses are pistachio-encrusted orange roughy with roasted red-pepper sauce, blackened chicken Alfredo, pepper steak sautéed in brandied mango chutney, beef or buffalo filet served with a mushroom Merlot demi-glace and smoked prime rib, the specialty. For a lighter dinner or for lunch you can order a charbroiled burger or chicken sandwich, Grandma's meatloaf, chicken-fried chicken or steak, or three-cheese and meat lasagna. Pumpkin cheesecake headlines their homemade desserts. Sunday brunch features eggs with hamburger or New York strip steaks, French toast, crab cakes Benedict, a host of omelets, a breakfast burrito and huevos rancheros.

Prompt service was provided by a pleasant and courteous young man. The dining area contains a mélange of colors: white tablecloths, pink cloth napkins, peach booths, black chairs and evergreen walls. Pastel watercolor paintings of water lilies, still-lifes and cobblestone walks lack a central theme but render a harmony of colors. Embellishing the setting are arched entrances, a gas-burning rock fireplace, paintings of lighthouses and curtains draped onto pinewood posts separating the booths along the wall. Windows on the south side of the building face the great scenic views of the Rampart Range and Pikes Peak.

NUTRITION AND SPECIAL REQUESTS

Everything is made from scratch at Austin's. Six salads are available for lunch and dinner, and most of their fish is grilled. Although they serve home-style cooking with mashed potatoes, gravy and sauces, these can be eliminated or served on the side. As for special requests, Shelly says, "If it is in the kitchen, we'll cook it."

Crab and Cream-Cheese Empanadas with Diablo Citrus Glaze

MAKES 24 EMPANADAS TO SERVE 5–6

For best results, freeze empanadas for 1 hour before frying.

¼ cup minced red bell pepper
¼ cup minced celery
¼ cup minced green onions
⅛ teaspoon butter
⅛ teaspoon ground coriander
⅛ teaspoon ground cumin
⅛ teaspoon black pepper; you
    may substitute ⅛ teaspoon
    crushed red pepper for a
    spicier empanada

⅛ teaspoon Old Bay Seasoning
8 ounces cream cheese, softened
12 ounces lump crab meat
24 wonton skins
4 cups peanut oil
Diablo Citrus Glaze (recipe follows)

1. Sauté red bell peppers, celery and green onions in butter. Cool.
2. Mix dry spices and add to cream cheese. Stir in sautéed vegetables and crab.
3. Lay out several wonton wrappers on a dry cutting board. Place one ounce of mixture in the center of each skin.
4. Dab all four ends of the wonton with water. Fold one corner of wonton over to make a triangle. Use a fork to press ends together, forming a triangle pocket. Place on sheet of wax paper and cover with a towel. Repeat with all wrappers.
5. If time permits, place empanadas in freezer for 1 hour before frying.
6. Heat peanut oil to 350 degrees in fryer or deep saucepan.
7. Place about 5 empanadas in oil at a time. Fry till golden brown. Remove with slotted spoon and drain on paper towels. Serve warm with Diablo Citrus Glaze.

Diablo Citrus Glaze

½ cup orange marmalade

½ cup apple jelly

½ teaspoon dry mustard

½ teaspoon prepared horseradish

⅛ teaspoon crushed red pepper
or cracked black pepper

Mix all ingredients well and chill for 1 hour. Makes 1 cup.

Recipe by Shelly and Dave Maki

Wine Recommendation: California Stag Leap Chardonnay

GLOSSARY OF RESTAURANT
PERSONNEL TYPES

THE FOLLOWING TERMS are used in finer restaurants, usually having chefs with culinary training who have served an apprenticeship.

Chef de Cuisine—Responsible for the restaurant and works under the executive chef, who has responsibility for the entire property. In charge of expediting the meals that leave the kitchen.

Executive Chef—The person in charge of overseeing all the operations. Designs the menu; does the majority of the public-relations work; delegates the menu to the sous-chef, in charge of all restaurant office functions, including monitoring food and labor costs. Oversees the cooking production, day-to-day operations and gives final say on all sauces and anything that leaves the kitchen. Goes over the menu with the sous-chef.

General Manager—Usually a term for someone who handles the front of the restaurant, not the kitchen. This person is responsible for seeing that all customers are pleased or satisfied with their dining experience.

Head Chef—The main chef who may or may not have any help in the kitchen. He is in charge of all aspects of running the kitchen, including food ordering, directing any assistant cooks, designing the menu and budgeting costs.

Kitchen Manager—A term used in both finer restaurants and small restaurants, it can refer to an executive chef or sous-chef who is in charge of organizing staff and obtaining products. The kitchen manager can also refer to the primary cook in a smaller kitchen with a staff of only one or two other cooks.

Line Cook—In charge of mise en place (i.e., having all the ingredients necessary for a dish prepared and ready to combine up to the point of cooking). Responsible for executing the menu according to the executive chef's wants and tastes.

Pastry Chef—In charge of daily breads and desserts as directed by the executive chef.

Sous-Chef—In charge of the line cooks, cooking production and day-to-day operations in the kitchen. Responsible for seeing that line cooks execute menu according to executive chef's wants and tastes. Acts as "referee" between line cooks and executive chef.

❧ RECIPE INDEX ❧

APPETIZERS

Yuppie-I-O Dip. Castle Café, Castle Rock . 70
Stuffed Portobello Mushroom. Buffalo Grille & Saloon,
    Crested Butte . 83
Vegetarian Egg Rolls. Thuy Hoa, Evergreen . 143
Escargot. Caroline's Cuisine, Grand Lake . 196
Crab and Cream-Cheese Empanadas with Diablo Citrus Glaze. Austin's,
    Woodland Park . 366

BEEF

Filet Mignon MacGregor. Twin Owls Steakhouse at the Black Canyon
    Inn, Estes Park . 135
Beef Wellington. The Inn of Glen Haven, Glen Haven . 171
Chive-and-Garlic–Marinated Top Sirloin with Sherry-Honey–Fried
    Potatoes, Beet Emulsion and Hill Top Compound Butter. Hill Top
    Café, Golden . 183
Meatballs. Italian Family, Parker . 290
Steak Diane. Russell's, Vail . 358

BREAKFAST

Jack's French Toast with Strawberries and Bananas and Lemon Syrup.
    Jack's at Sardy House, Aspen . 14
Blueberry Corn Cakes. The Village Smithy Restaurant, Carbondale . 66
Pasta Scramble. Christina's, Durango . 98
Huevos Kennebec. Kennebec Café & Bakery, Hesperus . 212
Cheese Crêpes. Karen's Country Kitchen, Louisville . 260

CHICKEN

Ginger Chicken with Black Bean Sauce. Taipei Tokyo,
    Carbondale . 61
Chicken Marco Polo. Sweet Basilico Café, Estes Park . 132
Chicken-Stuffed Pepper Italiano with Gorgonzola Polenta. Dream Café,
    Morrison . 273
Greek Chicken. B & E Filling Station, Palmer Lake . 287
Chicken Cacciatore. Grimo's, Poncha Springs . 298

DESSERTS

Chocolate Molten Cake. 937 Main—Ken & Sue's Place, Durango . 95
Margarita Pie. Grumpy Gringo, Estes Park . 118
Gratin Stube. Alpenglow Stube, Keystone . 222
Peach and Pistachio Pithiviers. Ski Tip Lodge, Keystone . 243
Flan. The Adobe Inn, Ridgway . 302
Apple Crisp with Caramel Sauce. Handlebars, Silverton . 320

LAMB

Wood-Oven Roasted Colorado Rack of Lamb. Splendido at the
    Chateau, Beaver Creek . 39
Loin of Lamb with Plum Sauce. The Peck House, Empire . 110
Moussaka. Tasso's Bistro, Georgetown . 165
Braised Lamb Shank. Paul's Creekside Grill, Granby . 192
Lamb Osso Buco Cremolata. La Bottega, Vail . 344

MEXICAN

Carne Asada over Seasoned Black Beans with Wild Mushroom–Ancho
    Chile Salsa. Pine Creek Cookhouse, Ashcroft . 4
Pechuga Suiza. Casa del Sol, Buena Vista . 58
Chihuahua Creek Chicken Enchiladas with Colorado Red Chile
    Enchilada Sauce. Ida Belle's Cantina, Keystone . 233
Rock Shrimp Chile Relleno Appetizer. Laughing Ladies, Salida . 309
Grilled Tequila-Lime Chicken. The Windmill, Salida . 312

PASTA

Liguini ai Crostacei. Campo de Fiori, Aspen . 10

Petti di Pollo alla Fragole (Strawberry Chicken). Ristorante Ti Amo, Avon . 21

Gnocchi with Cannellini Beans and Pesto. Mad Dog Ranch Fountain Café, Crawford . 78

Thai Chicken Pasta. Cascades at the Stanley Hotel, Estes Park . 114

PORK

Roasted Pork Tenderloin Stuffed with Apricot Chutney in Ginger–Red Wine Sauce. The Dinner Bell, Crawford . 74

Drunken Pork. The Other Side, Estes Park . 125

Pork Tenderloin Medallions in Sherry, Soy and Sweet and Sour Sauce. Peaceful Henry's, Guffey . 200

Cranberry-Glazed Pork Tenderloin with Shallot Confit and Potato Gnocchi. The Cliff House, Manitou Springs . 269

Rotisserie-Smoked Pork Loin Chop with Apple and Dark Cherry Sauce. J. J.'s Upstream Restaurant, Pagosa Springs . 282

SALADS

Baby Greens Salad with Granny Smith Apples, Gorgonzola Cheese, Toasted Walnuts and Fried Onions with Roasted Shallot Vinaigrette. 636 Main—Ken & Sue's East, Durango . 91

Seventh Street Salad with Honey-Glazed Walnuts and Honey-Poppyseed Vinaigrette. Juicy Lucy's Steakhouse, Glenwood Springs . 175

Watergate Salad. Haxtun Inn, Haxtun . 208

Grilled Eggplant and Roasted Red-Pepper Salad. Irwin Lodge Restaurant, Irwin . 217

San Juan Chicken Salad. Elk Creek Mining Company, New Castle . 277

Spinach Salad with Honey-Pomegranate Dressing. Il Poggio, Snowmass Village . 324

SAUCES

Smorian Beef (or Chicken) Sauce. The Silver Spoon Restaurant, Cuchara . 87

Jack Daniel's Sauce. The Woodlands Restaurant, Estes Park . 139

Marinara Sauce. Cables Italian Grille, Fort Morgan . 151
Creamy Mushroom Pepper Sauce (a.k.a. Chicken Enchilada Sauce).
    Old Capitol Grill, Golden . 188
Thai Peanut Sauce. Katie's Cookery, Gunnison . 205
Green Peppercorn Demi-Glace. The Stonebridge Restaurant, Snowmass
    Village . 327

SEAFOOD

Curried Shrimp. Café Bernard, Basalt . 25
Oven-Roasted Lobster with Purple Potato Puree and Sautéed Baby
    Fennel in a Red Wine–Cinnamon Reduction. Patina in the Hyatt
    Regency, Beaver Creek . 29
Sautéed Tilapia with Spinach, Crab and Pernod. South Ridge Seafood
    Grill, Breckenridge . 47
Mahimahi with Avocado Butter. Orlando's Steak House,
    Estes Park . 121
Scallops Milano. Silverado at the Lake Shore Lodge, Estes Park . 129
Ruby-Red Trout with Honey-Pecan Mustard Glaze. Backcountry
    Brewery, Frisco . 159

SOUPS AND SUCH

Spicy Red Chili. Breckenridge Barbecue, Breckenridge . 44
Santa Fe Chowder. Buffalo Bar & Grill, Buena Vista . 55
Miso Soup. Sato, Edwards . 102
Baked Potato Soup. Rollin Rich's Steakhouse, Florence . 147
Hot and Sour Soup. Panda City, Georgetown . 162
Creamy Forest Mushroom Soup. Keystone Ranch, Keystone . 238
Vince's Award-Winning Crab Soup. La Chaumière, Pinewood
    Springs . 294
Black Bean and Buffalo Sausage Soup. Yoder's High Country Restaurant,
    Silver Cliff . 316

STARCH

Roasted Vegetable and Fresh Herb Risotto. Wild Horse Bistro,
    Edwards . 105
Vermicelli. Mexico City, La Junta . 247

Blue Cheese and Artichoke Grits. Facing West, Lake City . 251

Jambalaya. Oskar Blues, Lyons . 264

Paella. Mediterranean Grill & Tapas Lounge, Steamboat
Springs . 332

VEAL

Breaded Veal au Citron. Rendez-vous Restaurant, Glenwood
Springs . 178

Veal Marsala with Rosemary Demi-Glace. The Bighorn Steakhouse,
Keystone . 226

Vitello Saltimbocco with Marsala Mushroom Cream Sauce.
Riggio's, Steamboat Springs . 336

Sautéed Sweetbreads with Caper–Brown Butter Sauce.
La Tour, Vail . 348

Veal Picatta. Mama Falzitto's, Winter Park . 362

VEGETARIAN

Baby Bok Choy and Black Mushrooms. Little Ollie's, Aspen . 17

House Cheese Fondue. The Swiss Haven Restaurant, Breckenridge . 51

Caramelized Asparagus. Antero Grill, Salida . 306

Spinach Quiche. Wazubi's Blue Cup Coffee House, Trinidad . 341

WILD GAME

Grilled Asian Duck Breast with Horseradish Mashed Potatoes and
Asian Slaw. SaddleRidge, Beaver Creek . 34

Grilled Caribou Chops with Cranberry Relish. The Meadow View
Restaurant at High Mountain Lodge, Fraser . 155

Venison Stew. Edgewater Café, Keystone . 230

Grilled Elk Tenderloin with Wild Blueberry–Sage Sauce. Tennessee
Pass Cookhouse, Leadville . 256

Fruitwood-Grilled Quail on Lavender Skewers with Mesclun-Herb
Salad, Peach Fritters, Stone Fruit–Viognier Sauce and Nasturtium
Confetti. Larkspur, Vail . 354

NOTES

ABOUT THE AUTHOR

DAVID GRUBER was born in Buffalo, New York, in 1951. His first time in Colorado was during the Christmas holiday in 1977 while on vacation visiting friends in Colorado Springs. He relocated there two months later and moved to the Denver area in 1982.

A former teacher of mathematics and accounting, he worked as an auditor and accountant for the state of Colorado before becoming a one-man book operation, writing, publishing, distributing, and tirelessly promoting his restaurant guide through four previous editions under the pseudonym Benjamin James Bennis. In all his research David

has dined at more than 900 restaurants in Colorado. His favorite hobbies are cooking, scuba diving, working on home improvements, and, of course, discovering new places to dine.

David is married to Linda Viray, his editor for the third and fourth editions of his restaurant guide. David and Linda are ardent dog lovers. They were devastated on October 1, 2001, when their beloved corgi, Cosmo, died at the young age of five. He was a very special dog who they miss dearly. David and Linda live in Denver.

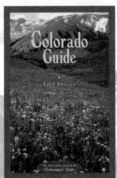